INTRODUCTION TO BRITISH POLITICS

INTRODUCTION TO
BRITISH POLITICS

P. J. MADGWICK

Senior Lecturer in Political Science,
University College of Wales, Aberystwyth

HUTCHINSON EDUCATIONAL

HUTCHINSON EDUCATIONAL LTD
3 Fitzroy Square, London W1

London Melbourne Sydney Auckland
Wellington Johannesburg Cape Town
and agencies throughout the world

First published 1970
Second impression 1971

Printed in Great Britain by litho on smooth wove paper
by Anchor Press, and bound by Wm. Brendon,
both of Tiptree, Essex

ISBN 0 09 096890 5 (cased)
0 09 096891 3 (paper)

Contents

Documents

CHAPTER II

CHAPTER 12

Diagrams, tables and facsimiles

Preface

I have attempted to write a flexible workbook rather than a traditional textbook. I hope that the student will be encouraged to work at and think about the material, rather than simply absorb it. It can serve as the basis for a whole course or as a collection of material to complement the teacher's own scheme.

This book is suitable for first-year undergraduates, A Level students, and Further and Adult Education. In compiling it, I have incurred countless debts to other writers on British politics. My thanks are due to many authors and publishers for permitting me to use extracts from their work.

I am also grateful to my former colleagues in the Nottingham University Department of Adult Education, for providing an environment in which it was possible to think seriously about teaching methods as well as content. I am particularly grateful to my present colleague, Mr Hugh Burroughes, for reading and commenting on the entire manuscript. Like every teacher, I am of course indebted to some hundreds of students who have shaped both the manner and the matter. Finally, like every author, I am thankful for a family which has accepted cheerfully the trials of having a writer in their midst, and even helped with the typing.

Mr Wilson's Government has been a great one for outdating books on British politics. The text of this book was completed in 1968, but I have taken the opportunity to emend certain details up to the end of 1969.

P. J. MADGWICK

Acknowledgements

Thanks are due to the following publishers and authors for permission kindly granted to reproduce extracts from copyright works:

Cassell and Company Ltd: The Earl of Avon, *Full Circle* (1960); The Earl of Woolton, *Memoirs* (1959); Sir Winston Churchill, *The Second World War*, vol. 1 (1948). Hamish Hamilton Ltd: R. H. S. Crossman, *Planning for Freedom* (1965). Longmans, Green and Co. Ltd: Francis Williams, *A Pattern of Rulers* (1965). Allen & Unwin Ltd: R. H. Tawney, *Equality* (4th ed., 1952). Frederick Muller Ltd: Hugh Dalton, *Call Back Yesterday* (1953), *The Fateful Years* (1957), *High Tide and After* (1962). Weidenfeld and Nicolson Ltd: Nigel Nicolson, *People and Parliament* (1958). Oxford University Press: Thomas Jones, *A Diary with Letters* (1954); Lord Morrison, *Government and Parliament* (3rd ed., 1964). Cambridge University Press: Sir Ivor Jennings, *The British Constitution* (1941); Lord Bridges, *Portrait of a Profession* (1953). Macmillan and Co Ltd: Keith Feiling, *The Life of Neville Chamberlain* (1946); David Butler and Anthony King, *The British General Election of 1964* (1965); J. Morley, *Life of Gladstone* (1903). Macmillan and Co Ltd and the Trustees of the Estate of the late Lord Keynes: J. M. Keynes, *The General Theory of Employment Interest and Money* (1951). André Deutsch Ltd: Lord Strang, *Home and Abroad* (1956). Penguin Books Ltd: Quintin Hogg, *The Case for Conservatism* (1947). Sweet and Maxwell Ltd: John Mackintosh, *The British Cabinet* (1962). MacGibbon and Kee Ltd: Peter Shore, *Entitled to Know* (1966). Faber and Faber Ltd: C. H. Sisson, *The Spirit of British Administration* (2nd ed., 1966); Allen M. Potter, *Organized Groups in British National Politics* (1961). Victor Gollancz Ltd: Clement Attlee, *The Labour Party in Perspective* (1937). Rupert Hart-Davis Ltd: G.M. Young, *Stanley Baldwin* (1952); Duff Cooper, *Old Men Forget* (1953). Hodder and Stoughton Ltd: Anthony Sampson, *Anatomy of Britain Today* (1965); Lady G. Cecil, *Life of Robert, Marquis of Salisbury* (1921). Collins: Walter Bagehot, *The English Constitution*, with an introduction by R. H. S. Crossman (Fontana, 1964). William Heinemann Ltd: Lord Hill of Luton, *Both Sides of the Hill* (1964); Lord Attlee, *As it Happened* (1954). Methuen and Company Ltd: J. Trenaman and D. McQuail, *Television and the Political Image* (1961). Jonathan Cape Ltd and the Executors of the Estate of Sir P. J. Grigg: P.J. Grigg, *Prejudice and Judgement* (1948). Hutchinson and Co Ltd: Lord Simon, *Retrospect* (1952); J. E. Wrench, *Geoffrey Dawson and Our Times* (1955); David Walder, *The*

16 ACKNOWLEDGEMENTS

Short List (1964). Arrow Books: Francis Williams, *Dangerous Estate* (1959). The Controller of Her Majesty's Stationery Office: Parliamentary Debates, Commons and Lords; Reports and Minutes of Select Committees of the House of Commons; Report of the Committee on the Machinery of Government (1918); Report of the Conference on Reform of the Second Chamber (1918); Agreed Statement on Conference of Party leaders (1948); Report of the Committee on Broadcasting (1949); Report of the Royal Commission on the Press (1961–2). National Opinion Polls Ltd: for the use of tables on voting behaviour. Institute of Practitioners in Advertising: Mark Abrams Booklet No 5 (1966). David Higham Associates Ltd: A. Christiansen, *Headlines all my life* (Heinemann, 1961). Political and Economic Planning: *Industrial Trade Associations* (1957). Royal Institute of Public Administration and Sir Edward Boyle Bart, M.P.: 'Who are the Policy-Makers'? (Public Administration, Autumn 1965). The British Broadcasting Corporation: Annual Report 1966–7. Consumers' Association: *Which?*, Seventh Annual Report (July 1964). The National Union of Teachers: Report of a Conference on Mass Media (1960). Independent Television Authority: *ITV 68* (1968). The *Sunday Times* for extracts from articles published on 8 October 1961, 17 September 1967, 1 October 1967. *The Observer* for extracts from an interview with Mr Harold Wilson, 24 October 1965; an article by Lord Home, 16 September 1965; and a letter, 28 May 1961. Mr Harold Wilson and Dr N. C. Hunt for extracts from a broadcast interview published in *Whitehall and Beyond* (BBC, London, 1964). The *Times* for an extract from an article, 1 August 1966; *The Times*, the Rt Hon Quintin Hogg, Q.C., M.P., and Professor Sir Alexander Haddow for letters published in the *Times* 26 July 1966. The Rt Hon Lord Aylestone, C.B.E., for an extract from a broadcast interview of 20 June 1963.

Thanks are due to the Controller of Her Majesty's Stationery Office for permission to make facsimile reproductions of pages of the Reports and Minutes of a Standing Committee, the Committee on Public Accounts, the Select Committee on Agriculture and the Select Committee on Science and Technology; also the Civil Estimates 1967–8.

Every effort has been made to trace the owners of copyright material. The author apologizes for any omissions, and would be grateful to know of them, so that acknowledgement may be made in future editions.

How to use this book

This book differs from most other textbooks: as well as a straight-forward exposition and analysis of the subject, it also contains *documents* and *exercises*. These are designed to encourage the reader to think about the topics for himself, and to learn by understanding, not by rote. The book may be taken as a complete text or in individual chapters; or the reader may find specific documents and exercises of value on their own.

The documents are mainly extracts from biographies, official publications and, in a few cases, figures and tables. They present evidence in a form which encourages independent thinking. Similarly, the exercises, many of them based on documents, invite the reader to formulate judgements and assessments on his own.

At the end of each chapter there is a *guide to exercises*, which suggests answers or advice on possible answers. Then comes a section of *assessments*, which are brief essays on particular themes and problems arising from the chapter. Finally, there are *recapitulation exercises* with a *key*.

The exercises are mainly not of the kind to which an exact answer can be given. They should set the reader thinking and, briefly, writing. He may then look up the guide, but should treat the answers given there as a point of departure, and not as necessarily the final and correct word. They are matters for argument, and may provide opportunities to justify conflicting points of view. While it is not cheating to look up the guide, there is obviously much to be said for the reader thinking about the exercises on his own to begin with. Generally, the exercises and their suggested answers should be read and understood before proceeding with the text, as they are part of the development of the argument.

The book is divided into five parts; this is for convenience of organisation and reference only. Politics is a continuous process, and it is necessary to see this process whole. The introduction provides an overall view, and may help the reader to relate one part to another. Part V is a collection of notes and cases which may be included in the study of individual chapters.

No textbook on its own is satisfactory for advanced study, and the reader is advised to go on from this book to deepen his knowledge of the subject. Most of the books and publications quoted or referred to in the text are suitable for further study, and there is also a select list of books on page 471.

PART I
Introduction

[1]
The nature of politics in Britain

i THE NATURE OF POLITICS

Politics is not a wholly respectable word. We are inclined to associate it with excessive partisanship, with devious plotting and unholy alliances, with dishonesty even, or at least a lack of straightforwardness. We accuse the other side of 'playing politics', or of 'dragging politics into' an issue which was properly above politics (politics being regarded as a 'low' activity). Now, these pejorative phrases do indicate some of the defects to which political activity tends, but it seems unfair to characterise the whole of an activity by its defects. This is prejudice, and no more desirable than the prejudice which characterises a favoured activity like cricket by all its best qualities, ignoring the defects. We need, for both politics and cricket, a balanced view.

Such a view must emphasise the necessity of political activity: we simply cannot manage without it. Politics is about society's conflicts and disagreements, and it is hardly imaginable that these should not exist. Some small groups with narrow objectives may be relatively harmonious. But even, say, the parochial church council or the Second XI selection committee have their disagreements— young Smith will not accept that Y is badly off form and should be dropped; old Smith will not accept that letting the parish hall for Saturday night hops is a (fairly) harmless way of promoting community life and paying off the mortgage. That smaller and allegedly naturally harmonious group, the family, is notoriously riven by conflict, ranging from trivial matters like the length of hair and skirts to where to go for a holiday, and to the supreme questions, who will lay the table and do the washing up? Whatever the group, conflicts arise: the nation, being so large and complex, contains within it conflicts both chronic and acute. Politics is the way such conflicts are contained, modified, postponed or settled, the way therefore in which the continued existence, the minimum cohesion, of the nation is promoted.

In many of the groups with which we are concerned in our daily lives, conflict is resolved by quite simple means. In a family of young children, a wise father will lay down a rule, and this will be accepted; in a school or college, the headmaster or the principal will decide many minor questions; in a business, the manager issues instructions. These are all situations in which authority is established and will be more or less readily accepted. In other situations conflict will be weak, friendliness strong, and natural harmony will prevail, so that a group of friends may have little difficulty in deciding which party game to play, or which beach to go to. However, even these situations in which conflicts are easily settled by authority or friendship can easily get out of hand. The Smiths we noted above are not necessarily perverse or obstinate: they simply disagree!

So political activity must take place. It follows that many of the topics which we say are being 'dragged into politics' (like comprehensive schools) are in fact already in politics: that is, they are fit and proper subjects for political activity, since people disagree about them.

So far, we have been concerned with definition: politics is the way a nation (or a group) manages conflicts and disagreements. Beyond this bare definition, the nature of politics depends on value judgements, on whether we favour broadly an authoritarian or a democratic society. These words, too, unfortunately have acquired connotations of approval and disapproval, so that we are all inclined to jump on to the democratic side without waiting to think.

In an authoritarian society, there is a disposition to settle conflicts through the enforcement of rules and orders by an established authority. This is justified because conflict damages the efficiency and integrity of society, and it is argued that the established authority is capable of settling disputes fairly, securing the consent of the protagonists. In this way, a father's or a headmaster's settlement of conflicts may be justified. Few people believe that this is an inhuman or improper method of settling the more violent arguments of the nursery or lower IIb.

In a democratic society, on the other hand, it is assumed that as far as possible conflicts should be resolved by rational discussion among those involved, with the final solution being accepted voluntarily. The process may well be time-consuming and untidy, but is justified because it respects the efficiency and integrity of the individual, his right to consent to the decisions which affect him and his need to feel committed to his social duties. In the democratic society, the Smiths are valued members, thinking, participating, standing up for their opinions.

Now the authoritarian and the democratic assumptions are not wholly antagonistic and mutually exclusive. In an authoritarian society, some attempt is made to modify decisions according to the wishes of the people; in a democratic society some decisions are going to be made and enforced whatever the people think. However, there is, especially at the level of nations and states, a fundamental difference. The authoritarian tends to limit the element of consultation and consent to the minimum he can get away with. The democrat, on the other hand, tries to maximise the element of consent.

At this point the democrat falls into difficulties. Maximising consent is by no means easy in practice, and democratic principles may easily fall into an idealism not firmly based on facts. The authoritarian can usually claim a superior realism.

The problem for the democrat is that on many issues the people's wishes are obscure, inarticulate or even non-existent; on other issues the people will be divided, some for, some against; and in some cases a democratic government may believe profoundly that all or most of the people are mistaken. The solution lies in a system of *representation* and *responsibility*. The wishes and views of the people are *represented* in the government; power rests normally with a majority; the exercise of power is subject to processes of *responsibility* (answerability) to the people. The device of responsibility allows a government to govern in an approximate and indirect accordance with the wishes of the people. A democratic government may thus, for example, abolish the death penalty despite a popular majority in favour of its retention, and expect to justify this decision before the next election (or hope that the public will not feel deeply enough to care or even remember).

This is a relatively crude example of democratic government. Democracy is not simply direct popular government, but neither is it simply government through a system of regular elections and elected assembly. The democratic assumption implies the existence of a complex range of institutions and processes: political parties, as well as parliament; an elaborate and powerful system of political communication; machinery for the articulation of demands of groups with ideas or interests; a network of committees, habitual processes of consultation, explanation, education; the acceptance of compromise and delay; even a respect for opposing views, and the ultimate recognition that you may be mistaken.

Democratic political systems

We should then expect to find in a democratic political system institutions of government linked to the governed by systems of responsibility and representation. Briefly these institutions and systems are as follows:

Head of state: ceremonial or part of the executive government.

Executive: a small group of directors, usually with one person at their head as chairman, or in a more exalted position as president.

Representative deliberating assembly, with some control over the executive, but also controlled to some extent by the executive. An important function of the assembly is usually legislation, i.e. the processing of laws, but these may be made (decided upon and fundamentally shaped) by the executive.

Electoral system providing for the popular election of part, at least, of the assembly, and perhaps of the chief executive too.

Political parties: groups seeking to win power in the government. In a democratic system this means an organisation to secure popular votes and to organise members of the assembly for government power.

Groups and individuals organised to bring pressure on government in favour of particular ideas or interests.

A system of political communication, including the press and broadcasting, and providing for the inter-communication of parts of the whole political system.

A judicial system to provide for the arbitration of non-political disputes.

This is the political system in outline. The essential processes are:

Identification and assessment of a problem and its solution.

Development of policy ideas by individuals and groups including the government.

Public ventilation of ideas, problems, solution.

Formulation of attitudes within organised groups, including political parties.

Consultation by government of political and other interested groups.

Assessment of the policy arguments, both on their intrinsic merits and in the light of pressures and representations.

Modification of policies by way of compromise with particular interests or adjustment to the general interest.

Formulation of policy within the administration.

Formulation and adoption of policy within high executive (decision making).

Processing of the policy decided in terms of law, regulation, finance, administration and information to those affected.

Communication of policy to public to secure acceptance.

Answerability to parliament and public for the policy.

Criticism of policy and scrutiny of its administration, by formal processes (parliament) and informally (press).

The process does not necessarily take place in this or any set order; sometimes the taking of a decision is the first step, rarely the last; often steps are missed out. The process is continuous, hence in a very rough way circular. But the most complicated lines on a single plane hardly represent the complexity of the political process. It is sometimes said that democratic politics is a dialogue between government and governed (where authoritarian politics is mainly a monologue). But a dialogue is too simple a concept. Politics is rather a multi-logue, a many-sided, many-centred dialogue.

The study of politics

It is difficult to exclude value judgements from the study of politics. The first task is to discover and describe what actually happens. This is important, worth knowing, and not at all easy to accomplish. We shall find, however, that discovery involves selection, description involves analysis; for example, we shall look especially hard at evidence of responsibility, effectiveness, power, or the absence of these. Words like democratic, inefficient, excessive will slip into our writing, and when they do, we must be aware that we are assuming and implying that some forms of political organisation are *better* than others, and be ready to defend our judgement. In the end, that judgement depends on the personal assessment of the kind of society we want to live in; and that assessment must be personal in the sense that it is yours, not the author's.

2 THE SETTING OF BRITISH POLITICS

Politics arises, then, from society and its problems and tensions. These provide the agenda of politics: they also influence the manner of political activity and the shape of the political system itself.

The most important feature of British society is its long history of independent existence as a more or less united nation. The last serious and successful invasion was by the Normans in 1066. Since then the English Channel has provided a sufficient barrier against invasion, but also an encouragement to a narrow separatism which has made England the perfect illustration of insularity. Within the islands of Britain, England itself has been united socially and administratively since at least the seventeenth century; Wales has been subdued since the early sixteenth century and Scotland since the early eighteenth century. Scotland, especially, is not wholly assimilated, but, like Wales, has accepted unification without serious resistance. Thus the main island of Britain has been governed as a unity from London for over 250 years.

Ireland has had a rather different history, in which conquest and colonisation have met and nourished a nationalist resistance movement. This movement triumphed after a bloody and violent revolt: Southern Ireland became independent as the Irish Free State in 1922. In the period 1800–1922 Ireland was part of a political union with England, sending Members to the Westminster Parliament. The effect on British politics was profound: the Irish left a permanent mark on the British Parliament and on the party system. Before 1800 Ireland was simply a disaffected colony; since 1922 she has been a revolted ex-colony: either way the disruptive effects on British politics were diminished and contained. The essential unity of the British islands was secure.

The unity which derived from insularity was reinforced by other geographical factors. Britain is not only an island, but a comparatively small one, with no great natural barriers to communication. The great mountain ranges of the west and the north bar the way to nowhere of any economic significance. Moreover, the natural endowment of the country has not led to profound conflicts between economic regions or interests. Britain has become a highly industrialised trading nation, and the interests of industry and trade have achieved an almost unchallenged predominance. This is not, of course, to say that sectional interests do not exist and clash, town with country, industry with agriculture, coal with gas, oil with electricity, and so on. But none of these interests engages in a permanent civil war of states within states, of the kind seen at times in American history.

One reason for this relative moderation of sectional interests is that they rarely coincide with identifiable regional interests. Hence Britain has avoided the formidable challenge offered in the US by Texan oil, southern cotton or mid-western cattle-ranching. Again, this is to imply not that regional interests do not exist, but that they do not detract much from the underlying unity of the political system. Within England, for example, Lancashire and Kent, Durham and Dorset, are remarkably uniform in their political behaviour: the problems vary but the responses do not. In Scotland and Wales there is a greater emphasis in political discourse on the separate interests of these areas, and some serious nationalism. Yet voting behaviour is not significantly different from England's—a slight leaning to the Liberals, no more. The recent (1966–8) political activity of the Welsh and Scottish Nationalists (with two by-election victories) is not yet substantial enough to suggest that permanent changes in regional political attitudes are taking place.

There are other ways in which Britain's basic unity has been preserved. Its population is now thoroughly mixed, and the tensions of the melting-pot long forgotten. The occasional mild resentments of Welsh, Irish, Jewish and English indicate plainly enough Britain's good fortune in overcoming early in her modern history the passions and tensions of a divided people. Recent immigration of coloured people, especially from the West Indies and Pakistan, might perhaps disturb this pleasant harmony. Such immigration has been comparatively small (about 2 per cent of the population up to 1968) and is now restricted. But there is a potential source of disunity, even conflict here, for in modern times the British people have not learned tolerance; they simply have not needed it.

Religion has been a powerful divisive factor in the past and remains so in many countries. In Britain, revolt first against the Catholic Church, then against the established Church of England, provided the mainspring of political history for three-hundred years. 'Non-conformity' in religion was a powerful force in industry, politics and society. Until late in the nineteenth century the cry of 'No Popery' was still potent as a rabble-raiser, and resistance to the dominant position in education of the Church of England led to a rate-payers' strike in the early years of this century. Politics was then about religion, and the Liberal Party was the party of 'the non-conformist conscience'. But the heart has quite gone out of the issue. Religious belief and observance have sharply declined, and distinctions between denominations are now of little account in England—except of course to the cause of Christianity.

Political history has reinforced the tendencies to unity. The violent, bloody, disruptive years of British history were virtually over by 1660 (except in Scotland and Ireland). The climax was the beheading of King Charles I in January 1649. This event was decisive in the struggle to establish constitutional limitations on the monarchy: kings have never felt the same since. Thereafter all has been a blessed anti-climax, in which the claims of Parliament against monarchy and of people against Parliament have been gradually and peacefully asserted. In 1688, the Glorious Revolution —a bloodless coup—established a new dynasty under limitations laid down by Parliament, notably in the Bill of Rights (1689) and the Act of Settlement (1701).

Thus Parliament successfully challenged the Crown. A century later Parliament itself was challenged by the people, and the series of Parliamentary Reform Acts from 1832 onwards transformed the political system into the modern parliamentary democracy, with government carried on by a Committee of Parliament, but subject to popular election. The authority of the Monarch was thus annihilated.

This was a revolutionary outcome, but there had been no prolonged or intense period of revolution since 1660. There was no sharp break with the past; institutions were accepted, trusted—but transformed; social relations were respected but modified. The pace of reform was maddeningly slow, but rarely so slow as to provoke a massive fragmentation of society (like 1789 in France; 1848 all over Europe; 1860 in the US; 1917–18 in Russia, Austria, Germany).

Britain, then, is a unified, cohesive, traditional and conservative society. This conservatism at once supports and is supported by an informal but powerful system of hierarchy and status. The British, it has been said, are a deferential people—they tip their caps willingly to the squire and his relations. The squires have almost disappeared from modern industrial Britain, but the habit of deference to the 'quality', the gentry, has not much abated. Such deference is encouraged by the system of private, fee-paying ('public') schools and the ancient universities. Conservative Cabinets still draw largely on Old Etonians (twelve out of nineteen in 1962) and many working-class Conservative voters regard this not as deplorable, quaint, or of no account, but as a positive virtue.

Lord Hill of Luton, a former Conservative Cabinet Minister, has written gently of the importance of birth and breeding within the Conservative Party. He recognised that 'within the larger community of the Commons ... there was the smaller community bound together by strong if invisible ties of birth and background and public school to which I did not and could never belong.' (*Both Sides of the Hill*, Heinemann, 1964, p. 11.)

Another feature of this system of status and deference is the exaggerated respect paid to voluntary public service. This has extended to Parliament itself, where the tradition of the gentleman amateur, helping to govern the country in his spare time, lingers on. The system is at its worst undemocratic, inefficient and snobbish.

However, old-fashioned deference may be a dwindling quality in British life. The sharpest outward sign of class difference was the employment of domestic servants, and that small army (nearly two millions in 1901) had almost disappeared by 1950. Affluence, 'angry young men', 'student-power', the teenage revolt against the adult world, these may well turn out to be permanent and profound shifts in social attitudes, which would inevitably be significant for politics too.

This account of British society suggests a degree of unity, cohesion, respect for hierarchy and authority, aversion from radical change and violence, which would provide little scope for politics. There would appear to be few disagreements and a reluctance to press these to open controversy. In fact, this is not the whole case. The unity and cohesion which history has conferred on British society provide only a framework of order. Within it, there are tensions and resentments. Politics repeats this pattern: an accepted framework within which fights (gentlemanly fights) go on. The fights are not normally about the framework and the fundamentals; hence comparatively little is at stake. Most of the participants are not fully committed and have little to lose: this may explain the lack of violence and corruption in British politics, and the tolerance extended to the less productive kinds of party warfare.

Some Britons are, indeed, ready to call a party truce and accept a coalition government of the 'best and wisest' men of all parties. This suggests a misunderstanding of their political system. Many others, inevitably, are apathetic and disengaged. For the rest, political attitudes are more specific and more complex. They include a respect for traditional institutions, both Crown and Parliament, but also a respect for universal suffrage and the right to vote; a preference for strong government, but a strong objection to direct government intervention in their personal affairs (taxes, 'breathalysers', conscription); a distrust of government *by* the people, but a ready acceptance of government *with* and *for* the people.

This is no doubt a confused inheritance for a pragmatic people little given to political theorising. The evolution of political attitudes has been further confused by the urgencies of imperial and foreign policies. Ireland, India, Germany, Russia, Africa—British governments and their peoples have often been too busy finding and keeping their place in the world to understand what they stood for at home.

The situation looks perhaps more confusing in the 1960s than for decades past—and this for a good historical reason. For a hundred-and-fifty years now, between the alarms and excursions of Empire, Britain has been coping with the problems of the first Industrial

Revolution. Her landscape is witness to this, so are her Labour movement, politically the strongest in the world, and perhaps her proletariat, with its world records in gambling and the consumption of newspapers. Domestic politics have been organised, on and off, around the consequences of nineteenth-century industrialisation. By the mid-twentieth century the old responses were no longer relevant; politics required new points of organisation—prosperity, modernisation, equality, quality of life—and political attitudes required new objectives and directions.

3 THE CHARACTER OF THE BRITISH
POLITICAL SYSTEM

It is difficult to characterise the British political system briefly— hence this book, like many of its fellows, is quite long. But it is as well to begin with some general notions about the system, even if these are only an approximation to, or part of, a truth attainable through a gradual refining of crude and imprecise notions.

Responsible government

British government is responsible, that is to say answerable, government. It is not, and does not try to be, direct popular government. The Government is responsible to Parliament, and Parliament to the people, in general elections. Within government, the administration (the Departments, the Civil Service) is responsible to Ministers, and Ministers through the Cabinet to Parliament. Thus in theory a line of responsibility runs from the humblest civil servant, via Cabinet and Parliament, to the people—and popular sovereignty is assured.

This is, of course, an overstatement. The line of responsibility is much too tenuous to support the supremacy of the people. Responsibility means answerability, and this implies something weaker than control, weaker because it is discontinuous, tentative, general; because it indicates rather than commands. The weakness of answerability is a matter both of theory or belief (few people want a stronger notion of answerability) and of practicality (answerability gets weakened in practice anyway for want of time, information, care and concern). Answerability is rightly seen as a way of providing for freedom *and* restriction, scope for initiative and independent action, but without complete loss of control.

Expressed less formally this might be: 'You are free to get on with the job as you please, but if anything goes wrong I shall know whose backside to kick!' This is, indeed, very much a matter of words and understandings. In a way, the term responsibility is a good one, because its other less literal meaning (capacity for reasonable conduct) emphasises independence and self-control—make (but check) your own mistakes.

Where the choice of words and their connotations are so important, diagrams are plainly misleading. We can draw a line of responsibility with electorate at one end and a humble civil servant at the other:

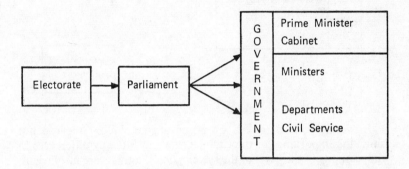

We can stand this on one end or the other, height signifying power:

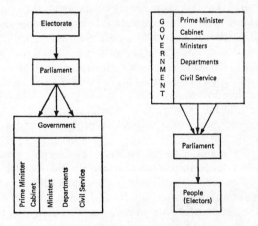

RESPONSIBILITY IN GOVERNMENT

Or we can escape from this dilemma and draw a circle instead of a line—this is sensible, for government is a continuous process:

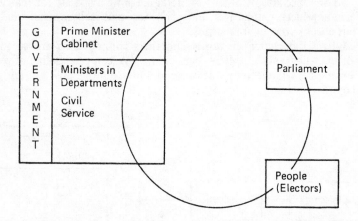

However, these diagrams are all unsatisfactory, for they do not show the importance of the Cabinet, nor indicate any differences in the relations of the parts of the system. Our diagrams are insufficient, but so too is the characterisation of British government simply as 'responsible government'.

Strong but restrained and responsive government

In its present stage (which may not be the last), the distribution of power in the British political system is transformed by the operation of political parties. It is normally possible for one of the two major parties to secure from a general election a majority of Members in Parliament. From these is drawn a government which can normally expect to control Parliament. The electorate itself cannot be controlled, but the Government has up to five years before it has to hold an election and has substantial advantages in the electoral contest, including some influence over relative prosperity and a free choice of date for the election.

Clearly, the majority party has very considerable power. Within the party the leadership, and particularly the Leader himself as Prime Minister, is supreme. There is a possibility here of unrestrained power ('dictatorship', to use an old-fashioned and emotive phrase) being in the hands of Prime Minister or Cabinet. But most of the time restraints seem to operate: the personal restraints of regard for principle and need for approval; the perhaps more dependable restraints of political colleagues and senior civil servants; the desire and the need to retain the ungrudging support of the party in Parliament; the pressures and persuasions of interest groups, journalists, advisers (asked and unasked); the constant reminder by the opposition that the electorate is the final arbiter.

British governments are enmeshed in this network of restraints, whether they like it or not. But mostly governments take a more positive attitude, and are willingly responsive to these restraining influences. This is not simply a matter of accepting the necessary or the inevitable with good grace: it springs in part from a genuine acceptance of democratic principles.

So we could go back to our diagrams and draw a slightly more complicated pattern:

At its simplest we are saying that
the acts of government

are modified by various
factors

and subject to a cut-off by
the electorate ⟶

So altogether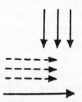

But on the next page is a more complicated diagram—which is still, of course, much too simple for the complex processes of politics.

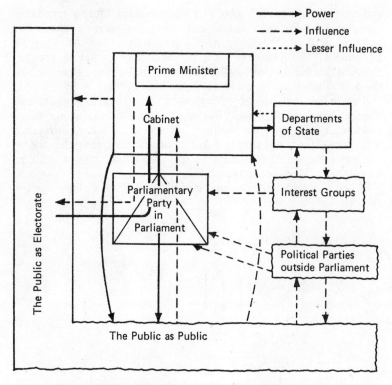

Power
Influence
Lesser Influence

Prime Minister

Cabinet

Departments of State

The Public as Electorate

Parliamentary Party in Parliament

Interest Groups

Political Parties outside Parliament

The Public as Public

RESTRAINING INFLUENCES IN GOVERNMENT

Constitutional morality and the rule of law

One of the restraints on government is its acceptance of a code of constitutional morality. Parts of this are central and almost always observed—the ceremonial prerogatives of the Crown, the formal sovereignty of Parliament. Other parts are marginal and may often be transgressed—for example, the 'convention' of ministerial responsibility (see chapter 3), the notion of a mandate (see chapter 12). According to some critics the mounting of the Suez intervention in 1956 was constitutionally improper, and according to others, the postponement of the London Borough elections of 1967 was unconstitutional. In the last resort, when hard pressed (as they often are), governments bend the constitution in the public interest and to save themselves (two matters which easily get confused). But there are limits on the bending, both prudential ('we may not get away with it') and genuinely moral ('we ought not to do it').

The collection of rules and precepts known as the 'rule of law' is one of the more important moral restraints on government. Again, the concept is a vague one, but not necessarily the less useful for that. Its meaning has been exaggerated in the past, in the belief that law was both relevant and sacred, that lawyers were less prejudiced than politicians, and that any obstacle to government intervention was good. None of these beliefs is wholly or consistently true. The 'rule of law' does not mean that law is sovereign (supreme), for Parliament can change the law; nor does it enshrine the principles of individual rights or liberty except in ways defined or accepted by Parliament. This old idea of the rule of law supported the principles of a *laissez-faire* state, unwilling to interfere with the liberties and privileges of subjects, and in which the judiciary was superior to the elected representatives of the people. Such ideas are no longer acceptable.

However the rule of law is still of the highest significance. It implies:

(a) The independence of the judiciary. Judges are appointed by the Crown, but are not normally removable by the Crown. The legal system is formally under the control of the Lord Chancellor, a distinguished lawyer holding Cabinet rank. The Lord Chancellor supervises the courts but does not intervene in the administration of justice. The judiciary does not have a duty to protect the interests of the State; in cases of doubt there is a strong tendency to protect the individual against the State.

(b) The law is the law as interpreted by the judges, unless and until Parliament changes the law. The law the judges interpret is the law the judges (and the citizens) see before them in the Statute Book. The judges are not normally concerned with the intentions of Parliament, except as they are conveyed in the law itself, nor are they often concerned with State policy—with what is desirable. In practice, of course, they must sometimes interpret an imprecise law in the light of common sense, or their understanding of the problem, or the prevailing notions of what is desirable. But the presumption that the law is set down in specific sets of words is a good one: it protects the citizen from uncertainty and the judge from pressures and persuasions outside the narrow context of the Statute Book itself.

(c) Imprisonment or any other punishment can be inflicted only for a specified breach of the law, established in court, according to the recognised procedures. This general statement includes such important legal safeguards as Habeas Corpus (no imprisonment without cause shown), and the rules of evidence. The importance of such safeguards is often overlooked by British people who have not experienced government by European dictatorship, African military junta or Chinese Communist Party.

(d) Freedom of expression, publication, assembly. These are freedoms secured by the ordinary law of the land, and not as in other countries dependent on a special declaration or section of the constitution. They are modified, but not fundamentally limited, by the laws of libel, slander, disturbance of the peace. There is obviously some advantage in reinforcing such freedoms by regarding them as part of 'constitutional morality' as well as plain law. But a government which might duck the morality is still bound by the law.

(e) Equality before the law. There are no privileged classes under the law. In a formal sense this is true, though not very meaningful. Litigation is so expensive that in practice the rich are privileged. For the rest, so much depends on the particular law involved. For example, try challenging the veracity of a policeman's evidence; or suing a barrister for negligence!

A centralised system, modified by local administration

The British political system is centralised: unlike a federal system, it has within it no autonomous or competing centres of power. Britain is governed from Westminster and Whitehall. There are, however, three ways in which this centralisation is modified.

First, the 'nations' of Scotland, Wales and Ireland have retained or secured modest elements of self-government. Scotland has been part of the Union (United Kingdom) since 1707, but has retained separate systems of law, religion and education. There is a Secretary of State for Scotland in the Cabinet, and a powerful independent administration, the Scottish Office. This is largely based in Edinburgh and most of the domestic Ministries do their work in Scotland through or under it.

Wales as a nation has had a thinner time, being governed as part of 'England and Wales' since the sixteenth century. In most important ways it is assimilated, but since 1964 it has, like Scotland, acquired its own Secretary of State and Welsh Office, with powers falling short of autonomy. The existence of a Welsh language and an historic culture have nourished national sentiment, which is perhaps the strongest centrifugal force in British politics.

Northern Ireland is the Protestant rump of independent Ireland (Eire). Having come so near to absolute separation, it has won the most substantial measure of independence—a Parliament and a Government of its own, with almost complete power in domestic matters. There are twelve Members for Northern Ireland in the Westminster Parliament: staunch Protestant Unionists, these MPs have not often been distinguishable from English Conservatives (who are of course also Protestant Unionists).

These elements of national devolution modify but hardly transform the strong centralism of British government. Similarly the system of local government, though deeply entrenched and important, is wholly subordinated to central government, and cannot move far on its own. The largest fields of local administration are education, planning, roads and police. In all of these the major decisions, and in some cases the minor ones too, are taken or reviewed in London. The reorganisation of secondary schools (the introduction of comprehensive schools) is a classic example of a policy choice taken by the central government which could arguably have been left to local government.

The power of central government over local government is formidable, and rests on statute and constitution. Local governments can do only what they are permitted to do by a Parliament buttressed by the prestige of the central government, its administrative capacity, and its immense financial resources. There is no strong popular challenge to the dominance of the centre: local government is loved by its practitioners but not by its clients.

This situation may be changing—but slowly and undramatically. Nationalist parties have had successes in recent by-elections. Economic planning is carried out on a regional basis in an attempt to correct 'regional economic unbalance' (the existence of long-term depressed areas), and this has led to the development of a tentative regional politics, and a demand for much more. Some Departments of Government (like the Ministry of Agriculture) have always operated throughout the country with strong provincial offices. Local government is to be reformed, and there may emerge from that reform a smaller number of comparatively large regional authorities. To these the central government would be more willing, and under more pressure, to grant greater powers. Thus it is conceivable that regional politics might eventually come to modify the centralisation of British politics, to a greater extent than nationalist devolution or the existing system of local government.

All this, for the moment, lies in the future. It is impossible to give an account of the government of the USA without describing the role of the fifty component states. For Britain what still counts above all are the few square miles around Westminster and Whitehall in London.

An unwritten constitution

As everyone knows, Britain has an 'unwritten constitution'. But what exactly does this mean and how significant is it?

Clearly Britain does not have a constitution in the sense of a single document, drafted and ratified at some point in history, and thenceforth established as 'the constitution'. In this respect, Britain is unique among the advanced nations. But, of course, parts of the constitution are written down, e.g. Statutes relating to the Crown and to the House of Lords, the powers of Ministers and the system of elections. And most other parts, e.g. the role of Prime Minister and Cabinet, could be written down, and indeed are written down in what are deemed authoritative books on the constitution. None of these has quite the authority of Sir Thomas Erskine May's standard work on parliamentary procedure[1], but an Erskine May equivalent on executive government is quite conceivable.

However, a piecemeal and 'written-down' system of government cannot claim nearly the authority of a single documentary constitution like that of the fifth French Republic (1958) and is a long way from attracting the reverence accorded a great historic document like the United States constitution of 1787. All the same there is in Britain a respect for traditional forms of government which seems to secure the advantages of stability and legitimacy. The British people show a marked pride in, and sense of loyalty to, their institutions, despite the absence of a revered document.

Britain has indeed lost little by its unwritten constitutional arrangements, and it may have gained much: a single written document is subject to interpretation and gives rise to endless and often profitless litigation. In countries like the USA, constitutional lawyers have haggled for years over the meaning of single words or phrases.

---

[1] *Treatise of the Law, Privileges, Proceedings and Usage of Parliament*, first published in 1844, now *Erskine May's Parliamentary Practice*, 17th ed., Butterworth, 1964.

Generally (because lawyers are cautious, conservative and well-to-do) their interpretations have held up the development of institutions to meet modern needs in social, economic and foreign policy-making. British institutions, on the other hand, have been developed and adapted with less time and travail.

This means that the British constitution rests in the care of the politicians more than does a written constitution. But the politicians are elected and responsible and they have not often abused their responsibility. In modern times Britain has avoided gross tyranny and accomplished great social reforms without undue tension or violence. This is as great an achievement as can be claimed by any other political system.

PART II
The executive

[2]
Prime Minister and Cabinet

1 OUTLINE

The office of Prime Minister is of crucial importance in the British system of government. We shall not understand how the system works unless we know the Prime Minister's functions and the Prime Minister's power. Both functions and power must be studied in relation to his colleagues in the Cabinet; the governmental machine as a whole; party and Parliament; the public, and the world at large. When this study and assessment is complete, it may be possible to answer the major question, whether this is an effective way of arranging the highest office in a parliamentary democracy.

The functions and powers of the Prime Minister

(a) He is the leader of the majority party, and will therefore have a hold on his party's loyalty, and command of the House of Commons.

But the Prime Minister does not hold his party's loyalty unconditionally. Revolts against the party leadership—mostly only tentative—have occurred. Some examples are;

the 'overthrow' of Asquith, 1916; and of Lloyd George, 1922;
tentative revolts against Attlee, 1948 and 1951;
rumbles of discontent under Eden, 1956; Macmillan, 1963.

Against this must be set the evidence that Prime Ministers can usually weather such storms—consider the careers of Baldwin, Attlee, Macmillan and Home—but not without some trimming of the sails.

(b) The Prime Minister has the power of appointment and dismissal. He makes the Cabinet when he comes to office. Traditionally he acts on his own when making appointments, though he will not be able to offend grossly some of his senior colleagues, or the more important wings of his party.

This is true of both Labour and Conservative Parties in Britain. Admittedly there is a strong element of elective democracy in the

Labour Party's constitution, and *in opposition* both Leader and Shadow Cabinet are chosen by vote of the Parliamentary Labour Party. In office, however, the Leader of the Labour Party has behaved like his predecessors, and chosen his colleagues without benefit of voting or advice.

The Prime Minister also has the power to dismiss Ministers. The only limitation on this power is the prudential one: he must avoid provoking effective revolt. The best example of this power is a recent one: in July 1962 the Prime Minister, Mr Macmillan, dismissed seven Cabinet Ministers at one sweep. One of the departing Ministers, the Lord Chancellor, Kilmuir, wrote in his autobiography, 'I once remarked ... that "loyalty was the Tories' secret weapon". I doubt if it has ever had to endure so severe a strain.'

But Macmillan survived as Prime Minister for more than a year, and then it was illness (mainly) which dismissed him.

(c) The Prime Minister is chairman of the Cabinet and controls its agenda and its discussions. He has considerable influence over the timing of decisions, or whether any decision shall be taken. He is in the position of arbiter when colleagues disagree. These are important powers and they go with the office.

Powers beyond this—the determination of the content of decisions—depend on other personal and political factors, most of which favour prime ministerial power.

(d) The Prime Minister inevitably becomes a person of high public prestige. He is 'the government'. At home he has a wide range of public duties, formal speeches, receptions, broadcasts, which are not subject to political criticism, and which can easily give the impression of power, dignity and a larger than ordinary humanity. Abroad, the Prime Minister is seen as representing the nation in its relations with the mighty.

Indeed, wherever he goes, even to play golf or shoot grouse, the Prime Minister is news, and the press, radio and television make the most of it, and him.

2 THE JOB OF PRIME MINISTER—
DAY BY DAY

....

DOCUMENT I

A DAY IN THE LIFE OF A PRIME MINISTER

(i) MR MACMILLAN

From an article 'by a supporter' in the *Sunday Times*, 8 October 1961

His working pattern is devised to keep the load from overwhelming him. He does delegate extensively, and does not harry his subordinates for progress reports on the telephone, as both Churchill and Eden used to do. Indeed, he uses the telephone far less than most politicians. The Downing Street (or Admiralty House) routine is that his five secretaries work the day shift on the papers, while the Prime Minister himself works the night shift on the boxes they leave each evening.

Mr Macmillan's day starts at six to six-thirty in the morning, when he wakes up. He then works on the boxes of papers which have been left for him the previous evening. He breakfasts in bed at eight o'clock, and reads the daily Press until nine o'clock. He usually rises between nine and ten, according to his appointments.

His day is then spent on seeing people, including an endless queue of foreign dignitaries who fly through London, and attending committees, with a regular Tuesday and Thursday Cabinet when Parliament is sitting. He has the Prime Minister's questions to take in the House, also on Tuesday and Thursday. He then gets back in the evening—often with an evening engagement—and finds the new day's boxes waiting for him. These he attends to in bed, wearing a comfortable old cardigan, before he goes to sleep or after he wakes up.

This is something like an eighteen-hour day, and it is no more than the standard day that any Prime Minister has to put in. Obviously it requires both fitness and a good organising sense to take the strain. The present Prime Minister is also concerned to find time to think—to get away on his own or to talk things over in a ruminative way with, perhaps, Lord Mills.

....

DOCUMENT 2

A DAY IN THE LIFE OF A PRIME MINISTER

(ii) MR WILSON

From an interview with Mr Harold Wilson by Kenneth Harris in the *Observer* Magazine, 24 October 1965

By the time Mr Wilson gets to the Cabinet Room at about 9.30 each morning, he has read some of the morning papers and any overnight telegrams brought in by the duty clerk in the Cabinet office. There may be some telephone calls too. 'An average morning's read usually sets off six or seven inquiries into what's going on.' Once a week, usually, there will be a Cabinet meeting, which will take up most of the morning. On a typical day when there is not a Cabinet—'There might be a Cabinet committee, or an *ad hoc* meeting of Ministers to settle some problem or other. Or a Minister has come to ask me about something—he wants to know how I would feel about him doing this or not doing that—or perhaps I have asked one to come and see me because I have something to say to him—or to ask of him. There may be a visitor from overseas—a Commonwealth Prime Minister, perhaps, who wants to talk, or an Ambassador. There may be a meeting of a Cabinet sub-committee—we often have two, three or four in a day, averaging from twenty minutes to an hour—longer of course if it's a big issue. Sometimes I have a lunch—visiting head of Government, say, sometimes an editor or a colleague. But I'm often free and if I am I like very much to go to the House of Commons when it's sitting. I ought to go as often as I can anyway, but I like it—after all, I've been lunching there now for twenty years.' There are no special places for Ministers; Mr Wilson may also go into the tea-room later in the day, using these meal-times for informal contacts with back benchers and 'getting the feel of things'. However, 'The one thing you've got to be careful about is not to let yourself become an individual court of appeal against Ministers or collective decisions of the party or the Cabinet.' On Tuesdays and Thursdays the Prime Minister will be answering Questions and must read his prepared answers and study the briefs for dealing with supplementaries. Sometimes he will be taking part in Debates.

In the evening, if there is no public or Parliamentary engagement, Mr Wilson withdraws to his flat with the red boxes of official papers. These may be proposals requiring a decision, or a comment (a minute); or appointments for the Prime Minister's approval; or letters requiring his signature. Some of the papers will be for information, for example, trade figures and Foreign Office telegrams. Finally, there will be briefs for Cabinet meetings and for Parliamentary Questions, if it is a Monday or Wednesday night. There is much for the Prime Minister to absorb and a good many items, perhaps forty or fifty, on which he must take a decision.

Towards midnight, if the boxes are cleared, the Prime Minister skims through the first editions of three newspapers; the *Telegraph*, the *Daily Mirror* and the *Sun*. 'It's a hard night's work,' Mr Wilson said, 'but it never gets dull.'

....

EXERCISE
THE PRIME MINISTER'S DECISIONS

1. Government and administration at the highest levels always involves making decisions, i.e. choosing one course of action rather

than another. The decision itself may be made in a moment, but preparing to choose (getting information, hearing points of view, arguing, discussing) can take hours, or days or years.

Which of the Prime Minister's activities involve him *individually* in the taking of decisions?

Since it is common to ascribe to top politicians an undue liking for office and power it is well to emphasise that the job of Prime Minister is arduous and exacting. Consider this conversation between Gladstone and Peel in the 1840s:

On Monday, I visited Sir R. Peel. . . . He said he had been twice prime minister, and nothing should induce him again to take part in the formation of a government; the labour and anxiety were too great. . . . I said, however, 'I can quite assent to the proposition that no one understands the labour of your post; that, I think, is all I ever felt I could know about it, that there is nothing else like it. But then you have been prime minister in a sense in which no other man has been it since Mr Pitt's time.' He said, 'But Mr Pitt got up every day at eleven o'clock, and drank two bottles of port wine every night.' 'And died of old age at forty-six.' (From Mr Gladstone's diary, 24 July 1846.)

3 THE PRIME MINISTER'S OFFICE, PERSONAL STAFF AND ADVISERS

Every Prime Minister works within a small circle of intimates and advisers, some of them Ministers, some officials, some neither. He usually accords an unofficial senior or special status to two or three of his Ministers, and may seek their advice (or have it thrust upon him) over a wide range of government business, including the most strictly reserved matters like appointments and dissolution. It is misleading to call this arrangement an 'inner Cabinet', since this would imply a formality which is not present. In this way, the Prime Minister preserves his right not to take or even seek advice.

Beside these political colleagues, a Prime Minister has on hand a number of Private Secretaries. These are usually Administrative grade civil servants, young and able, and specially assigned to Downing Street. But the Prime Minister will also have a Parliamentary Private Secretary, a favoured Member of Parliament, and some political assistants from the staff of his party.

The shape and size of the official prime ministerial and Cabinet Office staff is shown in the charts on pp. 48 and 49. Of Private Secretaries, one of their number, Thomas Jones, has written as follows.

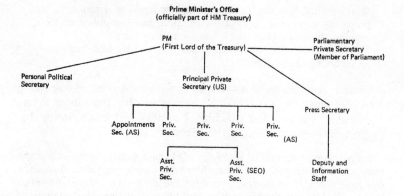

Prime Minister's Office
(officially part of HM Treasury)

The grades under secretary (US) and assistant secretary (AS) are explained in Chapter 4.
SEO is the Executive Class grade of Senior Executive Officer (senior to a junior Principal in the Administrative Grade).

....

DOCUMENT 3

THOMAS JONES ON PRIVATE SECRETARIES

From Thomas Jones, *A Diary with Letters*, Oxford University Press, 1954, pp. xix–xxi

The relations of the Prime Minister with his Secretaries are hardly less important than his relations with his Ministers.

The Private Secretaries arrange their master's daily timetable, form a barricade against unwanted bores, invent amusements for his recreation, assemble material for his speeches, guard his reputation, humour his foibles, tell stories, and talk nonsense as required. They have no settled hours or holidays and they neglect their families.

. . . his specialism should be omniscience. If a quotation from Burke is required, or the yield of sixpence on the income-tax, or the politics of the *Baltimore Sun*, or the name of a foreign ambassador's brand of cigar, the answer must be promptly forthcoming.

. . . he should never be in the way and never out of it. He is the one person whom the Prime Minister is glad to see enter his room; he will only enter at the right moment and on the right business; an unfailing instinct will dictate his withdrawal.

The Private Secretary does not seek public power; he nurses instead a passion for anonymity and secret influence. He would be horrified to see anything attributed to his own initiative. The reputation of his Chief comes

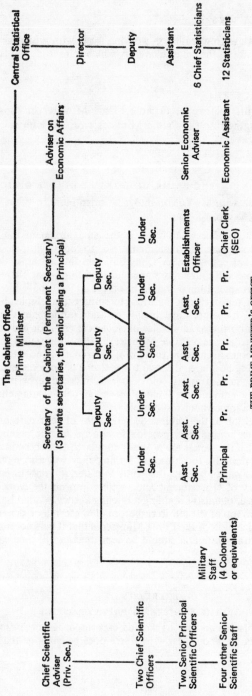

THE PRIME MINISTER'S OFFICE
THE CABINET OFFICE

first and last; his own reward lies in working freely with greatness in high places, in the service of the beloved country which transcends Minister and Secretary.

....

Mr Wilson, just before he became Prime Minister in 1964, contemplated strengthening the Prime Minister's private office:

....

DOCUMENT 4
MR WILSON ON THE PRIME MINISTER'S PRIVATE OFFICE
From an interview with Mr Wilson by Dr Norman Hunt in *Whitehall and Beyond*, BBC, 1964, pp. 18, 20

I am very worried about what I feel is the amateurism of the central direction of Government. If you compare No. 10 today with what it was under Attlee, or of course under Churchill, you find, I think, that it is much more remote and much more amateurish. I think that No. 10 is far too small. I'm not suggesting it should be on the scale of the White House with a staff of, I think, fifteen-hundred, to some extent duplicating and cutting across all the other departments of State (and again I'm rather against the idea of bringing in a series of *éminences grises* or Rasputins or court favourites to advise a Prime Minister); I think the right thing is to build up the Cabinet Secretariat to its proper strength. You see, perhaps the effect of having been a civil servant is that one is, to some extent in a Whitehall phrase, 'house trained', and one wants to see any experts properly dovetailed into the administrative machine—on an organisation chart, not floating about in a somewhat irresponsible way . . .

The traditional job of the Cabinet Secretariat is, of course, to brief—to service the cabinet committees, provide secretaries for the cabinet committees and see that the papers are properly circulated and a certain amount of coordination done by those means. I think they will also have to do much more in the way of briefing the Prime Minister, not only briefing him on the machinery of Government and briefing him on the work of any cabinet committee, but also providing a briefing agency, so that he is right up to date and on top of the job in respect of all these major departments of State. My conception of the Prime Minister is that if he's not managing director, he is at any rate and should be very much a full-time executive chairman.

....

EXERCISES
THE PRIME MINISTER'S PRIVATE OFFICE
2.1. Mr Wilson said that he wanted experts 'on an organisation chart, not floating about'. How or where does he envisage that the

members of the Prime Minister's private office should fit into an organisation chart?

 2.2. Where do the charts on pp. 48 and 49 show that the private office fits in?

Finally, Prime Ministers often look for advice (and hence concede influence) to individuals who may be neither officials nor Ministers. Thus Chamberlain kept closely in touch with Geoffrey Dawson, Editor of the *Times*. Churchill sought advice from the Oxford physicist, Lord Cherwell (and later brought him into the Government in a special 'statistical office'). Macmillan had a close confident in John Wyndham.

Chamberlain almost used Sir Horace Wilson, the Government's industrial adviser, as an adviser on foreign policy. Churchill evicted Wilson in 1940 as Hugh Dalton records:

....

DOCUMENT 5
THE EVICTION OF SIR HORACE WILSON

From Hugh Dalton, *The Fateful Years*, Muller, 1957, pp. 320–1

In Chamberlain's time Sir Horace Wilson occupied the small room opening out of the Cabinet Room at No. 10 Downing Street, facing towards the Horse Guards Parade. There every morning he reported for duty. But when he came, as usual, in good time on the morning of May 11th, he found that the paratroopers had arrived before him. On the couch, opposite the door through which he entered, sat Brendan Bracken, the new Prime Minister's Parliamentary Private Secretary, and Randolph Churchill, the new Prime Minister's son, the latter in uniform. They stared at Sir Horace, but no one spoke or smiled. Then he withdrew, never to return to that seat most proximate to power.

[Later Churchill appointed a senior civil servant to his private staff to work in Wilson's old room.]

....

DOCUMENT 6
THE RELATIONS OF A PRIME MINISTER WITH AN
OUTSIDE ADVISER AND CONFIDANT

From J. E. Wrench, *Geoffrey Dawson and Our Times*, Hutchinson, 1955, p. 373

Geoffrey [Dawson] remained in close contact with Neville Chamberlain during the latter's premiership. .... A study of the records available certainly gives the impression that Chamberlain valued the Editor's opinion and was strengthened in his own views by the knowledge that Geoffrey agreed with his policy and would support it in *The Times*.

[Extracts from Dawson's diary (quoted in Wrench, op. cit., pp. 376–7) show the relationship in operation:]

Sept. 14. Prime Minister decides to visit Hitler, Edward [Lord Halifax] imparted this momentous news to me at the Foreign Office in the afternoon under seal of secrecy till released but it enabled me to prepare for it, writing headlines and diplomatic notes and getting a leader started. . . .

Sept. 22. The Prime Minister's 2nd meeting with Hitler . . . drove down to see Neville Chamberlain off to Germany.

....

EXERCISES
PRIME MINISTERS AND OUTSIDE ADVISERS

3.1. Do these extracts from Dawson's diary support the view that Dawson influenced Chamberlain, or that Chamberlain used Dawson to secure support of the *Times* for his policies? (Answer briefly, unless you are able to consult the book itself for further evidence.)

3.2. Do you see anything wrong in a Prime Minister's seeking advice from a newspaper editor?

4 THE CABINET

Composition and functions

The Cabinet is the directing committee or board of management of British Government. It is composed of Members of Parliament (including some from the House of Lords) holding office in the Government. The size of the Cabinet has varied from sixteen to twenty-three (Mr Wilson's Cabinet 1964–6), except for the War Cabinets of 1916–18 and 1940–5. In most cases members of the Cabinet are heads of a major Department of State, bearing the title of Secretary of State or Minister. Some members of the Cabinet hold offices without heavy departmental duties, and their work is concerned either with advice or coordination at a high level, with the leadership of the two Houses or with special assignments (Lord President, Lord Privy Seal, Chancellor of the Duchy of Lancaster). The Prime Minister is chairman of the Cabinet.

The function of the Cabinet is (a) to take decisions at the highest level of government on matters of general policy rather than detail;

or (b) at lower levels of generality and importance, to take decisions which are on politically sensitive matters; or (c) acting as a court of appeal or arbitration, to decide between Ministers or Departments who have failed to agree on their own.

In addition to this high-level decision-taking the Cabinet (d) oversees and (e) coordinates the whole range of government operation and administration.

The Cabinet committees

The Cabinet works through a system of sub-committees and with the assistance of a small but powerful secretariat.

There have always been informal committees; the first formal committee was that for Imperial Defence established in 1904. Thereafter committees were set up from time to time; for example, one on foreign affairs in the 1930s. From 1942, first under Churchill and then Attlee, the committee system has been developed and formalised. In April 1968 Prime Minister Wilson announced a strengthening of the system, with the full Cabinet meeting less frequently than before, and a new Parliamentary and Political Committee.[1] The purpose of this committee would be to look at a future policy with some detachment from immediate departmental concerns, and to relate new policies to the support of the party in Parliament and the country. 'Relate' might here imply modifying the policies in deference to opinion in the party or modifying opinion, that is, actively seeking support for policies.

The system of Cabinet committees is private, if not wholly secret, so full information is lacking. Normally, it seems, there have been standing committees on Defence and Overseas Policy, Economic Affairs, a committee on Future Legislation (or an *ad hoc* committee on a particular piece of projected legislation) and other *ad hoc* committees, with particular jobs to do and more or less temporary. These sub-committees of the Cabinet will usually be composed of two or three Cabinet and senior Ministers, other Ministers concerned in the committee's agenda, and sometimes high civil servants. The chair is taken either by the Prime Minister or a senior colleague.

The function of the system is that of any sub-committee—to consider in detail matters for which the Cabinet itself would have no time. The Cabinet committee system has the particular purpose and advantage that it can bring into the discussion non-Cabinet

---

[1] This was itself replaced a year later by a Parliamentary Committee of six senior Ministers.

Ministers and civil servants, including some who are only indirectly concerned in the agenda. This ensures effective communication and a measure of coordination. It can also help to train junior Ministers for Cabinet responsibilities.

A system of sub-committees is by definition subordinate to the parent committee, in this case, the Cabinet. Committee decisions are reported to the Cabinet for ratification, and the Cabinet has the right of veto. In practice, objections to a committee's line of policy are likely to have been uncovered and met during its deliberations, and Cabinet approval is thus ensured. But, where this is not the case, the members of the Cabinet who do not sit on the committee are not in a strong position to resist its conclusions. Thus the development of the committee system has lessened the importance and power of the Cabinet as a whole. At the same time it may have increased the power of the Prime Minister, for he is at the centre of the system, taking a leading part in some committees and keeping in touch with the rest.

The Secretariat

The Cabinet Secretariat owes its origin to the pressures of war. It was established in 1917 by Lloyd George. Previously the work of the Cabinet had been conducted with what looks like terrifying informality. No minutes were taken and sometimes Ministers were not at all sure what had been decided.

The only official record was that sent by the Prime Minister to the Queen. Lloyd George, a 'master of the art of getting things done', changed this amateur and gentlemanly system. Taking over the Secretary of the Committee of Imperial Defence, he established a small team of civil servants to expedite the work of the Cabinet. Henceforth, the Cabinet Secretariat was responsible, under the Prime Minister, for preparing the papers for Cabinet meetings (agenda and supporting papers), making a record of the meeting and seeing to the initiation of action arising from Cabinet decisions. The Secretariat now has its own civil service head at Permanent Secretary level, the Secretary of the Cabinet. He is the engineer-in-charge of this government machine, but he takes his orders from the Prime Minister.

Coordination

One of the functions of the Cabinet is to coordinate—to see, for example, that the Minister of Transport's proposals for building motorways are related to the Economic Departments' plans for industrial development; or that the Minister of Agriculture's plans for farming fit into the Chancellor's Budget and the Board of Trade's import policies.

Coordination is carried out by the Prime Minister and by other senior Ministers, both personally and through the sub-committee system. The Cabinet Ministers without departmental responsibilities are, for obvious reasons, often given such inter-departmental functions. The senior Economic Ministers have a natural co-ordinating role in the allocating of finance. The Minister of Defence has a clearly defined coordinating function in relation to the other Service Ministers, who are not in the Cabinet—two Ministers and Parliamentary Under-Secretaries for the three Services.

Much unnecessary confusion has been caused by the so-called 'Overlords' controversy of 1951. Churchill announced the appointment of two Ministers to supervisory positions—Lord Woolton, the Lord President of the Council, was to supervise Agriculture and Food; Lord Leathers became Secretary of State for the Coordination of Transport, Fuel and Power. The arrangement was criticised partly because the two Ministers were peers (hence their nickname, 'Overlords'), but mainly because of the confusion of responsibility. Who was accountable for a coordinated Department, the Minister or the Coordinator? The arrangement was withdrawn. But this does not mean that coordination was abandoned—that would be absurd—but since then the arrangements have been less heavily publicised, in order to ensure the continuing responsibility of the named Minister for his Department. (Coordination may also be secured by the amalgamation of Ministries, as in the cases of the Foreign and Commonwealth Offices and the Ministries of Health and Social Security.)

Note: In October, 1969, the process of coordination by amalgamation was taken further with the incorporation in the Ministry of Technology of the Ministry of Power and industrial responsibilities of the Board of Trade. At the same time, Housing and Local Government and Transport were joined under a Secretary of State for Housing, Local Government and Regional Planning—a coordinating Minister, but in the Commons, and with certain specific responsibilities of his own.

Collective responsibility

The Cabinet functions under the convention of collective responsibility. This has been formulated by Prime Ministers past and present. Consider the following document.

DOCUMENT 7
THE CONVENTION OF COLLECTIVE RESPONSIBILITY

(a) *Lord Salisbury, 1878.* From Lady G. Cecil, *Life of Robert, Marquis of Salisbury*, Hodder and Stoughton, 1921, II, pp. 219–20

For all that passes in Cabinet each member of it who does not resign is absolutely and irretrievably responsible, and has no right afterwards to say that he agreed in one case to a compromise, while in another he was persuaded by his colleagues. . . . It is only on the principle that absolute responsibility is undertaken by every member of the Cabinet who, after a decision is arrived at, remains a member of it, that the joint responsibility of Ministers to Parliament can be upheld, and one of the most essential principles of parliamentary responsibility established.

(b) *Gladstone, 1883.* From J. Morley, *Life of Gladstone*, Macmillan, 1903, III, p. 113

. . . I should be as far as possible from asserting that under all circumstances speech must be confined within the exact limits to which action is tied down. But I think the dignity and authority, not to say the honour and integrity, of government require that the liberty of speaking beyond these limits should be exercised sparingly, reluctantly, and with much modesty and reserve.

(c) *Harold Wilson, 1951.* H.C. Deb. vol. 487, 24 April 1951, col. 230

. . . the principle [of collective responsibility] requires from each Minister a full and wholehearted acceptance of the measures decided upon by the Cabinet and of the policies underlying them.

A convention is a customary constitutional rule. The convention of collective responsibility developed originally as Ministers united in face of the Crown. The centre of power shifted to the Commons and the electorate, and it is in face of them that the modern Cabinet strives to retain its unity. Thus the convention serves a political purpose—otherwise it would, no doubt, have been modified. But the convention is also an essential feature of British democracy. It ensures that a Cabinet stands broadly on principles, not on personalities. In this way, responsibility for particular policies can be ascribed to the government, and the public may approve or reject these policies.

The convention has occasionally been flouted; notably in 1931–2 when three Liberal and free-trading Ministers joined the National Government, but with permission to oppose publicly any measure of tariff protection. This arrangement shortly broke down: the three Ministers found their position too embarrassing. Thus the convention was reinforced.

The Lord Chancellor, Lord Sankey, in defending this 'agreement to differ' said that the convention of collective responsibility was 'an ideal to be aimed at, but not always one to be realised.' He doubted whether it would ever be possible to get a large Cabinet to be unanimous on every subject.

A few years earlier, in 1928, Lord Birkenhead had confessed to the House of Lords that he was opposed to the Equal Franchise Bill, which it was his duty to commend to them:

... I have been a member of a Cabinet with a very slight interruption for thirteen years, and I can hardly recall a single measure of first-class importance on which all members of the Cabinet had precisely the same views. ...

Through my own attitude there runs a golden vein of consistency. I was against the extension of the franchise to women. I am against the extension of the franchise to women. ...

I have spent nearly the whole of my political life in giving wise advice to my fellow-countrymen, which they have almost invariably disregarded, and if I had resigned every time that my wise and advantageous advice was rejected I should seldom, indeed, during that critical period, have been in office.

EXERCISES

THE CONVENTION OF COLLECTIVE RESPONSIBILITY

4.1. What political or constitutional arguments would you have used in criticism of Lords Sankey and Birkenhead?

4.2. Is a rule still a rule if nothing happens when you disobey it?

4.3. Does anything happen if you disobey the convention of collective responsibility?

5 THE PRIME MINISTER'S JOB—OVERALL

The Prime Minister and the Cabinet

(a) The Prime Minister appoints the Cabinet. This is one of the few operations of the Prime Minister which by custom is in his hands alone. It could not be a matter for the Cabinet, since that body does not at that moment exist. It could be, but is not, a matter for the Parliamentary Party. Of course, the Prime Minister has to observe some limitations. One or two very senior colleagues will expect not only Cabinet membership but posts commensurate with their seniority. The Prime Minister may wish to seek advice on other appointments, and consideration of prudence and tactics will suggest other appointments, for example, so as to balance old- and middle-age, right and left. But within these limits, the Prime Minister is free to choose. He has thus an immense power of patronage: on him depend the political careers of perhaps a hundred or more serious contenders for office. But more important, on the quality of his choice depends the quality of his government.

The Prime Minister has the power to break as well as to make men. He can dismiss members of his Cabinet with no effective right of appeal against his decision, and with the approval and gratitude of the newly promoted replacements. The extent of this power was demonstrated in July 1962 by Mr Macmillan's sudden, brutal dismissal of seven Cabinet Ministers at one sweep.

(b) The Prime Minister is chairman of the Cabinet, in the strongest sense of the term chairmanship: he is leader and captain, as well as umpire. The functions of his chairmanship are indicated in the following document.

....

DOCUMENT 8
THE PRIME MINISTER AND THE CABINET

(a) From Lord Morrison, *Government and Parliament*, Oxford University Press, 1964, pp. 18–19

In a little while the Prime Minister or the Secretary of the Cabinet will appear and invite the Ministers to assemble round the long table covered with green baize. Each Cabinet Minister has his allotted place, having some relationship to ministerial status. The Prime Minister is in the Chair with his back to the fireplace, facing Horse Guards Parade.

An agenda and, probably, papers will already have been circulated. The relevant Cabinet Papers are indicated under each item and there may be references to earlier related documents. For most items there are papers, but sometimes a note will read, 'To be raised orally by . . .'

Sometimes the Prime Minister or, with his agreement, other Ministers will raise matters of urgency not on the agenda, or mention the settlement of some problem that had arisen at a previous meeting.

The Prime Minister will call upon the Minister principally concerned with the first item on the agenda, unless convenience requires that the order of business be changed. The normal and most appropriate course is for that Minister to make his case. If there is general agreement a conclusion is expeditiously reached. But there may be criticism, alterations in the course proposed may be urged, there may even be outright opposition.

To describe the ministerial contributions as speeches would not be quite right. They are, or at any rate, should be, to the point and in the nature of quiet, well-considered remarks, calculated to lead the Cabinet in the direction desired.

(b) From an interview with Mr Harold Wilson by Kenneth Harris in the *Observer* Magazine, 24 October 1965

P.M.: 'I've followed very closely what I learned from Lord Attlee when I was a member of his Cabinet: circulation of papers before the meeting; decisions not satisfactorily cleared at departmental level to be referred to the Prime Minister; extensive use of Cabinet sub-committees so that we can economise on the use of the time of the full Cabinet; re-introduction of his insistence—I say re-introduction because the practice seemed to have lapsed at some time since his day—that all Cabinet reports must have a price tag, meaning that the financial and economic implications must be previously agreed with the Treasury—which is a great time-saver in Cabinet, and a solvent of possible tensions outside it.

'I also followed Lord Attlee in putting emphasis on the attendance of all members whenever humanly possible, and on punctuality. And the key thing is that when the Cabinet takes a decision, that's it. There was one occasion when I noticed that a new Minister had referred to something that had been decided in Cabinet as a "proposal". I sent him a short note saying that the Cabinet makes decisions not proposals, and that was the end of the matter.'

Mr Wilson stressed that his Cabinet had 'talked a good deal less than Clem's did'; did not vote; had got through a good deal of work without bad temper or personal clashes. The sub-committees had been invaluable.

'This Cabinet, like every other, owes a great deal to the non-departmental Ministers. I've come to believe that the strength of a Cabinet is in its non-departmental Ministers. They are the half-backs of the Government team. They don't often score goals, or hit the headlines, but no team can be a success without a good half-back line.'

(c) From Lord Hill of Luton, *Both Sides of the Hill*, Heinemann, 1964, p. 235

... I thought Harold Macmillan's chairmanship of the Cabinet to be superb by any standards. If he dominated it (he usually did), he did not do it by *ex cathedra* pronouncements or by laying down the law or by expressing his views too early in a discussion or by any of the arts of repression which skilful chairmen are tempted to cultivate. It was done by sheer superiority of mind and judgement. He encouraged genuine discussion, provided it kept to the point. If he found himself in a minority he accepted the fact with grace and humour. If I have a criticism it is that, now and again, the Cabinet was consulted at too late a stage in the evolution of some important line of policy: he seemed to forget that many of us had not been present at the Cabinet committee concerned with the topic.

(d) From F. Williams, *A Pattern of Rulers*, Longmans, 1965, p. 147

Hore-Belisha told Francis Williams that to sit under Chamberlain in Cabinet was like being a departmental manager in a firm in which the chairman owned all the shares.

....

The part of the Prime Minister in Cabinet discussions is of course crucial. A strong Prime Minister will speak with authority either as one closely concerned with the matter whose views must weigh heavy, or as chairman formulating the sense of the meeting according to his own weighing of the arguments and of his colleagues. But with a less forceful Prime Minister, or on an issue which is not central to the Prime Minister's concerns, some other senior Minister, perhaps the chairman of the relevant committee, will give a lead. There is no constitutional prescription for the right way to run a Cabinet: this will depend on political circumstances and the peculiar alchemy of people under stress working together in a group.

EXERCISE
THE PRIME MINISTER AS CHAIRMAN OF THE CABINET

5. From the evidence of document 8, list the jobs done by the Prime Minister as chairman of the Cabinet.

The Prime Minister and the Government

The Prime Minister is also at the head of the Government—not only the Cabinet but the non-Cabinet Ministers and their Departments. He is:

(a) The creator of the Government, having powers of appointment and dismissal over all Ministers. His powers over the Civil Service are more restricted, but his approval is necessary for appointment of Permanent Secretaries. But the element of power should not be over-emphasised. He is personnel director of a very large organisation and his concern will be with efficiency, with finding the right jobs for the right men. Necessarily he will look to his Chief Whip for advice about filling over a hundred posts on the political side of the Government.

(b) The 'full-time executive chairman' of an immense organisation (the phrase is Mr Wilson's). Like any individual in such a position, he cannot himself attend to very much in detail. His job is to appoint an efficient staff, and see that they can get on with their work according to the general directions of the government. He must encourage, even inspire; he must coordinate, preserve a balance, keep the convoy moving steadily. Frequently he must step in to unravel acute problems and see that opportunities are taken. For all this he needs to keep in touch with his Ministers without taking over their work or working himself too deeply in one Department.

This is to ask a great deal of one man; not surprisingly, some Prime Ministers have not been good in this crucial role. Here are some illustrations of Prime Ministers at work, and in their relations with colleagues.

....

DOCUMENT 9
PRIME MINISTERS AND THEIR COLLEAGUES

(a) From Lord Simon, *Retrospect*, Hutchinson, 1952, p. 275

When Home Secretary for the first time I occasionally asked for an interview with Asquith to tell him of an impending difficulty and to ask his advice. Asquith would bring his sledge-hammer mind to bear and in a few minutes would express his view, usually, I am glad to say, agreeing with mine, but sometimes, as a matter of prudence, deciding that the question should be brought before the Cabinet. Baldwin, when I was Home Secretary for the second time, was equally considerate. But, in my experience, his method was to ask what I proposed and then, after a series of grimaces as he pulled in silence at his pipe, to say, 'well, carry on.' Neville Chamberlain, on such occasions, adopted a method different from either of these. He would go into the matter as though it was his personal problem, test it at every point, listen in a businesslike fashion to what one had to say, and then state his conclusion with the finality of a General Manager conducting a company's affairs.

(b) From Thomas Jones, *A Diary with Letters*, Oxford University Press, 1954, p. xxviii

[Bonar Law] was an admirable chairman of Cabinet and was not unlike Neville Chamberlain: painstaking, methodical, unhumorous, a master of detail, not entirely unconscious in a quiet way of his own competence. He gave clear, positive directions and summed up a discussion in Cabinet with such precision that his words were taken down verbatim by the secretary as the permanent record in the Minutes. He was a son of Martha. So were Neville Chamberlain and Ramsay MacDonald. They sat at the big table, unlocked red boxes, read papers, noted replies, wrote letters by hand, preferred the study of memoranda to the study of men. They liked to do their own drafting and to correct the drafts of others. MacDonald and Chamberlain sat up late at night entering up their diaries. Their time-tables were neatly filled with appointments whereas a son of Mary, Baldwin, for example liked a blank pad with leisure for the casual caller and the digressive friend.

(c) From a letter written by Ernest Brown, Minister of Labour, to Neville Chamberlain in 1940, quoted in K. Feiling, *The Life of Neville Chamberlain*, Macmillan, 1947, p. 303

You cannot know what a comfort it has been to hard pressed departmental ministers to know that, when their subjects have to be discussed, whoever else has not read their papers and digested them, one man had—the Prime Minister.

(d) From G. M. Young, *Stanley Baldwin*, Hart-Davis, 1952, p. 100

Sooner or later every one of [Baldwin's] colleagues could report the same experience. 'Why come to me? I have perfect confidence in you.' Letters laying some problem of administration before him for decision are answered always promptly, but not so helpfully: 'Go ahead as you propose in your letter just received' or, not infrequently, 'The P.M. has no time to study these papers, and leaves the matter to Mr A's discretion.'

(e) *On Prime Ministers' uneasy relationships with colleagues*

(i) [Macdonald] did not delight in the company of his colleagues. (Thomas Jones, op. cit., p. xxvii)

(ii) It is easier for me to talk these matters over with you than with any of my colleagues. (Baldwin to Dawson, Editor of the *Times*, quoted in Lord Vansittart, *The Mist Procession*, Hutchinson, 1958, p. 354)

(iii) There can be no friendship between the top five men in a Cabinet. (Lloyd George, quoted in Thomas Jones, op. cit., p. 52)

(f) From an interview with Mr Harold Wilson by Kenneth Harris in the *Observer* Magazine, 24 October 1965

P.M.: No. 10 should be a power house not a monastery. And though you've got to let departmental Ministers get on with their job, you've got to know what is happening.

Harris: The fact is that previous Prime Ministers have got out of touch. And that people writing about them have said how difficult it is to keep in touch. Baldwin. Lloyd George. Ramsay MacDonald. We were told that Harold Macmillan was in touch but got out of touch.

P.M.: The levers of power are all here in No. 10. In the Cabinet Room. The ability of the Prime Minister to use them depends on the Prime Minister being in touch with what is going on—and not going on—and if all those people around the Prime Minister—Cabinet officials, as well as Cabinet Ministers, departmental officials as well as Ministers, once realise that the Prime Minister wants to know what is going on, and intends to know what is going on, in all departments, they'll make sure that he gets to know. The more things you take an interest in, the more information comes back to you. A Prime Minister governs by curiosity and range of interest. You learn from what Ministers come and tell you, what advice they ask of you to enable them to make and carry out their departmental decisions. The more they sense that you care, the more they tell you.

EXERCISES
PRIME MINISTERS AND THEIR COLLEAGUES

6.1. What do you think Lloyd George meant when he said of Chamberlain: 'a retail mind in a wholesale business'?

6.2. Is there a case for preferring the Baldwin method of leadership to Neville Chamberlain's?

6.3. Would you expect a Prime Minister's relations with his colleagues normally to be better than those indicated in (e) above?

6.4. How does Mr Wilson's method (extract (f)) differ from Baldwin's and Chamberlain's?

The Prime Minister, party and Parliament

The Prime Minister has a part to play in the House of Commons as well as in the Cabinet Room. He must be chief spokesman and leader of his party on the floor of the House, taking part in major debates, making statements, answering questions twice a week.

Outside the House the Prime Minister must keep in touch with his backbenchers. Formally, he will sometimes attend party meetings; informally, he may circulate, talk and listen.

Some Prime Ministers have not been very good at 'keeping in touch'; it requires qualities of social ease, empathy, 'clubbability' and a willingness to sacrifice time which might be spent on apparently more urgent matters. Leadership on the Floor of the House is less likely to be neglected, and is usually carried out to the satisfaction of the Government side. A Prime Minister who is a good House of

Commons man will smooth the path for government business and improve his own public reputation.

....

DOCUMENT 10

LORD MORRISON ON PRIME MINISTERS AND

THE HOUSE OF COMMONS

From Lord Morrison, *Government and Parliament*, Oxford University Press, 1964, pp. 181–2

The House will forgive much in a Minister if it likes him and if it knows he likes the House. I remember an incident that shocked me during the lifetime of the 1929–31 minority Labour Government. I was sitting beside the Prime Minister (Mr Ramsay MacDonald) on the Treasury Bench. He had been rather cruelly and harshly attacked about the mounting unemployment by Sir Kingsley Wood from the Conservative Front Bench. Mr MacDonald had a rough time of it, but when at the end he whispered to me, 'Herbert, I hate this place', I was deeply shocked, and began to understand why in some way, considerable as he was as a writer on constitutional and parliamentary matters, Mr MacDonald, at any rate as Prime Minister, did not achieve an effective sympathetic relationship with the House of Commons.

....

Prime Minister and people

A Government will be judged in part by the performance of the Prime Minister (see chapter 12 on elections). He has therefore to project himself, or, rather, project an image of himself, which will be acceptable to millions of people. The medium of projection was once the public meeting and the press, reporting the parliamentary feats of the Prime Minister. Since 1959, television has supplanted both as the most important medium, projecting the Prime Minister directly in interviews and at meetings, reporting his parliamentary performances. Television also makes much of the Prime Minister as the embodiment of the Government. He is seen arriving at 10 Downing Street, greeting distinguished visitors, departing from airports, visiting foreign potentates. Much of this is purely visual news, available only to' cameras, and in its cumulative effect, quite potent.

The content of the 'image' has been much worked on recently by public relations experts. Previously, Prime Ministers from Gladstone through Lloyd George to Baldwin and Churchill had done their own public relations work. The productions of the experts have not been markedly different, but it may be said that the politicians (with the exception perhaps of Baldwin) have not treated their image as something only tenuously connected with their own political selves, and have regarded political issues as still quite important. (The corollary of the business of image-projection is that the other leader must be presented as unattractively as possible.)

The results of this work at election times may be studied in the pictures issued by the parties. Prime Ministers are presented, according to the possibilities of the raw material, as men of distinction and authority, as friendly chaps anyone might talk to over the garden gate, as trustworthy, as determined, as (whatever it may mean) sincere. All of this is understandable. Politics has to be reduced to very general terms and humanised, bearing in mind that the attitudes and policies which lie behind the faces should not be neglected.

Baldwin is interesting from this point of view because he took very seriously his role in relation to the people. He projected himself as a pipe-smoking countryman (though he was an industrialist); and he believed there was a reverse process, the people projecting their will through him. Consider the following extracts:

....

DOCUMENT II
BALDWIN AS MAN OF THE PEOPLE

(a) From Lord Vansittart, *The Mist Procession*, Hutchinson, 1958, p. 352
Baldwin wore a pipe as ships wear flags, could go rustic as Marie Antoinette went Shepherdess. . . .

(b) From G. M. Young, *Stanley Baldwin*, Hart-Davis, 1952, pp. 56–7
Baldwin was an Englishman not casually, by accident of birth, but deliberately and by election. To be an Englishman was the part he had undertaken to play . . . the gait, the accent, the scenery, the words—all were prepared. Within a few days this man from the provinces had become a national figure: a fond projection of everything that the common Englishman still believed himself to be. . . . They liked to talk about him; to see pictures of him smoking . . . he was once found before a looking glass, getting his pipe at the right angle for a photographer. . . .

(c) From G. M. Young, op. cit., p. 54
He was Prime Minister because none better could be thought of. But of all the gifts which that office seems to require, there was one he believed himself to possess in pre-eminent degree. 'My worst enemy could never say

that I do not understand the people of England.' And it was in corresponding terms that he conceived his duty. Whatever else the Prime Minister may do, or be, he must bring that knowledge into the Cabinet room, and make it tell in the deliberations of his colleagues . . . his colleagues must know and feel that this lonely man does embody the force to which they owe their offices: the will of the people, the sense of the nation.

[One reservation must be made about these passages (b) and (c) above. Except where indicated, this is not Baldwin speaking during his time in office, but G. M. Young, the historian, interpreting Baldwin's recollections of his time in office.]

....

EXERCISE
PRIME MINISTER AND PEOPLE

7. In what ways, in practice, can a Prime Minister discover the attitudes and views of 'the people of England'?

6 THE QUALITIES REQUIRED OF A PRIME MINISTER

One of the keys to effective politics is to find men of high capacity for the top political jobs. The processes of selection of Cabinet and Prime Minister are described in other chapters (3, 7 and 12). Some of the qualities of recent Prime Ministers have been illustrated. Some of the qualities required might be deduced from the nature of the Prime Minister's many functions. But each occupant of the office shapes the job to his own capacities and style and to the demands of a changing political situation. Drawing up specifications for an ideal Prime Minister is therefore hazardous work for the political scientist, and perhaps more appropriate for a party game. So this section is mainly a do-it-yourself one: make your own list of qualities. There are, however, a few firm points to be made.

(a) While an American President must needs be white, male and (until 1960 at least) Protestant, it seems a British Prime Minister must be white, male and conventionally religious.

(b) There is no general agreement that a Prime Minister must be of the highest intellectual calibre. Some judges plead for a certain ordinariness of mind, and Bagehot called for 'a man of first-rate capacity and second-rate ideas'. Some recent Prime Ministers— Eden, Macmillan, Wilson—have held first-class degrees; others— Baldwin, Douglas-Home—third-class degrees; Lloyd George, MacDonald and Churchill did not enjoy a university education. It looks as if academic distinction is not essential, but some force or nimbleness of intellect is needed.

(c) Besides vigour of mind, there must be a certain attack. A Prime Minister must be industrious, unlike Baldwin: 'Wake me up when you have finished with that' (of foreign affairs, in the Cabinet), and 'The PM is always being asked about the situation in Russia and would like to know what to say. Not more than a page.' But hard work is not enough; a Prime Minister must have the strength to push other people along and around. He must not, like Asquith, earn Amery's harsh comment: '. . . for twenty years he has held a season ticket on the line of least resistance.'

(d) A Prime Minister should not mind criticism, and certainly should not, like Chamberlain, resent it. More, he should accept the troubles and difficulties of politics as a necessary part of the job. The point is well made by Vansittart in his book *The Mist Procession* (Hutchinson, 1958, p. 354). He disagreed with Churchill's judgement that Baldwin was 'an adroit and relentless politician'. 'Adroit, yes, relentless no. Winston liked trouble; S.B. eschewed it. The difference was unbridgeable.'

(e) Beyond the above, a Prime Minister requires many other rare and imprecise qualities, judgement, patience, courage.

....

DOCUMENT 12

THE QUALITIES OF A PRIME MINISTER:

MR CHURCHILL AND MR ATTLEE ON BEING

APPOINTED PRIME MINISTER

(a) From W. S. Churchill, *The Gathering Storm*, Cassell, 1948, pp. 526–7

Thus, then, on the night of the 10th of May, at the outset of this mighty battle, I acquired the chief power in the State, which henceforth I wielded in ever-growing measure for five years and three months of world war, at the end of which time, all our enemies having surrendered unconditionally or being about to do so, I was immediately dismissed by the British electorate from all further conduct of their affairs.

During these last crowded days of the political crisis my pulse had not quickened at any moment. I took it all as it came. But I cannot conceal from the reader of this truthful account that as I went to bed at about 3 a.m. I was conscious of a profound sense of relief. At last I had the authority to give directions over the whole scene. I felt as if I were walking with destiny, and that all my past life had been but a preparation for this hour and for this trial. Ten years in the political wilderness had freed me from ordinary party antagonisms. My warnings over the last six years had been so numerous, so detailed, and were now so terribly vindicated, that no one could gainsay me. I could not be reproached either for making the war or with want of preparation for it. I thought I knew a good deal about it all, and I was sure I should not fail. Therefore, although impatient for the morning, I slept soundly and had no need for cheering dreams. Facts are better than dreams.

(b) From C. R. Attlee, *As it Happened*, Heinemann, 1954, p. 148

As the day wore on, country results confirmed our victory and by the middle of the afternoon it was clear that we had won a great victory.

Lord Portal, who was Chairman of the Great Western Railway, gave the family tea at Paddington, and presently I was told by the Prime Minister that he was resigning. A summons to the Palace followed. My wife drove me there and waited outside for me. The King gave me his commission to form a Government. He always used to say that I looked very surprised, as indeed I certainly was at the extent of our success. We went to a Victory Rally at Westminster Central Hall where I announced that I had been charged with the task of forming a Government, looked in at a Fabian Society gathering and then returned to Stanmore after an exciting day.

EXERCISE

DESIRABLE QUALITIES IN A PRIME MINISTER

8. On the evidence of these quotations only, who do you think would be the better Prime Minister, and why?

7 THE POWER OF THE PRIME MINISTER

DOCUMENT 13
HOW POWERFUL IS THE PRIME MINISTER?

(a) Lord Home, Foreign Secretary, in the *Observer*, 16 September 1962

Every Cabinet Minister is in a sense the Prime Minister's agent—his assistant. There's no question about that. It is the Prime Minister's Cabinet, and he is the one person who is directly responsible to the Queen for what the Cabinet does.

If the Cabinet discusses anything it is the Prime Minister who decides what the collective view of the Cabinet is. A Minister's job is to save the Prime Minister all the work he can. But no Minister could make a really important move without consulting the Prime Minister, and if the Prime Minister wanted to take a certain step, the Cabinet Minister concerned would either have to agree, argue it out in Cabinet, or resign.

(b) (i) From Lord Morrison, preface to 3rd ed. of *Government and Parliament*, Oxford University Press, 1964, pp. 9–10

. . . I have not thought it necessary to refer to exaggerated beliefs as to the role and status of the Prime Minister. He is clearly the most important member of the Cabinet unless—as has happened in some cases—he subordinates himself and prefers to leave the heavier burdens to some of his colleagues. It would be an illusion to accept the idea that the modern British Prime Minister has become as powerful as the President of the United States of America. And it would be wrong to assume that Gladstone and Disraeli were cyphers in the Governments over which they presided.

(ii) From Lord Morrison, op. cit., pp. 51–2

The first and most important non-departmental Minister is the Prime Minister himself. . . . As the head of the Government he is *primus inter pares*. He is the leader of his party. . . . He cannot know everything that is going on over the whole field of government and it would be foolish of him to try, but he must know enough to be ready to intervene if he apprehends that something is going wrong. . . . He is, of course, eminently a coordinating Minister. . . . He is not the master of the Cabinet . . . but (except on occasions of emergency) he ought not to, and usually does not, presume to give directions or decisions which are proper to the Cabinet or one of its Committees, even though his position is rightly one of special authority. . . .

(c) From Sir Anthony Eden, *Full Circle*, Cassell, 1960, p. 269

A Prime Minister is still nominally *primus inter pares* but in fact his authority is stronger than that. The right to choose his colleagues, to ask for a dissolution of Parliament and, if he is a Conservative, to appoint the chairman of the party organisation, add up to a formidable total of power.

(d) Stanley Baldwin, quoted in Reith, *Into the Wind*, Hodder and Stoughton, 1949, p. 129

No matter how much imagination or vision or energy the Prime Minister may have, it's like being stuck in a glue pot.

(e) From Earl of Oxford and Asquith, *Memories and Reflections*, Cassell, 1928, Vol. ii, p. 207

There is not, and cannot be, from the nature of the case, any authoritative definition of the precise relation of the Prime Minister to his colleagues. 'In practice', as Sir William Harcourt says, 'the thing depends very much upon the character of the man'. . . . The office of Prime Minister is what its holder chooses and is able to make of it.

9.1. What might be the *precise* possible meaning of *primus inter pares* (first among equals)?

9.2. Measurement of the views expressed.

For this we need an approximate scale of prime ministerial power, and for such a scale we need a point of reference. Now the important constitutional question is how powerful the Prime Minister is in relation to his colleagues, and this gives us our point of reference. (It would be possible but much more difficult, and less useful for our immediate concerns, to compare his power with that of, say, the Archbishop of Canterbury, or the Governor of the Bank of England, or the headmaster of a school.)

Here is a suggested scale of prime ministerial power:

(A) co-equal
(B) chairman or *primus inter pares*
(C) leader
(D) dominant
(E) supreme (dictator)

If you are not satisfied with this scale, make another!

Now indicate where the quotations in document 13 would go on the scale. Use more than one figure if you are uncertain:

(a) Home
(b) Morrison (i)
    Morrison (ii)
(c) Eden
(d) Baldwin
(e) Asquith

9.3. (a) Is there a tendency for men who were, or had been, Prime Ministers to rate the powers of the office high or low?

(b) Is there a tendency for post-1945 politicians to rate the powers of the office higher or lower than earlier politicians?

The factors affecting the power of the Prime Minister

The basic elements of the Prime Minister's power, as set out at the beginning of this chapter, were:

leadership of the majority party;
power of appointment and dismissal;
chairmanship of the Cabinet;
high public prestige.

Political elements have strengthened the Prime Minister's position:

the growing complexity of government enhances the Prime Minister's position as coordinator;

foreign and international economic affairs are of overriding importance and are essentially prime ministerial territory;

the development of television has given an impression of personal government, so that

elections have been fought to some extent as personal contests between rival leaders;

the Prime Minister makes the crucial political choice—the date of the next general election;

the Prime Minister's personal staff has been slightly strengthened.

However, powerful factors still operate to moderate the power of the Prime Minister:

the Cabinet has a tradition and a working philosophy of collective responsibility;

in particular, a Prime Minister must normally carry with him a number of his senior colleagues (who might claim his office);

the party must be carried along too, and no Prime Minister can persistently outrage his own backbenchers and (to a less extent) the party in the country;

the Departments must ultimately respond to prime ministerial direction, but they cannot be simply 'pushed around', especially if their Minister is on their side;

the sheer weight of the Prime Minister's job forces him to share the burden; and his colleagues are convenient, to say the least, for this purpose.

EXERCISES

STRENGTH IN A PRIME MINISTER

10.1. Does it make any difference to the powers of the office that the Prime Minister has a positive political personality? Look again at Asquith's remarks in document 13 (e).

Before answering, see how many of the factors listed above would be affected *substantially* by the PM's personality.

Now answer the first part of the question:

Yes, it makes a substantial difference
Yes, it makes some difference
Yes, it makes a little difference
No, it makes hardly any difference
No, it makes no difference at all.

10.2. Do you think that a 'strong' Prime Minister is preferable to a weak one?

First, consider what would be a proper basis of preference? What would be 'best for the country'? Refer back to the sections on the work and qualities of a Prime Minister.

Then, consider whether one of the following statements fits your own views:

(a) . . . on a question of policy there can be no doubt that the most successful administrations are those in which there is a strong Prime Minister and a subordinate Cabinet. (Harcourt, quoted in A. G. Gardiner, *Life of Sir William Harcourt*, vol. ii, Constable, 1923, p. 612)

(b) Indeed a Prime Minister in peace time ought not to have a policy. If he has able ministers he ought to rely on them, and policies should come from departmental ministers, assisted as they are by all the knowledge and experience that their Departments can offer. The qualities which made Lloyd George a great Prime Minister in wartime made him a disastrous Prime Minister in peace time. . . (W. I. Jennings, *The British Constitution*, Cambridge University Press, 1941, pp. 160–1)

(c) A Premier soon imparts his own tone to his government and if he fails to bind his ministers together, to tackle contemporary problems, or to ensure action, then there is no one who can, so to speak, steer the bus from a back seat. (J. P. Mackintosh, *The British Cabinet*, Stevens, 1962, p. 384)

GUIDE TO EXERCISES

1. Most of the time, it is important to recognise, the Prime Minister is acting as a member of a group of Ministers. On a strict interpretation of 'individually' therefore, the answer would be:

chairing of a Cabinet committee;
chairing an *ad hoc* meeting of Ministers;
interviewing a Minister;
approving appointments;
dealing by decision or comment with the submissions of Departments.

When he is acting as chairman the element of individual decision-making may be diminished by the responsibilities of the group; but it still seems reasonable, given the status of the Prime Minister, to include these functions among those requiring individual choice. (It is interesting, and possibly significant, that the extract from Mr Wilson is much more perceptive about power than the piece by Mr Macmillan's 'supporter'.)

2.1. In the Cabinet Secretariat. But Mr Wilson does not say how an enlarged Secretariat would relate to other parts of the machinery of government. For example, how far should the staff of the Secretariat go in initiating the execution of a Cabinet (or prime ministerial) decision?

2.2. The charts on pp. 48 and 49 show that there is a small but powerful private office apart from the Cabinet Secretariat. This is formally part of the Treasury, but is in practice genuinely the Prime Minister's office.

3.1. The latter; but it might be inferred that such a close relationship would be reciprocal. (Of course, as indicated by Wrench at the beginning of document 6, other evidence confirms this.)

3.2. No. But it should be expected that the Prime Minister would regard such advice as a small part only of the advice on which he should base his policy. In particular, a Prime Minister should look to his political colleagues and his senior professional advisers.

4.1. The most important argument is indicated in the text: the convention which Sankey and Birkenhead were criticising is valuable constitutionally in securing a government of policies rather than men. This preserves real choice for the public, in that policies and outlooks may be attributed to governments and criticised accordingly; also, the behaviour of governments is to some extent more predictable.

Other arguments for the convention are that it provides a way out of deadlock for a Cabinet, and may discourage the persistent postponement of decisions through failure to agree, and that it occasionally provides a welcome ray of light through the cloud of secrecy which blots out Cabinet activity from the public gaze (and the public attention).

4.2. This is a matter of definition, but it seems sensible to regard a rule as a kind of command, which ought to be obeyed, and which carries some kind of sanction. A much weaker interpretation is that a rule is simply a common or frequent mode of behaviour—'people *as a rule* do this or that'. But this weak interpretation does not fit the constitutional convention, which is intended and regarded as a kind of command (see the quotations from Salisbury, etc, in document 7).

So we may conclude that for constitutional purposes a rule is not a rule if nothing happens when you disobey it.

4.3. Yes: you are badly thought of if you disobey. If the breach is a minor one, then you may face the criticism and 'get away with it'. A more serious breach *might* lead to political difficulties, trouble with the opposition, a bad press, possibly trouble with one's own party. There is still a strong sense of constitutional propriety in Britain, and this cannot lightly be affronted. On the other hand, the solidarity of the majority party is normally shelter enough from any constitutional storm.

One practical point must be stressed. In practice a Cabinet has to be in agreement on major policies only to the extent that no member speaks publicly against its policies. Private disagreements do not count.

The nature of the convention is further discussed in chapter 3, pp. 96–7

5. The raising of matters of urgency, or agreeing thereto; chairmanship in the formal sense of calling upon speakers and summing-up; contributing himself to the discussion; leadership in bringing the Cabinet to an agreed conclusion.

(c) and (d) in document 8, on Macmillan and Chamberlain, suggest a stronger version of the same functions.

6.1. Too much attention to small-scale transactions, too little concern for the broader strategy.

6.2. Yes, certainly. Baldwin's method had the merit of delegation: much was left to individual Ministers, who were encouraged to use their own discretion and initiative. (The disadvantage is the lack of any overall control or guidance and encouragement to weak or bewildered Ministers.)

6.3. One may *hope* for a fruitful tension at the top. But there is no reason to *expect* that articulate and ambitious men, who have been fighting for power in the same organisation, will be compatible and naturally amicable. (Remember that in other spheres promotion often takes a person to another organisation: e.g. an assistant master rarely succeeds to the headship of the school he serves in.) Often tensions and resentments will be overcome for the sake of the common cause—but not always.

6.4. It seems that where Chamberlain intervened to take decisions and Baldwin left his Ministers on their own, Wilson tries *to keep himself well-informed.* Clearly this allows him to influence decisions, but perhaps short of the detailed intervention made by Chamberlain.

7. This is much more difficult than is usually thought and commonly claimed. A Prime Minister can read the papers, talk to MPs, travel about asking questions, see to his constituents' problems, commission opinion surveys. He will hope to 'keep his ear to the ground'. But political divination is quite difficult. And who are 'the people of England'; and which of them count? There are difficult problems here which are further discussed in chapter 11. Meanwhile, it seems fair to conclude that a Prime Minister has quite good opportunities for informing himself of 'public opinion', but at best he will remain isolated, confined to a limited section of the public— just as most of us are.

8. This is a matter of taste as well as political judgement. My own would be for the prosaic, unimaginative character of Mr Attlee, because most of the time the nation's problems are best solved by prosaic, unimaginative (but competent, cautious, tolerant) people. The eloquence and sense of drama and history conveyed in the first passage may have its uses at particular moments in a nation's history, but not often. Of course, an opposite view is arguable!

9.1. This over-used phrase is an unhelpful paradox. It has no precise meaning, and the contradiction in it needs to be resolved: but this is difficult. For example, it is unsatisfactory (because untrue) to say that the Prime Minister is equal in status but not in power.

9.2. The scale of power: suggested placings would be

Home		(D) (E)[1]
Morrison	(i)	(B)
	(ii)	(C)
Eden		(C) (D)
Baldwin		(A)
Asquith		(A) to (E)

[1] It is notable that Lord Home when Prime Minister himself did not behave in this strong manner.

9.3. (a) No.

(b) No: there is clear disagreement between Eden, Home and Morrison.

10.1. Almost every factor would be affected *to some extent* by the Prime Minister's political personality. It is just conceivable, but not very likely, that the Prime Minister's personal staff might provide an exception, with a powerful and able staff operating as a 'Prime Minister in commission', in support of a weak personality.

For the rest, only a Prime Minister of some personal force will be able to realise the potential strength of his position in relation to the public as a hero-figure and in relation to the Cabinet as master coordinator. So the answer must be: yes, it makes a substantial difference.

It should be added that political factors will affect the PM's powers too. If the country is thought to be in serious difficulties, especially in international affairs, then there will be more need and more scope for personal power. In relatively quiet times, the PM's power may be challenged. Party political factors will also count. A party in a low state of morale will perhaps be more inclined to criticise the leadership and resent too much personal power. Party morale itself is of course partly the product of leadership, but it will be affected by electoral prospects, the length of time in office, the balance of generations.

10.2. The question about the basis of preference depends on fundamental political outlook, and this, in the last resort, may be no more than a statement of 'I know what I like.' In very general terms, a Prime Minister must get the work of government done effectively and in a manner appropriate to a parliamentary democracy. (This statement means very little, without further definition.)

Harcourt's view (a) is no more than an assertion; it may or may not be right. Jennings (b), on the other hand, proposes that the heart of government lies in the Departments, hence a weak Prime Minister is preferable. Mackintosh (c) argues that the system requires a prime mover, so to speak, an initiator.

Both Jennings (b) and Mackintosh (c) would appear to be right: or rather a blend of the two views gives a plausible and balanced answer, which seems to fit with the nature of the job as indicated in this chapter. Further comment on this question will be found in the assessments below.

ASSESSMENTS

We are (or should be!) now in a better position to answer the question posed at the beginning of the chapter: is this an effective way of arranging the highest office in a parliamentary democracy?

This is rather a large question to be answered at one gulp, and it needs to be broken down. Here are four kinds of criticism:

(a) *The Prime Minister is too powerful.* If he is an able man, this is bad enough; if he is not, it is disastrous.

The evidence on the power of the Prime Minister has been reviewed above; and conclusions will have been drawn about the degree or extent of the Prime Minister's power. We are now enquiring whether that degree is excessive. Your answer to exercise 10.2. should provide some arguments. The extracts given there provide arguments from the nature of government work and policy (Jennings (b)) and the nature of the machinery (Mackintosh (c)). Here are further possible lines of argument:

(i) The power of the Prime Minister is more than one man can carry: the burden is simply too great, the span too wide. In the end, therefore, the PM will not be able to carry out the functions the system demands, and inefficiency will arise.

(ii) The power of the Prime Minister is so great as to be corrupting— 'absolute power corrupts absolutely.' This is not an impressive argument unless some precise meaning can be attached to 'corruption'. It could be argued that there is corruption of judgement, in particular that which arises from overweening self-confidence. There is evidence that some Prime Ministers acquire exaggerated notions of their own mission: they feel they have a destiny, as Churchill thought he must bring peace to the world before leaving office. Others fall victim to the hallucination of indispensability—Chamberlain perhaps, and Macmillan, dismissing seven of his Cabinet colleagues. Such arrogance might be regarded as not only corrupting judgement but damaging the notion of democratic government.

(iii) While not accepting either of these lines of criticism (i) or (ii), it might still be argued that the system does not secure the advantages of team-work at the top. Few opinions are not improved by exposure to criticism from other people, especially from those who count in the final decision.

It will be observed that all these lines of criticism are based on a high assessment of the Prime Minister's power: the assumption is that government is by one man rather than by the Cabinet. If you have made a lower estimate of the PM's power, then the arguments above may be invalidated.

(b) *The Prime Minister's private office and personal staff is inadequate.* This argument assumes that the Prime Minister has important functions in his own right, and not simply deriving from the Cabinet. Document 4 gives Mr Wilson's view. The comparison with the White House staff of the President of the USA is relevant, but of course the American system differs in important ways from the British: in particular, the Cabinet is not nearly so important.

Plainly the Prime Minister needs a staff; the question once again is precisely how much? If it is much expanded then its work would clearly duplicate in part the work of the Departments. For example, a Prime Minister wishing to determine transport policy, would have his own advisers and secretaries preparing papers for him. The Minister of Transport and the Ministry would not be the sole source of advice and initiator of policy.

Churchill, setting up Lord Cherwell in his statistical office, did something like this: the office was much resented by the Departments.

Mr Wilson in document 4 shows he is aware of the difficulties. In the event, he has not much expanded the Downing Street office, so it may be assumed that the advantages of an expanded office are not thought to out-weigh the difficulties.

(c) *The Cabinet is an inefficient directing body*. It is both too large and too closely concerned with departmental administration.

This line of criticism has had some distinguished supporters, including Amery and the Haldane Committee on the Machinery of Government (1918). Their argument is that a smaller Cabinet of five–eight people (like the War Cabinets of 1917–18, 1940–5) would be better able to take decisions, to coordinate government activity, to determine and impose financial priorities, and to formulate policy in the long term. Such critics envisage a small, high-powered committee, free of departmental respon-sibilities (though available for special assignments) and rather good at the broad sweep of thinking about policy.

Two points must be conceded at once. Large committees are indeed less efficient at taking decisions than small ones: this is a conclusion of common sense, of experience and of research into the behaviour of small groups. Second, the traditional large Cabinet is not often able to give time to long-term planning.

However, there are several weaknesses in the idea of a small Cabinet. First, it is certain to have uneasy relationships with the departmental Ministers. The latter would presumably sit in an inferior Cabinet and their decisions both on general policy and in departmental matters would be subject to the higher authority of the small Cabinet. If this were the case, the small Cabinet would soon be heavily loaded with short-term decision taking. But if the small Cabinet tried to avoid this position of supervisory responsibility, then it might soon find itself merely an advisory body on the margins of government. At best there would be serious difficulties over the extent of the powers of the small 'super-Cabinet'.

Second, it is by no means clear that a concern with departmental respon-sibilities is a disablement for higher policy-making. The implied dichotomy between 'entanglement with administrative detail' and 'creative forward thinking' is much exaggerated. A good deal of government is about administrative detail; forward thinking and higher policy cannot be divorced from day-to-day concerns. In any case, given an alternation of government between the parties, there is plenty of time in opposition for long-term planning divorced from administrative responsibilities. And the quality of some of it suggests the validity of the argument that adminis-trative responsibilities provide a necessary starting-point and background for long-term planning.

Third, it is a function of the Cabinet to represent, and this the larger Cabinet does better than the small. Prime Ministers who have persisted with large Cabinets have probably been most influenced by this need to represent sections of the party. In wartime this is not necessary. Politics of the usual kind are in abeyance and there is a general agreement on a national policy—to win the war. Hence the experience of small super-Cabinets in wartime is in a fundamental way irrelevant.

Fourth, the usual large Cabinet does already include Ministers without departmental responsibilities, and Ministers with coordinating functions. The Secretary of State for Defence is a coordinating Minister; so was the Secretary for Economic Affairs. Four Ministers in the Cabinet of 1966, including the Prime Minister, had no departmental responsibilities. These and perhaps others probably carry out specific coordinating functions, which are kept secret in order to avoid confusion over responsibility.

Thus the arguments would seem to favour a Cabinet of the customary size. But, of course, the working of the large Cabinet is profoundly modified by the system of committees. Perhaps this secures the best of both worlds; this is at least a possible consequence of the changes of April 1968 (a strong emphasis on committee decisions and a new supervisory 'Parliamentary Committee', a shadowy super-Cabinet).

Yet, whatever the prescription and the intention, the manner of working and the efficiency of the Cabinet depend on personal and political factors. In January 1968, major decisions on government economies were taken in full Cabinet in a marathon series of meetings lasting altogether for more than thirty hours. Within weeks of this demonstration of government by full Cabinet, the changes of April 1968 apparently reduced the Cabinet's role and influence. However, the change might be one of emphasis only. For the full Cabinet must remain the final court of appeal: it cannot be relegated to the sidelines unless half its members are unable and unwilling to contribute to the making of major policies. It seems unlikely that this will always (or even often) be the case.

(d) *The office of Prime Minister is insufficiently defined.* After all, it is the highest position in the constitution: the lack of definition cannot be denied. To some extent, the office is what the holder makes of it: some recent occupants have made it very powerful indeed; others have been more passive. But it does not follow that this flexibility is undesirable. Consistency and predictability would have advantages only if political situations were themselves consistent and predictable. It may be hoped that political parties will throw up the right kind of leader for the situation.

This is of course to expect too much—particularly as parties are sometimes saddled with leaders chosen in other circumstances. Selection for leadership is something of a lottery. But no amount of constitutional definition and limitation will remove this element of chance and of personality from the functioning of the office of Prime Minister. In that respect it is like many other offices of high authority—headmasters, captains of cricket teams, mayors, managing directors.

We have now largely rebutted these lines of criticism, and we may be justified in advancing two propositions about the British system of Prime Minister and Cabinet:

First, the system just avoids putting intolerable responsibility on one man, as in a presidential system.

Second, given incumbents of high quality (a considerable qualification), the system seems capable of providing effective, purposeful and responsible government.

RECAPITULATION EXERCISES

1. *True or False?* (mark T or F)

(a) A Prime Minister is usually too busy to spend much time in the House of Commons.

(b) Prime Ministers often seek advice from persons outside Parliament and Civil Service.

(c) The Prime Minister usually submits his list of ministerial appointments to a full meeting of his own party MPs.

(d) The Prime Minister takes the chair at several of the Cabinet sub-committees.

(e) A Minister who disagrees with Cabinet policy always resigns.

(f) In meetings of the full Cabinet the Prime Minister has no more power than any other member.

2. List four of the major sources of the Prime Minister's power.

3. List two arguments in favour of a small 'super-Cabinet'.

KEY TO RECAPITULATION EXERCISES

1. (a) F   (b) T   (c) F   (d) T   (e) F   (f) F.

2. See p. 70.

3. Better able to make decisions with force and speed.

Better able to look ahead, plan a broad, long-term strategy.

Free from detailed administrative commitment.

Coordinates better than a larger body.

Worked well in wartime.

[3]

Ministers and their Departments

1 OUTLINE

The Government now contains just over one-hundred posts. These may be divided by rank into:

Prime Minister.

Cabinet Ministers, including some non-departmental Ministers (the Lord President, the Lord Privy Seal, the Chancellor of the Duchy of Lancaster); departmental Ministers (mostly entitled Secretary of State or Minister; also the Lord Chancellor).

Ministers not in the Cabinet, mostly entitled Minister or Minister of State, but including four Law Officers. (The designation of some Ministers outside the Cabinet as of 'Cabinet rank' has been abandoned.)

Junior Ministers, entitled Parliamentary Secretary, or, if the senior Minister is a Secretary of State, Under-Secretary of State (Joint, if there are two such posts).

Government Whips, holding appointments as Lords Commissioner of the Treasury or as Assistant Whips. The Chief Whip is Parliamentary Secretary to the Treasury. (For the duties of Whips see chapter 5.)

Ministers may also have *Parliamentary Private Secretaries*: these are unpaid posts, with mainly political duties.

Most Ministers are members of the House of Commons, but a few (seven Ministers in 1966, eleven in 1969) are in the Lords. This is a consequence of the statutory limitations on the number of Ministers in the Commons (Ministers of the Crown Act 1937, amended 1965). In any case a government needs senior representatives in the Upper House.

With remarkably few exceptions, Ministers qualify for promotion by several years of service in Parliament, and Cabinet Ministers normally have behind them a period of ministerial service outside the Cabinet. Obviously this is less true when a party attains power after a long period in opposition, as in 1964. Parliament and junior offices thus serve as a school for the training and selection of senior Ministers.

81

The functions of most Ministers are both political and administrative. On the administrative side they have responsibility for Departments of State, or else may engage in the overseeing or co-ordination of a sector of public activity. On the political side they contribute directly or indirectly to the formulation of policy at Cabinet level, and to the representation of the Government in Parliament and outside. The constitutional conventions of collective and ministerial responsibility define and sustain the role of Ministers in the Cabinet and in the Departments.

The Departments are vast administrative structures. The pattern of their operations is determined overall by the responsibility of Government to Parliament. But below the highest levels, the principles of organisation and operation (hierarchy and specialisation, files and minutes) are less political, and the attendant problems are those of bureaucracy, administrative efficiency and economy.

2 HOW TO BECOME A MINISTER:
QUALIFICATIONS AND ROUTES OF ENTRY

Commons and Lords

....

DOCUMENT I
COMPOSITION OF THE CABINET AND OF THE GOVERNMENT

(a) *The Cabinet*

Prime Minister	Commons	Lords	Total
Gladstone 1868	8	7	15
Balfour 1902	10	10	20
Chamberlain 1937	15	6	21
Attlee 1945	16	4	20
Macmillan 1961	17	4	21
Wilson 1966	21	2	23
„ 1968	18	2	20

(b) *The Government (all ministerial appointments)*

Prime Minister	Commons	Lords
Attlee 1945	62	8
Churchill 1951	55	13
Wilson 1968	76	10

The number of Ministers in the Lords was maintained (as mentioned above) at a minimum figure by the 1937 Act, which limited the number of ministerial appointments from the Commons. This Act was amended by the Wilson Government in 1965. While the House of Lords continues in its present form, any Government must provide its presiding officer, the Lord Chancellor, a Leader, and sufficient representation to see its business through. It is also convenient for the Government to create as life peers some non-politicians whom it would like to appoint to office.

Experience before a Cabinet appointment

Normally a politician must prove himself in Parliament before getting office, and prove himself again in office before entering the Cabinet. This is an important aspect of British government, for it means that there is a built-in system of training and selection, and the continuous experience of colleagues working together is a valuable one. As a consequence, most politicians reaching high office are long-service professionals, who on average started their political careers at a comparatively early age.

A few people—bright young men usually—pass through the system very quickly. Sometimes, too, a party coming into office after a long period in opposition will perforce appoint inexperienced people to high office. Of MacDonald's first-ever Labour Cabinet (1924), only two (not including the Prime Minister) had sat in Cabinets before, and only three others had held some kind of office. Attlee was much helped in forming his Government in 1945 by the service of several leading Labour MPs in the wartime Coalition Government. Five of his Cabinet had previous Cabinet experience, and only two, Aneurin Bevan and George Isaacs, had no ministerial experience at all. Mr Heath entered the Cabinet in 1959 after long and successful experience as Chief Whip, but without departmental experience. Occasionally non-politicians are appointed to the Cabinet

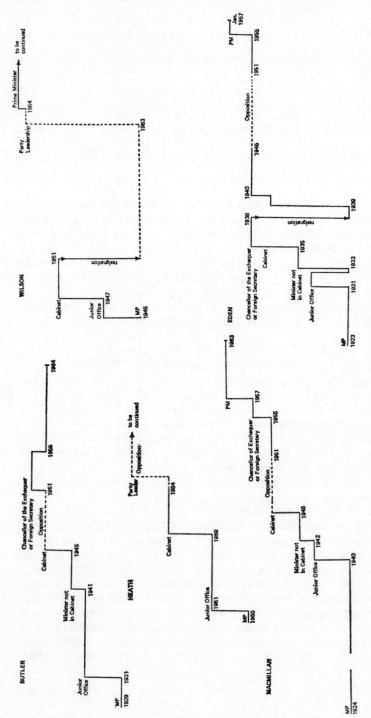

CAREER PROFILES OF SOME LEADING POLITICIANS

for special purposes without any previous parliamentary or ministerial experience. There were twenty-eight such appointments between 1916 and 1958 out of 173 new Cabinet Ministers. Many of these appointments can be explained by the special circumstances of war, the weakness of the early Labour Party and Mr Churchill's penchant for wartime colleagues. But there are more recent examples of such unorthodox appointments (Lord Mills as Minister of Power, Frank Cousins as Minister of Technology) which demonstrate the continuing possibility.

....

DOCUMENT 2

CARADER PROFILES OF SOME LEADING POLITICIANS

See diagrams, p. 84

....

EXERCISE

CAREER PROFILES

1.1. What, if anything, do the diagrams show?
1.2. Make some similar diagrams to illustrate the careers of other politicians, e.g. Winston Churchill, Lloyd George, Sir Alec Douglas-Home, Hugh Gaitskell, George Brown.

(Information may be obtained from, for example, D. Butler and J. Freeman, *British Political Facts*, Macmillan, 1968; *The Times Guide to the House of Commons*; and *Who's Who* (for appropriate years). Some histories of the period by Ensor, Taylor and Mowat include short biographies.)

The qualities required of an aspiring Minister

As in the case of the Prime Minister, there is no one perfect model, and it is all too easy to list not very meaningful general qualities. A Prime Minister on the look-out for ministerial talent might well say, like the person looking for an elephant, 'I can't define what I'm looking for, but I shall know it when I see it.'

The analysis, below, of the work of Ministers may indicate the particular qualities required of a Minister. Meanwhile, document 3 gives some extracts from a shrewd nineteenth-century account of 'the statesman'.

....

DOCUMENT 3
THE QUALITIES OF A MINISTER

From Sir Henry Taylor, *The Statesman* (first published 1836) in *The Works*, vol. iv, Kegan Paul, 1878, pp. 228–9, 237, 262, 277, 290, 291–2, 317–18

The most important qualification of one who is high in the service of the state is his fitness for acting *through others*; since the importance of his operations vicariously effected ought, if he knows how to make use of his power, to predominate greatly over the importance which can attach to any man's direct and individual activity.

It is of far greater importance to a statesman to make one friend who will hold out with him for twenty years, than to find twenty followers in each year, losing as many.

The conscience of a statesman should be rather a strong conscience than a tender conscience. For a conscience of more tenderness than strength will be liable in public life to be perverted in two ways:—1st. By reflecting responsibilities disproportionately to their magnitude, and missing of the large responsibilities whilst it is occupied with the small. 2nd. By losing in a too lively apprehension of the responsibilities of action, the sense of responsibility for inaction.

For the practice of looking at papers and handling them without disposing of them, not only wastes the time so employed, but breeds an undue impression of difficulty and trouble as connected with them; and the repetition of acts of postponement on any subject tends more and more to the subjugation of the active power in relation to it.

The rule . . . is that a statesman will do wisely for himself to walk by the broad lines of party distinction, and not imagine that the specialities of a case will exonerate him from the obligations of an adherent.

For a statesman should be by nature and temper the most unquarrelsome of men, and when he finds it necessary to quarrel, should do it, though with a stout heart yet with a cool head. There is no such test of a man's superiority of character as in the well-conducting of an unavoidable quarrel; and to be engaged in no quarrels but those that are unavoidable, though it be not the *experimentum crucis* which the other test is, affords however an evidence of some excellent qualities.

There are divers kinds of decisiveness; there is that of temperament, and that of reason, and there is that which is compounded of both; and this last is the best for a statesman.

....

3 THE FUNCTIONS OF A MINISTER—GENERAL

....

DOCUMENT 4
A DAY IN THE LIFE OF A MINISTER

A Minister's day is likely to be long and heavy—possibly too heavy for the efficient conduct of the office over a long term. A typical day might be as follows:

Glances at newspapers before leaving home, a duty and sometimes very far from being a pleasure.

On reaching the office, holds short consultation with Private Secretary about the morning's letters, messages and papers, about the day's programme, and the progressing of important correspondence.

There follows a longer discussion with the Permanent Secretary and one or two other senior officials about, e.g., problems in the preparation of the Department's estimates, progress with the early stages of consultation with outside interests about new legislation in the Department's field, or the possibility of political difficulties over some aspect of the Department's administration.

In the second half of the morning, a meeting of a Cabinet committee.

To the House for lunch, hoping to talk with old friends among backbenchers.

Stays on for Questions, though not himself engaged that day.

Back to office to meet a delegation from certain groups affected by the Department's work; fifteen minutes' briefing with senior civil servants beforehand.

Then two hours' solid reading and annotation of a draft paper on intended legislation, which will eventually go to the Cabinet.

A working dinner with ministerial colleagues.

No further parliamentary or speaking engagements (there is an unimportant division in the House and the Minister is 'paired') so home by 10 p.m., but with a briefcase of material for a speech in a major debate next week.

(On other days a Minister may go on visits to various parts of the country, to local offices, to meet local government authorities and so on; also to attend the unavoidable dinners and functions, some of which will be in his own constituency.)

....

A Minister's life is not indeed confined to Westminster and Whitehall (or wherever his Ministry is situated). An energetic Minister will want to investigate some of his Department's problems on the spot, to hear local opinion at first hand, generally to keep in touch, to 'keep an ear to the ground'. Here is an extract to show a tour by a very energetic Minister of Health, Neville Chamberlain.

....

DOCUMENT 5

A MINISTER ON HIS ROUNDS

From K. Feiling, *The Life of Neville Chamberlain*, Macmillan, 1947, p. 135

In 1927 his Lancashire and Yorkshire tour took in 30 institutions, 15 housing estates, and 6 slum areas. As of old he made a brief, legible, meticulous commentary. This town clerk is 'deservedly popular, but too old', this chairman 'old, deaf, and feeble', this medical officer 'kind-hearted and sympathetic', 'an excellent matron here'. At Bradford 'the worst slums I have come across yet', at Halifax 'rich and liberal citizens', at Liverpool 'the usual tale of nothing done by the Landlord'.

....

4 THE FUNCTIONS OF A MINISTER—POLITICAL

A Minister must have good and fruitful relations with the Prime Minister; with the Cabinet; with ministerial colleagues, including his juniors; and with the House of Commons.

The Prime Minister will wish to be kept informed of the main developments in the work of a Department, and to be forewarned of future problems and difficulties. The Minister must learn a fine discrimination between matters which ought to be referred to the Prime Minister and Cabinet, and matters which he should deal with himself. Decisions which may lead to political repercussions had best be made by the Cabinet, but a good Minister will learn to meet and survive a fair measure of criticism without recourse to the Cabinet. Equally a good Cabinet will not simply disclaim responsibility for a colleague who has run into trouble on his own.

A Cabinet Minister has to present his departmental point of view to the Cabinet, and to forward his Department's projects. But he must also contribute to the Cabinet's deliberations on other matters. On this Hugh Dalton has written bluntly:

I think I could name two, perhaps three, Ministers in the Attlee Governments who lost their jobs, at least for a while, because they talked too much in Cabinet, and one because he talked too little, except on his own departmental problems. To general policy he made no contribution. For a Cabinet should not be a band of specialists, each with no thoughts outside his own paddock. (Hugh Dalton, *High Tide and After*, Muller, 1962, pp. 17–18)

The Minister and the Treasury

Every departmental Minister must establish a good working relationship with the Chancellor of the Exchequer, for he is, under the Cabinet, the arbiter of the financial fortunes of the Department. A Chancellor, struggling to keep government expenditure within bounds, will scrutinise a Department's estimates carefully, and often prune some quite sharply. 'It may shorten discussion on this matter, Mr Prime Minister, if I say there is no money for it'—this was Snowden's rather brusque version of a Chancellor's regular Cabinet statement. But the Chancellor's position is by no means impregnable. He has to face eight or nine spending Ministers, and, individually or in alliance, they may in the end wear him down and defeat him.

DOCUMENT 6
MINISTERS AND THE TREASURY

(a) From an address by Sir Edward Boyle, Bart, M.P., at a conference on 'Who are Policy Makers?', printed in *Public Administration*, Autumn 1965, p. 252

When performing this vital function [of getting money out of the Treasury] Ministers have really got to know their stuff and have got to be able to argue in detail. The Minister must in my view do that very important homework himself. He must know and be ready to refute the sort of objections that the Treasury are likely to raise. I think, with great respect, that Ministers (particularly ex-Ministers) are far too inclined to abuse the Treasury. The truth is that Ministers—if they are to do their stuff—must know how to argue with the Treasury and must know their facts well enough to be able at any rate to get a reasonable settlement.

(b) From Duff Cooper, *Old Men Forget*, Hart-Davis, 1953, pp. 215–19

[The following extract illustrates the kind of campaign a Minister must fight to get money for his Department: Duff Cooper was then (1938) First Lord of the Admiralty, a Cabinet post.]

January 23rd. I had a discouraging letter from the Chancellor of the Exchequer (Sir John Simon) last week. He wants us to reduce our proposed estimates by £6,000,000 and I don't see how it can be done.

. . . a letter from the Chancellor saying he cannot possibly accept our building programme and we must produce a smaller one. This at a time when the Chiefs of Staff fear that our preparations for war are inadequate . . .

I have written to the Chancellor saying that I cannot produce what he asks for—'a very much smaller programme'—without a Cabinet decision. To reduce and slow down our preparations at this time seems to me to be indefensible.

At the Cabinet on Wednesday . . . the main subject of discussion was a report which Inskip has produced on the future of re-armament. The demands of the three services over the next four years amount to something in the nature of £2,000,000,000 and the Treasury say that £1,650,000,000 is all the money that can be made available. Inskip's simple solution is to divide that sum in certain proportions to be decided upon between the three services.

. . . the Cabinet eventually adopted the Inskip report and postponed consideration of my reconstruction programme as being affected by the report. I protested . . .

February 27th. At the Cabinet on Wednesday we discussed my construction programme. I put forward three [programmes] . . .

It was decided that Simon, Inskip and I must discuss it further and come back to the Cabinet if we couldn't agree.

There was another Cabinet on Monday, and before it I wrote the P.M. another letter, pointing out that more air construction wasn't going to impress anybody, that we probably shouldn't get delivery even if we gave the orders, and that if we did we shouldn't have the pilots. Also that our action would be interpreted as yielding to internal criticism. The increased naval construction on the other hand was easily practicable, and had in fact been contemplated, and it would be a direct reply to the aggressive policies of both Germany and Japan. He read it to the Cabinet but said that it didn't alter his views . . .

The bickering about naval expenditure continued all that summer.

....

A Minister should not fight for his Department without regard for Government policy as a whole; but a Minister who does not fight at all will often unduly weaken his Department. Sir Edward Boyle notes the comment of a colleague who divided Ministers into 'those who habitually get their way and those who do not . . . Ministers are strikingly different in their success at getting things through'.

All this may give the impression that Chancellors are always iron men disapproving in principle of all expenditure. This is not the case, of course. But a Chancellor must tread warily: Ministers will not be pleased with a Chancellor who seems to favour expenditure by one Department but not another. Consider the evidence in the next document that Chancellor Winston Churchill had departed too far from his proper role of arbiter between the Departments.

WINSTON CHURCHILL AS CHANCELLOR

From Neville Chamberlain's diary, quoted in K. Feiling, *The Life of Neville Chamberlain*, Macmillan, 1947, p. 131

26 November 1924: saw Winston Churchill ... about pensions for widows and old age ... I first gave him the history of the investigations ... and he then expounded to me the picture which, as he said, he had made for himself of his next budget. He was anxious to reduce direct taxation in order to relieve industry ... But he would have to balance the benefits by doing something for the working classes, and for this he looked to pensions ... it would have to be my bill, but he would have to find the money, and the question was would I start in with him, would I enter partnership and work the plan with him ... It seemed plain to me that he regretted that he was not Minister of Health. He spoke of the position, 'you are in the van, you can raise a monument, you can leave a name in history.'

The Minister and the House of Commons

A Minister should retain the support of his own side and deal effectively with the Opposition. In practice this means he must:

(a) persuade the party of the validity of his policies and of his own competence;

(b) deal effectively with Parliamentary Questions;

(c) take an effective part in debates; and, in particular,

(d) pilot his own legislation through the House, defending its general principles on the floor and establishing its detail in committee.

EXERCISES

THE POLITICAL FUNCTIONS OF A MINISTER

2.1. If you were Secretary of State for Education and Science, which, if any, of the following problems would you refer to the Prime Minister?

(a) A local authority has protested against your cutting of their proposed school building programme.

(b) Leaders of one of the religious denominations have asked you in the strongest terms to receive a deputation about their demand for more financial assistance for building denominational secondary schools.

(c) Negotiations for a salary increase for teachers have reached an impasse: and the teachers organisations are threatening to strike.

(d) Ten local authorities have formally declared they will not re-organise their secondary schools on comprehensive lines.

(e) You receive a report from your officials that primary education is likely to break down in some areas through a severe shortage of teachers.

2.2. You are Minister of Health. You are faced with a large number of resignations from the National Health Service by doctors going to work in the USA. What case would you make to the Chancellor of the Exchequer for increased estimates to meet a substantial rise in doctors' salaries?

2.3. If he refused, what would you do?

resign;

appeal to Prime Minister and Cabinet;

appeal to the backbenchers;

write to the *Times*;

secretly encourage the doctors' organisations to threaten strike action in order to strengthen your hand;

accept the situation.

5 THE FUNCTIONS OF A MINISTER— ADMINISTRATIVE

Most Ministers are at the head of major Departments of State. This imposes on them a dual responsibility—as politicians with duties in or towards Cabinet and Parliament, and as administrators directing a major organisation. A Minister comes to his Department as a trained and experienced politician, but with only his native abilities as an administrator and often with no special knowledge or experience of the work of the Ministry.

This arrangement is central to the British system of *responsible* government; for it provides a line of responsibility from the humblest section of the administration to Parliament. The line may be tenuous at times, but the principle of its existence is important. This political answerability is most significant at the higher levels, and there it depends for its effective working on the maintenance of a special kind of relationship between the Minister and the senior administrators of his Department.

The relationship is not one of master and servant. Rather it is based on the administrators' recognition of the political concerns and the final responsibility of the Minister: and on the Minister's respect for the information, advice and professional competence of his administrators. For the senior administrator is not concerned simply with the execution of policy but also with its formulation.

Clearly, there will be many variations of this relationship, depending on the capacities and temperament of the Minister, and the nature of the Department's work. The administrators, too, though carefully trained, will not have achieved complete homogeneity, and will also vary in talent and temperament. Yet an effective relationship is achieved more often than not. A distinguished wartime temporary civil servant, Sir Oliver Franks (Lord Franks), has testified to this. He acknowledged a paradox. Ministers could keep themselves informed and take decisions on a very limited number of topics: yet 'the effect of a change of Minister on headquarters was considerable.' (*The Experience of a University Teacher in the Civil Service*, Oxford University Press, 1947, p. 13.)

Here are three illustrations of the relationship.

....

DOCUMENT 8
A MINISTER AND HIS DEPARTMENT

(a) *Hugh Dalton imposes himself on his Department*
From Hugh Dalton, *High Tide and After* and Muller, *The Fateful Years*, 1962, pp. 15–16, and 1957, p. 435, respectively

A Minister has many necessary relationships which can be managed well or ill. First, his relations with his officials. I have already quoted Arthur Henderson's shrewd saying that 'the first forty-eight hours decide whether a Minister is going to run his office, or whether his office is going to run him.' A Minister should show his officials at the start that he has a mind of his own. Perhaps by refusing some early piece of official advice, as Henderson did on his first morning at the Foreign Office in 1929, when he was advised to congratulate the Pope and Mussolini on the conclusion of the Lateran Treaty and to refuse Trotsky a visa. Perhaps by making a fuss about the secretarial arrangements of the Minister and his Chief Adviser, as I did on my first morning at the Ministry of Economic Warfare in 1940, or in sharply reversing previous policy towards Italy as I did as soon as I could persuade the War Cabinet. But, having established an independent personality, the Minister should try to get all the help he can—and it will generally be a lot—out of his officials. There is great knowledge, naturally enough, and also great wisdom, not quite so naturally, in the Civil Service. But not in every Civil Servant equally.

[Dalton also insisted on choosing the young Hugh Gaitskell (then a temporary civil servant) as his Principal Private Secretary. Later, when Dalton was President of the Board of Trade, he discovered that the Board's evidence to the Barlow Commission in 1939 had] an extreme *laissez-faire* bias, opposing any serious control of industrial location. On becoming President, I told my officials that on this question I had firm views, based on long study, and that the policy of the Department, at all levels, must now change. [Dalton's mentor, Arthur Henderson, Labour's Foreign Secretary in 1929, sent round copies of his party's election manifesto, so that officials should know the Government's main principles and attitudes.

Dalton, admitting that officials could be helpful in putting the Minister's own ideas into good shape, warned that officials might point out 'formidable difficulties'. The Minister should] face these in a calm and honest mood, but may sometimes usefully invite those who have indicated the difficulties to indicate also how these can best be surmounted, or evaded. For it would be going too far to deny that the Civil Service contains a few congenital snag-hunters.

(b) *Ernest Bevin and his officials*
From Lord Strang, *Home and Abroad*, Deutsch, 1956, pp. 292–3

[Ernest Bevin, Foreign Secretary in the post-war Labour Government, was a man of powerful but untrained mind. In expertise in the use of words, in diplomatic finesse, his officials were his superiors. But he had the force of mind and personality, they had the skill, training and willingness to efface themselves. The result, suggested in this extract from Lord Strang's book was a remarkable combination which, in Strang's view, left the final decision to Bevin. Strang was Permanent Secretary of the Foreign Office at the time.]

He would call his advisers together and go round the map with them and look at the question at issue from the point of view of each of the other governments concerned. Again and again he would perceive connections which none of us had thought of; and if, as was sometimes the case, they were invalid, he would expect us to tell him so. In his exploratory peregrinations he had no ordered method of procedure. He might start from some remote point, wandering round and round the subject moving gradually nearer the centre, making up his mind as he went along, opening up his perplexities to us. These were the fruit of cogitations in the watches of the night or of perusal of the papers in the early hours of the morning. Before going into him, we would ask ourselves: 'Where is he going to start from this time?' But wherever the starting point might be, however unrelated it might seem, we learnt that it could not be lightly disregarded. As his mind cleared, he might put up some unacceptable solution and wait for us to give him our reasons for knocking it down. When these preliminaries had been exhausted, he would gather himself together and come to his conclusion. It might not always be very accurately formulated, but we knew his mind well enough to be able to interpret it and to translate it into executive terms. Some Secretaries of State stimulate; others devitalise; Bevin nourished.

(c) *Neville Chamberlain—the Minister-administrator*
From K. Feiling, *The Life of Neville Chamberlain*, Macmillan, 1947, p. 128

[Neville Chamberlain is an example of those Ministers who are more administrators at heart than politicians. He said:] '. . . my pleasure is in administration rather than in the game of politics.' [When he became Minister of Health in 1924, he made a five-year plan for the reform of local government, with twenty-five bills.] He could brief his bills better than his experts, to whom he would put every extreme possibility and demand an answer, while he explained to the Commons technicalities of rating or disease with a lucidity which the greatest advocates and medical consultants found enviable.

[All this is admirable, but there is a danger that a Minister with this kind of aptitude will neglect his political work, and take too little note of the advice of his experts. As Prime Minister conducting foreign policy a decade later, Chamberlain's disastrous foreign policy was due in part to his exaggerated confidence in his own ability to conduct policy personally.]

....

EXERCISES
MINISTERS AND DEPARTMENTS

3.1. On the evidence of the extracts in document 8 above, there are grounds for thinking that none of the three Ministers had an ideal relationship with his senior officials. What drawbacks do you notice?

3.2. Write, in the style *either* of an autobiography or diary *or* of a biography, a short piece by or about a Minister with a good (ideal, effective) relationship with his officials.

3.3. Here (in an extract from Sir Henry Taylor, *The Statesman* (1836), op. cit., p. 322) is the argument that the system of giving Ministers a dual role cannot work:
To what extent, if any, would you agree with this point of view?

A statesman who takes a part in consultations in the cabinet, or debates in a legislative assembly, or in both, ought to be relieved from all business which is not accessory to the performance of his duties as councillor and legislator. For those duties, if amply and energetically performed, must, by their nature if not by their magnitude, incapacitate any but very extraordinary individuals for performing others. The excitement of oral discussion with able colleagues upon deeply interesting and often personal topics, and still more the excitement of public debate, can rarely be combined with patient application to dry documentary business within the walls of an office. If the one class of business be transacted, in the duties of research and preparation with fidelity, and in those of execution with ardour, any other class will be almost inevitably neglected.

6 THE RESPONSIBILITY OF A MINISTER

The Minister is responsible in two important ways. As a member of a government, and in particular as a member of the Cabinet, he is responsible collectively with his colleagues for all government policy (collective responsibility). As a Minister he is responsible for all the actions of his Ministry (ministerial responsibility).

Collective responsibility

Collective responsibility has been discussed above (chapter 2, p. 54) in relation to the working of the Cabinet. In relation to the working of a Department, the convention makes the whole Cabinet responsible for the major policies of each Department. This encourages the Cabinet to take an interest in the Departments—or, to put it more strongly, this forces the Cabinet to exercise a general oversight of the Departments. A Cabinet will not wish to remain ignorant of and unconcerned with policies for which the Cabinet as a whole is answerable. In practice, however, this effect is not always very strong, for a Cabinet has a choice: it can apply its majority in defence of an erring Minister or else dissociate the Cabinet by removing the Minister.

The convention has another important effect. If a Minister is overruled by the Cabinet, he cannot campaign outside the Cabinet for the policies he prefers. He must submit—or resign. Normally he submits; occasionally he threatens to resign; more rarely he carries through his resignation. Since 1945 there have been only a handful of resignations: Bevan and Wilson (1951); Nutting and Boyle (1956); Salisbury (1957); Thorneycroft, Birch and Powell (1958); Powell and Macleod (refusing to join the Home Cabinet—1963); Mayhew (1966); Cousins (1966); Longford (1968); George Brown (1968). Usually, when resignations are pressed through, there are general grounds for discontent, sometimes personal grievances and party instability.

A Minister may resign on one or more of the following grounds:

Personal dissociation. He feels he cannot go along with a particular major policy, cannot bear to continue working with his colleagues. Sometimes this is a matter of honour, sometimes of anger, often quite simply a fundamental disagreement.

Tactical. He has threatened resignation as a way of persuading his colleagues, but his threat has failed and he cannot extricate himself. Alternatively, he may wish to appeal beyond the Cabinet to party or country. Such appeals are rarely successful. The best place to fight for policies is in the Cabinet, where you may hope eventually to persuade some of your colleagues that you are right. (A Minister would be unwise to threaten resignation often, for few men are indispensable, and no committee works harmoniously when subjected to bullying tactics.)

Constitutional. The preservation of the collectivity, the unity of the Cabinet. But this is preserved outwardly if a dissident Minister keeps silent. Plainly, there are many occasions when a Minister accepts defeat and lives on to fight again or fight on some other issue. There is nothing dishonourable in this—it happens all the time in professional life—unless the matter of disagreement is one of high principle.

It follows that the serious threat of resignation is not a frequent occurrence, and the carrying through of resignation is even less frequent.

Here is an illustration of the threat of resignation in play:

....

DOCUMENT 9

DALTON'S CAMPAIGN 1943–5, AS PRESIDENT OF THE
BOARD OF TRADE, FOR A DISTRIBUTION OF INDUSTRY BILL

Summarised from Hugh Dalton, *The Fateful Years*, Muller, 1957, pp. 446–54

In May 1943 Dalton began his campaign. First he put up a paper to his colleagues. There followed discussions at ministerial and at official level. A White Paper was produced in May 1944, and Dalton submitted a paper to the Prime Minister in November. He also wanted to promote legislation, a quite different matter, a Restrictive Practices Bill. The draft King's Speech mentioned neither, and Dalton was 'in the mood to resign . . . It would not help the Tories, I reflected, if I denounced them, both in Parliament and up and down the country, for refusing either to prevent post-war unemployment, or to cut the claws of the profiteers . . .'

Whether or not this threat had any effect, after further argument and some concessions on his own part, Dalton secured the inclusion of a Distribution of Industry Bill. A memorandum was prepared for the War Cabinet, which in December authorised the preparation of a draft Bill for consideration.

Two months later Dalton was preparing a third draft for the Cabinet, with a supporting paper. He 'also sent letters to a number of influential and not unfriendly colleagues . . . canvassing their support'. A few days later Dalton heard of a suggestion that consideration of his Bill by the Cabinet be postponed. So again, he contemplated resignation. To his Labour colleague and Deputy Prime Minister, Attlee, he wrote '. . . The day when it becomes clear that I have little or no hope of performing this duty I shall reconsider most seriously and most coldly, my personal position in the Government . . . If, after all my efforts, this Bill goes down the drain, I think the only right and honest course will be for me to cease to be a member of a Government which will have betrayed . . . the populations of the

Development Areas . . .' At the same time, Dalton told a Conservative colleague of his position, and asked him to pass this on. Next day the War Cabinet approved the Bill. It was now February 1945.

The Prime Minister, Churchill, who had been abroad during some of these negotiations, made a last attempt to delay the Bill after its First Reading, but Dalton had by then sufficient supporters to stand firm. The Bill received its Second Reading in March, went to Standing Committee early in May, and emerged shorn of one controversial clause three weeks later. In June 1945 the Bill went through the final stages of Report, Third Reading and Royal Assent.

....

EXERCISES
THE POLITICAL EFFECT OF RESIGNATION

4.1. If you had been in Dalton's place would you have felt that resignation was (a) simply an honourable dissociation from a government you no longer sympathised with; or (b) also an effective political strategy enabling you to fight outside the government for your policies?

4.2. If you had been Prime Minister, would you have taken Dalton's threat of resignation into account when deciding your attitude to the Bill?

Ministerial responsibility

Ministerial responsibility is the convention that each Minister is answerable for all the actions of his Ministry whether done with his consent or knowledge or not. All is done in his name: the officials begin their letters, 'The Minister directs me to say . . .' In Parliament the Minister must speak for his Department, giving information and rebutting (or occasionally accepting) criticism. This is a fundamental element in the political system, securing answerability (of Ministers, not officials) to Parliament. There is a strong form of the convention in which it is provided that a Minister whose Department commits a grave mistake is obliged to resign his office. In practice, this form of the convention does not operate consistently or often, and there is some dispute about its actual status.

The convention of individual ministerial responsibility, like that of collective responsibility, is regarded as an important and operative part of the British constitution. Both are conventions, i.e. non-statutory rules, but both operate in a manner largely determined by the underlying political condition of modern British government: the achievement of invulnerable government through Cabinet and party solidarity. Cabinets remain united, as far as possible, in order to present a bold front to Parliament and public. Just as Ministers do not resign on policy grounds every time they are in serious disagreement, so Ministers do not resign simply because an official in their Department has blundered.

This somewhat indeterminate position has come about because the conventions have no definable meaning. 'Responsibility' is a notoriously evasive word, though its political usage would suggest it must be held to imply answerability or accountability. There is another source of confusion in the margin between ministerial and collective responsibility, that is, between the work of a Department and the policy of the Government. Nor have the conventions any strong sanction. They operate if the majority party wishes. Since a resignation is a breach of solidarity, neither convention often operates in that way. The dissident Cabinet Minister is persuaded not to resign, and similarly the departmental Minister does not resign. Instead he accepts responsibility either by defending his Department in the House or by criticising it!

In the last century or so, only twenty Ministers have resigned in response to the convention of ministerial responsibility. Now, it seems likely that Departments have made major blunders rather more often than once every five years. Where such blunders have become public, either the Government has defended the responsible Minister, or the Minister himself has blamed his officials and promised disciplinary measures, or the Minister has been quietly removed in a re-shuffle. In the comparatively few cases where Ministers have resigned, this appears to be due to:

(a) the Prime Minister, or
(b) the party, being willing to see the Minister go;
(c) the Minister himself feeling he should go; or occasionally
(d) considerations of constitutional propriety or punctilio have operated.

The resignation of Sir Thomas Dugdale in 1954 (the Crichel Down case) is an example of all these in some combination. The resignation of Hugh Dalton as Chancellor of the Exchequer in 1947 is an example of (d). A recent example of the non-operation of the convention is the failure of Mr Lennox-Boyd to resign as Colonial Secretary in 1959 after revelations of maladministration and police brutality in prison camps in Africa. The present position is unsatisfactory—at least for the good reason that a much respected convention is in fact largely inoperative. Apart from this criticism, there are two possible views on resignation. First, it is quite unfair to expect a Minister to resign because an official has committed a blunder, without his knowledge but in his name. It is sufficient that the Minister can be questioned in Parliament about the matter and can take disciplinary action in his Department. The second view is that the strict operation of the convention for gross blunders is a necessary and salutary discipline which encourages high standards of action for both Ministers and civil servants, and publicly demonstrates, and so re-enforces, those standards.

To resign or not to resign: some case histories

(a) *Mr Hugh Dalton*, 1947. Mr Dalton resigned as Chancellor of the Exchequer in November 1947, because he had revealed details of his Budget to a lobby correspondent before presenting it to the House. It was clear that Dalton's action was at worst rather careless. As Dalton walked through the corridor of the House on his way to the Chamber, he met a correspondent whom he knew. The correspondent asked him about his Budget, and Dalton (according to his own statement) 'told him in a single sentence, what the principal points would be ... it certainly never entered my mind that he would telephone it to his paper ... or, indeed, that they would have time to publish it before my speech began to come through. ... My quick thought was ... to give him, in reply to his questions, the main points in advance, so as to help him to make a good note for his paper.'

Dalton offered his resignation at once. In accepting it, the Prime Minister wrote: '... the principle of the inviolability of the Budget is of the highest importance and the discretion of the Chancellor of the Exchequer who necessarily receives many confidential communications, must be beyond question.' This resignation has none of the difficulties of the other cases. The blunder was his own, not that of his officials; the blunder was one generally recognised to be such, a breach of a necessarily strict code. It is arguable, however, that apology rather than resignation would have been a more appropriate consequence.

(b) *Sir Thomas Dugdale*, 1954. Sir Thomas Dugdale was Minister of Agriculture in the Conservative Government. During his tenure of the office, some land on Crichel Down, Dorset, belonging to the Ministry, was sold to the Crown Land Commissioners. The land had a history: it had been compulsorily acquired in 1937 for military purposes and taken over by the Ministry of Agriculture in 1950. The (independent) Land Commission had advised that it should be equipped and sold for farming as a single holding. Representatives of the former owners then asked for the land to be sold back to them, to form part of existing farms. This request was refused, and after much delay and confusion, the land was sold to the Crown Land Commissioners who were to rehabilitate and re-equip the land as farming land and then lease it. Other applicants were not given an opportunity to bid for the land.

The Minister was himself aware of the problem of the disposal of the Crichel Down land, but was not fully informed of the matter. The decision to sell was taken on the grounds of the national need for efficient farming, but it looked as if the claims of the former owners were not considered with due care. The problem was not a simple one of black-and-white; tyrannical bureaucrat against long-suffering land-owner. Much depends on what rights a land-owner should have in these matters, and this is a matter of opinion, not law.

In the event, the Minister resigned, saying:

I, as Minister, must accept full responsibility to Parliament for any mistakes and inefficiency of officials in my Department. Any departure from this long-established rule is bound to bring the Civil Service right into the political arena ... [But] it should not be thought that this means I am bound to endorse the actions of officials, whatever they may be, or that I or any other Minister must shield those who make errors against proper consequences. (H.C. Deb., vol. 530, 20 July 1954, col. 1186)

The Home Secretary, Sir David Maxwell Fyfe, added to the theory of the convention in his speech:

We all recognise that we must have that principle [ministerial responsi-bility] in existence and that Ministers must be responsible for the acts of civil servants. Without it, it would be impossible to have a Civil Service which would be able to serve Ministries and Governments of different political faiths and persuasions with the same zeal and honesty which we have always found. ... There has been criticism that the principle operates so as to oblige Ministers to extend total protection to their officials [who in consequence] cannot be called to account and are effectively responsible to no one. That is a position which I believe is quite wrong ... [the civil servant] can be dismissed at any time by the Minister; and that power is none the less real because it is seldom used (the only exception being a small number of senior posts). (H.C. Deb., vol. 530, 20 July 1954, cols. 1285–7).

Sir David then laid down four categories:

(i) A Minister must protect and defend a civil servant acting on his explicit order or

(ii) in accordance with the policy laid down by the Minister.

(iii) In the case of an official who makes a mistake or causes delay on an unimportant matter where individual rights are not concerned, the Minister 'accepts responsibility' and 'states that he will take corrective action in the Department'.

(iv) Where an official's conduct has been 'reprehensible', in a matter of which the Minister has no prior knowledge: 'The Minister is not bound to defend action of which he did not know, or of which he disapproves. But, of course, he remains constitutionally responsible to Parliament for the fact that something has gone wrong, and he alone can tell Parliament what has occurred and render an account of his stewardship. The fact that a Minister has to do that does not affect his power to control and discipline his staff.'

Presumably Sir David intended that category (iv) should provide for more serious errors, but it is not at all clear how the procedure of parliamentary responsibility differs from (iii). Sir David's fourth category of errors does not necessitate resignation, although the traditional version of the convention (that accepted by Sir Thomas) calls for resignation in serious cases of this kind. Sir David had, in fact, propounded a modified form of the convention. This may or may not be justified; but the change must be acknowledged.

Thus Sir Thomas' resignation was not in accord with Sir David's convention. It seems that Sir Thomas himself wished to resign, particularly to register the seriousness of his Department's mistakes. It seems, too, that Sir Thomas was aware that these mistakes—infringing the rights of individuals in matters of property— were peculiarly abhorrent to Conservative philosophy. The offence was against deeply held party convictions, which were being pressed by influential Conservative backbenchers. Party sensibilities were confused with constitutional proprieties.

The significance of the Crichel Down affair is perhaps greatest in another way. During the Inquiry, civil servants had to give evidence and submit to questioning in public. This is as near as they have yet been to direct public scrutiny.

(c) *Mr Lennox-Boyd*, 1958–9. Mr Lennox-Boyd was Colonial Secretary in the Conservative Government. During his tenure of office, there were serious revelations of maladministration and brutality in the Hola Prison Camp, Kenya, resulting in the death of eleven men. At about the same time there were complaints of mal-administration in Nyasaland, where the alleged mishandling of political unrest and violence had led, among other things, to fifty-one deaths. A Commission of Inquiry under Lord Devlin investi-gated complaints and its report was, by implication, critical of the Kenya Administration (then under the Colonial Office).

In this case, the Minister offered his resignation, but the Prime Minister 'dismissed the idea as ridiculous and pointless and un-justified' (according to a report in the *Daily Mail*). The Prime Minister's attitude may have been influenced by the imminence of a general election. Perhaps under the same influence, the Opposition thought the Minister's resignation was required.

The best speech calling for resignation came, in fact, from the Conservative side, from Mr J. Enoch Powell, then a backbencher recently resigned from office. Mr Powell indicates, better than anyone, the case in political morality for ministerial responsibility to be carried as far as resignation—symbolic resignation, resignation to demonstrate concern, integrity, and in the widest sense, res-ponsibility:

... it is in the name of his personal blamelessness, that I beg of him to ensure that the responsibility is recognised and carried where it properly belongs, and is seen to belong ...

All government, all influence of man upon man, rests upon opinion. What we can do in Africa, where we still govern and where we no longer govern, depends upon the opinion which is entertained of the way in which this country acts and the way in which Englishmen act. We cannot, we dare not, in Africa of all places, fall below our own highest standards in the acceptance of responsibility. (H.C. Deb., vol. 610, 27 July 1959, cols. 236–7)

EXERCISES
MINISTERIAL RESPONSIBILITY AND RESIGNATION

5.1. Does the word 'responsible' mean the same in these three sentences?

The headmaster asked Thomas, a prefect, to be responsible for good order in the playground.

The works manager asked Bill, the foreman, to make himself res-ponsible for observance of the limitation of the tea-break to ten minutes.

The Prime Minister asked Sir Edward (a Minister) to undertake responsibility for government aid to research.

5.2. Comment on this extract from Sir Henry Taylor, *The States-man* (1836), op. cit., p. 324:

'The far greater proportion of the duties which are performed in the office of a minister are and must be performed under no effective responsibility. Where politics and parties are not affected by the matter in question, and so long as there is no flagrant neglect or glaring injustice to individuals which a party can take hold of, the responsibility to Parliament is merely nominal, or falls otherwise only through casualty, caprice, and a misemployment of the time due from Parliament to legislative affairs. Thus the business of the office may be reduced within a very manageable compass without creating public scandal.'

5.3. There is probably some agreement by now that:

(a) a gross blunder by an official acting on the instructions of a Minister should lead to resignation (though there is no agreement on what constitutes a gross blunder).

(b) A minor mistake made without the Minister's knowledge should not lead to the Minister's resignation.

The really difficult question is: What would be the political or constitutional justification for arguing that ministerial responsibility implies resignation for a gross blunder committed by an official without the Minister's knowledge or approval?

7 THE DEPARTMENTS

Ministers and civil servants meet and, indeed, overlap in the Departments. So what might be the last section of this chapter—the Departments of State—is, for convenience, taken over to the beginning of the next chapter covering the Civil Service.

GUIDE TO EXERCISES

1.1. The diagrams show a contrast between long and short careers; how politicians can arrive in high office with and without long ministerial experience; how long service as a backbencher is a usual prelude to office, but not indispensable; how resignations are not necessarily disastrous; how in general the ups and downs of any profession, the slow change of generations, are increased in politics by the intervention of periods in opposition.

2.1. (a) Minor problem: do not refer to PM.

(b) Do not refer to PM (but changes in such financial assistance by legislation or by administrative action would have to go to the Cabinet, probably via a sub-committee).

(c) Keep the Prime Minister informed of the situation. A decision to make a higher offer, or to stand firm in the face of a strike would probably go through the Cabinet.

(d) and (e) Again keep the PM informed, but do not simply lay the problem in his lap, unless you foresee the need for new legislation on finance.

2.2. The case is clear. Whatever the merits of a rise in doctors' salaries, your chief argument would be the real possibility of a breakdown in the National Health Service. However, the Chancellor might react unfavourably to this kind of arm-twisting, so it would be wise to argue the merits of the salary claim itself, too.

2.3. Appeal to Prime Minister and Cabinet: you could *threaten* resignation but this would probably not move the Cabinet (although it might move you). If your appeal fails, you must accept the situation—which after all, allows you to argue the case again later on. Appeals to the party, still more to the doctors' organisations, will not earn you the sympathy of the Cabinet.

3.1. Dalton was a little bumptious, a little of a bully. Bevin was too dependent on his officials: the formulation of a policy in words cannot be wholly separated from its formulation in substance. His methods also seem rather time-consuming. Chamberlain, as the text indicates, tried to do his administrators' job, thus neglecting his own proper role.

3.2. The faults just indicated must all be avoided, and your piece must suggest a happy blend: a readiness to receive and consider advice, to see the administrative point of view, but in the end to take your own decisions. A diary entry might go like this (with no apologies for the piousness and self-importance!):

'March 15th. Faced this morning with a memo from the Permanent Secretary, arguing very forcefully the case against the proposed Bill on Road Transport. I had him in and thrashed it out with him for two hours. I see now some minor weaknesses in our approach, but on the general principles I remain clear. Sir Thomas conceded (reluctantly but cheerfully) that my case was a stronger one than he had at first thought, and has gone to work on some amendments to the draft Bill, which he thinks will cover some of his points. We ended the day with mutual respect much increased.' (But, of course, Sir Thomas' entry in his diary for the same day might be more caustic!)

3.3. There is a good deal in what Taylor says: politics is a bad training-ground for administration. But politics, the public debate of matters in dispute, is essential to democracy, and either the administrators must engage in politics or the politicians in administration. You cannot have democracy any other way. While there is something to be said for administrators engaging in politics, this is open to the same kind of criticism: administration is a bad training-ground for politics. So, if Taylor is correct, the system has a serious defect. However, much of the Minister's administrative work is in fact political in nature, or closely related to politics. Taylor exaggerates the differences between the two kinds of work.

4.1. (b) is probably right, but Dalton over-emphasises the effectiveness of campaigning in the country. Of course, politics had been in abeyance during the war, and a public campaign would have had the additional effect of novelty.

4.2. Yes 'taken into account', certainly. The reasons indicated in **4.1.** apply. But a Prime Minister has to balance the displeasures of his colleagues, and Dalton was not an indispensable member of the Coalition Government.

5.1. In each case the person in authority indicates a job to be done and implies accountability for doing the job. The accountability is the same in each case, only the importance of the job varies. But in the last example the special meaning of responsibility in politics—answerability in Parliament—is added. So the answer is almost, but not quite, yes.

5.2. Taylor's comment is a just one, in the sense that there is not likely to be political answerability for most administrative action. But there is still the answerability of a civil servant to his superior (and his superior to his superior), and the general *sense of responsibility* of the Civil Service. All this does not invalidate Taylor's point about political responsibility.

5.3. That this is the only way in which pressure can be applied to a Minister to oversee his Department effectively.

ASSESSMENTS

(a) *Ministers as heads of Departments of State*

Let us take an exaggerated version of the criticism that the system is 'amateur': 'It is absurd that the great Departments of State should be at the mercy of the personal whims, political prejudices and administrative inexperience of Ministers chosen on party-political grounds.' This statement (just made up by the author) puts the criticism at its sharpest: rebutting it will show the contrary arguments.

(i) 'at the mercy of' is not an exact description of the relation of a Minister to his Department. A Department is not a Minister's poodle: it has its own integrity, competence and strength.

(ii) 'personal whims': the same comment applies. The Minister is supreme, but the Department can stand its ground on important matters, yielding only after a case is put. For example, if a Minister thinks the entrance-hall should be painted blue not cream, he will have his way, if he insists (though he may have to wait his turn for redecoration). But if he thinks the Department's administrative procedures are wrong, he must make a case. Courtesy is a necessary element in a satisfactory relationship.

(iii) 'political prejudices': this is what you call political principles you do not like. A Minister's job is to modify the work of his Department according to his political principles. Some would put it more strongly: that a Minister's job is to impose his political principles on his Department.

(iv) 'administrative inexperience': true, but a man able enough to be chosen as a Minister can acquire a sufficient competence in administration to direct his Department. He will have at his disposal the administrative expertise of his permanent officials.

(v) 'chosen on party-political grounds': this is to use 'party-political' as a pejorative word. In fact, there is nothing necessarily wrong with party politics. Ministers selected for capacities demonstrated in party politics will be reasonably good at making speeches, at committee-work and even at the drafting of papers.

Thus, arguments for and against the criticism of amateurishness have been deployed. The truth no doubt varies with the Department and the Minister.

Much of what has been said on this theme in this chapter is relevant to the discussion of the Civil Service in chapter 4.

(b) *Conventions of responsibility*

Is either convention—of collective or of ministerial responsibility—still effective in British government?

(i) *Collective responsibility*. This still applies, in that dissident Cabinet Ministers do not speak in public against Cabinet policy. Thus Mr Cousins, Minister of Technology in Mr Wilson's Government, October 1964 to July 1966, was widely thought to be opposed to the government's incomes policy and eventually resigned. But until his resignation he did not openly campaign against the policy. Even in the Opposition's Shadow Cabinet, Mr Enoch Powell's request to be allowed to speak freely was not allowed.

Dissident Ministers do not always resign. In July 1966, Mr George Brown offered his resignation, because he disagreed with the Government's economic policies (the 'squeeze' of July 1966). The Prime Minister refused to accept the resignation, and Mr Brown was persuaded to stay on, but he was shortly moved to the Foreign Office, where acquiescence in, rather than active support for, the economic policies would suffice. (When Mr Brown eventually resigned in March 1968, this was due to personal tensions and temperamental incompatibilities, rather than simply to policy disagreements.)

Clearly, on many issues it is not dishonourable to accept the majority view, or to hope to continue the argument later. But, depending on the issues, the persons and the political situation, resignations do still occur, e.g. Thorneycroft, Birch and Powell (all the Treasury Ministers) resigned in 1958 in protest against the size of the Estimates. Thus the convention still applies, but it operates mainly to preserve the solidarity of government and so inhibit criticism. However it has also the important constitutional effect of preventing the formation of Cabinets based only and publicly on a loose collection of men rather than measures.

(ii) *Ministerial responsibility*. The present position of this convention, as the cases showed, is more difficult to fix. In the strong and specific form, involving resignation, it would seem to apply only to:

major blunders;

personal corruption (e.g., cases not cited above of J. Thomas 1936, Belcher 1949, Profumo 1963);

breach of constitutional punctilio.

The first case is one purely for the judgement of the Government, and the political rule of minimum vulnerability applies: don't give the Opposition and the press a chance to attack if it can be avoided. This is the most important area for the operation of the convention, and here it operates only infrequently. In the general sense, of Ministers answering to Parliament for their conduct of government (offering information and justification), the convention is a basic element in the British political system.

RECAPITULATION EXERCISES

1. *True or false?* (mark T or F)

(a) Some Ministers are of Cabinet rank, though not in the Cabinet.

(b) Parliamentary Private Secretary is an unpaid office held by Members of Parliament.

(c) It is quite unusual to have members of the House of Lords in the Cabinet.

(d) The Chancellor of the Exchequer makes the final decision on a Minister's estimates.

(e) In the Crichel Down case (1954) the Minister's resignation was in accordance with the convention of ministerial responsibility.

(f) A Minister who resigns according to the convention of collective responsibility has no right to campaign against the Government.

2. List the two main alternative consequences of the convention of collective responsibility for a Minister disagreeing with Cabinet policy.

3. List the main political functions of a Cabinet Minister.

KEY TO RECAPITULATION EXERCISES

1. (a) F   This designation has been abandoned.

   (b) T   (c) F

   (d) F   Since the Cabinet's decision is the final one.

   (e) T

   (f) He has the right to make a statement to the House, explaining his resignation, and is free then and thereafter to say what he pleases, subject to the limits of Cabinet secrecy, and the hope of later preferment.

2. (a) A Minister who disagrees does not publicly oppose Cabinet policy.

   (b) A Minister, in certain personal and political circumstances, wishing to dissociate himself from, and campaign against, a policy he dislikes, will resign.

3. To pursue his departmental policies with his colleagues, especially the Chancellor of the Exchequer.

To participate in the Cabinet, both in general and in the pursuit of his own Department's policies.

To participate similarly in Parliament and in the country.

(This is not so very different from the political functions of a non-Cabinet Minister. The Cabinet Minister is distinguished by his contribution to general policy-making outside his own Department, and mainly in the Cabinet.)

[4]

Departments of State and the Civil Service

1 OUTLINE

British central government consists of a score or so of major Departments and about a hundred minor ones. The division of functions between the Departments is, in detail, always somewhat arbitrary, with blurred and overlapping edges. The major Departments are headed by a Minister, and in this way the administrative machine is linked to the political parties and Parliament.

The chief official of the Department is the Permanent Secretary, a career civil servant, who is responsible to the Minister for the work of the Department. The Minister has a small personal office, including a young official serving as Principal Private Secretary. Departments are organised vertically by the division of work into a number of coherent sections, and horizontally in a hierarchy of coordination and control. The formal procedures of administration are concerned with taking a decision at the lowest point in this organisation which gives a reasonable chance of a correct and coordinated decision.

The top officials belong to the small Administrative Class.[1] Specialists (e.g., economists, architects, accountants) are recruited and graded separately: their advice is available at the highest levels but the final decisions are usually taken by the general administrators of the Administrative Class. This class is recruited mainly from the lower Executive Class, or direct from university graduates.

By the highest professional standards, the Administrative Class is a very able and devoted group. But there are doubts about its suitability for the tasks it confronts. Its members tend to lack specialised training, and to be drawn predominantly from the higher social ranks and from the ancient universities.

Departmental officials help in the formulation of policy as well as in the routine administration of their Department. Senior officials

[1] For recommendations of the Fulton Committee on the Civil Service, see p. 144.

are therefore concerned with politics, with the political implications of administrative decisions, the translation of party policy into departmental policy, or the support of the Minister in Parliament and in the country. In all this, however, the official himself remains uncommitted, serving governments of either side with equal devotion. The Minister retains the ultimate power of decision and the continuing responsibility for defending his policies in Parliament and in the country, Thus the British Civil Service is characteristically 'non-political', working anonymously behind the scenes. It has some special imperfections of its own as well as its share of the usual defects óf large bureaucracies. Nevertheless, it has the great merits of keen intellect, hard work and integrity.

2 THE DEPARTMENTS OF STATE

Major and minor Departments

There are now twenty-one major Departments[1] in the central Government. These are Departments headed by a Minister—in all but five cases, by a Cabinet Minister. In addition, there are about a hundred minor Departments, not headed directly by a Minister, but of course fixed somewhere in a line of responsibility to a Minister. They range from the National Assistance Board and the Board of Customs and Excise to the Stationery Office and the British Museum.

Despite the look of permanence which Whitehall wears, some Departments are quite new, some rise while others fall. Thus, between 1900 and 1956, twenty-five new Departments were created. Between 1964 and 1968 Mr Wilson's Government has done much construction and some demolition in Whitehall. In 1964 five new Departments were created: the Department of Economic Affairs, the Ministries of Technology and of Land and Natural Resources, the Welsh Office and the Ministry of Overseas Development. None of these Ministries was to do work which had never been done before: the changes were mainly intended to provide new emphasis, new vigour and new spans of coordination. Since 1964 several Ministries have disappeared, not in fact demolished but merged in others: these include the Colonial Office, the Ministry of Aviation, the separate Service Ministries and the (new) Ministry of Land and Natural Resources.

The overall change between the beginning of the century and 1968 may be studied in the following document.

[1] March, 1968. This figure excludes the Departments of the Lord Chancellor and the Law Officers. The position at October, 1969 is given at p. 137.

DOCUMENT I
CHANGES IN THE DEPARTMENTS OF STATE, 1902–68

Major Departments	
1902	*1968*
Treasury	Treasury
Home	Home
Foreign Office	Foreign Office
India	Commonwealth
Colonial	
Ireland	
Admiralty	Defence
War	
	Economic Affairs
Board of Trade	Board of Trade
Scottish Office	Scottish Office
	Welsh Office
Education (Board)	Education
Local Government	Housing and Local Government
	Employment and Productivity
	(Labour until April, 1968)
	Agriculture
	Transport
	Power
	Technology
	non-Cabinet departments
	Overseas Development
	Health
	Social Security
Post Office	Post Office
Works (First Commissioner)	Public Building and Works

EXERCISE
CHANGES IN THE MAJOR DEPARTMENTS

1. What are the important differences between the two lists and how would you explain the differences?

A rational division of function. It may seem at this point that the central organisation of government is untidy and illogical, or that the changes suggest no clear principle of organisation: Whitehall is shaped and reshaped by politicians in a hurry, and having regard only to persons and political gestures.

Half a century ago the Haldane Committee thought it had found the answer—a principle for the allocation of functions.

THE ALLOCATION OF FUNCTIONS TO DEPARTMENTS

From the Report of the Machinery of Government Committee (Haldane Committee) Cmd. 9230, 1918, pp. 7–8

... Upon what principle are the functions of Departments to be determined and allocated? There appear to be only two alternatives, which may be briefly described as distribution according to the persons or classes to be dealt with, and distribution according to the services to be performed. Under the former method each Minister who presides over a Department would be responsible to Parliament for those activities of the Government which affect the sectional interests of particular classes of persons, and there might be, for example, a Ministry for Paupers, a Ministry for Children, a Ministry for Insured Persons, or a Ministry for the Unemployed. ...

The other method, and the one which we recommend for adoption, is that of defining the field of activity in the case of each Department according to the particular service which it renders to the community as a whole. Thus a Ministry of Education would be concerned predominantly with the provision of education wherever, and by whomsoever, needed. Such a Ministry would have to deal with persons in so far only as they were to be educated, and not with particular classes of persons defined on other principles. This method cannot of course, be applied with absolute rigidity. ...

But notwithstanding such necessary qualifications, we think that much would be gained if the distribution of departmental duties were guided by a general principle, and we have come to the conclusion that distribution according to the nature of the service to be rendered to the community as a whole is the principle which is likely to lead to the minimum amount of confusion and overlapping.

The structure of Departments

At the head of each Department is the Minister or Secretary of State, in most cases with Ministers of State and junior Ministers to assist him. Immediately below the Minister is the chief official of the Department, the Permanent Secretary (or Permanent Under Secretary if the Minister is a Secretary of State). Below him come the Deputy and Assistant Under-Secretaries, each supervising a defined section of the Ministry's work.

In this scheme the part of the Permanent Secretary is crucial. He is in the highest grade of the Administrative Civil Service (see below) and is the highest official in the Department, responsible to the political head for all its work. Given the Minister's absorption in political work and lack of time for any but the most important departmental business, then the Permanent Secretary's responsibility amounts to the direction and supervision of most of the Department's normal work. If these things could be measured, 'most', in terms of quantity, would here mean perhaps ninety-five per cent. The Permanent Secretary's administrative responsibility is fixed not only by his place at the top of the hierarchy, but also by his being formally the Department's Accounting Officer. As such he appears before the financial committees of the House of Commons.

Apart from these duties as chief administrator, the Permanent Secretary has a close and special relationship with the Minister. This has two aspects. One is advising the Minister on the other five per cent of business, the major departmental decisions, the formulation of new policy, the handling of politically live issues. The other is advising and assisting the Minister on the parliamentary and political business of the Department—speeches, questions, legislation, committees. The Minister will of course deal with other senior civil servants, but he will normally do so through the Permanent Secretary.

The Minister's Principal Private Secretary[1] is an important link between the Minister and the Department. The Private Secretary is usually an able young civil servant, marked out for rapid promotion but still relatively junior. Thus he does not fit neatly into an hierarchical chart, for he is by rank junior, and very much the servant of both political and official heads, yet access to the bosses gives opportunities for acquiring information and influence. We need not look here for powers behind the throne: rather we may discern how the machine actually works. The following account of the work of a Principal Private Secretary is by Sir James Grigg, later both a Permanent Secretary and a Minister.

....

DOCUMENT 3

THE WORK AND INFLUENCE OF A
PRINCIPAL PRIVATE SECRETARY

From Sir James Grigg, *Prejudice and Judgement*, Jonathan Cape, 1948, pp. 56-7

It was the business of the Principal Private Secretary to take a pre-view of all drafts and memoranda. . . . He was (or so I held) entitled to offer

---

[1] Not to be confused with Parliamentary Private Secretary, an unpaid office filled by a Member of Parliament.

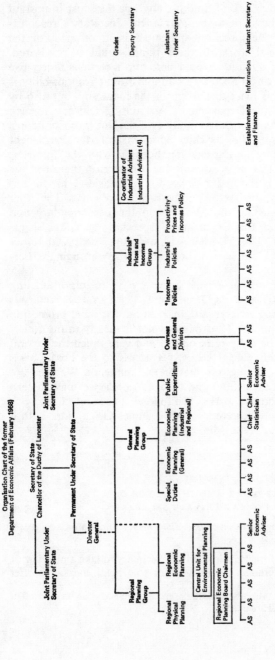

Organisation Chart of the former
Department of Economic Affairs (February 1968)

DEPARTMENT OF ECONOMIC AFFAIRS (FEBRUARY, 1968)

*In April, 1968, Prices and Incomes Policy was transferred to the new Department for Employment and Productivity. This may seem logical. There is no agreement on the proper allocation of economic functions among the Departments.
Instability was a characteristic of the DEA and it was abolished finally in 1969, its functions going to the Treasury and the Ministry of Technology.

Note: For explanation of grades, see Chapter 4.

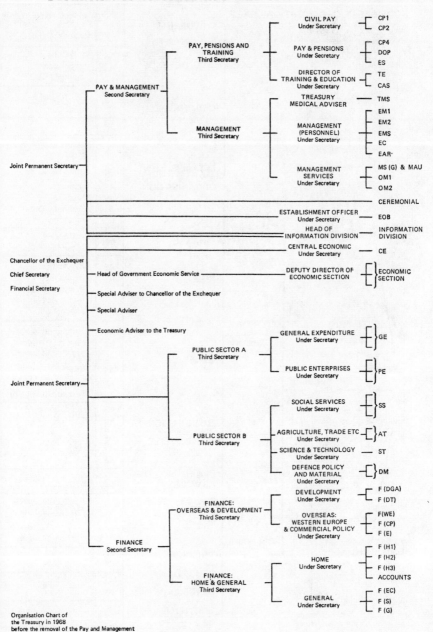

Organisation Chart of
the Treasury in 1968
before the removal of the Pay and Management
Division to the new Civil Service Department.

H.M. TREASURY ORGANISATION CHART (1968)

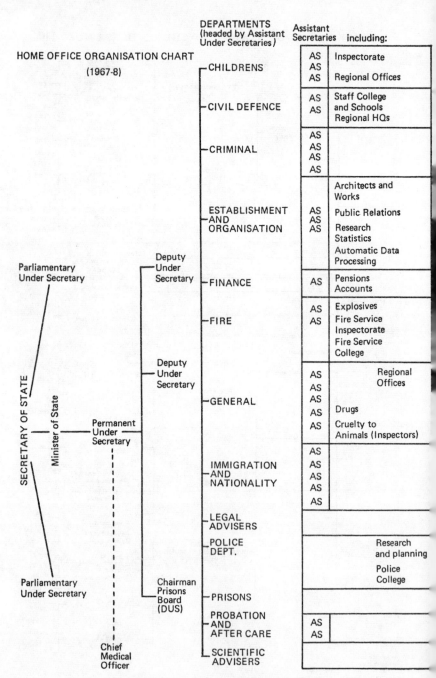

HOME OFFICE ORGANISATION CHART (1967–8)

suggestions to the authors of the documents for making them more acceptable or convincing to Ministers or more calculated to meet their requirements. In my view, the Private Secretary was never justified in re-vamping the work of his official superior and the most I ever permitted myself was to give the Chancellor a short written summary of the case . . . I could also supplement the official recommendations by oral exposition of them and if the Chancellor was still unconvinced I could get him to send for the expert concerned. In course of time one actually acquired great knowledge and experience and in consequence great influence both with the Minister and with the office hierarchy. But . . . it was essential that the Private Secretary . . . should strictly confine himself to being an efficient link between the Minister and the machine. . . .

The division of labour. The work of a Department is usually divided into blocks, which are as far as possible meaningful and co-herent. Most Departments have sections for finance and establish-ments. The establishments section is concerned with staffing matters, such as training, promotion, welfare, organisation and methods, and with buildings, furnishing, supplies, cars and so on. Most Departments also have sections for statistics and public relations, as well as a library.

DOCUMENT 4
ORGANISATION CHARTS OF MINISTRIES
see pp. 116–18

EXERCISES
THE ORGANISATION OF DEPARTMENTS

2.1. What are the main principles of organisation evident in these charts?

2.2. Organisation charts can be misleading. They imply patterns and relationships which may not exist in practice. As an indication of this, consider what is implied by the vertical and horizontal lines in the charts.

Principles of administration

The work of Government Departments is conducted according to three general principles of administration.

First, the processes of administration take place within certain horizontal and vertical divisions—as the organisation charts show.

The vertical divisions indicate *specialisation*, and the horizontal divisions are *levels* within a *hierarchy*. This simple pattern determines the location or routing of each problem, with important and general problems going towards the top of the pyramidal structure.

Second, the system works by communication, in letters, meetings, personal discussion by telephone or face-to-face, but characteristically in the circulation of a file. This is simply a folder containing the relevant documents, to which are added 'minutes' (i.e. notes or comments) as the file goes around (up, down or sideways). Its destination is the officer who must take the final decision based on the contents of the file—or pass it up to a higher level. Most large bureaucratic organisations are based perforce on these two principles.

The third principle distinguishes the Civil Service from most other bureaucracies: it is political accountability. For every problem, and at every point, there is the awareness that the Department must be ready to defend all its actions in Parliament. This, for the public administrator, is the equivalent of a businessman's need to make a profit. Hence some of the civil servant's tendency to make written records, and some of his caution.

EXERCISES

COORDINATION AND COMMUNICATION

3.1. How would you arrange for the coordination of the work of two civil servants below the level of Assistant Secretary in the Home Office, one dealing with naturalisation problems, the other with a treaty affecting aliens?

3.2. In broad terms, how would you arrange good lines of communication to the outside world?

3 THE TREASURY

The Treasury is the most important of the Departments of State. Its First Lord is Prime Minister. The Treasury's unique role in British government deserves a separate, though brief, section.

The Treasury has important functions which place it at the centre of government administration:

(a) the raising of revenue;
(b) the control of public expenditure.

(c) the oversight of the national economy (the removal of part of this function to DEA in 1964 was abandoned in 1969, though other Ministries are still concerned in economic policy).

Until 1968, when the Government adopted the Fulton Committee's recommendation for a Civil Service Department, the Treasury also managed the Civil Service. This function dated from 1919–20, when the Service was centralised under the Treasury. Previously, each Department looked after its own staff, and was a miniature civil service on its own. This was probably not good for efficiency, since it bred departmental narrowness, and it was bad for careers because there were no short cuts to the top. The regulations of 1919–20 changed this. There was to be a single Service, with movement and promotion across departmental boundaries, and the Permanent Secretary of the Treasury was to be head of the Civil Service. Appointments to the top posts in every Department could be made only with the Prime Minister's consent—which meant in practice the consent of the Head of the Civil Service. Thus, the Treasury acquired as a substantial part of its functions a 'Pay and Management side'. After 1956 this 'side' had its own Joint Permanent Secretary, who was also Secretary of the Cabinet. Another Permanent Secretary headed the Finance and Economic side. In 1962 the post of Secretary to the Cabinet was separated from the pay and management post, so where previously there was one, there were three Permanent Secretaries—two in the Treasury and one in the Cabinet Office.

The Treasury was, then, the directing organisation of the Civil Service. This position was not affected by the existence of the Civil Service Commission, which is simply a recruiting and selecting agency for the Civil Service as a whole. The Treasury controlled promotion and appointments, especially at the highest levels. It supervised establishments policy for the Service as a whole, operated a powerful Directorate of Organisation and Methods, and watched over discipline. This position has been changed by the establishment of the Civil Service Department under the Prime Minister. In the long term the preeminence of the Treasury will be modified.

In financial matters the Treasury remains a dominant force. Departmental estimates must be approved by the Treasury. The total expenditure of a Department is necessarily a matter of high policy, and the major decisions will be fought out at ministerial level, or in Cabinet (see chapters 2 and 3). But, in addition, Treasury officials are involved in discussions with the Departments. The Treasury's main concern is with overall totals, but its examination of estimates extends to questioning the major heads of expenditure. It is also concerned with seeing that actual expenditure is consistent with moneys voted (with the help of the Comptroller and Auditor General).

The financial powers of the Treasury are not limited to the review of the annual budgets of Departments. Since the Plowden Report of 1961 on the Control of Public Expenditure, Government has recognised the need to project its financial plans several years ahead. The broad decisions on expenditure are now part of a five year rolling programme, with more specific decisions being taken up to three years in advance. Such forward planning is obvious good sense, but inevitably enlarges the influence of the planners and restricts the discretion of the Departments. Of course, the planning of expenditure on this scale is a matter for the Government as a whole including the Cabinet and its committee on public expenditure.

In the exercise of financial control, the Treasury clearly has very great powers. Such powers might provide a salutary discipline for Departments, or induce in them excessive caution if not paralysis. The Treasury has indeed acquired over the years an unenvied reputation for caring too much about 'candle-ends'. Until 1939, a Department could not hire an extra charwoman without approval, and more recently the Ministry of Works had to seek approval for any building project costing more than £1000. However, the Plowden Committee recommended replacing close financial control by a more vigorous policy of management—that is, seeing that Departments were well run by competent people.

Thus, Treasury control in the form of directing the Civil Service or controlling expenditure, or in the form of 'management', has been a force to be reckoned with, and the overriding force in the administrative aspect of British government.

EXERCISE
THE MANAGEMENT OF THE CIVIL SERVICE

4. Is there a case for transferring the management of the Civil Service from the Treasury to a new Ministry for the Civil Service?

4 THE CIVIL SERVICE: CLASSIFICATION, RECRUITMENT, TRAINING[1]

History and classification

There have always been administrators, but the modern Civil Service dates only from the nineteenth century. In 1854 the North-cote–Trevelyan Report recommended (a) the separation of the intellectual from the mechanical side of administration; (b) the unification of the Service, with unified recruitment and inter-departmental promotion; (c) recruitment by competitive examination, not by patronage; and (d) promotion by merit.

These were recommendations only, but in the next seventy years (the time-scale on which a cynic might think British governments always work) they were virtually all adopted. The Civil Service Commission was set up with commendable speed in 1855, and in 1870 the first competitive recruitment was established. In 1919–20, the Service was in effect unified under the Treasury.

By then the clerks of the mid-nineteenth century had been converted, some of them, into twentieth-century administrators (with girl typists to do the purely mechanical job of copying). The important distinctions of function implied in this process are well indicated in this extract from a lecture by Sir Edward Bridges, a former Permanent Secretary to the Treasury.

....

DOCUMENT 5
FROM CLERK TO ADMINISTRATOR

From Sir Edward Bridges, *Portrait of a Profession*, Cambridge University Press, 1953, p. 14

The Clerk who at first had done nothing except copy letters, despatch them and file them, makes himself useful in collecting precedents and previous papers. The next stage is that he becomes a clerk who can describe accurately what has happened in the past, who can collect together the information required by the officer who is going to reach a decision on the matter in hand; and before long you have an adviser who presents his senior colleagues or his Minister with a carefully documented appraisal of the position, who tests all the statements made and sets out what seem to him the possible courses of action and the likely consequences of each. There remains a final step. To sum it all up and say which course has behind it the

---

[1] The text was completed before the publication of the Fulton Report on the Civil Service. The Report is summarised and assessed at pp. 144–8.

backing of all the knowledge and experience that the Department can give to its Minister.

....

The modern Civil Service is divided and classified in several ways.

The *Treasury classes* include the general practitioners, ranging from the high administrative arts to the humble skills of the office cleaner. The *departmental* and *specialist classes* include officials doing work special to one Department (e.g. tax inspectors, agricultural advisers) and people with specialist qualifications (e.g. scientists, lawyers, accountants, economists). The specialist classes include over 130,000 people and some of these work on the same problems as the general administrators of the Treasury classes. Central government is not in fact without specialist advice.

In addition to these administrators and specialists of the *non-industrial* Civil Service, there are *industrial* civil servants, such as postmen[1], and dockyard and ordnance workers. Most civil servants are 'established', having a right to a pension and a certain security of tenure: a few are temporary and 'unestablished'.

For the student of politics, the most important civil servants are those in the Treasury classes, especially the Administrative Class. This is the highest of the Treasury classes, and includes the Permanent Secretaries, Assistant Secretaries and so on, working in the major Departments. Its numbers are small—only 2,300, with about another thousand in the Diplomatic Service. Below it is the Executive Class of 77,000, ranging from senior accountants and managers of Labour Exchanges to responsible Executive Officers dealing with routine claims for insurance benefits. Below again, is the Clerical Class (130,000), the Ancillary Clerical (102,000, mostly typists and machine operators), and a smaller army (34,000) of messengers and cleaners.

The original distinction between Administrative, Executive and Clerical classes was between university graduates, school leavers at eighteen (with Advanced Level qualifications) and school leavers at sixteen (with Ordinary Level qualifications.) This is still a rough guide to the kind of official in each class. But the tendency for many more bright eighteen-year-olds to go on to university is changing the pattern of recruitment. The Executive Class increasingly recruits university graduates.

[1] Until 1969, when the Post Office became a public corporation.

The rest of this chapter is concerned with the Administrative Class, the higher levels of the Executive Class and the relation to those of the specialist classes.

Recruitment and training for recruitment to the Administrative Class. The Administrative Class of the Civil Service is recruited in three ways:

(a) by promotion from the Executive Class (about forty per cent of entrants to the class);

(b) from young university graduates (about sixty per cent);

(c) from persons in senior positions outside government, in their late thirties or forties, direct to the senior rank of Assistant Secretary (very few)—also a small but increasing number of 'outsiders', of lesser status, direct to the rank of Principal.

Of these, the second category is most important, because of the weight of numbers, especially at the higher levels (eighty-seven per cent of posts of Permanent and Deputy Secretary in 1966) and because the tone of the Service tends to be set by this category. Entrants in this category are selected by two methods:

Method 1. Candidates take a short qualifying examination, a written examination similar to that of an honours degree (in the candidate's own subjects) and have a final interview board.

Method 2. Instead of the degree-type written examination, groups of candidates attend a selection centre for two-and-a-half days and have a series of interviews and tests. Some of these are designed to simulate actual administrative problems and candidates draft papers, chair committees, make speeches and so on. Method 2 is increasingly favoured by candidates and in 1966 eighty-two were successful in this way, compared with only eighteen by Method 1.

EXERCISE

METHODS OF SELECTION

5. If you were (a) a candidate and (b) a selector for an administrative post which method of selection would you prefer—a written academic examination and an interview, or tests based on administrative problems?—and why?

There is an important principle of British public administration involved in this process of selection: the administrator is regarded as a man of general ability, not with specialist abilities or training: he is an 'amateur' (to use that term loosely). The principle and some practical consequences are illustrated in the following document.

....

DOCUMENT 6

THE RECRUITMENT OF THE 'GENTLEMAN AMATEUR'

(a) From Lord Macaulay, *Report on the Selection and Examination of Candidates for the Indian Civil Service*, 1854

We believe that men who have been engaged, up to twenty-one or twenty-two, in studies which have no immediate connection with the business of any profession, and of which the effect is merely to open, to invigorate, and to enrich the mind, will generally be found in the business of every profession superior to men who have, at eighteen or nineteen, devoted themselves to the special studies of their calling. The most illustrious English jurists have been men who never opened a law book till after the close of a distinguished academical career; nor is there any reason to believe that they would have been greater lawyers if they had passed in drawing plans and conveyances the time which they gave to Thucydides, to Cicero, and to Newton.

(b) Table derived from Sixth Report of the Estimates Committee, H.C. 308, 1964–5

Recruitment of Assistant Principals		
	1948–56	*1957–63*
attended		
Oxford or Cambridge	78%	85%
Boarding schools	31%	37%
Local authority schools	42%	30%
with fathers in		
Registrar General's Class I (higher professional)	38%	46%
Manual work	22%	15%
with degrees in		
Classics	21%	24%
Social science	24%	17%
Science, technology, mathematics	4%	3%

....

EXERCISE

'AMATEURS' AND 'SPECIALISTS'

6. Macaulay's view is now unfashionable, and it is sometimes argued that the Civil Service Commission ought to be seeking

graduates in economics, public administration, accountancy, aeronautical engineering, and the like—persons with direct training in the matters they may be called on to administer. So, to swim against the tide, set down arguments against the recruitment of specialists to the Administrative Class.

Social bias in recruitment. The table in document 6 shows what is called a 'social bias' in recruitment to the Administrative Class, an enormous preponderance of entrants from Oxford and Cambridge universities and a substantial preponderance from the public and 'direct grant' schools.

It is undeniable that a strong imbalance exists with respect to the backgrounds of the successful candidates. For example, a selection proportionate to all universities would reduce the representation of Oxford and Cambridge to a small minority. A similar comparison can be made for schools.

However, none of this proves that the selectors are biased toward private schools and ancient universities. The selectors claim, first, that the field of candidates is largely biased in the same way. This is true, and, of course, the selectors cannot choose people who do not apply (but this is not a complete explanation, for a further bias shows among the successful candidates, i.e. candidates from local authority schools and newer universities are less likely to be successful than others). Second, the best candidates happen to be in many cases from Oxford or Cambridge and from private schools. Thus, say the selectors, *we* are not biased, we select what the system throws up: if there is a bias, it is in the educational system.

This is a plausible, perhaps a convincing, line of argument, and it raises questions about the educational system. In particular, do all the best (by Civil Service standards) pupils go to private schools and ancient universities, or does the education provided in these institutions convert average pupils into potentially successful candidates for the higher ranks of the Civil Service? It seems unlikely that educational institutions alone can turn sows' ears into silk purses. It seems more likely that these institutions have more than a fair share of the nation's talent. At university level, in particular, places at Oxford and Cambridge are much sought after, and there is to some extent a 'creaming-off' of talent.

In spite of all this, it is incredible that *all* the nation's highest talents (including the administrative talent required by the Civil Service) should be confined to these institutions. The conclusion must be that the present selection process fails to recognise some talent outside the private and ancient educational system.

This is a puzzling conclusion: for there can be no doubt that the selectors themselves are scrupulously fair, and the processes of selection highly developed. The explanation possibly lies in the figures on father's occupation. Successful candidates tend to come from the highest levels of society, in status and income. It may be that selectors look for qualities such as social poise, self-confidence, range of experience (all desirable in high-level administrators, but most likely to be found in the children of well-to-do families). It might then be objected that candidates from humbler homes and newer universities might, *given two or three years to find their confidence*, turn out to be at least as good at administration as these golden youths.

But this conclusion is speculative—perhaps worth a try-out, for example, through a temporary cadet-grade. There is firmer ground for the belief that the field of candidates must be widened, and the Civil Service Commission is now endeavouring to do this.

EXERCISE
SOCIAL BIAS IN RECRUITMENT

7. Does social bias matter? The Civil Service is recruiting men (and a few women) of high capacity. Why should it be a matter of concern that there should be no bias in the recruitment?

Subject bias in recruitment. Does it matter that so many recruits have not graduated in relevant subjects? The arguments in the answer to exercise 6. point to the conclusion that subjects do not matter much at all. But there is a case to be made for training, both in the technique and the subject matter of government—i.e. in political, economic and social studies

Training. The tradition of the higher Civil Service is that a person of the right calibre will acquire the art of administration by doing the job of an administrator. The recruit is not trained, he serves an apprenticeship. In recent years the tradition has been modified. Direct entrants to the Administration Class now undergo at least one short period of training. This takes place at the Treasury's Centre for Administrative Studies in Regent's Park. Despite the title, most of the training is in economics.[1]

This paucity of post-entry training, and in particular of specialist training in public administration, is in marked contrast to the

---

[1] For recommendations of the Fulton Committee on the Civil Service, see p. 145.

procedures of other countries, notably France. It implies that little can be learned by formal training which cannot be learned as well while doing the job. This is hard to believe, and more than one distinguished civil servant has argued the need for more post-entry specialist training. The Treasury, in its evidence to the Fulton Committee on the Civil Service (submitted in 1966), accepts the point and proposes the development of training courses directly related to the work of the Civil Service, including courses in management for middle and higher ranks.

If the choice is between subjects of the arts group, say classics, literature or history, then the difference in practice is probably quite small. There is no fundamental difference between an understanding of Homer, Cicero, Edward I, or Wordsworth in their educative potential (or lack of it) as subjects for administrators.

However, in the social sciences the universities now teach subjects directly related to the concerns and techniques of administrators: economics, sociology, social and public administration, statistics, and (of course) political science. It is likely, to say the least, that these subjects help young administrators to understand their problems and develop their techniques quickly, and avoid some elementary mistakes in their early years.

Of course, a good deal must still be learned on the job, and the entrant without this specialist background will have caught up most of the way within five years or so. Still, one would expect a certain advantage to remain with the social scientist—a deeper, more reflective understanding of his trade. There is an analogous situation in the education service, and here the prejudice is now very heavily —and rightly—on the side of professional training for teachers.

The case of science is less clear. This is highly relevant to the subject matter of some government operations. We certainly need civil servants with a general understanding of science. But specialist knowledge may well hamper an administrative decision. Thus, making a policy recommendation on, say, the Concorde project, requires an understanding of the economics of the transport and aircraft industries, and the relation of these to the national economy and the national interest. It does not require a special knowledge of aeronautics. All the same, an awareness of the technical limits and possibilities of supersonic flight would help the administrator in assessing the validity of the technical advice. Similarly, the administrator of the Lime Subsidy does not require a technical knowledge of lime; but there needs to be someone in the Department who can question the value of lime on some kinds of soil.

In all these cases—science, economics, public administration—specialist advice can easily be provided. The question really is how far such advice is required, not on the outside, but within the Department, in the man actually taking the decision. It has been implied above that the social sciences may have a greater relevance than science itself inside the administrator's office.

Grading. At present the direct entrant to the Administrative Class becomes an Assistant Principal (at about £1,000 p.a.). This is a training grade, and most recruits can expect promotion after three to seven years to the grade of Principal (£2,599 rising to £3,596 p.a.—1970). A good Principal may expect promotion to Assistant Secretary (£4,045—£5,200) in his early forties. Beyond this are the senior ranks of Under, Deputy and Permanent Secretary, with salaries up to £9,800: these heights will be reached by only a few.

5 KINDS OF WORK AND KINDS OF MEN

The work of the Administrative Class

The work of higher civil servants was indicated in chapter 3 in relation to the work of Ministers. A re-reading of section 5 (p. 92) will show how the relationship of senior civil servants to Ministers may vary. This variation affects the whole range of the work of the Administrative Class. The major fields of work are:

(a) *Administration.* The overseeing of the day-to-day work of the Department or some part of it; dealing with difficult, non-routine cases; conferring with colleagues; corresponding with, or talking to, persons and groups with an interest in the Department's work.

(b) *Policy.* Helping in the *development* of the Department's work and the *formulation* of policy—by surveying the possibilities, assessing alternative lines of policy, estimating costs, foreseeing practical problems and the reactions of Parliament, people, pressure groups. (Here the politician's or the columnist's bright idea, the academic's 'perception' do not suffice—a line of policy must be worked out in detail.) Terms may be confusing here. The Civil Service uses 'administration' to cover (a) and (b), and sometimes 'management' for (a). In industry, the term 'management' applies to functions (a) and (b) and this is a normal use of that term. Hence it is quite proper to regard Administrative Class civil servants as 'managers', and this indicates better than the term 'administrator' that they are not mere executants.

(c) *Politics*. Preparing legislation, answering Parliamentary Questions and letters from Members of Parliament, briefing the Minister.

The strong Minister tends not to lean on his Department much for advice on policy and politics. But it is not a sign of weakness for a Minister to look to his staff for assistance over the whole range of his work. Thus, the administrative civil servant is also an adviser, and advises on political as well as administrative matters. For example, a senior civil servant may be expected to be aware of the relative acceptability of policies within the parties. A good Department will not be taken by surprise at a change of government: it may already have carried out some studies on the possible applications of new political direction in the Department's work.

The fundamental differences between the two kinds of men—politicians and civil servants—show most clearly only when party policy is in question, and parliamentary or political answerability is required. The following document illustrates the nature of the work of the administrative civil servant. It is from an account by a higher civil servant, but one who moved from being Permanent Secretary to the War Office to the Ministerial Office of Secretary of State for War.

....

DOCUMENT 7

MINISTER AND PERMANENT SECRETARY—THE DIFFERENCES

From Sir James Grigg, *Prejudice and Judgement*, Jonathan Cape, 1948, pp. 351–2

I could get nothing done without persuading those whose primary concern it was that it was the right thing to do. After that we had to go hand in hand to the Secretary of State and convince him that it was the right thing to do. But once he had decided . . ., they became his own and he assumed the entire responsibility for them *urbe et orbi* . . . . Those of us who had advised or pressed the decisions upon him hid ourselves behind the cloak of the unique but universal accountability of the Secretary of State.

Now I was myself Secretary of State. I had no longer to go through a whole chain of private persuasions. In the administrative sphere I could decide things for myself and I could give orders in any sense and at any time I liked. But I had to recognise that I might be called on to justify what I had done to the Prime Minister and the War Cabinet or to defend it publicly in the House of Commons. From now on it was I and not another who had to answer for everything that went on in the War Office and the Army.

....

MINISTER AND PERMANENT SECRETARY

8. What are the chief differences between the two jobs indicated by Sir James Grigg?

Ministers as prisoners of Departments? The Labour Party's evidence to the Fulton Committee suggested that civil servants could control a Minister by controlling the flow of information to him, hiding facts from him if necessary. This point was put to Prime Minister Wilson in a broadcast interview in March 1967. Mr Wilson replied: '. . . if you'll tell me the names of any Ministers who allow their civil servants to keep back information, or any civil servants who would do it, I think the time has come for a rapid change, whether of the Ministers or of the civil servants or both.' (*The Listener*, 13 April 1967.) On the other hand, at least one former Minister has referred sharply to the distinction between Ministers who run their Departments and those who are run by them— 'Everyone knows which are which: you could make two lists.'

CIVIL SERVANTS AND THE MAKING OF POLICY

9. Do higher civil servants make policy?

Distinctive features of the role of the Civil Service in Britain

The British Civil Service is distinctive in its approach to recruitment and training: there are also distinctive features in its manner of operation, some of which have already been described.

First, the formulation of policy is closely connected with the practical experience of execution of policy. This has the advantage of ensuring that policy is normally practicable, and changes in policy arise naturally from day-to-day practice. Those who accept this approach would argue that there is little to be said for superior, detached policy-planning bodies, especially those composed partly of outside experts (non-career civil servants)—nor, it seems, for the policy-planning functions of a political party. Clearly there is a case to be made the other way, arguing that administrators buried in routine tasks have neither time nor vision for forward planning, and lose their taste for change. This is an unresolved argument in British government.

A second distinctive feature is the anonymity of the civil servant. He offers, even urges, advice, but is not answerable in Parliament and in public for the major policies, or even the minor acts, of his Department. This is the job of the Minister, and is part of ministerial responsibility (see chapter 3). The arrangement is both admired and criticised. It is criticised because it seems to make for secret and irresponsible government. For example, the decision on a local planning appeal of some significance will be taken by a civil servant, but conveyed to you in the name of the Minister. If you wish to continue arguing (which will not normally change the decision), you must argue with the Minister (who will be briefed by the civil servant). You may feel you are talking with shadows. The situation is indeed a curious one, although on lesser and local matters—e.g., a National Insurance claim or a passport problem, where the Ministries concerned have local offices—it is much easier to interview the civil servant taking the decision. It is a further anomaly that organised pressure groups find it much easier to gain access to decision-taking civil servants. They circulate within the private system, which is barred to individual citizens.

Nevertheless, the system has substantial advantages. It divides the labour of government between Ministers and their advisers. The Ministers take the decisions finally, are responsible to the Prime Minister and Cabinet, and answerable in Parliament and in public. Their job calls for qualities of strength of personality, skill in public advocacy, the temperament and skills appropriate to politics. The adviser, on the other hand, characteristically has the qualities of a seeker after truth, an assessor of conflicting arguments, a dispassionate and uncommitted technician. This division of labour is maintained by the devices of civil service anonymity and ministerial answerability. If you change the devices, you change the division, hence change the location of responsibility and the type of person carrying out the functions of government. The case for the system is a strong one, but it applies with less force at levels below those of political sensitivity, controversy or struggle: there is much more scope for the civil servant's direct answerability to the public at these levels.

A third characteristic of the British Civil Service is that the civil servant is non-political. He is a permanent career official, serving all governments with equal vigour. Prime Ministers Attlee, Churchill and Wilson (who have taken office after Prime Ministers of opposite parties) have all testified to the capacity of the Civil Service to keep faith with this tradition. Again, this could be done differently. For example, in America an incoming administration changes many of the top advisers of government for men of its own political views. Thus, professional competence is vitalised by personal conviction.

The men who do the work

The last section especially indicates that a higher civil servant must have, or develop, very special qualities if he is to fill his role effectively.

EXERCISES

THE QUALITIES REQUIRED OF A CIVIL SERVANT

10.1. In the light of the foregoing account of the work of civil servants, what three qualities would you look for in a candidate for the administrative Civil Service? First, attempt an answer on your own, then read on.

10.2. Following, in document 8, are some descriptions of actual or desirable qualities by many hands. Choose up to three qualities from these which *you* would regard as desirable. Would you regard this as an adequate list of necessary qualities?

DOCUMENT 8

THE JOB OF THE CIVIL SERVANT

Remarks by Ministers on their civil servants, made to Anthony Sampson and reported by him in *Anatomy of Britain Today*, Hodder and Stoughton, 1965, p. 272

(a) You know, they've got a wonderful political sense, without themselves being political. They can get the feel of your ideas very quickly.

(b) They're extraordinarily adaptable. I remember when we took office in 1951, the same civil servant who had been looking after nationalisation had already got out a plan for de-nationalisation. He went about it with just the same enthusiasm.

(c) Civil servants aren't passive by nature. They're do-gooders, they're Benthamites at heart. They want to reform the world.

Remarks by civil servants on their job, taken from Sampson, p. 276:

(d) It's our job to provide the brake rather than the spur. A lot of our time is spent pointing out the snags.

(e) You have to spend so much time understanding what other men think that you sometimes forget what you think yourself. But I don't think that matters too much.

Mr Marples, when Minister of Transport, quoted in the *Sunday Times*, 18 June 1961

(f) I have no brains myself, I don't need them. Other people [i.e. civil servants, advisers, etc.] have brains, I have judgement.

C. H. Sisson, a senior civil servant himself, in his book *The Spirit of British Administration*, Faber and Faber, 1966, pp. 20, 23 and 127

(g) He had better not be in the habit of seeing things with his own eyes unless he has abnormal disinterestedness which enables him at once to set aside his own vision.

(h) He is a man who has been trained to a practical operation not to the exposition of a theory or a search for truth.

(i) [The administrator need not be] a man of ideas. His distinguishing quality should be rather a certain freedom from ideas.

(j) It is the absolute non-entity of the British administrator that is his chief merit.

....

6 SOME PROBLEMS OF THE CIVIL SERVICE

It is clear already, and no cause for surprise, that the Civil Service has not satisfactorily solved all the problems arising from its efforts to manage the massive and complex operations of modern government. So far, two main problem areas have emerged. First, there are problems of recruitment and training. These include methods of recruitment, kinds of people, in terms of education, social origin, professional expertness, methods of training, the kind of career structure to be offered and who should rise to the top. (Professor Brian Chapman has described the Civil Service as 'by European standards, an over-specialised, parochial, closed corporation'— *British Government Observed*, Allen and Unwin, 1963, pp. 23–4.) Second, there are problems of role and power. These are the problems of the relation of civil servant to politician and to public; the source of ultimate decision-making; the secrecy and anonymity of the Service.

There is a third important problem area, the methods of work of the Civil Service, which are the characteristic methods of most bureaucratic organisations. They are open to some of the criticisms popularly linked with the word 'bureaucracy'. This is often used as a term of abuse for governments, though bureaucratic systems are a normal feature of any large organisation. Still it is true that such organisations are prone to certain faults, which may be technically labelled 'bureaucratic dysfunctions':

(a) There is a tendency for bureaucracies to grow in size without any increase in (valid) output. By 1967 the non-industrial Civil Service had grown to 466,000, some 50,000 more than in 1964. Some, perhaps most, of this growth is directly related to increases in work and responsibilities under new government programmes. But at least a little of it is not justified and has to do with human failings of a general kind (e.g., desire for the status of a large staff) and of a particular kind (e.g., those indicated in the famous Parkinson's Law[1] that 'work expands so as to fill the time available for its completion.') It has also to do with the techniques of routine administration, the addiction to forms and formal procedures, recording and consulting.

(b) There is a tendency to excessive caution, suspicion of innovation, lack of initiative, devotion to precedent, and, in routine clerical work, to time-consuming procedures and excessive use of forms. These faults may be lumped together in the phrase 'red-tape'.

EXERCISE

RED-TAPE

11. Do you see any justification for 'red-tape' in the sense of forms in triplicate and decision by precedent?

(c) There is a tendency for the insulation of the bureaucracy from important aspects of the life of the community. Thus, the Civil Service is still overwhelmingly London-based; most civil servants have not experienced any other kind of employment; contacts with regional offices, with local government and with industry are still only slight.

However, these problems and criticisms should not be exaggerated, and we should bear in mind that the Civil Service is capable of self-criticism and self-modification, if not of radical self-reform. The Treasury has a strong sense of economy, and a strong Organisation

[1] C. N. Parkinson, *Parkinson's Law*, Murray, 1958, p. 4. This law applies to many organisations, including schools and colleges. Professor Parkinson predicts, jokingly of course, that the whole adult labour force will be in the Civil Service by the year 2195.

and Methods Division. The Departments have similar sections, and establishments officers have responsibility for the pattern of staffing. Promotion is keenly competitive. But there is no continuing strong pressure for revision of methods and, as in most organisations of this kind, there is steady pressure from the civil servants themselves to create 'zones of comfort' in which they may live out their professional lives without too much stress.

The Wilson Government in 1966 set up the Fulton Committee to review the Civil Service, the first review of this kind since 1931. It seems likely that more frequent general reviews would strike a better balance between salutary scrutiny and undisturbed 'getting on with the job'.

Some larger questions of reform are considered in the assessments.

GUIDE TO EXERCISES

1. The differences are:

Department of Economic Affairs, a new Ministry; India and Colonial Offices transformed into Commonwealth and Overseas Development; War and Admiralty into Defence; a new Welsh Office. New Departments for Labour, Agriculture, Transport, Power, Technology, Health and Social Security.

Most of the explanations are obvious enough. Governments have increasingly chosen to intervene in, subsidise, encourage, manage, and take over the economy, and to provide welfare for the citizens. The colonies have almost disappeared, and aid (development) is more important than ownership. The armed forces have at last been coordinated. The Welsh Office is a tribute on the Scottish model to regional devolution and Welsh separatism.

These explanations are not necessarily justifications.

[Note: In October 1969, the number of major Departments was eighteen. The Foreign and Commonwealth Offices had been amalgamated; so, too, Technology and Power. The DEA was abolished. There was a new Department of the Civil Service, and two 'super' Ministers, for Social Services, and for Local Government and Regional Planning.]

2.1. The division of labour (specialisation); levels (of control and coordination); hierarchy. See text following the exercise.

2.2. The lines indicate communication of some kind, and vertical lines normally indicate control and coordination. Of course lines are a very crude expression of highly complex relationships.

3.1. As a minimum, they must talk to one another directly, and circulate files between the two sections. As a maximum, there should be a small inter-section committee, perhaps chaired by the Assistant Secretary in charge of both sections. But in the maximum scheme, too much time and formal organisation is devoted to coordination, at the expense of what is being coordinated.

3.2. There are two important problems: communication with the section's clientele, and communication with the general public. The latter is a simple 'public relations' operation to explain and justify the work of the sections. It could be done on a small scale by providing news stories and information for the press, circulating leaflets and so on. Communicating with the clientele requires finding the customers and providing them with more detailed information, designed to promote personal application to regional offices, and so to face-to-face communication.

4. Yes. The Treasury is already heavily loaded with work, and (in the view of some critics, including former Permanent Secretaries) excessively powerful. Much of its work and expertise is, moreover, in the fields of economic and financial management, which are very different from, and even counterproductive to, good personnel management.

A separate Department would meet these objections, and provide more effective parliamentary responsibility. Presumably such a department would include the present Civil Service Commission. But one more Ministry means one more problem of coordination. It might be better to put the management of the Civil Service into the Cabinet Office or the Prime Minister's Office, thus strengthening the influence of the Prime Minister (which some critics think is essential).

This case is not, of course, unanswerable. For example, it may be argued that the Treasury has the capacity to do the job (now it is aware of the problems of management); and that the coordination and financial centre of government is clearly the right place for running the Civil Service. Again, there are objections to placing the Service in the hands of the Prime Minister. Is he not overworked and excessively powerful too?

[Note: The answer of the Fulton Committee and the Government was, Yes. See p. 145.]

5. (a) Candidates seem to prefer tests based on administrative problems (the distinctive feature of method 2), probably because they think they can do better that way, and because they have had enough of academic examinations. They are probably right to suspect the accuracy and fairness of an external academic examination.

(b) Selectors seem to agree with the candidates. In any case, they can obtain information on a candidate's academic qualities from the schools and colleges.

But, either way, the judgement of persons is very difficult; and 'social bias' is more likely to enter into assessments of method 2 tests than the purely academic assessment.

6. (a) Administration is an art or skill on its own, and may be equally discovered or developed in the classics graduate as in say, the biochemist.

(b) University education provides a broad intellectual training. What is required of the subject matter of this training is that it should involve clear

thinking, judgement, precision and some force of written and spoken expression. If anything, these may be better developed in arts subjects than in
sciences. In particular, it may be argued that some arts subjects help to
develop judgement, both in respect of other people, and in situations where
the evidence is incomplete and untested.

(c) It is not possible in many cases to arrange that an administrator
should confine himself to certain special fields. Indeed, if he does so, he
may be less useful as an administrator for coordination and communication *among* specialists.

(d) It is by no means certain that the special knowledge acquired by a
university first degree is usefully 'special' by the standards of government.
(And as with most specialisms, it will go out of date very quickly.)

(e) The non-specialist recruit can acquire relevant special knowledge
after entry to the Service.

(f) Moreover, civil servants in the specialist classes can work alongside
the generalist, providing all necessary special knowledge and techniques.

These points are not of course the whole of the argument. There is more
to be said for the specialist, and about the problem of fitting him into the
Civil Service. But the Government did not accept the (not unanimous)
Fulton recommendation for recruitment by 'relevance' of University degree.

7. (a) There is at the moment a shortfall of candidates of the right calibre.
This might be made up by a system which got over or round the social
bias and provided a larger field of potentially successful candidates, without lowering standards. (The text argues that this must in fact be possible.)

(b) The present system is unfair to many good candidates, who, it is
arguable, would make good administrators.

(c) The highest ranks of government administration ought to be more
widely representative of Britain, of schools and universities, of social
classes and of regions (the existing social and educational bias carries with
it a regional bias in favour of the south-east). Of course, there are limits to
the applicability of this point. A Cornishman or a Liverpudlian would
presumably prefer to be administered by a Londoner of sharp intellect and
sound judgement than by a local lad who had neither. But nationalists
might not argue in this way.

8. The Permanent Secretary had the task of formulating policy and persuading the Minister. The Minister had the ultimate decision-taking and
the responsibility.

9. It depends, of course, on what is meant by 'make policy'. As the text
indicates, civil servants at the higher levels take part in the formulation of
policy—i.e. the formulation, discussion and deciding-upon new courses of
action for their Departments. The Minister will seek, consider and respect
their advice, but he may reject it all the same. He is most likely to accept
their advice in the detailed direction of his Department's work and to pass
over departmental advice in the case of important party principles or programmes, or where he has deep personal convictions (which he knows to be
acceptable to his political colleagues).

This is the normal situation. But sometimes a Minister does not know in what direction he wants to lead his Department. Then the higher civil servants may lead him, or opt for immobility. In either case, the civil servant then makes policy. How often does this situation arise? It is hard to say: one guesses that 'never' would be an unsatisfactory answer.

10.1. See answer to 10.2.

10.2. (a), (b) and (e) seem desirable, but you may disagree. The choice between (c) and (d) is an important matter of political judgement. In (f) Mr Marples is mistaken: civil servants need judgement too. Sisson's ideal civil servant is too passive and self-effacing for some tastes.

Of course, the list is not exhaustive. Among many which might be added are: capacity to inform oneself quickly of the outlines of a problem and understand its essential nature; administrative judgement, in particular, the assessment of expert advice; skill in drafting letters and memoranda; skill as a personnel manager.

11. It is simply not possible to carry out large-scale administration without standardisation of forms and procedures, records and accounts. These may need to be in multiple copies for communication and coordination. The doctor who complains about filling in and signing National Insurance forms would complain louder if he had to write a letter each time; or if there was no official check on claims for Sickness Benefit. But, of course, some of these procedures are unnecessary, the consequence of inertia and self-importance.

With regard to caution and conservatism, it is fair to say that civil servants have a duty to be fair and consistent and this is best achieved by administering according to precedent. Novelty is here a much less desirable quality than predictability. But, of course, such adherence to established procedures needs to be modified by humanity and a readiness for change when change is justified.

ASSESSMENTS

Reform of the Civil Service

The reform of political institutions is not the main job of the political scientist. He must above all *understand* them. But making a case for reform which will stand up to critical examination may help understanding. So here is a statement on the case for reform of the Civil Service. It is followed by a summary and brief discussion of the Report of the Fulton Committee on the Civil Service.

(a) *Recruitment*. Recruits to the higher Civil Service need to be drawn from a wider range of universities, of degree subjects and of social class. It would, of course, be absurd to argue that a bishop's son, with an Oxford degree in classics, is unsuited to high official position; but it is difficult to believe that the present heavy bias of the Administrative Class towards the highest social class, and to classics and history at Oxford and Cambridge, serves the nation well. It imposes on the Civil Service a narrowness of experience and outlook which can hardly be overcome in every case and is not compensated by the gain of a homogeneous corps of administration.

However, it is not at all easy to devise ways of bringing about rapid change. The Civil Service Commission is already making strenuous and well-directed efforts to widen the field of candidates. A beginning has been made too on the direct recruitment to the grades of Principal and Assistant Secretary from industry and the professions. But a more radical policy is surely required.

(b) *Training*. The British Civil Service has worked for too long on the principle that administration is an art to be acquired solely in the performance. The evidence from industry and from other countries is that some training helps. Hence, there is a need for a more extensive training and executive development policy. This should include some teaching and training in the field of public administration to supplement the courses now given at the Centre for Administrative Studies, which concentrate on economics and statistics.

(c) *The structure of the higher Civil Service*. The distinction between Executive and Administrative grades no longer corresponds to educational differences among potential recruits and imposes a rigid division of duties and status in the middle ranges where the two classes overlap. The Treasury proposed the abolition of the distinction in its evidence to the Fulton Committee. Their suggestion is for a unified Service, divided into grades. But the old distinction has crept back in a proposal for 'starred' entrants, who should be paid more than others (though on the same scale) and be prepared for faster promotion. Only thus, it is thought, can the Civil Service hope to attract the most able people.

The place of specialists in the higher ranks of the Service is still uneasy. Their advice is increasingly drawn on without their being accepted as policy-formulators and decision-takers, a function carried out by the Administrative Class. Now it is clear that the inventor of, say, the 'swing-wing' principle in aircraft is not the best man to decide to adopt it. Nevertheless, the decision needs to be arrived at with the advice of men having some understanding of aeronautical engineering and air defence needs. The Service needs to provide more opportunities for specialists to transfer to administrative posts, and easier and more flexible working relationships. In this respect the Department of Economic Affairs and the Ministry of Transport have recently used 'mixed' groups with some success. This development would be assisted if more senior officials specialised within particular policy fields—e.g., economic, social services, defence—only after going through a period of inter-departmental mobility to gather experience. There is also scope for specialising in particular aspects of administration, political, research, policy development, and adjustment. All this would provide for a more open profession—in contrast to the traditional mystique about what makes an Administrative Class civil servant.

(d) *Strategic planning and the formulation of future policy*. In a Civil Service which is probably overburdened in the higher ranks, there is too little provision for long-term planning. This is done in Britain, if at all, mainly by political parties in opposition when all the apparatus of government is lacking. To compound the matter, the Service has tended to develop a tradition which glories in the short term of administration. There has been an emphasis on neat patterns of administration, on coordination (whate'er is best coordinated is best). C. H. Sisson, a distinguished civil servant, has written impressively of the claims of balancing and of survival: '. . . at the end he is still upright and the forces around him have achieved a momentary balance. . . . The operation [is] nothing less than the preservation of the state.' (*The Spirit of British Administration*, Faber, 1966, p. 23)

But if the fault can be diagnosed with some certainty, its cure is by no means clear. It may be possible to recruit and train a different kind of civil servant for this function. However, in the British system the sources of initiative ought to be close to the Minister, and a possible solution may be in the building-up of ministerial offices (or *cabinets* in the French sense). These could include experts recruited from outside the service, and personal political advisers, as well as carefully selected civil servants. Their function would be to act as a ginger group for the Minister's Department. There would certainly arise some overlapping and disputing of jurisdictions, some personal discomfort, and competition for the Minister's ear. This might be salutary.

(e) *Efficiency*. The Civil Service is, of course, inefficient at times and in parts, like every other large bureaucratic organisation—perhaps more so, because of the demands of politics and public accountability, and the immensity of the whole operation. It is doubtful whether anything different can be done to ensure greater efficiency. The Treasury and the Committees of Estimates and Public Accounts are good watchdogs, and the Organisation and Methods apparatus has some effect. The parliamentary committees could well be developed for this function, and more frequent full-scale enquiries of the kind now being undertaken could be effective.

Again, recruitment and training policies and efficient Ministers will help. But there is no panacea in calling for more businessmen or university dons to bail the Civil Service out—after all, there are great areas of inefficiency in the commercial and academic worlds.

(f) *Power*. A common criticism of the higher Civil Service is that it is too powerful in relation to the politicians, who, being elected, ought to have the supreme power. Anthony Howard has referred to 'the twin state of Whitehall'. Mr Peter Shore, when a junior Minister in Mr Wilson's Government in 1966, published a book in which he described civil servants as 'permanent politicians', dominating the 'temporary politicians', i.e. the Ministers: '. . . it is not difficult to see how even the most ruthless Ministerial will and the sharpest Ministerial cutting edge can be frustrated and blunted if they conflict with the conventional wisdom of Whitehall'. (*Entitled to Know*, MacGibbon and Kee, 1966, p. 156)

We ought not, at this stage in the book, to be surprised or alarmed at this kind of statement. It is equally pertinent that some high civil servants have left government service for industry just because they felt frustrated at their *lack* of power. The real danger is not of take-over by the Civil Service but inaction and paralysis at the top, when the Minister cannot, and his Department will not, act.

However, this kind of discussion of power, lack of power, action and inaction, does not go far enough. The issue is not simply power, but power to take appropriate and effective action in a situation which secures an adequate measure of public accountability. This definition suggests two major defects in the higher Civil Service. First, it is lacking in initiative, force and readiness to innovate. This—the emasculation of the civil servants—is partly the price paid for the supremacy of the politicians, but partly too it stems from a tradition of caution, conservatism and self-effacement taken to extremes.

Second, the Civil Service is too remote from the public. Top civil servants need to be seen and heard more frequently explaining policies and problems. The extension of the specialist committee system of the House of Commons (see chapter 7) should provide opportunities for this to happen.

Government is an enormous operation. Some Departments are several times larger in size and financial turnover than the major industrial corporations (e.g., ICI, BMC). They cannot be run by Ministers alone, lacking experience and expertise, and immersed in the essential political activity of Westminster and the nation. The Civil Service must have power, including the power to press the case for radical and long-term policies, subject to the measure of accountability that would be secured by greater visibility as well as to the still overriding power of the Minister.

(g) *The management of persons.* Change in the Civil Service cannot be determined simply by prescribing a desirable role. It is necessary to develop new kinds of civil servants to fulfil new functions. Hence the main instrument of Civil Service reform lies in 'management', more precisely in 'personnel management'. There are many suggestions in this field. Some remedies appertain to recruitment and training, in particular the direct recruitment to senior grades of, for example, executives in private industry. The career development of recruits might be modified to give greater responsibility earlier in the career. At the higher levels there could be greater power, more opportunities for creative action, and perhaps less mobility, in order to build up strength through experience.

Altogether, the Civil Service has probably placed too little emphasis on the management of persons. This should become one of the major responsibilities of the Permanent Secretary. Sir Henry Hardman, Permanent Secretary to the Ministry of Defence, has written recently of this 'establishment' role: 'If [the Permanent Secretary] is to further the policies of Ministers, he must do it in part through appointments and the management of staff—guiding them, keeping up confidence in areas where the burden is greatest, showing that his own morale is unquenchable . . .' (*Sunday Times*, 1 October 1967).

Some critics (including former Permanent Secretaries) believe that a revised personnel policy must involve structural changes, and notably the demotion of the Treasury as manager of the Civil Service. Too many Treasury men, it is said, get posts as Permanent Secretary. Lady Sharp, formerly a Permanent Secretary herself, has said: 'I don't believe that 20 years in the Treasury is the best training for taking charge of some quite different department.' The remedy lies in the establishment of a central management section, coming directly under the Prime Minister and in his Office.

Here, as elsewhere, however, discussion of reform tends to blacken what exists and brighten the consequences of change. We all deplore excessive caution in civil servants, until an energetic, creative, imaginative official does something positive to *us*: then we talk of excessive zeal, high-handedness, dictatorship. There is much that is highly creditable about the Civil Service today; and much that is doubtful in the proposals of the reformers. It is necessary to remember the scale and complexity of the tasks of government, and the overriding need to fulfil these tasks within a framework of political democracy. Efficiency may often appear to be impaired by democratic processes, but it goes without saying that in a democracy the definition of efficiency must include democracy.

Notes on the Report of the Fulton Committee on the Civil Service (HMSO, Cmnd. 3638, 1968)

The Committee was appointed in 1966 to 'examine the structure, recruitment and management, including training, of the Home Civil Service, and to make recommendations'. Its membership was typical of similar committees, and included distinguished academics, businessmen and civil servants, with two Members of Parliament, one of them a former Minister. Besides its observation, study and discussion, the Committee commissioned several major research projects and a report from a Management Consultancy Group.

The findings of the Committee and diagnosis. The Committee says in its opening paragraph: 'The Home Civil Service today is still fundamentally the product of the nineteenth-century philosophy of the Northcote–Trevelyan Report. The tasks it faces are those of the second half of the twentieth century.'

Specifically, the Committee noted six major defects:

the Service is too much based on the philosophy of the amateur, i.e. the gifted and experienced layman, called pejoratively the generalist or all-rounder;

the system of classes impedes the efficient use of individuals;

the specialist classes, e.g. scientists, accountants, are denied opportunities for full administrative (managerial) responsibility;

too few civil servants are, or see themselves as, skilled managers;

there is not enough contact between the Service and the community it serves;

personnel management and career planning are inadequate.

The Committee proposed a basic guiding principle for the development of the Civil Service: 'look at the job first'. (Translated into official English: 'The Civil Service must continuously review the tasks it is called upon to perform and the possible ways it might perform them. . . .')

Proposals in the Report for reform

(a) *The higher direction of the Civil Service.* A new Civil Service Department should be set up, replacing the Civil Service Commission and the Pay and Management side of the Treasury. The main functions of the Department would thus be recruitment and personnel management, but it should be concerned positively with the matching of staff and tasks, and the promotion of flexible career development throughout the Service. The Permanent Secretary of the Department would be Head of the Home Civil Service, with a day-to-day responsibility to a senior non-departmental Minister; but also having a direct responsibility to the Prime Minister for senior appointments, the machinery of government and problems of security.

(b) *Classification, training and recruitment.*

(i) All classes should be abolished and replaced by a single grading structure for all non-industrial civil servants. The existing rather rigid boundaries, both horizontal and vertical, would disappear, and the differences in qualifications, skills and kinds of work between specialists and general administrators would be diminished. Thus, promotion from what is now the Executive to the Administrative grade would be facilitated. Specialists, e.g. accountants and engineers, would have opportunities of becoming general administrators; and the generalists would be expected to specialise to some extent. (The Committee suggested a division of general administrators into the economic/financial and the social fields).

(ii) A Civil Service College should be set up, to provide courses mainly in administration and management, and to conduct research into problems of government machinery and policy.

(iii) Recruitment. There should be greater mobility between the Civil Service and other employments by means of late entry, temporary appointments and interchange. Such mobility requires interchangeable pension schemes.

The practice of a Minister's personal and temporary appointment of experts and advisers was approved.

The recruitment of able young graduates of the kind at present joining the Administrative Class should be encouraged by the granting of additional salary increments, within a 'training grade' for graduates and the best of the non-graduate entry (cf. the Treasury's scheme, submitted to the Committee, for 'starred' entrants.)

Movement out of the Service for those who fail at the probation or later stages should take place more frequently than at present.

A majority of the Committee considered that, in the recruitment of some graduates, 'more account should be taken of the relevance of their university courses' to their prospective jobs. All agreed that increasing importance should be attached to 'numeracy'.

(c) *The organisation of Departments.*

(i) The principles of 'accountable management' should be applied to the work of Departments. Accountable management is defined as a 'system in which individuals and units are held responsible for performance and output measured as objectively as possible'. The system requires the identification and establishment of accountable units.

Further, management services should be set up in all major departments.

(ii) Departments should establish Planning Units, with comparatively young staffs. 'The Unit's main task should be to identify and study the problems and needs of the future and the possible means to meet them. It should also be its function to see that day-to-day policy decisions are taken with as full a recognition as possible of their likely implications for the future. The Planning Unit should not carry any responsibility for the day-to-day operation of the Department,' but must not become 'too detached from the main stream of the department's work.' (Report, p. 57.)

(iii) Most Departments should have a 'Senior Policy Adviser' to assist the Minister. He would normally be Head of the Planning Unit, and his job would be similar to that of the Unit. He should be an authority in the Department's field of work, familiar with other experts and new trends in thinking and practice in that field. Such Advisers would usually, but not invariably, be career civil servants. The Permanent Secretary would retain overall responsibility for the Department, under the Minister.

(iv) The administrative process should be more open, with less secrecy and more consultation. 'The convention of anonymity should be modified and civil servants, as professional administrators, should be able to go further than now in explaining what their Departments are doing, at any rate so far as concerns managing existing policies and implementing legislation.' (Report, p. 93.)

(v) The 'hiving-off' of responsibilities from Government Departments to autonomous public boards (like the BBC and the nationalised industries) is tentatively approved and further inquiry recommended.

Assessment of Report

The recommendations of the Committee meet a number of the criticisms raised in this chapter. The Committee goes further in pressing the introduction into the Civil Service of modern managerial technology, and especially the principle of accountable management. This is a valid updating of the rather flaccid and ineffectual notion of 'responsibility'. Against this must be set some doubts in detail. For example, the division of administration into economic/financial or social does not seem precise enough to be useful. The problem of recruiting very able people is not faced. The opening of recruitment may damage the unappreciated virtues of the 'élite corps', its aloofness and incorruptibility.

More serious criticisms may be made. The weakness of the amateur or generalist is exaggerated. This was argued in a note of reservation by a member of the Committee, and has been discussed above (see especially exercise 6.). The removal of the control of the Service from the Treasury might be regarded as a removal from financial discipline (but if this is really the case, then every Department except the Treasury is without financial discipline).

Another of the Committee's recommendations for fundamental reform, the proposal for Planning Units and Senior Policy Advisers, is open to criticism as unworkable. The Permanent Secretary is allowed the final responsibility, but the SPA would be only marginally below him in pay and status, and would have access to the Minister. The Policy Adviser's work is certain to involve him in criticism of the Department; so there is likely to be an awkward triangle at the head of the Department. There are indeed serious practical difficulties but these are not insoluble, given stable personalities and a wise and skilful Minister: after all, he, not the Permanent Secretary, is supposed to direct the Department. Such overlapping and competing relationships may, in fact, have positive value in securing competition and challenge at the highest levels of policy-making.

Finally, the Report may be criticised like most reports, for not going far enough. In particular, the Committee did not develop their views on the diminution of Civil Service anonymity and on the 'hiving-off' of responsibility from Government Departments. To the student of politics rather than management, these would have been the most interesting speculations. Should we admit that the Civil Service governs us, hence abandon our notions of ministerial responsibility, and devise a new kind of publicly communicative civil servant? Should we admit that the existing government machine cannot cope with the tasks now forced upon it, and begin to break it down into separate units, answerable in varying ways to a public seen as clientele (customers) rather than as electorate (voters)? The Committee, understandably in view of its terms of reference, left these questions to hover over the future of British government.

The response of the Wilson Government to the Report

The Wilson Government accepted immediately the Committee's proposals for a new Civil Service Department, and designated an official Head, and a Minister (the Paymaster General), with day-to-day responsibility. The Government also accepted the proposals for the abolition of classes and for a Civil Service College. The student of this book may now determine his own reaction to the Report of the Fulton Committee, in the light of the arguments of this chapter and the summary of the Report.

RECAPITULATION EXERCISES

1. *True or False?* (mark T or F)

(a) There are no specialists or scientists in the higher ranks of the Civil Service.

(b) 'Each Department is a little Empire in itself.'

(c) A substantial proportion of recruits to the Administrative Class are recruited from the Executive Class.

(d) Candidates for the Administrative Class do not favour the non-academic tests of 'method 2'.

(e) Senior civil servants are involved in the formulation of policy.

2. How would you defend the Civil Service's present recruiting policy for the Administrative Class?

3. What are the features of the Civil Service which may require reform?

KEY TO RECAPITULATION EXERCISES

1. (a) F

(b) F, but this is a question for discussion rather than an exact answer.

(c) T (d) F (e) T

2. It appears to select able people; it is a reasonable selection from the (admittedly narrow) field of candidates; it takes great trouble to be fair and efficient; it seeks out qualities of mind and personality which are essential in the higher administration of the State.

3. See assessments (pp. 140–4).

PART III
The legislature

[5]
The Commons: Members, parties, procedure

1 OUTLINE

Being a Member of Parliament is in some respects like being a school teacher or an engine-driver. It is a job of work, a way of earning a living, employing one's talents, serving the community, filling in time between week-ends. In short, Parliament can be assessed as a profession from the point of view of those persons occupied in it, as well as by its political functions. Judged in this way, membership of Parliament does not rate highly. Nevertheless, there is still keen competition to secure adoption as a candidate, although some comentators have doubts about the general quality of the candidates. Others think membership of Parliament should not be regarded as a profession at all: it should be equivalent to voluntary service in local government or as a magistrate. Parliament should not be a corps of specialists cut off from ordinary life: Members should be engaged in other occupations and activities. Whatever the virtues of this theory, in practice Members are able to pursue only a limited range of outside work, and even this may preclude them from the proper fulfilment of some of their parliamentary duties.

Members of Parliament are, on average, better educated and of a higher social class than most of their constituents. Perhaps this is not surprising. But in some ways the educational and occupational background of the Commons is very odd. There is, for example, an absurdly high number of Old Etonians, and the number of ex-service officers and trade union officials is, to say the least, not a good reflection of the electorate as a whole. (This is not to imply that the Commons should proportionately represent the back-ground of the adult population.)

The House of Commons has an 'atmosphere' which many Members regard as an important influence on the functioning of Parliament. The atmosphere might be compared with that of a school or a club: in one, the atmosphere permits, say, running along the corridors, in another it does not. Members of Parliament are often keenly aware of the atmosphere, and while some of them find it helpful, a gentle moulding of respectful conformity, others resent it as inhibiting liveliness and innovation.

The building itself is a part of this atmosphere. The Commons was rebuilt, after its destruction during the war, in its Victorian mock-medieval style. It is oblong and small. Members must sit on one side or the other, and speak from their places. It is very poorly provided with office facilities.

The work of Parliament is determined by the functioning of party and of procedure. The House is largely in the hands of the majority party, which sustains, and is directed by the Government. The effect is that great questions are not decided on the floor of the House. Debates contribute to the whole long-term nation-wide process of political argument, but no more. The voting, and to some extent the speaking, of Members is subject to the control of the party in the House. This is the way the British system of Cabinet responsibility works. There is much to be said for it, but it cannot be claimed that it leaves political questions to the free decision of the people's representatives. The Commons is the source but not the arena of sovereign power.

House of Commons procedure broadly divides the business of the House into legislation, control of finance, and oversight of policy and administration. About half of the time is devoted to matters initiated by the Opposition and by Private Members; the rest is the Government's. Procedural devices provide, sometimes in rather indirect ways, for major and minor debates. The Speaker presides over the House and acts as umpire: though an MP, he is not a player. The Leader of the House arranges the business of the House on behalf of the Government but with some regard for the rights of the Opposition and of Private Members. The Government, by the use of its majority, can push through the Commons most of what it wants. This includes changes in procedure (e.g., closure devices and the extension of the session) to expedite its own business. But there are limits to what the House will stand for: or, to put it more realistically (cynically?) governments deal moderately with the House, so that they may enjoy similar treatment when in opposition. In this way the alternation of governments provides a check on constitutional marauding.

2 THE MEMBER

The profession of Parliament

Membership of Parliament is a temporary professional occupation. By October 1964, seventy-four of those elected in 1959 had already left the House, by resignation, ennoblement or death, and another sixty sitting Members did not seek re-election. Thus over a fifth of the membership of 1959 had already withdrawn on the eve of the 1964 election. A day later, electoral defeat had removed another tenth—sixty-three Members.

Thus a substantial number of the new Parliament—127—were 'new boys' and 103 had not contested a seat before 1959. Well over five-hundred had not stood before 1945. This left a large minority—ninety-two Members—who had been active in politics as candidates and Members for thirty years or more, but only fifty of these had entered the House as long ago as that.

The temporary nature of the occupation for the majority is in part due to the choice of the Member's constituents, in part to his own choice. Judged as a professional man, a Member of Parliament is moderately well paid (£3,250 per annum, with free travel to and from his constituency, free London telephone calls, but no other substantial expense allowance); poorly equipped (no office, no secretary[1], no car); and hard worked (up to fourteen hours a day or even more for some Members during the session). To balance this, however, Parliament is in recess for five months each year, and there is nothing but conscience to stop a Member from pursuing another occupation (paid or unpaid) at the same time. Some theorists believe an outside occupation to be positively valuable. Lord Morrison, for example, has argued in favour of such part-time MPs, believing that it is of advantage to the nation that its Members of Parliament have close links with the world outside Westminster. For some occupations in the world outside, it may be added, Parliament makes an excellent complementary activity, since membership confers prestige, access to information, material for writing, and opportunities for travel.

Those who argue for Parliament as a part-time profession are not convinced that the demands Parliament makes on the time of the ordinary Members are excessive. Commander R. T. Bower, M.P. wrote, in a letter to the *Times*, 24 July 1957: 'There are many

---

[1] Limited improvements made in 1969 include an annual allowance of £500 for a secretary.

days when there is no necessity to attend the House at all; others when only a perfunctory visit for an important division may be required: the main business of the day does not begin until about 4 p.m. and the House is in recess for long months'. In recent years the House has in fact sat for only about seven months each year.

Members of Parliament do not, however, view their job merely as one, more or less satisfactory, way of making a living, whether part- or whole-time. Most of them see in Parliament the possibility and attraction of engaging in political activity and rendering political service. Many, perhaps, foresee a career ending in ministerial office. But this is a prize for the few. In the length of a decade, only a few score of men will reach senior ministerial office, and the chances of politics may leave unsatisfied a generation of aspirants (see chapters 2 and 3).

The attractions of Parliament as a means of earning a living and of engaging in political activity are limited, but still considerable enough to make candidacy eagerly sought after, except in 'hopeless' seats. Bagehot, writing in 1874, added prestige to knowledge and power as the gains of being a Member of Parliament. Then the job was unpaid and shared in the respect still given to unpaid public service. Then, too, Parliament itself was perhaps held in greater respect as an institution. Today, its prestige, and that of its Members, may be lower—but, perhaps fortunately, prestige cannot be measured.

....

DOCUMENT I

LENGTH OF PRIOR SERVICE OF 1959 HOUSE OF
COMMONS AT TIME OF ELECTION

Prior service (in years)	0	1–4	5–8	9–12	13–16	17–20	21–24	25 and over
Number of MPs (out of a total of 630)	108	103	72	117	149	30	27	24

(In interpreting this table it is worth remembering the years between 1959 and other elections—four to 1955, nine to 1950 and fourteen to 1945. The latter appears as a watershed in these figures for political reasons and because the end of the war concentrated the change of generations more than usually into one year.)

....

DOCUMENT 2

LIFE IN A MARGINAL CONSTITUENCY—
THE PARLIAMENTARY CAREER OF SIR FRANK MARKHAM,
FORMER MP FOR BUCKINGHAM

Sir Frank Markham contested every election from 1924 to 1959 inclusive, and a by-election in 1934—ten elections in all. He was successful five times, and sat as MP for twenty-five of the forty years for which he engaged actively in politics. Buckingham is a marginal constituency (majority 1,746 in 1959): seventy-eight members had majorities of less than 2,000 in 1959. In 1964 Sir Frank gave up the seat. It was won by Labour in 1964 and 1966.

....

DOCUMENT 3

PROFESSIONAL FACILITIES IN THE HOUSE

From Mr R. J. Mellish's speech, H.C. Deb., vol. 620, 31 March 1960, cols. 1590–1

I have the services of a secretary for one hour a week. My postage is about 120 letters a week. I have been to Germany on a 10-day trip, thanks to the generosity of a parliamentary delegation, and I returned to a pile of about 180 letters. This girl can give me one hour a week. To be fair, she has done a remarkable job and helped me a great deal, but I am faced with the fact that I have to write about 100 letters by hand. I have to do that, for I have no secretary and, I will be frank, I cannot afford one. I think it is about time my constituents knew that.

Where am I to write these letters? I will explain. I shall go into the Library. If I go there at certain hours, I shall find nowhere to sit. In any case, when I sit down I am always worried in case I am occupying a seat which belongs to someone else who has just gone out for a cup of tea. Usually they leave a lot of books around. Once I start writing I shall be there for about three hours.

May I turn to the method by which we do our work? We all know that there is congestion in the Library. I see no reason at all why some facilities should not be provided for Members—a room which it is possible for three or four Members to share, for example. I do not ask for a room of my own. That would be asking far too much. Such a room would be used only for a few hours of the day and for the rest of the time it would be empty. But I ought to have the right at least to sit down somewhere in some reasonable measure of comfort and to dictate my letters on behalf of my constituents.

My next comment concerns research. These days, one has to try to find out a great deal about subjects in which one has not interested oneself before. I certainly find that that is the case. At the moment, I am engaged in trying to find out about transport. I pay tribute to the people who work in our Library, but it is so short of staff and there are limitations. They render us magnificent service.

The Library staff say to us, in effect, 'read this, that and the other.' They give us the sort of books which we ought to read so that we might learn something from them. I am very grateful to the staff in the Library for doing that. We then go away with a pile of books. I remember once going upstairs to one of the Committee rooms. The custodian thought this rather strange. He came in about four times. He thought that I had gone mad. I was sitting there on my own. He said, 'Are you all right, Sir?' I said, 'I am trying to look for somewhere quiet so that I can read.' I was not talking to myself, which is a habit of some members who are trying to prepare speeches. I did not want anyone to see me there, because I might have been locked up.

[See also section 3 below on the inadequacies of the House as a workshop.]

The advantages of being an MP

It is clearly of some importance that Parliament should attract men and women of high quality, for apart from its own job, Parliament is the reservoir of ministerial talent. But the prestige of Parliament has probably declined in the last fifty years, and the respect once paid to Members of Parliament has been replaced by a contempt for 'politicians'. To this extent, Parliament is no longer a glamorous calling. The following documents illustrate the change.

Nevertheless, there is no shortage of candidates for Parliament—this is a solid fact to set beside the impressions of the last paragraph. And there is little firm evidence of a decline in the quality of Members.

DOCUMENT 4

THE ADVANTAGES OF BEING AN MP

(a) *A mid-Victorian view*
From W. Bagehot, *Works*, vol. ix, Ed. Mrs Russell Barrington, Longmans Green, 1915, pp. 32–5

The real gains at the present, as they affect most men, are three. First, a man gains far more social standing, as it is called, by going into Parliament than he can gain in any other way. 'I wrote books', said a politician of the last generation, 'and I was nobody; I made speeches and I was nobody; I got into Parliament and I was somebody'. . . .

Secondly a member of Parliament has the means of acquiring much valuable knowledge which it is difficult to learn in other ways at all, and which can in no other way be learnt so easily and perfectly. . . . The knowledge of public men, so freely given by newspapers, is a knowledge of masks rather than realities—of actors as they seem on the stage, rather than of those actors as they really are. Something may be learned out of Parliament to remedy this, but an able and active member can see, with ease and certainty, five times as much as can be gathered in any way. . . . What *ought* to be done can often be sufficiently seen by persons not in Parliament, but the final problem of practice, what *can* be done, is not often fully seen except by those who are there.

Lastly, members of Parliament have a certain amount of power; not indeed enough—indeed of the sort to satisfy men of eager minds and despotic temperament—but still considerable. They can take part in the business of legislation; if they have any sort of real knowledge, and any kind of regular industry, they can easily find work which will be in itself valuable, and which they will be respected for doing by those around them. If they aspire to and obtain office, they have of course much more power. No doubt it is very rarely even then of the sort which tyrannical disposition, the disposition which most longs for power, most likes. An English statesman can only in very rare cases impose on others original plans of his own. His work is either to co-operate in committee with other men, or to embody in legal form the ideas of other men. Even in administration he has to cope with many obstacles, and has to consult with and consider many other minds. Still this power, even so lessened and so defined, is a sufficient object of a wise ambition.

(b) *A view in the 1950s*
From Sir Robert Boothby's speech in debate on Members' expenses, H.C. Deb., vol. 528, 24 May 1954, col. 42

When I first entered this House, thirty years ago, it was possible to live quite comfortably on one's Parliamentary allowance.

Happy days those were. It was also possible to work in another profession, and many Members did. I should say the majority did, and this was of great value to the House and to the country. In those days it was quite a thing to be a Member of Parliament. One had prestige and social cachet. The doors of a society which no longer exists were open to one; and if one was so minded, one could eat and drink and spend one's holidays entirely at other people's expense. They were delighted and honoured to have you, and you were delighted and honoured to consume their food and drink.

I have been talking recently in some of our universities. In the old days, in the 1920s, any student or undergraduate of outstanding promise was at once considered as a potential candidate for this House, perhaps not in the immediate future but in the near future; and it was natural that he should consider entering public life, and be encouraged to do so by his tutors and by the heads of colleges and universities. I am assured that nowadays the question of public life simply does not enter in, in any of our universities. No young man however brilliant or promising who contemplates marriage and bringing up a family, even begins to think in terms of entering this House. I cannot help thinking that that is a great tragedy from the point of view of our democracy.

[Lord Boothby's description of an MP's life in the 1920s was referred to later in the debate as 'golden mist.']

EXERCISE

THE ADVANTAGES OF BEING AN MP

1. There is no shortage of candidates for Parliament:

Why? For what reasons would you consider or reject going into Parliament?

Parliament as a full-time paid profession

In British politics, as in sport, there is a traditional respect for the amateur. In the case of Parliament, it is argued that Members should engage in other occupations. Parliament should not be a monastery, and its Members should be closely in touch with, indeed involved in the world outside, 'the life of the people'. Thus they may bring to the House the illumination of representative experience. It is also argued that a Member should not be dependent on his salary, since this restricts his independence—he could not afford to lose his job. Finally, there is in this view something of the tradition of unpaid 'service' which has shaped British institutions from the Middle Ages to the present day. Members of Parliament were not paid at all until 1911, and the notion lingers that payment for such opportunities of service and honour is slightly improper. This is the tradition which puts justice in the hands of lay magistrates and consumer protection in the hands of the volunteers of the Citizens Advice Bureaux. The tradition is at once admirable, inefficient and just a little snobbish.

DOCUMENT 5

THE CASE FOR THE FULL-TIME MP

From Mr Hugh Gaitskell's speech in debate on Members' salaries, H.C. Deb., vol. 556, 12 July 1956, cols. 615–16

We are often lectured by the newspapers and told to get another job in order to earn some extra money. Let us examine that suggestion for a moment.

There are three points to be made about it, none of which can, I think, be disputed. First, it is a simple fact that only a limited number of Members can do other part-time jobs. If one is in business and can find a congenial partner, it is, of course, possible to do some part-time work in that business. It is possible to be a lawyer in practice at the Bar, though not always very easy, and still play some part in the House of Commons; there are variations in the extent to which those who are barristers do come to the House —no doubt with perfectly good reasons. It is possible, in some cases, for hon. Members to earn some extra money in journalism, though I venture to suggest that that is a rather overcrowded profession.

It is impossible for a Member to take on any ordinary salaried job. It is impossible for a miner to go back to the coal mines. It is impossible for an engineer to go back to the bench, or for a factory worker to go and work in a factory again. I think we must recognise this and we must tell the country that there are very strict limits to the extent to which hon. Members can do other jobs. The second point, which, I think, is equally unchallengeable though seldom appreciated, is that the House of Commons simply could not work if everybody had part-time jobs. After all, on Tuesday and Thursday mornings, and sometimes on Wednesday mornings as well, there are, in the normal way, Standing Committees which must be manned; and there are many other meetings of one kind or another which we all have to attend. The plain fact is that if it were not for those full-time Members who carry the burden today, the House of Commons would not function as it ought. That is an important point, and, incidentally, a point which I was interested to find was made with great clarity by Mr Lees-Smith in the 1937 debate.

My third point follows from the others. We may not wish to insist on all being full-time politicians—I understand the arguments against that—but we must, surely, have some full-time politicians and we must have sufficient pay and allowances to make it possible for those who wish and who are able to do so to become full-time politicians. That seems to me to be the essential point.

....

Mr Gaitskell put a convincing case: on the other hand, a Member with other means of earning a living might be expected to be more independent of his party. It may be significant, for example, that Mr Stanley Evans, who resigned his seat because he disagreed with the Labour Party's attitude to the Suez intervention, was not dependent on his parliamentary salary. But if this argument were generally valid, the Conservative Party would suffer from back-bench revolts much more than the Labour Party (which has fewer Members with other sources of income). This does not appear to be the case.

Moreover, dependence on the party may be exchanged for an equal dependence on an outside body.

....

DOCUMENT 6

'KEPT MEN' IN THE HOUSE OF COMMONS

From Mr Walter Elliot's speech in debate on Members' expenses, H.C. Deb., vol. 528, 24 May 1954, col. 75

There are still many hon. Members representative of every walk of life in this House today. But there is a strong tendency towards journalism. I have nothing against journalism, but I think that a House composed entirely of journalists would be a very bad House of Commons. There is also a tendency towards 'kept men' in this House, and a House composed entirely of 'kept men' would be dangerous, especially if men are kept by bodies able to pay more than the State is willing to pay for their services. It would be a great risk.

....

Many Members engage in journalism or the law or accept paid service in industry or commerce. This must have some effect on their conduct as MPs, both in limiting their parliamentary work and, to some extent, influencing their opinions. It also affects the type of Member recruited to the House: there is a tendency for a disproportionate number of MPs to be drawn from London-based professional men. The notion that outside work keeps a Member in touch with the outside world is thus possibly mistaken; certainly the 'outside' world for some Members is a narrow one.

The payment of MPs.

Members of Parliament must be paid an adequate salary in order:

(a) to make it feasible for poor men as well as rich to become MPs, and to attract men of talent from all social classes;

(b) to enable Members to do their parliamentary work without the diversion of other paid employment.

The salary should not perhaps be so high as to attract Members for money alone, but given the nature of the work this seems unlikely. Moreover, rather different arguments are put forward (sometimes by the same people) when the salaries are those of industry and commerce: high salaries are then viewed as an indispensable incentive.

The work of a Member of Parliament involves heavy personal expenditure—two homes (except in the case of London and Home Counties MPs); secretarial assistance and office facilities; public relations work in the constituency. This is met at present (1968) out of the salary of £3,250 per annum. Members may claim income-tax relief for expenses actually incurred. A few MPs spend a good deal for professional purposes, but many are forced to pare their professional to meet their personal expenditure. Evidence of this kind is reinforced by comparisons with other countries: the inescapable conclusion is that British Members of Parliament are still not well paid.

EXERCISE

THE PAYMENT OF MPS

2. There are some disadvantages in paying high salaries to Members of Parliament. What are they? and do they outweigh the advantages?

The MP himself

There is no average Member of Parliament: they are a various collection of people from many 'walks of life'. But the following tables of occupation and education show some major classifications within the variety. A majority of MPs are middle-class by occupation and have had a university education. Almost three out of four Conservative MPs are from the public schools; one in three Labour Members finished his normal education at the elementary stage. There are notable clusters in each party—barristers, brigadiers and businessmen in the Conservative Party; trade unionists and teachers in the Labour Party. There are only twenty-six women MPs. Parliament in this and other ways is not a true image of the nation: this is not to imply that it should be.

Even a distorted image, however, must change as the object changes. There is some evidence that the social composition of Parliament is responding slowly to the revolution in educational opportunity which has gone on in Britain since 1939.

....

DOCUMENT 7

OCCUPATIONS OF MEMBERS OF THE 1964 PARLIAMENT

(*1959 figures in brackets*)

[This is a summarised version of the table in D. E. Butler and A. King, *The British General Election of 1964*, Macmillan, 1965, p. 235, to which the reader should refer for fuller information]

	Conservative	Labour	Liberal
Professions			
Law	79(86)	46(37)	4
Armed Services·	28(37)	2	—
Teaching	5	51(36)	1
Medicine	3	9	—
Government (inc. local government)	18	7	—
Other	11	13	—
Total: professions	144	128	5
Business	80(113)	34(26)	2
Miscellaneous			
Publicists, journalists	20(26)	27(25)	—
Farmers	35(38)	2	1
Housewives	—	5	—
Others	20	18	—
Total: miscellaneous	75	52	1
Workers	2	103	—
Total number of MPs	304(365)	317(258)	8

For comparative purposes the figures may be converted to percentages.

(Note: There is an element of inaccuracy in a table of this kind because some Members have more than one occupation—e.g. a barrister who accepts a directorship after election to Parliament; or a miner who became a trade union official before election—and others do not reveal all their activites.)

DOCUMENT 8

THE EDUCATIONAL BACKGROUND OF THE 1964 PARLIAMENT

(*1959 figures in brackets*)

[This table is derived from Butler and King, op. cit., p. 237]

	Conservative	Labour	Liberal
Elementary only	—	39	—
Secondary only	34	52	2
Elementary or secondary with further education (at evening classes or adult colleges)	5	84	—
University	192 (218)	134 (101)	7 (6)
of which Oxford and Cambridge	159	60	4
Public school (including those who went to university)	229 (263)	56 (47)	3 (4)
of which Eton	68 (73)	2	2

EXERCISES

THE REPRESENTATIVENESS OF PARLIAMENT

3.1. Should Parliament be socially an image of the nation?

3.2. What, if anything, is wrong with the educational and occupational background of Members of Parliament?

3.3. What would you regard as an ideal composition?

3.4. Express the following figures for 1959 and 1964 as percentages and say whether there is any significant change: (The figures for the Liberal Party are too small for analysis in this way.)

Soldiers in the Conservative Party

Teachers in the Labour Party

Members with a university education (each party and the House as a whole)

Conservative Members with public school education

Etonians in the Conservative Party.

3 THE BUILDING AND THE ATMOSPHERE

The atmosphere of the Commons

The six-hundred-and-thirty Members of Parliament might be sorted in several ways besides party affiliation and social background; for example, by commitment to Parliament (full-time professionals, and side-liners); by attitude to authority (rebels and conformists); by House habits generally (those who speak, and those who do not; those who eat well in the dining-room and those who take snacks in the tea-room). Ministers, too, are MPs, but distinctively a class apart.

....

DOCUMENT 9

A WEEK IN THE LIFE OF A BACKBENCHER

Here are some of the activities a backbench Member might engage in during the week. Many backbenchers would not, however, participate in House affairs to this extent, some being actively engaged for part of every day in other business or professional interests:

travel to and from the constituency;

gathering information informally by reading the newspapers, and talking with colleagues (of all parties);

gathering information formally by study in the library, or by specially arranged visits, e.g. to a school or a defence installation;

dealing with letters, especially from constituents with grievances;

dealing with constituents and lobbyists in person;

addressing various gatherings outside the House, and meeting people;

in the Chamber, speaking or just sitting; or in committee upstairs;

attending meetings of the parliamentary party or its committees;

about the House, waiting for the division bell;

to the constituency for the week-end, to interview constituents, attend meetings and display himself at public functions.

....

The House, like most great institutions, has its own atmosphere, a compound of its rather stuffy, mock-medieval architecture and ceremonial, the sense of being on the edge of the centre of politics, the respect for the status and *savoir-faire* of the old hands. Any pupil in an old-established school with a high regard for itself would know the feeling. As in schools, such intangibles can be powerful agents in moulding the pattern of life and in setting standards and codes of conduct, but they can also be powerful in inhibiting critical thought and innovation, and in ritualising the vitality out of life. Both kinds of view appear in the following document.

DOCUMENT 10

THE ATMOSPHERE OF THE COMMONS

(a) From Hugh Dalton, *Call Back Yesterday*, Muller, 1953, pp. 156–7

Parliament is a very comfortable place. The historic dignity of its procedure and its precincts is very soothing. The sense of unreality in debates, where speeches turn no votes, is enervating. The physical atmosphere of the House itself, through which no fresh wind ever blows, seems designed to subdue the will and banish discontent . . . Why kick against the pricks? Parliamentary tactics make a pleasant game from day to day. Asking Ministers a few questions, scoring a few points in debate, voting in a few divisions, attending a few committees—what more need one do?

(b) From Sir Thomas Moore's speech, H.C. Deb., vol. 393, 28 October 1943, cols. 460–1

My only object at the conclusion of this Debate in which Private Members have taken part is to offer one thought which is the result of 19 years' experience in the House of Commons, and that is the value of atmosphere. There has been something in the atmosphere of the whole House and of the surroundings as a whole that has managed to discover the best that is even in the worst of us. I, and most other hon. Members, have seen great reforming spirits come down to this House as new Members. They have come possibly from the Clyde and the Tyne and from Ipswich, where they have been inspired or embittered by social injustices prevailing in their own districts. They come with an exaggerated idea of what they are determined to do, sometimes even to destroy not only the constitutional structure, but the material structure of our Chamber. I have watched for years and seen the way the atmosphere has got hold of these wild spirits, has tamed them and brought them into a constitutional frame of mind in which they become proud of the structure, of the atmosphere and of the constitutional methods adopted by this ancient Mother of Parliaments. I agree with some of the criticisms which have been made, although on the whole I am entirely behind the Prime Minister in the outline of what we should do. Whatever may be the future and whatever the Select Committee may decide, I hope they will try and preserve, as far as possible, that atmosphere which has enabled the negotiations, consultations and Debates in this House to be conducted in the interests of and the advancement of our people.

The building

'We shape our buildings and afterwards our buildings shape us'— so Mr Churchill said in the debate of October 1943 on the rebuilding of the House of Commons. It is not at all easy, however, to say to what extent and in what ways (if at all) British political life is influenced by the buildings in which it goes on.

The oblong shape *symbolises* the division of the House into two parties: this is true. But it is not the *cause* of this division: the cause is to be found in British social and political history and in the electoral system. Moreover, three parties existed for a time between the wars, despite an oblong Chamber; and so did coalition government which would best flourish, it might be supposed, in a semi-circular chamber.

The second point made by Mr Churchill in the debate of October 1943 (see document 11 below), about the size of the Chamber and its effect on speaking styles, is less open to challenge. Most people with a varied experience of speaking in public are aware of atmosphere and seem to adjust their speeches to it: but it is an adjustment of manner rather than of matter. Comparisons of speeches made in other assemblies do not suggest that the difference is a substantial one. Moreover, such differences of manner are partly due to the conventions of the House, notably that all remarks are addressed to the Speaker and no Member is addressed by name.

There is a third point which Mr Churchill omitted, but which was raised by backbenchers: it concerns the facilities of the House of Commons outside the Chamber. These were, and still are, inadequate for a profession which at its best demands both learning and administrative skill. A backbench MP, lamenting his lack of an office, a telephone, an interviewing room, might well mutter to himself 'we shape our buildings and afterwards our buildings shape us.'

DOCUMENT 11

THE DEBATE OF 28 OCTOBER 1943 ON
THE REBUILDING OF THE HOUSE OF COMMONS

From Mr Winston Churchill's speech, H.C. Deb., vol. 393, 28 October 1943, cols. 403–4

There are two main characteristics of the House of Commons which will command the approval and the support of reflective and experienced Members. They will, I have no doubt, sound odd to foreign ears. The first is that its shape should be oblong and not semi-circular. Here is a very potent factor in our political life. The semi-circular assembly, which appeals to political theorists, enables every individual or every group to move round the centre, adopting various shades of pink according as the weather changes. I am a convinced supporter of the party system in preference to the group system. I have seen many earnest and ardent Parliaments destroyed by the group system. The party system is much favoured by the oblong form of Chamber. It is easy for an individual to move through those insensible graduations from Left to Right but the act of crossing the floor is one which requires serious consideration. I am well informed on this matter, for I have accomplished that difficult process, not only once but twice. Logic is a poor guide compared with custom. Logic which has created in so many countries semi-circular assemblies which have buildings which give to every Member, not only a seat to sit in but often a desk to write at, with a lid to bang, has proved fatal to Parliamentary Government as we know it here in its home and in the land of its birth.

The second characteristic of a Chamber formed on the lines of the House of Commons is that it should not be big enough to contain all its Members at once without overcrowding and that there should be no question of every Member having a separate seat reserved for him. The reason for this has long been a puzzle to uninstructed outsiders and has frequently excited the curiosity and even the criticism of new Members. Yet it is not so difficult to understand if you look at it from a practical point of view. If the House is big enough to contain all its Members, nine-tenths of its Debates will be conducted in the depressing atmosphere of an almost empty or half-empty Chamber. The essence of good House of Commons speaking is the conversational style, the facility for quick, informal interruptions and interchanges. Harangues from a rostrum would be a bad substitute for the conversational style in which so much of our business is done. But the conversational style requires a fairly small space and there should be on great occasions a sense of crowd and urgency. There should be a sense of the importance of much that is said and a sense that great matters are being decided there and then, by the House.

....

Mr Churchill was concerned about the essential political nature of the House and its traditions. He carried his view, and the House was built in imitation of the nineteenth-century imitation of the medieval Palace of Westminster. A few concessions were made to the twentieth century—well-upholstered benches, central heating and a system of sound amplification. But hardly anything was done to provide professional facilities in the House for its Members. Hence there has been a long history of complaints, especially by those Members who are full-time professionals.

Here is an extract from one Commons debate in 1960, and a summary of another. This is hardly out of date, except for the precise numbers of filing-cabinets, desks and so on—which have improved slightly (1968): Mrs Castle, a Cabinet Minister since 1964, has some power now to promote her sympathies. (See also document 3 above.)

....

DOCUMENT 12

FACILITIES FOR MEMBERS IN THE REBUILT HOUSE OF COMMONS

(a) From Questions in the House, H.C. Deb., vol. 479, 23 February 1960, cols. 170-1

[This exchange is quoted in full, because it reveals other things about British government besides the inadequacy of its accommodation for Members of Parliament.]

Mrs Castle asked the Minister of Works how many desks are now provided in the Palace of Westminster for the exclusive use of hon. Members or their secretaries; and how many are on order.

Lord John Hope: There are 72 desks allocated to hon. Members in desk rooms and 109 for the use of their secretaries: in addition, there are 232 writing places in various parts of the House. Another 16 desks are on order for hon. Members, and 24 for their secretaries, for No. 6–7 Old Palace Yard.

Mrs Castle: Is the Minister now aware that what hon. Members are anxious to have is desks exclusively for their own use, not merely a place in which they can perch like a bird of passage to do a bit of writing? Is he aware that as long ago as 1954, in answer to a questionnaire by the Stokes Committee, 295 Members said they wanted such a desk for their own exclusive use, yet, according to his own figures, 100 hon. Members are still without one? Is it not intolerable that 100 hon. Members have not even a desk of their own, let alone an office?

Lord John Hope: There is a great deal to be said for the point of view of the hon. Member.—(An hon. Member: 'Then say it.') Most hon. Members on both sides of the House, would like to have some place of their own where they can keep their own things.

Mr Leavey: Is my right hon. Friend aware that it seems that we are arriving at a situation where, in view of hon. Members opposite, an Englishman's desk is his Castle?

Mr F. Noel-Baker: Is the Minister aware that my hon. Friend the Member for Blackburn (Mrs Castle) is being far too modest in this matter? What hon. Members want is not one desk crowded out by others in close proximity, but a properly appointed office in which we can have two desks, one for a secretary, with a telephone and facilities not inferior to those enjoyed, for example, by medium-rank officials of local authorities? Otherwise, we cannot do our jobs properly on these premises and will have to go elsewhere.

Lord John Hope: The possibility of office accommodation is one of the things I am looking at. The hon. Member perhaps rather over-egged the pudding when he spoke of telephones and that sort of thing, but office accommodation is a different thing.

Mr Tiley: Is it not possible at the moment to take steps at least to have telephones on the desks we now use? We waste hours waiting to get hold of secretaries, those few of us who are lucky enough to have them.

Lord John Hope: Yes, I shall bear that in mind.

(b) Summary of debate, 31 March 1960

A debate a few weeks later revealed a considerable division of opinion in the House. This does not exactly follow party lines, but no Labour Member spoke against radically improved facilities in the House, and few Conservative Members spoke in favour of improvements. This division may reflect different habits of mind, the Conservative being conservative, and the Labour Party radical and reformist. More likely, it reflects the fact that there are more Members on the Labour side than among the Conservatives who depend wholly on their parliamentary salary and the facilities of the House for carrying out their duties.

It was argued from the Labour side that the existing House of Commons is inadequate as a workshop. There is a shortage of rooms and offices for Members and secretaries; there is even a shortage of desks, filing-cabinets and telephones. (There is a shortage of secretaries, too, but Members must provide these themselves.) The Chairman of the Selection Committee (which selects Members for committee-service) has nowhere to keep his papers; a Member finding himself without a carbon can obtain one only on personal application to the Serjeant-at-Arms. The House, though it is the sovereign power in the nation, does not have full control over the Palace of Westminster, of which the House forms a part.

Governments have done something since 1960 to meet these criticisms; in particular, more offices, desks and filing cabinets have been provided. But there was a disinclination to accept that the House was a workshop or business place. Mr Butler said: 'Even if we try to improve the filing system, the research system and the general work of the library, I believe that we still must not ignore the fact that these things are not at the core of the real spirit of the House of Commons.' Members who agree with this kind of statement are inclined to regard the preservation of a row of catalpa trees or the view of Westminster Hall and the Clock Tower as more desirable than the extension of the House as planned by Barry. 'Rubbing shoulders' in the lobbies and 'falling over each other' in the tea-room, smoking-room and in the library are also considered of some advantage.

....

Thus, there are several possible differences revealed here—between tradition and change, between vague sentiment and precise thought, between Ministers and backbenchers, between those who have offices, and those who do not.

EXERCISES
THE BUILDING

4.1. What is the case for a mock-medieval Parliament building?

4.2. Which of the following facilities would you regard as important in a Parliament building?

seats for each Member in the Chamber
offices for each Member
desks for each Member in shared writing-rooms
telephone booths
dictating rooms
research facilities (including the preparation of briefs)

4.3. The text claims that document (a) tells us other things about British government. What?

4.4. Can you think of any arguments against regarding the House of Commons as a workshop?

4 THE PLACE AND PURPOSE OF THE PARTY IN THE HOUSE OF COMMONS

The purpose of parties

There is a classical dispute about whether a Member of Parliament puts forward his own view or those of his constituents. Burke made a famous pronouncement on the Member's independence of his constituents (see chapter 9, p. 318). Sir Winston Churchill, 150 years later, provided a slightly more modern version, with the claims of party included, but only in third place! Sir Winston asserted that 'in any healthy manifestation of democracy' the first duty of a Member was 'to do what in his faithful and disinterested judgement he believes right and necessary for the honour and safety of our beloved country'. Second he must serve his constituents, but as a representative, not a delegate. Third he had a duty to the party.

It is difficult to accept this as accurately representing the present function of a Member of Parliament. There are two immediate practical objections. First, if a Member is to express his own views, he may find difficulty in coming to conclusions genuinely his own on every topic. Second, if a Member is to represent his constituents, he will find some difficulty in representing those (often nearly half) who voted for the other candidate, and he will need to consult his constituents frequently on issues arising after the election. In fact, Members of Parliament act primarily as members of a political party, and in doing so they normally carry out the wishes of a majority of their constituents.

In the eighteenth century, political parties in the modern form did not exist, but were foreshadowed by groupings or connections of political friends. These were shifting, ill-organised groups without common and defined political attitudes. In this situation, the King could usually secure the nominal cooperation of Parliament, which was a pre-requisite of government, by the judicious use of patronage and political management. Parliament could be persuaded not to obstruct, if not to support either, the course of royal government.

In the first half of the nineteenth century, due to the decline of patronage, the growth of a democratic public sentiment, and the slow enlargement of the electorate, the Crown found it increasingly difficult to arrange a majority in the House: political power had slipped into the hands of the Commons.

The changed distribution of power became apparent in 1835, when Peel found he could not go on as Prime Minister with the support of the King but not of the Commons, and again in 1841, when Queen Victoria found that holding a general election was no longer a guaranteed method of arranging parliamentary support for the royal candidate for Prime Minister.

The keys to this newly defined political situation were:

(a) the organisation of a majority of voters in the constituencies;
(b) the organisation of a majority of Members in the Commons.

Modern political parties have developed in order to grasp and use these keys. The change is a profound one, indeed a revolution: the source of Government had been the Throne and was now the People. The purpose of the political party became, and still is, to make and sustain a government in the name of popular sovereignty.

Common criticisms of the party system are that it has made Parliament powerless in face of the Cabinet; that the individual MP has become 'mere lobby-fodder'. But there are major advantages deriving from the operation of political parties:

(a) The system imposes a limit on discussion and expedites the taking of decisions on policy.

(b) The decision-takers are answerable in the end for their decisions through the House of Commons and to the electorate.

(c) The elector is confronted with a clearly marked set of choices —he knows for what as well as for whom he is voting.

(d) Government is relatively stable (and this is not simply an acceptable way of saying that government is immune to criticism and inflexible).

Party organisation within Parliament[1]

Party meetings. Both Conservative and Labour Parties have regular general meetings of their Members of Parliament; the Conservatives have a Private Members' committee, usually referred to as the 1922 Committee, and Labour has its Parliamentary Party

[1] See also chapter 9.

(PLP). These bodies meet once or twice weekly during the session to discuss the business of the House, and particularly matters on which there is not general agreement within the party. In these meetings, Ministers or front bench spokesmen have an opportunity to meet the backbenchers. But this opportunity is carefully restricted, especially in the case of the party in power.

The influence of the parliamentary party varies. On a major issue, on which there is deep feeling, and which cannot be solved by a party formula, the front bench must come to terms with its backbenchers. The backbenchers may often accept a statement of policy produced by the front bench; but such a statement is likely to incorporate concessions to the known backbench points of view. Here, as elsewhere, 'what you can get away with' is more important than 'what is constitutionally correct'. Most of the time a wise and skilful front bench can 'get away with' the policies they want, although there seem to be periods when backbenchers are awkward and unwilling to conform. These periods sometimes look like moods, bearing little relation to the issues, but some relation to electoral security, length of time in office, infrequency of ministerial reshuffles (with the prospect of promotion for others), and alleged erosion of the party's ancient principles.

Government and party meetings. There is agreement on both front benches that the parliamentary party should not instruct or control the Cabinet. This would be regarded as unconstitutional and inefficient. The Cabinet is responsible to the House, but not its instrument: government by even half of a large assembly is unlikely to be consistent, coherent and well-judged. These are generally acceptable arguments, though there are other dangers for a government which gets out of touch with its supporters—or indeed with the House as a whole.

Mr Wilson put the point to a meeting of the PLP as follows when the party was restive, even rebellious, over the Government's East of Suez and other defence policies.

....

DOCUMENT 13

GOVERNMENT AND PARTY MEETINGS

From Mr Wilson's speech to PLP, June 1966

Although we want to proceed in harmony with the Parliamentary Party, this means two-way, not one-way, cooperation, and it must be based on the recognition that the party meeting, however important, cannot become itself a government, or substitute for government. Such a concept is neither in the Labour Party Constitution, nor in the British Constitution, and any attempt to operate on that basis would rapidly make the Government, and I believe the party, a laughing-stock in the country, with all the inevitable consequences.

The Government must govern, and there can be no substitute for it. . . .

There are still, even in the Parliamentary Labour Party, certainly in the movement in the country, worthy dedicated Socialists, who do not see the Labour Party as a party of power, who see it more as a party of protest, who are much happier in opposition. . . .

[The comment at the end of the extract is interesting evidence of the tradition and ethos of the Labour Party.]

In addition to full meetings of the parliamentary parties, there are numerous area and subject groups or committees. These are subordinate to the party: in describing their function, Lord Morrison uses the terms 'making representations' and 'making recommendations'. What evidence there is of conflict between a group and a Minister seems to point to the likelihood of ministerial victory (for a resignation in protest by a backbencher is equivalent to defeat).

The Whips and discipline. The relation of front and back bench is also the continuing responsibility of officers of the parliamentary parties, known as Whips. Their title implies a disciplinary function, though this is somewhat to misrepresent their work. Their job is to organise the party in the House, 'ensuring the maximum practicable attendance of members of the party, promoting support for government policies, and seeing to it that Ministers are aware of the opinions and apprehensions of backbenchers' (Lord Morrison). The Chief Whip may sit in the Cabinet, but in any case will be constantly in touch with the Prime Minister. Conservative Whips are appointed by the Leader: Labour Whips are appointed by the Prime Minister, but in opposition they are elected by the PLP.

The Chief Whip of each party sends to his Members each week a document also known as a 'Whip', which sets out the business of the coming week, indicating with one, two, or three underlinings how important a Member's attendance may be. The Whip's job is thus to provide a channel of communication and consultation from front to back bench. The object is to keep back bench in line with front, and this is where the disciplinary element may come in. The ultimate sanction which carries the relationship of Whip and backbencher beyond the level of friendship and persuasion is the withdrawal of the Whip. This is, in effect, expulsion from the parliamentary party,

DOCUMENT 14

MINISTERS AND THE PARLIAMENTARY PARTIES

	In office	*In opposition*
Conservative Party	Ministers attend meetings of the parliamentary party to discuss policies for which they are responsible. Prime Minister attends occasionally, especially just before the recess.	Members of the Shadow Cabinet (appointed by the Leader) may attend, but they have no special position and may not stand for office in the committee. The Leader does not normally attend.
Labour Party	When the party is in office, the PLP elects a chairman separate from the Leader/Prime Minister. The chairman is senior and respected, but not himself an aspirant to high government office. In 1945–51, Ministers including the Prime Minister attended, but there was 'no question of Ministers seeking Party approval for their actions'. A liaison committee was set up to ease the relations of Ministers and backbenchers. The position has been similar in 1964–8. When there was acute unrest over the Government's economic policies (also its defence and Rhodesian policies), the Prime Minister spoke to the PLP at great length in support of his policies. But the voting was made a matter of confidence, i.e. the PLP was invited not to approve the policy but to approve Mr Wilson's continuing in office. Inevitably, Mr Wilson won the vote and continued with his policies.	Formal democratic machinery, with elected parliamentary committee (in effect the Shadow Cabinet) chaired by the elected Leader. This committee reviews resolutions from the subject groups and submits them to the Parliamentary Party.

and, if it is not rescinded, will entail almost certain loss of the seat at the next election. But this dire consequence depends on the maintenance of the withdrawal, and acceptance by the constituency association of the parliamentary party's decision (see chapter 9, pp. 316–8).

The machinery for withdrawal of the Whip is different in the two parties. In the Conservative Party the Whip is withdrawn by the

Leader, and this will normally be sufficient to ensure that the local association will no longer adopt the Member as an official candidate. But the Whip is very rarely withdrawn. What is more likely to happen is that the local executive will ask a Member for an explanation if he has been consistently out of line with party policy. If the explanation is regarded as unsatisfactory, the executive will recommend the association to adopt another candidate, and that means almost certain defeat at the next election for the Member, should he still decide to stand.

Discipline in the Labour Party is as strong as in the Conservative Party, and the procedure for taking away the Whip is more formalised. Under standing orders, 'the privilege of membership of the Parliamentary Labour Party involves the acceptance of the decisions of the party meeting'. There is a 'conscience' escape clause, which since 1966 has been interpreted fairly broadly to include deep convictions beyond the traditional narrow grounds of conscientious objection, pacifism and private morality (which used to mean temperance). This liberalisation was balanced by the banning of unofficial 'organised groups', as defined by the Whips. Minor offenders may be merely reprimanded by the Chief Whip, or for more serious offences, suspended temporarily from party meetings. A persistent and serious offender against standing orders risks heavier punishment. He may be asked to appear before a meeting of the Parliamentary Labour Party, and that body will decide whether or not to recommend the withdrawal of the Whip. This constitutes expulsion from the Parliamentary Party: expulsion from the party itself involves another formal hearing before the national executive committee. In practice, the effectiveness of these standing orders is limited. It is difficult to hand out these punishments to more than a dozen or so at a time—as every misbehaving schoolboy knows, there is always safety in numbers. Members have defied the Whip, had it withdrawn or even been expelled from the party, and eventually have been re-admitted, one or two going on to achieve Cabinet rank.

....

DOCUMENT 15

THE WHIPS

From Lord Morrison, *Government and Parliament*, Oxford University Press, 1964, pp. 184–5

It is a widespread belief that the Whips have no other duty than to bully and coerce Members against their will into voting in the party lobby and speaking in accordance with the 'party line'. This is an inaccurate and incomplete picture of the functions of the Whips. It is persuasion rather than bullying that is the rule; it is reasoning with a recalcitrant Member rather than coercion that is the general practice. The good Whip seeks to avoid a situation in which the troubled or troublesome Member is driven to choose between humiliating conformity, and flagrant revolt which may raise all the difficult problems of official disciplinary action. There are extreme cases from time to time which may justify and, indeed, necessitate straight speaking, but peaceful persuasion, friendly reasoning, and argument based on the need for keeping the party together, are far more normal and effective.

Moreover, the Whips' office conducts a two-way traffic. During the nearly six years that I was Leader of the House of Commons I impressed upon the Labour MPs and the Whips that the Whips had just as much a duty to convey to me and to other Ministers the anxieties, worries, and unhappiness of back-benchers as they had to convey to the back-benchers the wishes of the Government. I would myself see troubled—or troublesome—MPs if necessary. Such interviews were normally pleasant and helpful. This part of the Whips' functions was fully discharged. They were the ears and eyes not only of the Government but of the back-benchers.

....

The distribution of power between front bench and back bench is obviously, and no doubt justifiably, uneven. The front bench will be dominant most of the time and especially when in office, for the following reasons:

(a) through its superior information (and ability?);

(b) through the force of the general agreement that underlies a party's thinking, and the general desire to preserve party unity as an electoral asset;

(c) through the absence for most of the time of issues of contention within the party;

(d) through the 'tact of the ambitious';[1]

(e) in the case of the Conservative Party, through the ready acceptance of the principle of front bench leadership: (this works the other way in the Labour Party, where the psychological force of a tradition of democracy must not be discounted).

Lord Morrison argues that this balance (or unbalance) is right and proper. It may at least be considered efficient.

[1] A nice phrase from P. G. Richards, *Honourable Members: A Study of the British Backbencher*, Faber, 1959.

....

DOCUMENT 16

A RUEFUL COMMENT

From Captain De Chair's speech in the Commons, H.C. Deb., vol. 393,
28 October 1943, col. 461

It is more than a year since I spoke in this House, because I belong to the
Dumb Chums' League who sit behind the Government Front Bench,
which makes freedom of expression somewhat difficult.

[This may be compared with the animal simile used by Mr Wilson in
addressing the Parliamentary Labour Party in March 1967 (See chapter 7,
p. 249).]

....

There is another problem: the balance between Parliament and
public. Whether decisions are taken by front or back bench, they
are taken in secrecy, broken only by the faint gleams of leakage,
and the speculations of the political correspondents. The development of the parliamentary party as the only body in which ministerial or front bench decisions may be immediately and effectively
questioned and modified has seriously reduced the possibility of
public participation in the political process. Where the public does
not know, the consequence may follow that it will not care.

EXERCISE

PARTY ORGANISATION IN THE HOUSE OF COMMONS

5. What advantages and disadvantages do you see if a substantial
number of Members were independent of parties?

5 THE BUSINESS OF THE HOUSE OF COMMONS—
A SUMMARY

The business of the House

The time of the House is divided roughly in the following proportions:

(a) Legislation	50%
(b) Financial business (including Supply Days)	20%
(c) Policy and administration	30%

The following summary gives the main procedures under which the House works. These are amplified in chapters 6 and 7.

(a) *Legislation.*

Public Bills (Government or Private Members')

1st Reading (formal)

2nd Reading (principles of measure debated)

Committee Stage (details debated either in Committee of the Whole House or in small Standing Committees)

Report Stage (Bill as amended in Committee reported to House)

3rd Reading

(b) *Financial business.* Estimates considered by the House (not now in a Committee of the Whole). Twenty-six days in the year are allotted for consideration of the Departments' estimates of their expenditure. These 'Supply Days' are less a discussion of finance than an opportunity for a debate on Government policy. The Opposition chooses which Department's estimates will be discussed on any particular day. All estimates, when agreed to, are put together in the Appropriation Act for the year.

The means to pay for the estimated expenditure is considered (again by the House as such and not, since 1967, by the Committee of Ways and Means) beginning with Budget Day and ending with the budget resolutions incorporated in the Finance Act for the year. The detailed financial administration of the Departments is considered in the Select Committees on Estimates and Public Accounts.

(c) *Policy and administration.*

Address in reply to the Sovereign's Speech—a general debate at the opening of each session.

Adjournment Motions—daily half-hour debates at the end of each day's business.

Adjournment under Standing Order No. 9—on specific and important matters that should have urgent consideration.

Substantive Motions—moved by the Government to secure agreement of the House to some item of policy.

Ministerial statements—by leave of the House, a Minister may make a statement on Government policy and be asked questions on the statement immediately afterwards.

Question Time—Questions and supplementaries.

Private Notice Questions—an opportunity for the Minister to give a longer and more detailed explanation.

Procedure and the organisation of business

People cannot discuss a subject effectively without some elementary rules of procedure. These should ensure, for example, that everyone wanting to speak has the opportunity to do so; that the order of speeches is not unduly influenced by the power, prestige or strength of voice of the speakers; that speeches are relevant and avoid gross personal abuse; and that a conclusion is reached at an appropriate moment, which may be when a consensus is possible, or when time is up. A chairman is necessary to control the discussion and enforce the rules. The House of Commons has rules of this kind, though in more complicated form, and the office of chairman is filled by the Speaker.

Many chairmen hold positions of authority, and exercise leadership functions in the organisation over whose committees they preside. This is true, for example, of a chairman of a school's board of governors, and of the Prime Minister in the Cabinet. Their position as captains of the side may overlay their position as umpires. The Speaker of the House of Commons, however, has no governmental responsibility, and is able to act as umpire impartially with respect to contenders in the House of Commons, committed only to the preservation of parliamentary methods and manners. This is a position which has evolved since the eighteenth century. Originally the Speaker was the Spokesman of the Commons, and a man of influence with King and Commons. His importance lay in his political role: now it lies in his non-political character.

A good Speaker is a man able to gain respect from all parties, but not required for high office by his own party—a colourless man, in short, but capable, and preferably with a good presence and voice. In general, the Speaker ensures fair play, gives rulings on the proper conduct of debate, suppresses disorder and has some regard for the rights of backbenchers. Some arrangements—for example, the order of speaking, or notice by a backbencher of an intention to raise a point of order—may be made privately 'behind the Speaker's Chair'. To enforce the orderly conduct of debate the Speaker may call for order; call for the withdrawal of 'unparliamentary' language or for a Member's withdrawal from the Chamber; or, in extreme cases of general disorder, he may suspend the sitting. These sanctions against disorder depend on the moral authority of the office, supported by the House, whose servant the Speaker is. The House has a strong sense of self-discipline.

While the Speaker ensures that debate is orderly and correct according to the Rules of Procedure, the Leader of the House, on behalf of the Government, controls the time of the House in accordance with the needs of Government. Something like two-thirds of the time of the House is in the hands of the Government, and is used to further Government business. The remainder of the time (mainly the twenty-six Supply Days) is available to the Opposition to raise matters of their choosing. A very little time is left over for Private Members. The latter now have twenty-four Fridays in each session for the introduction of Bills or Motions. There is little chance that these will have more than an afternoon's airing, unless the Government is convinced by other evidence that the matter is a proper one for government-sponsored action.

The dominance of the Government (in effect the Cabinet) in the arrangement of parliamentary business is sometimes regarded as improper. It is more accurate, however, to regard it simply as one more or less satisfactory way of conducting business: the job of a Cabinet is to govern, subject to its answerability to Parliament by way of criticism, and to the public by way of election and dismissal. If the Cabinet did not control the time of the House, the system would not be Cabinet-government, but government by assembly: this is another and different way of conducting business, again more or less satisfactory. The less and the more is a matter of detailed argument, but both systems *may* provide good government, that is, government which is both efficient and democratic.

The Leader of the House, together with the Government Whips, plans the timetable of the House, in some degree of consultation with the Opposition Whips. These are the 'usual channels' through which informal agreement is made. The Leader of the House is bound to respect the sentiment of the House as a whole, whilst not forgetting that he is the agent of the Government. The Government has a majority, and, in case of disagreement, the sentiment of the House is what the majority says it is. Occasionally, the Government has to show its procedural teeth. For example, the National Health Service Contributions Bill of March 1961, which doubled the charge for prescriptions under the National Health Service, had to be forced through the House by the adoption of the 'guillotine' procedure. So too the Prices and Incomes Bill (August 1966) was forced through the Commons, fundamentally amended at the Committee Stage, and then passed by the House of Lords in one day. The guillotine procedure provides for the ending of debate on each clause according to a timetable, and is the complete answer to Opposition 'filibustering'. The filibuster is the American device of talking at length to delay and perhaps prevent government action, and only works in the American Senate, with its tradition of unlimited debate. For the record, the longest speech by a backbencher in recent times was possibly that of Mr Malcolm Macmillan, who spoke for two hours and forty minutes, on the night of 15/16 March 1961, in a debate on the Crofters (Scotland) Bill. The debate went on for another 3½ hours and there were 139 Members still about the House at 5.20 next morning to vote on and reject Mr Macmillan's amendment.

GUIDE TO EXERCISES

1. Probably because some people see politics as the highest form of public service, giving opportunities to take part in the shaping of society; because, too, some people find politics a peculiarly satisfying activity both intellectually and emotionally; because quite a few people come from backgrounds which encourage a political career, e.g., trade unions, journalism, the forces.
The second part of the question is for you to answer unaided.

2. Some Members may be attracted by the financial reward alone, and be in other ways unsuited. This is only, of course, to make Parliament comparable to most other professions, except perhaps school-teaching and the Church. We do not expect, say, ICI, to attract better executives by paying them low salaries.
The more serious objection is that some Members may not be able to afford antagonising their party or their constituents, or they may be reluctant to resign or retire.
These arguments derive from the notion that membership of Parliament should be different from that of other professions, even that it should not be considered a profession at all. This does not seem to be a good way of attracting into Parliament persons of high calibre.

3.1. Parliament is both a representative and a 'deliberative' body. In both functions it needs to contain within it knowledge and experience of life as it is lived by masses of ordinary people in Britain. This does not mean that Parliament must be proportionately representative of the nation by social class, education, occupation or interest. It does mean that people with direct experience of, say, working-class life in Bradford as well as of the farming community of Wiltshire ought to be in Parliament. No amount of perception, humanity and good intention could make a Scottish landowner properly aware of, for instance, the problems of primary schools in the Black Country. Conversely, of course, a school-teacher from the Black Country cannot fully appreciate problems of land and agriculture in the Scottish Highlands.
Inevitably, Members of Parliament will be better educated on average than their constituents: otherwise they might not be able to carry out effectively their representative and deliberative functions.

3.2. and 3.3. On these assumptions, Parliament is at present rather uneven in its representation, with some backgrounds and interests under-represented. The comparatively high level of education *may* be regarded as acceptable to ensure effective deliberation. True the Civil Service can provide the brains, but an ill-educated Parliament might well be unduly

influenced by educationally and intellectually superior officials. Ultimately
a much higher level of popular education might enable Parliament to be at
once more genuinely representative and more effective.

3.4.

Soldiers in the Conservative Party

1959:22%   1964:19%

Teachers in the Labour Party

1959:37%   1964:40%

Members with university education

Conservative	1959:60%	1964:63%
Labour	1959:40%	1964:42%
Whole House	1959:51%	1964:53%

Conservatives with public school education

	1959:72%	1964:72%
Etonians	1959:20%	1964:22%

Almost everything is the same, or a little more so, except for the number
of soldiers in the Conservative Party. On these figures the persistence, not
change, of social background is the most significant fact. The figures for the
1966 Parliament (available in D. E. Butler and A. King, *The General Election
of 1966*, Macmillan, 1966, p. 208) should now be studied to see whether there
is alteration due to the sharp change in the number of Members on each
side.

4.1. It encourages an awareness of the great history of the institution of
Parliament, and this ought to be a constant factor in the activities of the
House—serving as a warning to governments tempted to apply their majority in defiance of the rights of the House; an indication, too, to new and inexperienced Members that some of the irritating convolutions of parliamentary life might be a proper institutional adjustment to complex and
contradictory functions. An historic-looking building may also secure the
respect and affection of the people, demonstrating the continuity of their
institutions. It may be good for the tourist trade too.

4.2. Not perhaps the first, for the good reason given by Mr Churchill—
in any case, seats for each Member would not often be in demand. Similarly
many Members do not require offices, but, for those who do, a desk or a
shared writing-room is not a satisfactory substitute. On research facilities,
it might be argued that the Member should aim to be an informed layman,
not an expert, and that he ought to do his own 'homework'. But without
research, how is a Member effectively to tackle the Minister with his
departmental brief?

4.3. The dilatoriness and complacency of governments in causes they regard as worthy but not urgent; the ministerial soft, evasive answer; the use made—and comparative ineffectiveness—of supplementary Questions.

4.4. That Parliament's function is separate and different from that of the executive. It ought not to concern itself with expertise and administrative detail, but with the wider, more philosophical criticism implied in the word 'deliberation'. This is the 'amateur', as opposed to the 'expert', view of Parliament. Given the expansion and complexity of government activities, this amateur view now seems out of date.

5. The advantages would be that viewpoints not deriving from party doctrine and assumptions would be heard more often, and that voting would not be more or less fore-ordained and predictable. However, the political parties already contain a great range of opinion, and even on rather hoary points of party conflict a debate normally (with the cooperation of Mr Speaker) includes a number of viewpoints which are not straight down the party line. One of the snares here is the word 'independent', which is very much a word of approval (hence its use by commercial television, which is dependent on advertising but not on license fees).

All this suggests that the advantages are much overrated. The only serious disadvantage is that arising if the number of 'independent' Members were sufficient to affect a government's majority. The system would then be changed from a two-party system to a coalition system: by the arguments advanced above this is a change for the worse.

ASSESSMENTS

(a) *Should there be more free votes?*

Free votes are already held on a few matters of conscience, e.g. hanging, sexual offences. These are matters of fundamental morality or of purely private morality, on which parties have no line of policy, and on which governments are reluctant to take sides. Free voting is possible since the Government, having no policy, cannot be defeated. Free voting could not be extended far without running into matters on which a government must have a policy. And if it has a policy, it would soon have to accept the possibility of defeat of that policy by vote of the House. If such defeats were both fundamental and persistent the Government would be forced to resign—like Peel in 1835. 'Good!' say the advocates of free votes, 'this is precisely what ought to happen more often. It says little for the British system of government and the Governments responsible for Suez in 1956 and for the economic crisis of 1966 did not have to resign.'

The judgement between this point of view and that advanced in the text (pp. 170–1) is a difficult one. The choice is between answerability to the House of Commons immediately, or to the electorate quinquennially. Two arguments seem to be decisively in favour of the party-organised system (with comparatively few free votes). First, this gives the elector, rather than the Commons, a genuine if infrequent choice; second, combination in parties to advance particular lines of policy is going to happen anyway.

(b) *Should there be a coalition government based on experts, not parties?*

Politics and political parties are not in great favour. It is an old and popular notion that political parties distort government, making it doctrinaire, bigoted, inflexible, and concerned with sectional advantage rather than public interest. Two remedies are advanced, sometimes together. The first is that governments should be based on a coalition of existing parties (survey evidence shows strong popular support for this). The second is that government should be handed over to a small committee of wise and knowledgeable men.

This second notion is easily disposed of. For many of government's most serious problems there are no 'right' solutions, discernible even by the wisest men. In many cases, e.g., economic problems, quite formidable experts disagree. Government is, more than we may like to admit, a process of compromise, adjustment, and temporising: governments live a hand-to-mouth existence enlivened by occasional leaps in the dark. In any case, the practical objections to the 'Wise Men' solution are insurmountable: wise and knowledgeable in what way? and in what subject? chosen by whom?

If we could assemble a dozen philosopher-kings who knew the right answers to our problems, we should be pleased to have them as the government. We cannot do so.

The coalition argument looks at first sight more attractive: an end to doctrinaire policies and party bickering, a concentration of the best talents on the problems. But much would be lost, as the text indicates (section 4, p. 171). Politics provides machinery to enable disagreements to be argued out and decided. For example, if people disagree about the merits of comprehensive education, it is right and proper and democratic that the question becomes a political one. Of course, the argument will be comparatively crude, and ignorance and prejudice will be displayed. But the question cannot be left to the experts (who have prejudice if not ignorance), because the experts disagree.

Now if politics is a necessary mechanism for arguing out disagreements, coalition politics restricts the argument, encourages a complacent sense that there is not a case to be made on the other side. This is satisfactory in wartime: the only recent peacetime experience of coalition—the National Government of 1931—is less encouraging. Effective opposition was destroyed while the Government carried out policies which are now seen to be wholly mistaken. The opposing cases are well illustrated in this exchange of letters to the *Times* which occurred during the severe economic crisis of July 1966.

Professor Sir Alexander Haddow, F.R.S., wrote:

We have many politicians but too few statesmen. Present policies are unbelievably materialistic, conflicting, and to boot unsuccessful, and ill reflect the latent qualities of the nation. If the history of the past twenty years has anything to teach us, surely it is that this nation will not respond to cajolery, muddled exhortation or financial and economic bluster. Men yearn for the expression of a purpose, through a calibre of leadership which they have not known since the days of the war.

Certainly we must have the books in order, but this cannot be done—and in any event will be of no avail—without the stimulus of a higher aspiration. Our aspiration should be towards the affairs of the world, influencing them no longer through arms and Empire, but by more subtle means which that world still needs and without which it will be an even sadder place.

I believe these questions could profitably be considered at once by men of all parties and none, in conference. I also believe that no single party, as at present constructed, alone has the talent or objectivity necessary to reform. We should, therefore, look forward to a National Government for a period of some five years, with partisan emotions for the moment subdued, and having the health of our country and (I repeat) of the world, as its prime intention beyond a per-adventure. A move must come soon, and it must be dramatic and decisive.

In reply, Mr Quintin Hogg, Q.C., Conservative MP for St Marylebone, wrote:

... A national Government is only a politer name for a coalition. There are no doubt cases where coalitions are desirable—the paramount importance of a single clearly defined objective (victory in war, for instance) the means to which cannot be defined by political reasoning, is clearly one example.

But, like other Governments, coalition Governments depend for their survival upon agreement on a common policy. This agreement must exist precisely between the members of the Government *inter se*—and, more generally, between the members of the Government and the political forces outside the Government supporting it. In the absence of such agreement, a Government becomes, as Disraeli pointed out long ago, nothing but an organised hypocrisy. Coalitions are particularly prone to this form of hypocrisy, and it is for this reason, as Disraeli also pointed out, that they are not loved in this country.

The ultimate fallacy ... is that there is anything normally dishonourable or petty about political differences, whether about means or ends. Such differences are the badge of a free society. Parties exist in order to give effect to them, and if we want Parliamentary Government, we must also opt for Party Government.

These arguments do not of course imply that party government has no faults and unerringly ensures both good and democratic government. Plainly it does not. The faults ascribed to it by coalitionists are all true in part. Its justification depends on these being outweighed by its advantages.

RECAPITULATION EXERCISES

1. List very briefly the arguments for:

(a) full-time Members of Parliament;
(b) party government;
(c) party discipline.

2. What are the main duties of:

(a) The Whip;
(b) The Speaker;
(c) The Leader of the House?

(The answers are indicated in the text.)

[6]

The Commons at work (I): legislation, policy, finance

1 OUTLINE
(for chapters 6 and 7)

The House of Commons sits for about 160 days each session, from late October to early August. The time of the House may be divided in several ways. Public business (which includes the Opposition's business) takes up about ninety per cent of the time available; Private Members' business takes up the remaining ten per cent. Of the ninety per cent of time available for Public business, the Opposition has at its disposal about twenty-five to thirty per cent. Of the whole business of the House, about half is devoted to legislation, about thirty per cent to finance, and twenty per cent to administration. These figures do not take into account time spent in committees, except those 'of the Whole House'.

This rough analysis indicates some of the main functions of Parliament—making laws, enacting the Government's proposals for taxation and expenditure, and scrutinising administration. These are the formal activities of Parliament which account for most of its official time. But through these activities Parliament indirectly fulfils other functions of crucial importance. It sustains a government chosen from its ranks. It engages in a 'Grand National Debate', which, whatever its immediate outcome in the voting lobbies of Parliament, shapes the political climate in which further decisions are taken, and in which the next general election eventually takes place.

A Government has about half of Parliament's time for legislation. There will be a programme of legislation indicated by the party's programme, and some Bills from Departments to effect minor improvements and tidying-up in, for example, the regulation of factories. Some outside groups, say the professional organisations of estate agents, may also be pressing for legislation. A great deal of work is done before a Bill reaches the House of Commons: discussion of general aims in party meetings and Cabinet committees;

more detailed discussion with Departments and with interested bodies outside government; trial drafts, each perhaps going to Departments and the Cabinet. The procedure in Parliament itself (two general debates on Second and Third Readings and detailed consideration in Standing Committee) is thus the last stage of a long process.

The financial procedure of Parliament provides for the consideration of estimates of expenditure and proposals for revenue (taxation). Here, more than anywhere, the historical origins of parliamentary procedure are ill-adapted to modern circumstances, in which government spends over £10,000 millions each year. Much of the parliamentary discussion of finance is in fact about policy. This is of course closely related to finance, but the financial content of policy is subject to little acute scrutiny. Arguments about 'too much' or 'too little' have insufficient impact, because so imprecise. The fault here lies not in parliamentary procedure alone, but also in the defects of government's own financial information and analyses. For example, until recently, nobody knew the precise cost of individual defence commitments.

Finance is again subject to scrutiny in the Select Committees on Estimates and Public Accounts. Some of the work of the Committees provides an effective check on the Government's 'housekeeping', running over from questions of financial economy to administrative efficiency. Administration is also subjected to criticism—and made to answer—in Parliamentary Questions and Adjournment Debates. Here the Commons are also concerned with justice and humanity, for a Department dedicated to efficiency and economy may well in its zeal act without a proper regard for fairness and compassion. In all these matters, Parliament functions mainly as the instrument of the Government, providing explanatory and critical publicity, minor amendments, formal approval for laws, policies and pronouncements initiated and promoted by the Government. The apparent independence of the Commons is of course overlaid by the operation of a party majority. In the scrutiny of administration, however, the Commons have more freedom, as long as they avoid the areas of major policy.

A consideration of the parliamentary round of work raises questions about the purpose and effectiveness of Parliament, the role within it of the backbench Member, and ways in which Parliament could be made more efficient. The reform of Parliament is still on the agenda of politics, still a good cry for a true Radical.

2 MAKING LAWS

The genesis of legislation

Governments arrive in office committed to making changes—all the more so, because the election campaign will have exaggerated the differences in the policies advocated by the parties. A good deal can be changed without legislation. For example, new financial priorities might switch spending from defence to education, or vice versa: this change in policy would go through the House in the Estimates (see section 4, p. 204). Foreign policy can be changed by new initiatives or a new emphasis, or have changes forced upon it: these again would be debated in the House—though not necessarily immediately. A policy of comprehensive education may be introduced by administrative means, that is, by asking local authorities to carry out the reorganisation, and providing finance most readily for comprehensive schools. This too may well be debated in the House. But none of these cases involves making a law.

There is a limit, however, to what a government can do without legislation. Only laws can provide for enforcement in the courts, and only laws can provide a regular authority for spending money. Thus, the Government which took office in October 1964 secured, in its first parliamentary session, the enactment of Bills to establish an Airports Authority to run the London Airports; to enlarge the borrowing powers of the Gas Council; to regulate race relations; to protect tenants from eviction; to regulate early closing days in shops—and sixty or so more.

This brief, but not unrepresentative, list gives some clue to the sources of legislation. Some laws are the culmination of major items of party policy, developed by the processes of dialogue and criticism between parliamentary leaders, backbenchers and the party in the country. The Protection from Eviction Act was one of these. Other laws arise from the policies and administrative problems of the Departments; for example, the Airports Authority Act. The Shops (Early Closing Days) Act was of a similar kind, but arising also from the problems and objects of interested groups (shopkeepers, shop assistants, even consumers).

Every government has to carry through a good deal of legislation of this undramatic but necessary kind—hence the clogging of the parliamentary time-table. Mr Wilson's Government, poised on its majority of three, enacted sixty-five Bills in the session 1964–5, and in addition the Private Members' Bills included the abolition of the death penalty. In the session 1966–7, with a large majority, the

Government secured the enactment of 103 Bills; few people would be able to name more than three or four of them.

The process of legislation begins a long time before a Bill makes its first formal appearance in Parliament at the First Reading. By then a Bill in its draft form must approximate to its final shape. It will have proceeded from original ideas through lengthy consultations with Departments of State and interested groups; its general provisions may have been commented on by the majority parliamentary party; and it will have gone to the Cabinet via a committee of the Cabinet. The parliamentary stages of legislation constitute the final amending and registration process. But the legislative process is much longer than the parliamentary process and much more important; and it takes place mainly outside Parliament.

.....

DOCUMENT I

THE GENESIS OF LEGISLATION

(a) *The National Health Insurance Act, 1911*

This was one of the major social reforms of Asquith's great Liberal Government, formed in 1908. The Act was the first large-scale introduction of modern welfare provision based on insurance. It can claim to represent a minor social revolution, for what is familiar now was sufficient then to cause the most heated and hysterical opposition.

The Act was inspired by Lloyd George, from the unlikely office of Chancellor of the Exchequer. He discovered the insurance principle at work in Germany, liked it and promoted a Bill. The success of the Bill was above all due to his skilled and powerful backing in Cabinet, Commons and country. Without him the Bill would not have reached the Statute Book.

Lloyd George was assisted by one or two ministerial colleagues, and by the great socialist intellectuals, the Webbs. Also a Royal Commission on the Poor Law had reported in 1909, and its views in a general way indicated the value of an insurance scheme. The Liberal Party had very little to do with the inspiration of the Bill; it was much more concerned at the time with the Lords, Ireland and Licensing.

In detail, the Bill owed a good deal to others besides Lloyd George, especially to one or two able and industrious civil servants. Of these the most important was R. Braithwaite, who was seconded from the Board of Inland Revenue to the Treasury to work on the scheme. In fact, Braithwaite worked himself into a breakdown, and at the end of it all was 'dropped' by Lloyd George—one of whose qualities as a Minister was his capacity to 'use' other men ruthlessly.

The Bill, in its final form, was also the product of a long series of consultations with, and representations by, the National Conference of Friendly

Societies, the Industrial Insurance Companies, the British Medical Association, the Trade Unions and Women's Organisations.

Lloyd George began work on the Bill towards the end of 1908. By April 1909 he had submitted a general outline to government actuaries. A year and a half later, in December 1910, Braithwaite started the detailed work. After five more months of drafting, the Bill was ready for introduction in Parliament. It passed its Third Reading at the end of 1911, three years after Lloyd George had initiated the project.

The promotion of this Bill clearly owed a good deal to one energetic and individualist Minister. The modern Cabinet system, with its committee structure, gives less scope for such legislative enterprise. The process is more formalised, and more closely related to the Departments and Cabinet committees. (The history of the Bill is set out in W. J. Braithwaite, Ed. Sir H. Bunbury, *Lloyd George's Ambulance Wagon*, Methuen, 1957.)

(b) *The legislative programme of the Labour government, 1945–50*

The Labour Government was committed when it came to office to a vast programme of legislation. In its Election Manifesto, *Let Us Face the Future*, the party had promised to bring under public ownership the coal, gas and electricity industries, all forms of public transport and the Bank of England. The Cabinet set up a future legislation committee, which worked on the assumption 'that, subject to unforeseen circumstances, we would seek to implement the legislative aspects of *Let Us Face the Future* within the lifetime of a single Parliament.' (Lord Morrison, *Government and Parliament*, 3rd edn., Oxford University Press, 1964, p. 235.) And so they did—in the seven major nationalising statutes. This is a classic illustration of legislation originating in a party programme. But it is untypical of a government's normal legislative activity.

[See chapter 9, p. 309, for some account of how the origin of one of these Acts related to the peculiar power-structure of the Labour Party.]

....

Drafting legislation

The first stage in making a law, then, is this decision in principle to enact a law, for example, to nationalise the coal industry, or to regulate shop hours. The next stage overlaps the first, and involves the working out in detail of the principles of the Bill and its embodiment in precise language. This second stage is in many ways the more difficult. The detail is worked out partly by the Minister and the Department concerned, partly by specialist civil servants, the parliamentary counsel or draftsmen. The Department is concerned with policy aspects, the draftsmen with the technical matter of language. At all stages, the Cabinet has to give its approval to the draft.

In the example given in document 1 (a), the National Health Insurance Act, 1911, Braithwaite began work on a draft in January 1911. This was discussed with other Ministers, officials and interested parties. About a month later a revised draft was ready for the Prime Minister to see. Three more weeks and a new draftsman was appointed, and *his* draft eventually went before the Cabinet. A month later it was approved, and a fortnight after that the Bill was ready for the Commons.

This is not the end of the road, of course, for the Commons too have then to go through the two stages of general principle and detailed drafting, within their own procedural forms.

EXERCISE

DRAFTING LAWS

1. The necessity and the difficulty of drafting laws in exact and meaningful language is often underestimated. Try drafting a clause which would compel employers to provide somewhere to sit down for those employees who could reasonably sit from time to time in the course of their work—a shop assistant serving at a counter for example.

(Do not spend more than ten to fifteen minutes on your draft— long enough to appreciate the problems. Part of an actual clause used in a statute is given in document 2 on pp. 198–9.)

Legislative procedure

Bills are of two kinds, Public and Private. Private Bills are concerned with private interests, for example, local authorities seeking new powers, or a company seeking power to acquire land, The rest are Public Bills, except for a few which are deemed hybrid. Public Bills may be promoted either by the Government or by a Private Member. Thus a Private *Member's* Bill is a Public Bill.

All Bills go through the following procedure, or a variant of it:

(a) *Introduction and First Reading.* The Clerk reads out the short title of the Bill and the Minister names a day for Second Reading. This is a formal signification that the Government intends to bring in a Bill. No debate takes place. The Bill is then printed and published, and the Opposition can study it with a view to criticism and amendment. (Occasionally a Bill is introduced 'on a motion': this procedure allows for immediate debate of the general case for legislation.)

(b) *Second Reading*. This is the main debate on principles, the only amendment being one amounting to complete rejection. The amendment may be in the simple form 'declining to give a Second Reading'; or it may be in the form, 'that the Bill be read a second time upon this day six months' (meaning that the Bill be rejected). The latter is a good example of the characteristic and baffling procedural convolutions of the House of Commons. The Second Reading of some non-controversial Bills may be taken in Committee.

(c) *Financial Resolution*. If the Bill involves expenditure, then the expenditure must be authorised by the House. Formerly (before 1966–7), 'Money Resolutions' were taken by a Committee of the Whole House. This meant precisely what it said: the whole House meeting as a committee with the freedom and relative informality that allows. In particular, Members might speak more than once in Committee; so it was possible to have a to-and-fro discussion, rather than the set speeches of formal debate. Thus, there was a justification for the committee procedure: but why the absurdity of a committee as large as the parent body? The traditional answer was that finance is too important a matter to be left to a subcommittee. The Government must initiate all proposals for expenditure, and no Private Member should be excluded from their consideration. These are not entirely convincing rationalisations. The truth is, here as in other matters, that the House acquired a procedure of this kind for historical reasons, probably to do with its earlier conflicts with the Crown, and was until recently (and perhaps still is) afflicted by a deep institutional conservatism.

(d) *Standing Committee* (see facsimile on p. 194). Most Bills are then sent to a Standing Committee for detailed consideration and amendment.

The House has six Standing Committees, labelled A to F. They have no specialised functions. Indeed, in the ordinary sense they are not 'standing' committees at all, for they are reconstituted for each Bill as it comes up. Usually between twenty-five and forty-five Members are appointed by the all-party Committee of Selection run by the Whips. The membership is in rough proportion to the balance of parties in the House, with the Government always in the majority. A Chairman is appointed by the Speaker from an all-party panel.

Many of the members of a Standing Committee will have a special interest in, and sometimes special knowledge of, the subject of the Bill. Most members who are not in the Government itself take some highly improper if the Minister determined the nature of the organisation in every detail, without consulting those who are to be responsible for the administration.

On the question of consultation with the employees, I repeat that it is inconceivable that a National Coal Board, responsible for the administration of this great industry, should not consult with workpeople. The workpeople would remind them very forcibly if they failed to consult. I do not think it is necessary to put that in the Bill, but I am prepared to put this. It may be necessary, in order to satisfy all the people concerned. It is not a matter only of those employed in the colliery industry, if the Bill is accepted in its present form, possibly with slight modifications. We shall have to consider the employees in a vast number of ancillary undertakings, not only in the National Union of Mineworkers, but maybe the General Workers' Union, technical organisations, professional organisations. It is not unlikely that we may be taking over farms. We may have to consider consultations with the Agricultural Workers' Union. Therefore, I am prepared to consider a form of words which will make it clear that there must be some appropriate machinery for consultation. I am satisfied that it ought not to come in this Clause. I will tell the Committee why, and then I will conclude.

The Board is not being established for purposes of creating consultative machinery, but for the purpose of getting the coal, and administering the industry. Therefore, consultation comes in as a general principle, and if I can get the right form of words as no doubt I can, with the assistance of my officials, or perhaps entirely because of them, I shall ask the Committee to consider a new Clause at a later stage in our proceedings. I think that that should satisfy the Committee. I beg hon. Members to understand that is no fault of ours that we are unable to furnish every detail of the future organisation. Hon. Members opposite have agreed that this is an experiment. There has never been anything like it, and I defy anyone to say in minute detail what should be done. We have some conceptions of the matter, and I assure hon. Members that in due course these will be put before the Committee in more detailed form.

Mr. Macmillan: I think the Committee will feel that this Amendment has been well worth discussion, even if its sole purpose was to hear the useful and illuminating speech which we have just had from the right hon. Gentleman. Committee stages of Bills are considered by some who have not had a very long acquaintance with our procedure as a waste of time. They afford an opportunity for raising these important issues, an opportunity for Ministers, as the right hon. Gentleman has so agreeably done, of saying that this is an important point to cover which he will consider in a new Clause.

I would like to make one or two observations about his arguments because, as he has told us, he is now such an old hand that he knows well how to cover a strategical retreat by a series of tactical counter-attacks. He said that it was not essential that the words of our Amendment should be included in this Clause of the Bill. I do not see why. Most of his speech was to say that it would be foolish to put in a detailed account of the regional organisation either for the consultative machinery or for the arbitration and conciliation machinery. We did not ask for that. All we said was, Where the duties of the Board are declared as three in number, to add a fourth.

12.45 p.m.

What are the three? He says it is obvious that the Board would take into account the necessity of regarding as a prime duty the making of a proper system of conciliation and labour arbitration. Look at Clause 1 (1, *b*). He might have said it was obvious that the Board's duty will be to secure the efficient development of the coalmining industry. Why put those words in? What else are the Board for? Are they supposed to be inefficient, to play bagatelle, to enjoy themselves in an agreeable way on a summer evening? In view of those words, which might have been said to be rather otiose, it seemed to us strange to have such an omission on this great occasion of this great experiment.

I was glad to have the friendly and honest tributes of the Minister and the hon. Member for Gower (Mr. Grenfell). We have accepted the Second Reading; we are trying to improve the Bill. We accept the experiment, that is the system of the House of Commons, that is how it runs, but it seemed to us strange that on this great occasion which the whole part in this committee work, but some do much more than others. Some, though appointed, do not attend at all; others may put in thirty or forty attendances. Here the part-time MP finds it difficult to do his share of the essential work of the House.

The Standing Committees meet in the morning, twice a week, sometimes longer and more often. The Minister in charge of the Bill will go through the Bill clause by clause, sometimes himself proposing amendments, and urging the rejection of Opposition amendments. Most Bills are not highly contentious, and will be approved by the Committee in one or two sittings. Others may be fought clause by clause. For example, in the session 1964–5, half the Bills were despatched at one sitting, but a quarter took up six or more sittings, and one, the controversial Rent Bill, as many as twenty sittings.

The proceedings of Standing Committees can be restricted by the methods of closure described below. The moving of amendments is at times severely restricted by the rule that only the Government may propose new or additional expenditure.

The Committee Stage is an important part of the legislative procedure of the House. It is unlikely, given party-based government, that Bills will be rejected on principle at Second or Third Reading. In effect, the electorate has empowered the Government in advance to enact certain broad policies and to meet other problems as they see fit. The function of the House is to make the execution in detail as effective and as just as possible. This is a restricted function, but it is an important one.

(e) *Report Stage*. The Bill as amended by the Standing Committee is formally 'reported' to the House. The Government may introduce further amendments, based on its second thoughts, or the prompting of the Committee's discussions. Often the House proceeds directly to the Third Reading.

(f) *Third Reading*. This is a general debate on the Bill in its final form, rather like the Second Reading.

(g) *The Bill in the Lords*. The Bill goes through similar stages in the House of Lords, except that there is no Financial Resolution (the Lords cannot deal with financial matters) and the Committee Stage is usually taken by a Committee of the Whole House.

The Bill may be amended in the Lords, often on the initiative of the Government. These amendments must be submitted to the Commons. If they are not accepted, the Houses exchange messages, and if there is still no agreement the Commons may resort to the procedure of the Parliament Acts, and thus override the Lords (see chapter 8). Normally Bills pass through the Lords quite quickly.

(h) *Royal Assent*. The Bill has then completed its journey through Parliament and shortly receives the Royal Assent.

The Government's control of a Bill's timetable

Parliamentary procedure provides the Government, through its majority in the House, with several weapons to expedite the passage of its Bills. These are all to do with the closure of debate, which may be moved at any time, though the Speaker may refuse to accept the motion if he thinks the matter has not been sufficiently debated. If he does accept the motion, it will be decided by vote, normally, of course, in the Government's favour. In the case of debate on an amendment, the Speaker (or the Chairman) decides, when asked, whether 'the question be now put'. These arrangements clearly might not meet the needs of a Government in a hurry, faced with an Opposition determined to fight every inch of ground. So the Government has some reserve weapons, dating from the 1880s when the Irish used obstructive tactics in the Commons. The Government may propose a restrictive timetable for the consideration of a Bill. This is known picturesquely as the 'guillotine', and it may be operated by compartments (grouping clauses and amendments) or by 'kangaroo' (leaping from one selected amendment to another).

These devices are normally used only when the Government is in serious difficulties with its legislative programme, or has 'emergency' Bills to enact, or when the Opposition is engaged in obstruction. Of course, the judgement of what constitutes an emergency, and what obstruction, lies with the Government. The devices are unpopular, restricting valuable criticism and amendment as well as obstruction, and negating the legislative role of Parliament. Hence governments use these closure procedures infrequently, out of 'respect for the rights of the House as a whole', and a prudent awareness that they must do as they would be done by.

....

DOCUMENT 2

FROM BILL TO ACT—THE PASSAGE OF THE
OFFICES, SHOPS AND RAILWAY PREMISES BILL, 1962–3

Introduction and First Reading (1 November 1962)

This being only the third day of the session, there was no Question Time. Business began with a Private Notice Question about the steel industry. Then, as is customary on Thursdays, the Leader of the Opposition asked the Leader of the House to 'state the business of the House for next week.' Some discussion followed. Then the Offices, Shops and Railway Premises Bill was presented, read a first time and ordered to be printed, and a day for Second Reading named.

The name of the Bill, its long title and its sponsors appeared on the Order Paper for the day. The long title is explanatory—'Bill to make fresh provision for securing the health, safety and welfare of persons employed ... etc.' The Clerk read out the short title, and a Minister named the day for Second Reading.

The Bill was published next day together with a short explanatory memorandum.

Second Reading (15 November 1962)

Business began with Questions, and, this being again a Thursday, the business for the next week was announced and briefly commented upon. Then, by leave of the Speaker, the Home Secretary announced the membership of the Tribunal of Inquiry set up to look into the security problems of the Admiralty (the Vassall case and the Radcliffe Inquiry). This led to some discussion, and it was 4.22 p.m. before the Minister of Labour rose to move the Second Reading of the Bill. He spoke for a little over half-an-hour, giving way to interruptions several times. He explained the Bill in very general terms: it aimed to provide for cleanliness, ventilation, sanitation, seats, first aid, and so on, in certain premises.

The Bill was not a matter of party controversy, and it extended and improved previous legislation on similar lines. It was one of the many Bills which are the product of Government Departments, working with interested groups, within the limits of what both parties will accept as non-controversial. (The Government itself will not have much parliamentary time for Bills which may be fought clause by clause.) The Minister claimed in this case that he had consulted about 130 organisations.

The front bench spokesman for the Opposition, Mr Gunter (who was to become Minister of Labour himself two years later), welcomed the Bill generally, but found it too limited and imprecise. Thirteen backbench Members spoke and the debate was wound up by another leading Opposition spokesman, and for the Government, by the Parliamentary Secretary to the Minister of Labour. It ended at about 9 p.m.

The Bill was then, without a division, read a second time and committed to a Standing Committee.

Financial Resolution (15 November 1962)

Since the Bill involved some expenditure by the Government, the House straightway resolved itself into a Committee of the Whole House, and approved a resolution covering the financial aspects of the Bill. Only the Government can initiate spending, so this was formally the approval of the 'Queen's Recommendation'. This resolution was later, on 19 November, 'reported to the House, and agreed to'.

Standing Committee (16 November 1962 to 12 February 1963)

The Bill was referred by the Speaker to Standing Committee D, which had forty-one members, Mr H. Hynd as Chairman. The Minister and other front bench spokesmen were, of course, included. The Committee met for the first time on 29 November and agreed to meet subsequently on Tuesdays and Thursdays at 10.30 a.m.; normally they adjourned at 1 p.m. The Committee met thirteen times altogether and, with a month's break at Christmas, their last meeting was on 12 February 1963. It was then agreed that the Bill, now much amended, mainly on the initiative of the Government, 'be reported'. The Committee had considered the Bill clause by clause, rejected a number of Opposition amendments, accepted some proposed by the Government.

Report Stage and Third Reading (6 March 1963)

On its return to the floor of the House, the Bill was first further amended by the House, meeting as a Committee of the Whole House. These were amendments without prior notice, representing the Government's second (or third) thoughts, and conceding points pressed on the Government by the Opposition in Standing Committee. Then the Bill 'reported as amended' was considered. This Report Stage was in effect a more formal repetition of the Committee Stage, but some new amendments, of which notice had been given, were moved. Most of these were quite technical and detailed. For example, the Minister of Labour moved that:

'Where persons who are employed to work in office, shop or railway premises have, in the course of their work, reasonable opportunities for sitting, without detriment to it, there shall be provided for their use suitable facilities for sitting sufficient to enable them to take advantage of those opportunities.'

The most important intention of this clause was to extend the provision of 'sitting facilities' to men (women were already provided for in other legislation). The clause was criticised, reasonably enough, on the grounds that it was ill-expressed. As one Member said, the good Lord has already provided us with suitable sitting facilities. And is a wooden box a sitting facility?—and if there is to be no detriment to the work, then assistants in busy shops will not be entitled to sit down. The Minister claimed that anyone who had attended the discussions of the Standing Committee on these matters would understand and approve the clause. It was duly agreed to.

The Bill was 'exempted business' (by the wish of the Government)—i.e. the House was not able to adjourn at 10 p.m. In fact, the debate, which had started at 4.15 p.m., went on to 12.38 a.m. next day—over eight hours. The House then went straight into a fifteen-minute Third Reading debate, and the Bill was passed without a division at 12.55 a.m. (A half-hour Adjournment Debate on the fluoridation of water then took place.)

The Bill in the Lords:
First Reading (11 March 1963)

The Bill brought from the Commons, read and ordered to be printed—a formal introduction, as in the Commons.

Second Reading (18 March 1963)

A debate on general principles, as in the Commons, lasting about three hours.

Committee Stage

The Bill was discussed in detail in a Committee of the Whole House on 2 April (4½ hours), 4 April (5½ hours), 8 April (3 hours). In this stage a number of amendments were moved on behalf of the Government, and many other amendments were defeated. When meeting in the evenings, the Lords usually took an hour off for dinner.

An amendment to the 'sitting facilities' clause is a good illustration of the drafting amendment most commonly made at this stage. In order to prevent employers providing seats in inaccessible places, the following words were inserted between 'use' and 'suitable' in the clause quoted above: '. . . at suitable places conveniently accessible to them . . .'

Report Stage (29 April)

3 hours.

Third Reading (13 May)

The Government was now anxious to get the Bill out of the way, so that they could push on with the London Government Bill. The Whips allowed no break for dinner, and used their majority to end discussion of the Bill with a series of divisions. Two days later, 15 May, the Bill was finally given a Third Reading and returned to the Commons. This stage had taken in all 2⅓ hours.

Final Stages

The Commons agreed to the Lords' amendments and made some more of their own, 26 July 1963 (1½ hours).

The Lords accepted the newly amended Bill in just eight minutes on 30 July 1963.

Royal Assent was given by commission on 31 July 1963. Thus the Bill became an Act of Parliament.

....

EXERCISES

THE LEGISLATIVE PROCEDURE OF THE HOUSE OF COMMONS

2.1. In the light of the above account and illustration of legislative procedure, what points can you make for and against the procedure?

2.2. Can you devise better procedures for the making of laws?

Private Members' Bills

Nine tenths of Parliament's time is devoted to the business of the Government and the official Opposition (technically this is all Government business). In the brief remainder of time, the Private Member can take the initiative in asking Questions (see chapter 7) and in introducing Bills and motions. Here, above all, the Private Member has his day.

In the context of British, government-dominated politics, this meagre ration of time looks to be fair. However, compared with the kind of system which operates in the United States, the scope allowed to the British Private Member acting on his own seems ludicrously inadequate. The restrictions are not of recent origin, the present position having been almost reached by 1902.

Since 1950, Private Members have usually had twenty Fridays in each session for introducing Bills and motions. In 1959 the time available was slightly increased. These times are shared by ballot, and a Member has about a 1:11 chance of being successful. It is also open to a Member under the 'Ten-Minute Rule' to introduce a Bill with a ten-minute speech at certain specified times. A ten-minute speech may be made in reply, and the House then votes, or accepts the Bill unopposed.

These devices all allow a Member to 'ventilate' a subject, to publicise a cause or a grievance, to show a need for legislation and test the extent of support. They lead only infrequently to the enactment of legislation, for which the obstacles are considerable. No Bill may propose the spending of money (a Government prerogative). Official help with drafting is not normally available. The ballot is another hazard, and even with good fortune the time available on the allotted days is short for a Bill to go through all its stages, and it is easy for opponents to obstruct and destroy. If the Bill antagonises the majority party, the Cabinet, or a powerful pressure group, it is likely to be sunk. A Bill may be talked out if the debate is kept going until 4 o'clock and the Speaker refuses to put the question; it must anyway be supported by at least a hundred Members; the Committee considering it must keep a quorum; and, like all other Bills, if it is not completed in one session it lapses.

Nevertheless, the difficulties are not insurmountable. Sometimes a Bill has widespread sympathy, both in and outside the House, and the Government itself may step in to facilitate its passage. About half of the Bills which are balloted do in fact become law, a dozen or so in each session. An example—the Public Bodies (Admission to Meetings) Bill, 1960—is illustrated in Part V (General

Notes) at the end of this book. There has been a long line of minor legislation, on fireguards, litter, protection of birds, pool betting, mock auctions and so on, as well as one or two outstanding laws, introduced by Private Members. Of these the most justly famous is the Murder (Abolition of Death Penalty) Bill of Mr Sidney Silverman (1965). Also notable was Mr Duncan Sandys' Civic Amenities Bill, and Mr David Steel's Bill on Abortion Law Reform.

EXERCISE

PRIVATE MEMBERS' BILLS

3. Do you see a case for the extension of facilities for Private Members' legislation?

3 THE 'GRAND NATIONAL DEBATE' ON MAJOR POLICY

One of the functions of Parliament is to inform and educate opinion in Westminster and in the nation as a whole. This is a function which is not inhibited or invalidated by the inevitable vote of the majority party for the Government's policy. But its effectiveness outside Westminster depends on the reporting of Parliament in the press and on radio and television. This is adequate only when there is high political tension or a situation the reporters can build up as a crisis. There is in consequence a strong prima facie case for televising the proceedings of Parliament in some form.

This function of political education, the 'Grand National Debate', is not tied to one procedural form. The debate on the Queen's Speech, a debate on a major Bill (see section 2), a Budget or Supply debate (see section 4), a tempestuous Question Time (see chapter 7, section 3)—all these can contribute. In addition, Government or Opposition frequently use time available to them for a motion of a general character, for example, taking note of, or welcoming, a Report or a Government White Paper, or (from the Opposition) 'regretting the Government's continuing failure' to do this or that, or 'having no confidence in' a policy (a censure motion). The contentious motions will be voted on and of course the Government will win. But all is not in vain: a case against the Government will have been expounded, and the Government itself will have had an opportunity to defend itself at some length.

These are all examples of 'motions' in the ordinary sense used by debating societies. The House also conducts business by the procedural device of a motion 'to adjourn'. This is a technicality which enables the House always to 'proceed upon questions put from the Chair upon a motion made by a Member, and resolved in the affirmative or negative' (Erskine May). One of the most famous debates of modern times, that of 8–9 May 1940, which led to the fall of the Chamberlain Government, took place on a motion to adjourn. The insignificance of the motion does not imply an insignificant debate; and it is the speeches, not the voting, which contribute to the 'Grand National Debate'.

Illustrative material in the form of a document is both too abundant and too long for repeating here. So find and study your own documentary material. Among newspapers, *The Times* has the most comprehensive parliamentary reports, but even these are not complete. The BBC, fulfilling its statutory duty, gives an excellent summary of the day's proceedings in both Houses at 10.45 p.m. each sitting day. Best of all, of course, get hold of copies of Hansard.

EXERCISES

PARLIAMENT AND THE 'GRAND NATIONAL DEBATE'

4.1. Take one day's proceedings in the House of Commons and check how they were reported by the daily newspapers and by the broadcasting authorities. Avoid Fridays. You will need the *Times* report at least as a control. Consider:

(a) the amount of reporting;

(b) the prominence given;

(c) the selection made;

(d) the total 'slanting' or bias introduced by selection, editorial comment and headlines.

You could supplement this analysis with an informal survey among your acquaintances: ask them questions designed to elicit how much they know about the previous day's proceedings.

In the light of your analysis would you say that the reporting of Parliament is:

(a) in amount and prominence given
   adequate,
   barely adequate,
   inadequate,
   grossly inadequate?

(b) in selection and treatment
   perfectly fair,
   just about fair,
   a little unfair,
   quite unfair?

(1)

DEPARTMENT OF EDUCATION AND SCIENCE

I. ESTIMATE of the amount required in the year ending 31 March 1968 for the salaries and expenses of the Department of Her Majesty's Secretary of State for Education and Science; for grants and loans in connection with education, &c.; for sundry services; for a subscription to an international organisation and for certain grants in aid.

Sixty-eight million seven hundred and sixty-seven thousand pounds

(£68,767,000)

II. Subheads under which this Vote will be accounted for by the Department of Education and Science, and additional detail.

1966-67 £	SUMMARY	1967-68 £
8,375,000	A. to E. ADMINISTRATION	8,974,000
21,418,000	F. to H. PRIMARY AND SECONDARY EDUCATION	23,560,000
2,957,260	I. FURTHER EDUCATION	2,950,760
19,047,000	J. and K. TEACHER TRAINING, &c.	21,004,000
1,625,000	L. AWARDS TO STUDENTS	1,015,000
336,010	M. GRANTS TO MISCELLANEOUS ESTABLISHMENTS	363,010
95,594,000	N. and O. SCHOOL MEALS AND MILK	8,150,000
4,695,390	P. to U. OTHER GRANTS AND SERVICES	5,042,390
840	V. INTERNATIONAL SUBSCRIPTION	840
153,349,000	Gross Total	71,060,000
	Deduct:	
2,464,000	Z. APPROPRIATIONS IN AID	2,293,000
150,885,000	Net Total	68,767,000

Decrease £82,118,000

		1966-67 £	1967-68 £
		7,151,000	7,151,000
A. SALARIES, &c.		29,250	27,250
(1) Ministers	Nos. 1966-67 / Nos. 1967-68		
Secretary of State (£8,500)	1 / 1		
Ministers of State (£5,625)	2 / 2		
Parliamentary Under Secretaries of State (£3,750)	2 / 2		
(2) Staff *See Appendix.*	2 / 2	7,121,750	7,452,750
B. GENERAL ADMINISTRATIVE EXPENSES		616,000	663,000
(1) Travelling and subsistence, &c.		327,000	358,000
(2) Post Office services		156,000	154,000
(3) Miscellaneous expenses		133,000	151,000
C. NATIONAL LENDING LIBRARY FOR SCIENCE AND TECHNOLOGY: SALARIES, &c.		162,000	211,000
D. NATIONAL LENDING LIBRARY FOR SCIENCE AND TECHNOLOGY: GENERAL EXPENSES		446,000	470,000
E. DOCUMENTATION PROCESSING CENTRE		—	150,000

C. The number of staff provided for is 195 including a Director at £4,175–£4,625 and 35 industrial at 1 April 1967 (176 at 1 April 1966 with provision for a further 16 in 1966–67) increasing to a total of 217 at 31 March 1968.

D. General expenses (including Russian Translation service £190,000) (£170,000 in 1966–67).

E. Expenditure on the setting up and running of this Centre in 1967–68.

PRIMARY AND SECONDARY EDUCATION

		1966-67 £	1967-68 £
F. GRANTS TO DIRECT GRANT AND SPECIAL SCHOOLS		8,128,000	8,340,000
(1) Direct grant schools		7,703,000	7,821,000
(2) Special schools:			
(a) Current		50,000	69,000
(b) Capital		375,000	450,000
G. AIDED AND SPECIAL AGREEMENT SCHOOLS: BUILDING GRANTS		10,400,000	12,720,000
H. AIDED AND SPECIAL AGREEMENT SCHOOLS: LOANS		2,890,000	2,500,000

FURTHER EDUCATION

		1966-67 £	1967-68 £
I.1. GRANTS TO COLLEGES OF ADVANCED TECHNOLOGY		159,010	10

I.1. Token provision for remnant payments for period prior to 1 April 1965

4.2. List any advantages and disadvantages you can see in the televising of Parliament by means of a programme edited each night by the BBC.

4 FINANCE

Finance is a peculiarly important subject for Parliaments. It is the historical source of their being, for it was above all the need for money that drove medieval and Tudor and Stuart monarchs to summon parliaments and listen to their grievances. Finance is still the essential element in a government's policy: governments can do what they can afford to do and no more. Parliament is formally the judge of what can be afforded.

It is understandable, therefore, that financial procedure is hedged about with some fundamental and ancient maxims and the awesome accretions of the centuries. It is, above all, a function of Parliament, not the Crown (i.e. the Government), to grant money and impose taxes, but in practice only the Government initiates financial proposals. Before granting money, Parliament has the right to the redress of grievances—in practice, the right simply to express them. Finance is a matter for the Commons, not the Lords.

Parliament is in some ways the prisoner of its own procedures. These are based on an annual cycle, running from estimates to public accounts. But public expenditure is a continuing and long-term process. This is now formally recognised by the executive which makes its financial plans three to five years ahead (see p. 122). So far Parliament has not devised, or been allowed to devise, special procedures for reviewing the Government's plans beyond the current year, and is without detailed information about those plans.

Financial procedure is complex and a short glossary will make clear the main elements:

The financial year runs from 1 April to 31 March. Note that the parliamentary session normally runs from October to August, thus straddling two financial years.

The Queen's Speech, written by the Government, read by the Queen, indicates at the beginning of each session the main points of Government policy, including financial policy.

The Estimates are estimates of the Government's spending, presented in tabulated form, under the main heads of the Defence Departments, the Revenue Departments, and the Civil Estimates. The latter are divided into classes, votes and sub-heads (see facsimile illustration on p. 203). The whole presents a massive documentation of over a thousand pages of high technicality—a factor having some bearing on the degree of effectiveness of the Commons' scrutiny of finance.

Select Committees on Estimates and Public Accounts: see chapter 7, section 1.

Supplementary Estimates: additional estimates to cover changes in policy or previous under-estimates.

Excess Votes: to cover unforeseen deficits.

Supply Days: until 1966–7, twenty-six days were allotted each session to consideration of supply (i.e. expenditure). Most of the time was taken up by debates on the policies of the Departments, at the choice of the Opposition. The form of the debate was financial (e.g., on a motion to reduce a vote, or even the Minister's salary, by a few pounds), but the substance was policy. Since 1966–7, Supply Days have been recognised procedurally (but not in name) for what they are, debates mainly about policy, at the choice of the Opposition. Thus only a few of them are now strictly part of financial procedure.

The Consolidated Fund is a common account into which taxes are paid and from which payments are made. It is an accounting procedure, but one which shows that taxes are not normally applied to meet specific expenditure. Thus, a government does not double the petrol duty in order to build more roads, and you cannot give up smoking to avoid supporting nuclear armaments.

Vote on Account is presented in March to provide authority to the Government to go on spending money after 1 April, since the full financial programme cannot pass through Parliament until July or August. The Government cannot pay a single soldier or civil servant without the authority of Parliament. Having a majority in Parliament means that the Government is normally sure to get all it asks for, but the procedures of seeking authority cannot be skipped.

The Committees of Supply and of Ways and Means were abolished in 1966–7. Both were Committees of the Whole House (see p. 193). This procedure was used by the House for the consideration of financial matters: Supply for estimates of expenditure; Ways and Means for raising and for finally granting money. In the session 1967–8, the Finance Bill was considered in a specially appointed Standing Committee of fifty members.

Budget: the Government's statement of accounts, with proposals for taxation and spending. Particularly since 1945, the Budget Statement and accompanying papers represent a review of the state of the economy, for the purpose of a modern budget is to regulate and influence the economy as well as to provide for Government expenditure. The Budget Statement is made by the Chancellor of the Exchequer early in April. There is now a tendency for Chancellors to alter (usually increase!) taxation at other times, to meet the fluctuations of the economy.

....

DOCUMENT 3

THE COURSE OF A TYPICAL FINANCIAL YEAR IN PARLIAMENT

(a) *October to January*

Preparation of next financial year, and completion of current financial year (ending on 31 March).

October. Queen's Speech—addressing the Commons only, the Queen says, 'Estimates will be laid before you.'

October to January. Preparation of Estimates in the Departments, and negotiation with the Treasury.

November to December. The Select Committees are set up (see chapter 7).

November to January or February. Consideration of Supplementary Estimates and Excess Votes. The debate on these, in the Committee of the Whole House, is mainly financial.

(b) *February to March*

Presentation of Estimates for the next financial year and passing of Consolidated Fund (No. 1) Bill. These are the first of the Supply Days, in which the Opposition chooses to debate the work and policies of a selected Department, usually at this stage an armed services Department. This is done under a motion to reduce the work or the cost of a Department, since only the Government can move to increase expenditure. The Consolidated Fund (No. 1) Bill grants supplies (i.e. money) for the first five months of the next financial year, thus keeping the Government going while the complete programme of finance is debated and approved. This part of the Bill is the Vote on Account (see glossary above). The Bill also gives approval to the Supplementary Estimates for the year just ending and excess expenditure for the year before that.

Since the Consolidated Fund Bill involves the expenditure of money, it has to be passed in the Committee of Ways and Means as well as in the Committee of the Whole House.

(c) *April to July*

Consideration of Estimates goes on; and the Government indicates how it will raise money, first in the Budget, then in the Finance Bill.

April. The Budget presents the Government's general plans for its own spending, and for the regulation of the economy. The Government's proposals are given immediate effect by resolutions.

April to July. The resolutions are then incorporated in a Finance Bill, which goes through the normal procedure for legislation. The Committee Stage of this Bill is a serious and detailed consideration of finance, a laborious and time-consuming task in which only experts can take an effective part. It is therefore suitable work for a small committee and was removed from the 'Whole House' in 1968 (this experiment has not since been repeated). At the end of this process, the Bill becomes the Finance Act. Meanwhile, the House will go on considering the Estimates, especially now the Estimates of Civil Departments. As before, much of this consideration will be concerned with policy rather than finance: for lack of time, many estimates will not be discussed at all. At the end of these labours, the House will have produced what becomes the Appropriation or Consolidated Fund No. 2 (Appropriation) Act.

(d) *November to July*

While all this is going on in the Chamber itself, the two financial Select Committees, on Estimates and on Public Accounts, meet regularly 'upstairs'. The Public Accounts Committee considers the previous year's accounts. Both Committees are mainly concerned with detail, with 'value for money', hence with administrative efficiency. The work of these Committees is discussed in chapter 7 below.

EXERCISE

THE FINANCIAL PROCEDURE OF THE HOUSE OF COMMONS

5. On the evidence given above, what criticisms would you make of the financial procedure of the House of Commons? This is quite difficult: try your hand for a while, then refer to the guide to exercises below.

GUIDE TO EXERCISES

1. You might assess the effectiveness of your draft clause by pretending to be an inhuman and grasping employer. Do you see a loop-hole?

Part of the clause actually enacted is given in document 2.

2.1. Against the procedure:

It is complicated and long—so long, in relation to the time available for major legislation, that important Bills are often postponed. The Offices Bill of document 2 had itself been promised for the previous session and dropped for lack of time. Yet this time-consuming procedure does not seem to give the Bills a sufficient consideration in detail.

For the procedure:

A procedure for legislation quite properly takes up time, enabling criticisms and representations to be made, and giving the Government time for further thoughts.

There is a logic in the procedure: it moves from notice and publication to discussion of general principles, to amendment in detail, then general debate on the amended Bill. These are all necessary stages, carried out in a meaningful order and then repeated by the other House.

Further argument would involve fundamental appraisal of the whole machinery of Parliament. For example, it may be suggested that the House as a whole is an inefficient body for even a general debate, and that more should be done in committees. Again, it might be suggested that a Standing Committee on a Bill needs to carry out a much more highly informed and technically qualified scrutiny—in fact, that senior officials could do the job better. These suggestions might be supported with evidence drawn from legislative proceedings.

However, there are strong, if not overwhelming, counter-arguments. The House is a representative institution. A loss in efficiency of discussion may be compensated by a gain in efficiency of representation. As for the officials, they will have discussed the drafts of the Bill in departmental and interdepartmental committees. They have had a turn.

2.2. The answer depends, of course, on what criticisms you regard as justified. If we accept that legislation ought to take up a good deal of time, and that Parliament has not at present sufficient time for legislation, several changes are possible:

(a) Longer sittings. But this change is made difficult by the need of Ministers to give time to their Departments; by the need for all Members to visit their constituencies, to travel and to study; also by the need of some Members to give time to their other occupations.

(b) Giving the House of Lords more and more serious work and responsibilities in law-making. (Already some Bills of a non-contentious character go through their first stages in the Lords.) But clearly the Commons cannot give up any substantial part of their legislative work to a Second Chamber constituted largely on a hereditary basis.

(c) Giving much less attention to the details of a law which could be worked out instead by the Departments. In a Memorandum to the Select Committee on Procedure of 1958, the Clerk of the House wrote: '. . . sooner or later I am ¦convinced the House of Commons will have to approach legislation from the angle that Parliament lays down very general principles, and that it is the business of the Executive to administer the law inside principles.'

The objection to this lies in the possibility of 'bureaucratic tyranny', the fact that law would not be openly made by the representatives of the people. This objection is easily exaggerated. Departmental officials already have considerable power: what is needed is to subject that power to ministerial responsibility and supervision.

(d) Extending and improving the use of Committees. More Committees could be used for more stages of the Bill. The Report Stage could perhaps be taken in Committee. In the case of non-contentious Bills, there is now provision for the Second Reading to be taken in a Committee. It would be difficult to extend this to contentious Bills, but in practice few Bills are contentious in the sense of being at the centre of party principle and argument.

The Committee system itself could well be reformed. Large Committees of forty or fifty members are really miniatures of the Whole House, and could be used accordingly in a representative function. But for detailed consideration of Bills, much smaller Committees of fifteen to twenty at most would be more effective. It might make for greater efficiency too—it would certainly make for greater knowledge and expertise—if all Committees had special functions in relation to Departments or groups of Departments.

(e) Having a general debate at the beginning of the cycle, based on a White Paper or explanatory memorandum, and leading to a series of resolutions on the main lines of the proposed legislation. This could be done either before the first official draft, so that the draft could be immediately adapted to meet lines of criticism, or at the time of the presentation of the first draft. Debates at Second or Third Reading could then be much reduced.

3. Yes. The history of Private Members' Bills suggests that there are a number of matters demanding legislation on which governments have no wish to legislate: they are preoccupied with other matters, or reluctant to interfere in matters like divorce or Sunday Observance for fear of antagonising vociferous pressure groups. Private Members may step in and do good where governments fear to tread. In many cases, these are matters which do not excite opinion on party lines, and the prestige and authority of the Government is not at stake.

The possibility of making laws is also important for the morale of the backbencher. For much of his time he must follow the lead of the front bench. Private Members' Bills give him a chance to take the initiative. This is important in a profession which is in many ways frustrating for most of the time for two-thirds of the people involved.

The overall case for the extension of these facilities is indeed a good one, but it comes up against the problem of shortage of time discussed above. There is too the problem of finance. Private Members cannot propose the expenditure of money. If they could, they would doubtless be hounded by pressure groups wanting a share. So the scope of Private Members' legislation must necessarily be limited, and the problem of time remains unsolved.

4.1. This you must do for yourself!

4.2. The advantages lie in the improvement in public interest and information about Parliament itself and the affairs it discusses, since for most people television is now the main source of political news.

The disadvantages lie in the difficulties of editing, and in the possible effects of television on the proceedings of Parliament. The editorial problems are serious. Eight hours or more of debate would have to be reduced to at most perhaps an hour, and this would require most skilful summarising and selection. The presentation would have to be fair to both sides, and would have to convey some difficult argument and procedures. The television producer's natural tendency is to look for the exciting moments and, in particular, the visually exciting: this might well make for distortion and sensation. Already, television reports, like those of newspapers, distort the truth by reporting (and hence exaggerating) the 'newsworthy'. For example, one dissident speech gets more attention than half-a-dozen in support of the party line.

These possibilities indicate the likely effects on parliamentary proceedings which might follow the introduction of television into the Chamber. For television could not be simply a reporter; it would itself affect the material it was reporting. There would be a tendency for Members to address the television audience rather than their fellow-members, and hence to play to an undiscriminating gallery. There might well be more scoring of party and debating points, more insults, less serious debate. Thus public information about Parliament might be increased, but it would not be improved.

These arguments have force—but some parliamentarians argued on rather similar lines when it was a matter of admitting the press. Two things are clear: first, public ignorance of Parliament and of public affairs is abysmal, and it would be worth paying a price to increase and improve public knowledge. Second, since much of the argument is speculative, an experiment is certainly justified.

It seems possible that in the end Parliament will be televised, and will respond, like local councils faced with the press, by retreating into committee. This might be no bad result.

5. There is clearly a good deal in financial procedure which has only a historical justification; no one devising a financial procedure on a clean slate would choose this model. The main criticisms are these:

(a) The procedure is both complex and confusing. It may be mastered in the end by most Members; but the proceedings of Parliament ought to be intelligible to the ordinary newspaper reader.

(b) It all takes up a great deal of parliamentary time, at the end of which most of the Government's spending programme has not been fully considered. In particular, the Commons gives very little attention to the major questions of priorities between different areas of government spending (e.g., defence; social services; transport) and of total expenditure on particular services (e.g., education). It is indeed doubtful whether the Whole House is a proper body in size and speed of operation for work of this kind, and the removal of the Finance Bill 1968 to an 'upstairs' Committee implied the acceptance in part of this point. Moreover, the procedures are based on one year, while major financial plans are now related to three to five year projections at least.

(c) Supplementary Estimates often get a closer scrutiny than the main estimates, because they are smaller in scope and available for consideration apart from the main financial business. In consequence, Departments may inflate their main estimates to avoid the embarrassment of Supplementaries.

(d) The work of the Select Committees, however effective, simply does not cover enough ground quickly enough.

There are some points to counter these criticisms:

(a) The procedure is only complex and confusing in its form and mannerisms; and recent changes (the abolition of the two financial committees of the Whole House and associated procedures) have made it more straightfoward. There is now, it may be argued, a comprehensible and manageable structure of debate.

(b) The extent to which finance can or should be debated on its own is much exaggerated. Finance is meaningful mainly in relation to the state of the economy, the policies of the Government and the detailed administration of these Departments. It is unreasonable, therefore, to include these matters in debate and discussion under financial procedures. The narrowly financial subject of raising money (taxation) is considered in detail on the Committee and Report Stages of the Finance Bill. Thus, in a way, Parliament deals with finance in the manner of those many organisations which have finance *and general purposes* committees.

(c) The problem of time and overall adequacy of discussion is more difficult to counter. It seems fair to say that the present system makes the best of a procedure involving the Whole House in financial business. Any improvement would need to be by way of an extended committee system (see chapter 7).

ASSESSMENTS

Note: There is an assessments section relating to the whole work of the House at the end of chapter 7.

RECAPITULATION EXERCISES

1. *True or False?* (mark T or F)

(a) The general principles of a Bill are debated on the First Reading.

(b) The detailed consideration of Bills usually takes place in a Standing Committee.

(c) Backbench Members are permitted to move amendments in Standing Committee.

(d) Private Members' Bills publicise a subject, but never reach the Statute Book.

(e) Supply Days are occasions for debate on finance.

2. List the sources from which a government may draw its programme of legislation.

3. Explain the terms: guillotine; kangaroo; motion to adjourn; Vote on Account; Supplementary Estimate.

KEY TO RECAPITULATION EXERCISES

1. (a) F   (b) T   (c) T   (d) F   (e) F

2. Party programmes, departmental concerns, pressure groups, also problems and opportunities arising while in office.

3. See text, pp. 196, 201–2, 205.

[7]
The Commons at work (II):
Committees, Questions, and the
backbencher

1 THE SCRUTINY OF ADMINISTRATION
BY COMMITTEE

The analysis of Parliament by functions

The House of Commons usually manages to do more than one job
at the same time. For example, it is constantly contributing to the
function of public political education; and its financial debates are
usually also about policy. Similarly, the function of scrutinising
government administration is mixed up with other functions. The
Select Committees on Estimates and Public Accounts are (as their
name implies) financial committees, but they are concerned mainly
in the scrutiny of administration. Question Time and Adjournment Debates also here come under this heading, though financial
matters and major policy sometimes arise.

The Select Committee on Nationalised Industries works in a
similar way to other Select Committees, but has special problems,
and a separate and clearly defined field of work. It is therefore
dealt with separately in the General Notes, p. 453, at the end of the
book.

The Committee system of the House of Commons

The House of Commons does a good deal of its most effective work
in committees, not on the floor of the Chamber itself. The Committees are called Standing or Select Committees, but these terms
are misleading. It is more meaningful to describe them as legislative
or scrutiny committees.

The Standing, or legislative, Committees were discussed in chapter
6, pp. 193–5. They are concerned with producing a Bill in its final
form, with the revision and amendment of legislation. The Minister
in charge of the Bill directs the work of the Committee, applying
his party majority to secure his objectives.

The Select Committees are mostly concerned with the investigation of a particular aspect of government administration, and their object is to produce an agreed report. The Committees are not partisan, and are not led by Ministers. This mode of operation, now conventional, effectively restricts the work of the Select Committees to detailed 'administration' rather than grand policy—in practice, to matters which are not the current object of partisan attachment.

Two of the Select Committees are concerned with Finance—the Committee on Estimates and the Committee on Public Accounts (PAC). In practice, they proceed from finance to matters of administration. Recently, some specialist Select Committees have been established—e.g., on Agriculture, on Science and Technology, and on Education and Science. These are specialist in that they deal with one subject area, related to a single Department of Government. In other respects, their work is similar to that of the Financial Committees.

Besides these Committees, there is a Select Committee on the Nationalised Industries, and another on Statutory Instruments. For these, see Part V, pp. 453 and 462.

The Committee on Estimates

The Select Committee was first established in 1912, and has been reconstituted in each session since then, except for the war years. It now has thirty-six members, chosen by the Whips in rough proportion to the balance of parties. The Chairman of the Public Accounts Committee is a member. The Chairman of the Estimates Committee is chosen by the Committee, and is always a Government backbencher. The Committee is served by two of the clerks to the Financial Committees, and a Treasury official is 'in attendance'. There is no other staff.

The Committee, like all Select Committees, has the power 'to call for persons and papers': 'persons' includes civil servants, but not normally Ministers or even junior Ministers. Most of the work of the Committee is done in sub-committees, coordinated by a sub-committee of chairmen. Each sub-committee is allocated one main field, e.g., economic, social, defence. Sometimes they travel at home or abroad in pursuit of their enquiries.

The formal terms of reference of the Committee are:

To examine such of the estimates presented to this House as may seem fit to the Committee and report how, if at all, the policy implied in those estimates may be carried out more economically and . . . to consider the principal variations between the estimates and those relating to the previous year and the form in which the estimates are presented to the House. . . . (Standing Order No. 80)

The Committee is concerned with the Estimates, a massive and complex task, which must be done for the main Estimates between February (when they are presented) and July (when they must be passed). But the Committee works *to*, rather than *on*, the Estimates. It selects a few each session for detailed investigation and calls for papers and questions witnesses. The Chairman and the clerks play an important part. The clerks guide the Chairman, and draft the Reports. The Chairman leads the questioning. The effectiveness of each sub-committee depends a good deal on how well he has studied the papers and briefed himself for the sitting, and how skilfully he presses the questions.

Some of the questioning does little more than elucidate for the benefit of members the estimates of a Department, and the kind of activities they cover. But the Committee tries to discern cases of overspending, or of spending with a poor return, and will concentrate questions on these aspects. The concern is with 'value for money'. The Committee does effective work if it merely elicits and clarifies the factual material and other considerations on which policy is based. But sometimes this concern conflicts with the basic limitation of the Committee: that it should not concern itself with policy. 'Policy' is a loose word, and the practical limitation for the Committee is that it does not work on party lines. It does not therefore question the major decisions for which the Government is responsible, for normally such decisions are matters of controversy between the parties. Thus, the Committee, reporting in December 1965 on the rise in the cost of prescriptions dispensed under the National Health Service, did not comment on the Government's controversial policy of abolishing the charge to patients. But they did analyse the causes of the rise in costs, showing that there had been increased demand for prescriptions and also increased sickness. Their conclusion was concerned with the inaccuracies of the estimates for the pharmaceutical services.

The Reports of the Estimates Committee are submitted to the relevant Departments for their observations. These may accept or 'note' some of the Committee's strictures and recommendations, or they may indicate their disagreement, adding a brief justification. Unless Parliament itself intervenes, the Committee's recommendations carry no sanction. But they do not go quite unheeded, for the Department has had to explain itself before the Committee, a salutary proceeding, and will not wish to attract the Committee's further notice by a show of unconcern. Moreover, the Treasury, with its perennial concern for financial economy, normally backs the Committee with pressures of its own. The Committee examines the Defence Departments almost every year, and the Treasury in two out of three years on average. Other Departments may escape scrutiny for two to five years. But they can never be sure of immunity, so the deterrent effect is not much weakened.

The main effect of the Committee is, thus, in its direct relation to Departments. Parliament itself does not spend much time in the Chamber on the Committee's proceedings. Three days altogether are devoted to debating the reports of both Financial Committees, and sometimes Questions are based on them. The political rewards of service on these Committees are slight; reputations are not made, and offices are not won. There is little incentive for the energetic and ambitious Member to devote himself to committee work.

....

DOCUMENT I

THE COMMITTEE ON ESTIMATES

(a) *Grants to the British Travel and Holidays Association*

From Minutes of Evidence of Sub-Committee C, 3 February 1960 (Sir Frank Lee, Joint Permanent Secretary to the Treasury being examined), H.C. 258, 1959–60, pp. 28–9

Mr Thornton: I have one question on the grants in aid. I notice in the case of the British Travel and Holidays Association and in one or two other cases that the grants in aid are quite substantial but there is nothing in these figures to indicate what contribution is made by the industry itself. For instance under subhead A.1—the British Travel and Holidays Association—the Government contribution is limited to £1,050,000, part of which is to be made up of a block grant. Could you give us any idea what contribution the British Travel and Holidays Association itself makes?

Answer: Apart from a certain income it may get from the sale of publications it is not a very great deal. I will have to check this figure, but it is something of the order of £75,000 or £80,000 a year which it gets from a variety of industries or other bodies subscribing to it. The difficulty is that the efforts of this Association—because of its nature—have to be spread in relation to the whole of the United Kingdom. . . .

Mr Thornton: What is concerning my mind is that in these cases where the grant in aid extends to 75, 80, 90 and 95 per cent, what is the extent of public control and checking of the expenditure, because I see that it says in the footnote on page 28 of Class VI of the Civil Estimates: 'Expenditure out of these grants in aid will not, except in the case of the Council of Industrial Design, be accounted for in detail to the Comptroller and Auditor General.' . . .

Answer: Might I say this, and this does not exclude the taking of detailed evidence later: What we do is to work out in relation to each of these bodies a code of rules about the conduct of its financial affairs—what is to be the procedure about consultation with us on estimates, what power has it to incur new expenditure on new projects during the year . . . and what power, if any, has it over the salaries and numbers of its staff. There are fairly elaborate codes which are often tailored, as was implied might be the case, to the circumstances of each association. Our particular object is, as I indicated earlier, to satisfy ourselves as best we can that that money which very largely is public and taxpayers' money is properly and sensibly spent without getting into the position that we are interfering with the day-to-day work of these bodies. That answer could be elaborated by more detailed information on a subsequent occasion.

....

EXERCISE

THE COMMITTEE ON ESTIMATES

1. Within the limits of the evidence given above:

(i) Is the Committee concerned in these proceedings with policy, administration or finance, or some combination of these?

(ii) Would you regard the questioning as searching and effective, or ill-considered and ineffective? Does it show any signs of party bias? (Try guessing the party of the Member speaking.)

(iii) Do the officials respond, in your view, efficiently and openly, or efficiently but guardedly, or evasively?

(iv) Would you say that the proceedings show the Committee's lack of (and need for) expert advice?

....

(b) *Anglo-French project for a super-sonic aircraft* (*the Concorde*)

From Minutes of Evidence of Sub-Committee B of the Estimates Committee, 8 July 1963 (three Treasury officials being questioned), H.C. 42, 1963–4, p. 147

[The Committee was concerned that in projects of this kind, a Department may become committed to substantial expenditure over a period of years, in advance of specific Treasury authorisation. Here is one exchange on this subject:]

Mr Millan: But it is somewhat artificial to say that Treasury authority has not been given. This agreement has now been signed between the two countries and some of the details have been announced publicly. It would not be open to the Treasury to come along now and say, 'We are not going to give authority for these moneys', would it?

Answer: I accept that this is to some extent a formality. Nevertheless, for better or for worse, Treasury assent is required before a Department can sign a development contract, and the Ministry of Aviation are not at the stage of being able to seek our authority.

EXERCISE

THE COMMITTEE ON ESTIMATES

2. Answer questions 1. (i), (ii) and (iii) in relation to this extract.

(c) *Increase in the number of civil servants*

From Departmental Observations on the Sixth Report of the Estimates Committee, July 1964, H.C. 304, 1963–4
[Here is part of the Committee's recommendation and the Treasury's Observation:]

Recommendation (para. 41): Last Session your Committee commented on the steep increase which had taken place in the number of non-industrial civil servants (excluding the Post Office). They also drew attention to the fact that in 1963 the numbers published in the Estimates and in the Financial Secretary's Memorandum, although they represented Departments' estimates of the staff likely to be employed at the beginning of the financial year, exceeded by more than 5,500 those who were actually in post in April, 1963. . . .

Observation: The Treasury has noted the Committee's remarks on the difference between the staff numbers shown in Estimates and the numbers actually in post on 1st April, 1964. This difference, although slightly greater than last year, is less than one-and-a-half per cent., or about one for every 70 staff. . . .

EXERCISES

THE COMMITTEE ON ESTIMATES

3.1. Was the Committee concerned with policy, finance or administration?

3.2. Was the Treasury's Observation concerned with policy, finance or administration?

(d) *Grant to London Transport to cover the postponement of fare increases*

From Minutes of Evidence of Sub-Committee on Supplementary Estimates, 7 December 1965 (three officials from the Ministry of Transport being questioned), H.C. 31, 1965–6, p. 26

Chairman: Are we to take it then that so far as you know it is not intended to legislate on this subject [i.e. the approval of the grant]?

Answer: No, Sir. I do not think I can say what the intention is. What I can say is that there is no intention to legislate to give retrospective cover to the payment of £3,850,000 to London Transport in respect of 1965.

Chairman: I am right in thinking that the payment in question only goes up to the period ending December 31st, am I not?

Answer: Yes, that is so.

Chairman: What is the intention for the next three months?

Answer: I do not think this is a question that an official could be expected to answer.

Chairman: May I put it this way? Has a decision been taken about the next three months?

Answer: Ministers have not yet announced what they are going to do about the next three months. There is a Debate in the House on Thursday, and I expect the Minister will be speaking then about London Transport, but I cannot forecast what he will say.

EXERCISE

THE COMMITTEE ON ESTIMATES

4. Answer questions (iii) and (iv) from exercise 1. in relation to this extract.

The Committee on Public Accounts

The Committee on Public Accounts was first established in 1861, and has been re-appointed annually since then. It has fifteen members, all backbenchers, appointed in accordance with the balance of parties. The Chairman is a member of the Opposition, usually with ministerial experience on the financial side: thus, the Chairman 1964–6 was a former Chief Secretary to the Treasury, and before that, a former President of the Board of Trade (Harold Wilson).

The PAC, like the Estimates Committee, is served by clerks from the staff of the Clerk to the Financial Committees (equivalent to Administrative grade civil servants) and an official from the Treasury is in attendance. In addition, the Committee has the services of the

Comptroller and Auditor-General and his staff. The Comptroller is a senior official, appointed by the Crown but, according to the ancient formulae, holding his appointment 'during good behaviour' and not 'at the pleasure' of the Crown. He can be removed only on an Address by both Houses. Thus, historically and formally, his independence is emphasised. His staff consists of well over four hundred auditors specialising in government accounts. The Comptroller and his staff audit the accounts of each Government Department, present reports to the Committee, and act as its expert advisers. So, unlike the Estimates Committee, the PAC is able to base its inquiries on the extensive preliminary work of an expert and authoritative staff.

The Committee, as a Select Committee, has the power 'to send for persons, papers and records, and to report from time to time'. Its terms of reference defined by Standing Orders are:

... for the examination of the accounts showing the appropriation of the sums granted by Parliament to meet the public expenditure, and of such other accounts laid before Parliament as the Committee may think fit. ... (Standing Order No. 79)

The PAC deals with accounts (of money already expended), not with estimates (of proposed expenditure). Formally, its inquiries are concerned with seeing that the money has been spent as appropriated (in amount and purpose); with excess votes; with the exercise by the Treasury of the power of virement, i.e. transfer of money by Defence Departments from one Vote (head or category) to another; and with the method of presentation of the national accounts.

In practice, the Committee does more than carry out this rather limited and technical audit. It is concerned more generally to see that government money has been spent economically, that is to say, that it has not been spent carelessly, that proper accounting principles and techniques have been applied, and that what has been purchased represents value for money. These inquiries into good housekeeping sometimes lead the Committee on to matters of 'policy'. As with the Estimates Committee, this is unavoidable, for the crucial part of public questions is so often a matter of 'how much, and in what way?' For example, almost everyone agrees that the Government should build roads, hospitals and schools, and the important questions are of priorities and finance; these come in their detailed form into the view of the PAC. However, like the Estimates Committee, the PAC does not work on party lines. Party controversy, and hence matters of major government responsibility, are avoided.

The proceedings of the Committee are similar to those of the Estimates Committee. The major differences are that the PAC is less hampered by shortage of time and much assisted by the work of the Comptroller and Auditor-General. The questioning, the work of the clerks, and of the Chairman—these are all similar. Again, the Committee's Reports are sent to the Treasury and the Departments. The Treasury comments on the Committee's recommendations in a formal Annual Treasury Minute. The Committee has here both a direct and immediate, and a continuing deterrent effect. Parliament debates the Reports for one or two days each session, and questions arising from the Reports may be asked. A good deal of the Committee's work is, as its founder, Mr Gladstone, said, 'dry and repulsive': but sometimes the PAC makes the headlines of the daily press by revealing some 'scandalous' waste of public money. Such cases may be of no great moment for a government spending £10,000 million annually; but the high cost and technical complexity of modern defence requirements have opened up possibilities of waste on an unprecedented scale.

....

DOCUMENT 2

A CHAIRMAN OF THE PAC ON ITS WORK

From Sir George Benson's speech in debate on the Reports of the PAC, H.C. Deb., vol. 686, 11 December 1963, cols. 457–8

The function of the Public Accounts Committee . . . is an extremely narrow one. It is concerned with the expenditure of money by Governments. Its first purpose is to see that the money is spent according to the Appropriation Bill which allocates the money for certain purposes, and its second is to see that the money is spent economically.

This is a unanimous Report. It is based on the draft report of the Chairman which we discuss and modify. We have established a tradition of unity, and a tradition that in the PAC there are no politics. We represent the House against the Government, and that is the strength of the PAC in this country.

....

EXERCISE

THE PAC COMPARED WITH THE ESTIMATES COMMITTEE

5. List the differences between the two committees.

....

DOCUMENT 3

THE WORK OF THE COMMITTEE ON PUBLIC ACCOUNTS

(a) *The development and production of guided weapons*

Second Report of the Committee, H.C. 256, 1959–60, pp. xxx–xxxi
[The need for close scrutiny and control of government expenditure is demonstrated in this extract:]

Treasury approval for the placing of the main development contract for a guided weapon for the Navy was sought in November 1948. The Ministry told the Treasury that the total cost of development might be of the order of £1–1.5 million, spread over a number of years. The Treasury approved the proposals in December 1948, and in February 1949 a contract covering development up to March 1950 was placed with a member firm of a large group. The Ministry was assured that the full resources of the group would be behind the firm responsible for the project. Development thereafter continued under contract up to March 1953, when a contract was placed covering development to completion. . . . Production contracts for the missile were eventually placed, under which delivery is planned in good time to meet the date when it is now required by the Navy; but that date is some five years later than the one originally called for, which the Ministry described as extremely optimistic. In the meantime development is being continued. The latest estimate of the direct cost of developing the missile and its control and guidance system is £40 million, while the total estimated all-up cost is £70 million, including the ship-borne radar developed by the Admiralty.

(b) *A reconstruction scheme at a teaching hospital*

From the same Report, pp. xxiii–xxiv
[A case-history to demonstrate the same point on a lesser, and more typical, scale:]

A scheme, approved by the Treasury in December 1955, at an estimated cost of some £80,000, for the reconstruction of the operating theatres on the fourth floor of a teaching hospital involved substantial alterations to a building over 75 years old. The scheme required the construction of a new concrete fourth floor, and to counter-balance this the existing heavy roof was to be replaced by a lighter structure. On 1st April, 1957 the Ministry of Health were informed by the Board of Governors that opening up the structure had revealed weaknesses not shown in old drawings. As it was thought that the stresses being put on the building were likely to get rather high the architects acting for the Board were authorised to consult structural engineers. The engineers recommended that work should be stopped, and in a report dated 7th May 1957, they stated that work already done on the new fourth floor loaded the brickwork of parts of the lower levels to such a degree as to make it unsafe by accepted standards. The additions at fourth floor level were not in themselves the only cause of overstressing, which was also due to the original design of the building. The terms of the report suggested that expert superficial examination before the work started would have caused doubt as to whether the building would bear the additional load entailed by the scheme.

After considering further reports by the engineers consulted by the architects and by an independent consulting engineer called in by the Ministry, the Board concluded that it would be more satisfactory and no more costly to erect a new building instead of proceeding with the scheme, and that the old building should be reinforced only so far as necessary to provide a limited life, the fourth floor being sealed off and abandoned. The Ministry approved this alternative scheme in principle in August 1958.

The total cost of the abortive scheme was £41,109 . . . Your Committee draw three conclusions from this unfortunate affair. First, there should be no such delay in investigating responsibility for the waste of public money. Secondly, when dealing with old buildings about which information may be lacking or misleading—and presumably there are many such in the hospital service—no alterations should be authorised until the Ministry have assured themselves that the stability of the building will not be affected. Thirdly the Minister should advise Hospital Boards that they should not continue to employ professional advisers whose competence is in question, until such time as investigations show that the professional advisers were not at fault.

....

EXERCISES

THE COMMITTEE ON PUBLIC ACCOUNTS

6.1. In the above extracts (a) and (b), is the Committee concerned with policy or administration?

6.2. Do these extracts show the value of the work of the Comptroller and Auditor-General and his staff?

....

(c) *A case history of apparent ineffectiveness*

Extracts from Reports of the Committee, H.C. 251, 1961–2, p. 15; and H.C. 31–I, 1964–5 etc., pp. 203 and xxxiv

From the 1961–2 Report

The Committee of Public Accounts of Session 1960–61 considered it essential that the Ministry of Health should obtain full information about the expenditure by drug manufacturers on advertising and on the sales promotion activities of door-to-door representatives, so that it could be judged whether extravagant advertising costs were inflating the prices paid by the

National Health Service. The Ministry furnished Your Committee with certain information provided by the Association of the British Pharmaceutical Industry about the cost of advertising and sales promotion in 1961. This showed that on sales amounting to about £67 million the cost of advertising amounted to 9.78 per cent or about £6½ million . . .

The Ministry did not think that if they or the medical profession provided doctors with information on new drugs it would cost the £6½ million spent by the industry.

From the Minutes of Evidence, 11 March 1965

A member of the Committee: [Some representatives of drug firms] keep on saying 'We are progressively reducing our expenditure on sales promotion.' Has your Ministry any evidence that that is the case?

Answer: The evidence we have is the collected evidence from major firms who are members of the A.B.P.I., and there has been some small increase . . .

From the Report for the same year

As regards sales promotion costs, the Ministry stated that they were being provided by the Association with figures for the industry as a whole, and that when negotiating prices the Ministry would examine a firm's figures in rather more detail and compare them with the general level of the industry.

....

EXERCISE

THE COMMITTEE ON PUBLIC ACCOUNTS

7. Would you say that the PAC had made any serious progress in this matter over five years?

....

(d) *The Chiswick Fly-over*

From Minutes of Evidence, 29 March 1960 (Mr Harold Wilson in the Chair, and nine members present, the Permanent Secretary and Director of Finance, Ministry of Transport being examined)

Vice-Admiral Hughes Hallett: The general impression, I think it would be fair to say, of the general public who have had to use this road during the long years when it was being constructed was one of almost unthinkable leisureliness in the whole process. To what extent do you think that was a fair impression, and to what extent do you think it was responsible for some of the increased costs?

Answer: I do not think it was responsible for the increased cost. If I may express a personal view, it appals me how long we take to do things, but I am bound to say I do not think we are quite free. I am told, week-end working and double shift working would substantially increase the cost of a project, and that is the explanation I am always given when I raise that particular point.

(e) *The excessive profit made by the Ferranti firm on the Bloodhound missile project*

This is one of the cases which hit the headlines. Due to inefficiencies of the civil servants concerned, and, it was alleged, the unethical conduct of the Ferranti firm in keeping quiet, the firm made a profit of about seventy per cent (a figure disputed by Ferranti). The Committee called Mr Sebastian de Ferranti before it, and for part of its proceedings, it operated as an inquisition into operations of private industry—this was quite relevant and proper since Government contracts were involved. But the immediate concern of the PAC was as usual with the efficiency, cost-effectiveness and cost-consciousness of the Department. An examination of this kind is illustrated in the facsimile extract on p. 226.

....

EXERCISES

THE COMMITTEE ON PUBLIC ACCOUNTS

8. How would you assess the questioning and the answering in the extracts (d) and (e)—sharp or obtuse? ill-informed or knowledgeable? aggressive or passive? effective or ineffective?

THE TWO FINANCIAL COMMITTEES

9.1. On the evidence you now have, is there a case for amalgamating the two Committees?

9.2. In these Committees, officials and Members of Parliament come face to face, with the officials submitting to questioning by the Members. What advantages and disadvantages do you see in this?

The new 'specialist' Committees

In 1967 the House established 'specialist' Committees dealing with Agriculture, Science and Technology and Education. These Committees are intended to provide for closer scrutiny of the work of some Departments by backbenchers, without being tied to estimates or accounts. It is hoped thus to make the operations of the Departments better understood at least, and hence, ideally, more efficient; and to give backbenchers some worthwhile work and a greater contact with the administration.

The Committees consist of between fourteen and twenty-one members, chosen by the Whips, with senior Government backbenchers as Chairmen. Their procedures are investigatory, like the Financial Committees; the object being to produce an agreed

I.T.B.P.—H

deal of work to do before we could define the extent of work allow for. In the event we obviously under-estimated the ability of the contractor to reduce his production costs.

I would just become really use to we only say that the total figures to us whereas the contractor with the Exchequer and Audit Department started last August. (Sir *Edmund Compion*.) I would say that the figures in my Report which were checked with him at the time as being correct, reflected the state of knowledge at the time; they also are an actual record of the figures of labour and overhead costs which, as a matter of historical fact, were provided myriad professional accountants with those figures were available. When the price models mentioned were not historically in that position. That is the validity of these figures. Also I would say this, on the new figures we have just heard. Sir Richard has stated that the amount of costs actually incurred was £6,848,000, whereas the amount actually paid to the contractor was £11,770,000; that is the difference between amounts to a difference of £4,922,000, in other words, the magnitude of that he is speaking about now—the gap between what they were paid, which is my figure of 70 per cent.—is about the same on the new sets of figures as it was on the old sets of figures.

577. Do you agree, Sir Richard?— (Sir *Richard Way*.) I agree that the percentage has not substantially changed; although in paragraph 52 the 70 per cent. is related only to the direct labour and overheads, to include the figures I have quoted do include the cost of materials and sub-contracting; but we are talking of the same order of magnitude; this is the important point.

Mr. *Thornton.*

578. Was there any failure to appreciate the significance of falling costs on a very long run of production, which no doubt some of these contracts involved?— There should not be a failure because the falling cost of production, the same particular contracts the prices for the later production models were lower than those for the first production models. The prices were on a downward curve. There should not have been

factors that should allow for. In the event we obviously under-estimated the ability of the contractor to reduce his production costs.

Mr. *Cledwyn Hughes.*

579. When you consider these contracts at the outset you start on the assumption that they are going to be fixed price contracts. There is no discussion with the contractors as to whether they should be fixed price contracts or cost-plus contracts?—I do not think in the case of a production contract of this kind that we seriously contemplate a cost plus contract, not to the extent of discussing it with the contractor. It would be assumed that we should try to fix the prices.

580. From the very beginning?—Yes.

581. And the basis of your thinking on this is not only what this Committee has said over the years but also the fact that you think that this provides a greater incentive for the contractor?—Yes.

582. And do you still adhere to that?—Yes.

583. Notwithstanding the discrepancies which have been disclosed in this case?—Yes, because when one considers discrepancies of this kind it really ceases to be a fixed price contract, does it not?—But I am convinced that this is probably a unique case, and that even if it is not absolutely unique, over the whole industry the Government gains as much financially by fixed price contracts as it loses, and I think the country gains certainly. There is a balance of advantage in terms of the efficiency of the firm concerned.

585. But it is a case which has disclosed deplorably weaknesses in the system, is it not?—Yes.

586. And you are in no position to say there are not similar cases?—I am in no position to say that I am sure that there are no similar cases.

587. Because the weaknesses which are disclosed could well apply in other contracts; this is the case, is it not?—This is the case. One asks oneself: What weaknesses are disclosed? Our failure to compare these two sets of figures is not the weakness disclosed;

contractor was able to beat the technical costs estimate by such a great amount. But since it is important to look at the position of the contractor. The contract provides for fair and reasonable prices. The contractor should quote fair and reasonable prices. The object of the technical costs officers is to act as our advisers on whether the prices the contractor quotes are fair and reasonable prices; and I think it would be a great pity if we got the impression that the primary task of the technical costs officers was to say that the prices should or to say what the prices should be. The weakness is that we have failed to apply a sufficiently rigorous check.

588. In the sense that the technical costs officers and the accountants seem to work quite apart from each other?—I do not think that this was the weakness at all, because this would not prevent other cases of this sort arising, not once in a thousand times, because normally the two figures are not comparable.

589. The technical costs officers were applying their minds to this Bloodhound weapon contract?—Yes.

590. And the accountants were applying their minds to this Bloodhound weapon contract?—No.

591. *Inter alia?*—*Inter alia.* They were applying their minds to the Ferranti Guided Weapon Product Group, not to the Bloodhound weapon contract.

592. When you say that they were not applying their minds to the Bloodhound weapon contract, you mean that when they were scrutinising out their examination, were applying their minds to the accounts relating to the Bloodhound weapon contract?—The accountants were asked to advise what the overheads should be in a particular part of the Ferranti organisation, and the accountants went to the Ferranti organisation to extract from the firm's accounts figures which would enable them to arrive at the overheads rate. It so happened that the whole of this group were employed on this Bloodhound contract, but the accountant was not specifically asked to look at the accounts relating to the Bloodhound contract; he was looking at the whole of that part of the Ferranti organisation.

593. But in fact he was immediately realised that he was dealing with the

Bloodhound weapon contract?—Yes, he must have done.

594. How soon afterwards was it that the fact that the figures were closely related was discovered in your Department?—It was not discovered at all in my Department; it was discovered by the Comptroller and Auditor General's staff.

595. How can it be in your Department that you have the accountants working on this Bloodhound contract and the technical costs officers working on this Bloodhound contract, and yet there is this complete lack of liaison between the two sets of estimates?—Of course, the accountants' figures were not estimates, but there is no satisfactory answer to your question. Obviously it should have been realised by somebody that these figures were comparable (very unusually), but it clearly was not the technical costs officers, who did their work early in the contract and who, once they had submitted their report, had done their job. I believe that the accountants should have realised that in doing their overhead calculation they had costed the contract, but they did very nearly extracted figures which they had costed the contract, but they did not.

596. This is, therefore, the obvious basic weakness in the system?—It is a failure, yes, but not the main failure, and it is a failure which now, you can and rather too late in the day, we have remedied.

597. In paragraph 53 of the Comptroller and Auditor General's Report, he says: "Investigation of the discrepancy was continuing"—is it still continuing?—No. It has taken a long time, because it has been a very complicated picture. There were 64 separate items on the two major contracts; it was not just one simple contract for Bloodhound Mark I. It is a difficult picture to assess but I think the figures which I have given to the Committee are now fairly final.

598. What steps have you now taken to make sure that this sort of thing does not happen in the future in your Department? How have you now corrected the system in order to make sure that where these accountants are working in the same field there is liaison between them?—There are two main things which we must do. I have mentioned one of them, that is to say that

A 6

Report. The formal terms of reference of the Committees are quite general—'to consider the activities of the Department and report thereon'—but the Committees have so far observed the restrictions of the other Committees in avoiding partisan proceedings. This is recognised to be a condition of their effective operation. In any case, their subject-matter—e.g. the Inspectorate of the Department of Education and Science; defence research; how to increase home food production—is not fruitful of partisan attitudes. All the same, as with the financial committees, administrative detail always leads to policy implications: the Inspectorate's influence on local education authorities, the cost of the defence programme, the system of subsidies to farmers—these are policy matters arising naturally from the subjects mentioned above.

None of the Committees has yet made any dramatic impact on the Government, but all have begun their work with skill and vigour. It has been established that the Committees may meet in public, summon even Ministers as witnesses, and may appoint specialist staff and undertake visits in pursuit of their enquiries. This is an impressive list of procedural reforms and the older Estimates Committee has gladly profited by the example.

It is early yet to assess the ultimate impact of the Committees on British Government. Plainly, some Departments will undergo a salutary scrutiny and MPs may be better informed. Over the years there may be a cumulative influence on the formulation of policy as well as on administration. However, the resistance of the executive to such incursions is strong, and it is always likely that party loyalties will deflect the Committee from the consideration of matters touching policy, or even prejudge the results of such a consideration. Although new committees have been set up, including one on Race relations and immigration, the Committee on Agriculture has been disbanded. The strength that arises from permanency may be denied this new system of committees. In any case, it is not intended that specialist Committees shall yet be established in the vital fields of defence and economics. (Examples of the work of the Committees are given on pp. 228 and 229—extracts from a Report and from Minutes of Evidence.)

2 THE SCRUTINY OF ADMINISTRATION BY QUESTION AND MOTION

Parliamentary Questions

Question Time is often regarded as one of the glories of the British Parliament: at the very least, it is an important opportunity for the

2. Economic Effects of the Common Agricultural Policy

43. The *M.A.F.F.* memorandum (See Ev. pp. 88-97, dealt fully with the general organisation of markets under the Common Agricultural Policy (C.A.P.) and with the economic effects of applying the C.A.P. as it stands to British agriculture but considerably less comprehensively with the more general financial effects of the C.A.P. This was because these matters were regarded as being within the province of other Departments and as being covered by other sections of the Government's overall assessment which have been mentioned but which, unfortunately, have not been published. However, in oral evidence (Q. 375-579, 681-799), M.A.F.F. officials amplified the views expressed in their memorandum, and some evidence was also received from other bodies on the economic effects of applying the C.A.P. to British agriculture and the consequences for British consumers.

(a) General Effects on Producers

44. The evidence of the *M.A.F.F.* was expressed in paragraph 63 of their memorandum:—

"In view of the uncertainties regarding the effects on particular com- modities any assessment of the overall effect that Community membership might have for British agriculture as a whole must inevitably be speculative. Farmers total revenue (aggregate gross income) could be expected to be **substantially greater** because of the higher level of prices, particularly for cereals. But production costs would also be affected. . . . On the assump- tions made in this paper the aggregate net income of the industry might be expected to be at about the same level as if we were outside the Com- munity." (Ev. p. 91, para. 63).

The memorandum goes on to say that the aggregate income would be distributed very differently as between commodities, types of farm and areas from the way it is now if the C.A.P. was applied as it stands to the U.K.

45. The *National Farmers' Union* (N.F.U.) did not altogether share this view. In a published booklet which they submitted as evidence to the Committee, "British Agriculture and the Common Market," they summed up their assessment of the position: "It is the Union's view that acceptance of the present E.E.C. regulations would have grave consequences for large sectors of British Agriculture. Later, in a detailed commentary on the M.A.F.F. evidence, they amplified this and stated that they expected some decline in net income (Ev. pp. 319-20). They agreed with the Ministry's evidence that the main effect on production costs would come from the increase in cereal feed prices, but considered that there were likely to be increases in other cost elements such as wages and home produced machinery. Also the N.F.U. thought that the advantages of the C.A.P. for beef producers would not be as great as the M.A.F.F. indicated, and they doubted if sheep producers would in fact gain (Q. 1076, Ev. pp. 313, 315).

The Ministry of Agriculture, Fisheries and Food in analysing the N.F.U.

measure of agreement. There were, however, certain differences of view, and the main one was, as described above, on the net income of the farming industry. (Q. 1168).

47. The assessment of *the Farmers Union of Wales* was pessimistic about the impact of the C.A.P. on Welsh Farmers and ended with the statement "that for Welsh agriculture as a whole . . . . it must be concluded "that if Britain does enter Europe it will be a retrograde step" (See Appendix 21). *The Country Landowners Association* did not express a view directly but hoped the Ministry was justified in expecting that should Britain eventually enter the E.E.C., the prosperity of her agriculture within the Community would bear at least equal comparison with that which might be antici- pated under the National Plan and the Selective Expansion Programme (Appendix 8.)

(b) General Effects on Consumers

(i) Cost of Food

48. The *M.A.F.F's* estimate was that, assuming world prices continued at their current levels and that the E.E.C's common prices remained un- changed, (a premise about which the *Country Landowners Association* expressed doubts) the increase in the cost of food to the consumer might be within the range of between 10 and 14 per cent., which was equivalent to an increase of 2½ to 3½ per cent. in the cost of living. (Ev. p. 93, Q. 786-7).

49. Comparing this estimate with that of others, the M.A.F.F. said that the *N.F.U's* calculation of a 25 shillings per week increase for a family of 4 came within their range of 10 to 14 per cent., as did the Unilever calculation of 10 per cent. The calculation of Mr. T. K. Warley, in a pamphlet published jointly by Chatham House and P.E.P., fell more or less in the middle of the M.A.F.F. price range in assessing wholesale prices (Q. 787). The N.F.U. calculation did not take account of possible changes in consumption (Q. 787-8) and to that extent the M.A.F.F. assessment was "dynamic" and the N.F.U's "static". The M.A.F.F. emphasised that there was a speculative element in any calculation of this sort (Q. 788). Details of the way in which the M.A.F.F. assessment was built up were given by the Chief Economist and other M.A.F.F. representatives. (Q. 786-787, 791-793).

50. *The N.F.U's* evidence was that they chose a "static" basis because their resources were more limited than those of the Ministry, and also because assessments of changes in patterns of consumption were necessarily speculative (Ev. p. 320). The N.F.U. considered that if "dynamic" estimates were to be used they should be accompanied by a rider that no account was taken of changes in the standard of living which, the N.F.U. felt, would be lower under the E.E.C. system since it would involve reduced consumption of meat and dairy products (Ev. p. 321).

51. *The Co-operative Union* criticised the M.A.F.F's assessment as falling short of that of the N.F.U. and Unilever both in scope and adequacy

think so. They, of course, have to consider the question in the wider context of the fuel policy, but this is inevitable.

184. Would you like to do rather more than they are allowing you to do in the nuclear field?—Concerning the second nuclear power programme, the latest White Paper published postulated a nuclear programme of 8,000 MW by 1975. We regarded this as completely rational in the then situation. Since then the situation has evolved and it could well be that in the light of recent increases in coal prices and increasing knowledge and development, some increase in that programme would be economically justified.

185. Of course, you are not free agents and we quite appreciate that it is very unlikely that you ever will be free agents. It is not necessarily in the public interest that you be absolute free agents, or freer agents, would you be ordering more nuclear plant than you are ordering?—Not today. However, before 1975, as free agents, we would wish to increase the postulated programme of 8,000 MW.

186. It has been reported—I do not know how accurate the figures are—that of new generating plants ordered in the United States at the present time between 50 per cent. and 60 per cent. are now for nuclear plants. It will be some time before we are in that position. If the Americans are doing this they must have a reason for it. Is not this causing the C.E.G.B. some thought?—Frankly, I do not recognise the figure of 60 per cent.

187. A figure of between 50 per cent. and 60 per cent. has been referred to us?—There has been a very sharp increase in the ordering of nuclear plant in the United States, in spite of the fact that their coal prices are very significantly lower than our coal prices.

188. They have plenty of natural gas?—Yes. Another factor in the equation is that their interest rates are lower than ours and this is a factor which weighs heavily in favour of the high capital cost of nuclear power stations. However, their orders have certainly increased sharply. We are certainly interested in that fact, but, on the other hand, the shape of development in the United States tends to go rather more in fits and starts than it does in this country.

189. These new nuclear stations in the United States are going to last for quite a time. This is a very solid basis for the future of their programme?—Yes, this is not in any way an inference of criticism of the United States. It is merely a fact that when the economics of a given technology are accepted as proved in the then situation, that technology is applied very rapidly indeed and I think this is what has happened. A couple of years ago in the United States there was what could perhaps loosely be described as a "breakthrough" on prices and as a direct result of that there has been a very large increase in nuclear orders in the United States.

Mr. Lubbock.

190. Am I right in assuming that by the end of 1975 system capacity will be 80,000 MW of which 12,000 MW will be nuclear?—(Mr. Booth.) You are not far off.

191. At that point in time what will be the load factor of the marginal nuclear power plants coming into commission?—(Mr. Brown.) 75 per cent.

192. Only 75 per cent?—This is the figure that is taken for the basis of all our economic assessments.

193. How much of the plant of that type will be operating at load factors of above 80 per cent?—(Mr. Booth.) The system will allow nuclear plant in operation in 1980 to operate at the highest load factor possible. There will be no marginal nuclear plant in service in 1980.

194. In looking at the amount of nuclear plant that you are going to bring into operation, you surely take into account the fact that it is economic as a base load plant and not as a plant that is only going to be used for a small proportion of the time. Therefore, you must make forward estimations of how much of the plant will be operating at more than 75 per cent., if that is the assumption you are going to make in costing your nuclear power?—Yes. The bulk of the nuclear plant which we shall have in service in 1980 will be base load plant and it will operate as continuously as its reliability will allow it to be operated.

195. What do you mean by "base load plant" and what percentage load factor do you assume when talking of base load plant?—We do not assume the load will cover it all. We simply say that at the time the plant is available for operation. We are not obliged to limit the output of any nuclear plant because of shortage of load.

196. At what point would this happen? Supposing that you doubled the second nuclear power programme from 8,000 MW to 16,000 MW, would that still represent the base load capacity?—Yes.

Mr. Atkinson.

197. It may be useful to put a general question to Dr. Rotherham at this stage. Could you explain to us your mechanism of decision-making in relation to various fuels? Perhaps you could give a general outline of the methods which you use to present evidence and to whom you present it?—(Dr. Rotherham.) It is a very long story and I should have to take the historical sequence of events to give you a full description. When I joined the Board about a year ago the situation was that we had a research organisation which mainly dealt with transmission problems. Following the establishment of the Generating Board, it was decided that we should have a more substantial organisation to meet our needs. Being a new boy, I did not really know what the needs were. I started on the assumption that if I only had scientists working in the Industry I would have to have a place for them to work in. This would have to be of the nature of a laboratory and therefore, we started building the first laboratory. Things have evolved from that point onwards. A late decision was taken that we should establish a nuclear laboratory. We took this decision on the basis that we should have some interests which were not identical with the interests of the Atomic Energy Authority and we would be wise to cultivate our own interests. Over the years we have had to decide the extent to which we could afford to provide monies for research and approximately 1 per cent. on our expenditure went on research. We then have to spend on research. We then have to calculate a balance of judgment as well as calculation as to how much of this should go into nuclear research, how much should go into coal research and how much should go into transmission or other interests. If you take the extent of the capital investment which we see in the future, we are probably spending too small a proportion on our total research, but this is because we obtain a great deal of assistance from the Atomic Energy Authority on future systems. This is one of the factors that should be taken into account. If you want a comment on the economic basis for decision-making, you will recall that at an earlier session Sir William Penney described their system of discount and cash flow which establishes the very large sum of money justified in research and development. We would agree that that is a, correct method of doing it and we do to some extent, practise the same method, but we do not postulate the outcome of our research when we make calculations.

198. Briefly, you subscribe to Sir William's evidence on that matter?—Yes.

Mr. Ginsburg.] I should like to put three points to you arising from Mr. Lubbock's point with particular reference to paragraph of his memorandum. Could we be told something about the costs of nuclear and conventional generation for 1985, if estimates have been made: could we be told something about what the bases of these calculations are; my third point is, is there now a consensus of agreement between the interests concerned? I have in mind not only the A.E.A. but the Ministry and the Coal Board. Would you say that they, by and large, accept the estimated projections and calculations?

Chairman.] We are still dealing with paragraphs 1 and 2.

Mr. Ginsburg.

199. Yes, but Mr. Lubbock's point did bring up the position in 1985? (Mr. Brown.) If the question is, "what are the views on the capital costs of the stations we shall be building in 1985?" the answer is that we have no such estimates. I think that any attempt to estimate costs as far forward as 1985 at present is basically unreal. It is, further, unnecessary. I do not believe in taking decisions in advance of the

backbench Member to probe aspects of the Government's administrative record.

Question Time takes place from Mondays to Thursdays each week
(except at the beginning of the session), immediately after Prayers
and Private Business. It begins at about 2.40 or 2.45 p.m. and goes
on until 3.30 p.m. Members 'put down' Questions, giving not less
than forty-eight hours' notice (and no more than twenty-one days').
Questions for oral answer are 'starred'. Members are limited to two
oral questions each day. Ministers reply on a rota system, with the
more important Ministers appearing frequently, the Prime Minister
twice a week. Further questions may be asked after the Minister has
given his reply. These Supplementary Questions (with supplementary
answers) take up a good deal of time. If the later Questions are not
reached, the Minister will furnish written answers. It is thus in the
interests of the House to get through the Questions. At present it
requires high skill and judgement to ensure an oral answer for your
Question.

A Parliamentary Question is much more than simply a question.
It must indeed be interrogatory in form, and not in substance a
statement or speech. It must seek information or press for action on
a matter within the responsibility of the Minister. It must not be
argumentative, or a rhetorical question, and it must not refer to a
debate in the current session or be critical of a decision of the
House. It must not be based on rumour or unauthenticated reports.
A Question must not contravene constitutional usage or parliamentary etiquette.

EXERCISE

THE ADMISSIBILITY OF PARLIAMENTARY QUESTIONS

10. Which of the following Questions would you regard as admissible under the above rules?

(a) To ask the Minister of Defence if he is aware that the Government's defence policy is both costly and wholly irrelevant.

(b) To ask the Minister of Power what plans he has for a coordinated national fuel and energy policy.

(c) To ask the Secretary for Education what action he proposes
to take to improve discipline in the Long Puddleton Secondary
Technical School.

(d) To ask the Prime Minister if he would consider resigning in
order to recover the country's international standing.

(e) To ask the Minister of Public Building and Works what plans
he has to provide that the national stockpile of 500 million bricks
will be used for building houses.

(f) To ask the Postmaster-General to give directions to the British Broadcasting Corporation to discontinue the programme known as 'That was the week that was'.

(g) To ask the Chancellor of the Exchequer if he would agree that Britain now bears a burden of taxation so high as to cripple incentive and productivity.

(h) To ask the Minister of Labour to prevail upon his colleagues to repeal the recent legislation on prices and incomes.

(i) To ask the Minister of Health whether he will make a statement on the present outbreak of influenza.

(j) To ask the Minister of Aviation whether he will publish the terms of the agreement between BOAC and Fortes on the formation of Bofort Catering Company Limited.

Answers to Parliamentary Questions are prepared in the Departments as a matter of urgency. The Minister will also be given information to assist in answering Supplementary Questions. Here the civil servant preparing the Minister's brief will assess political factors, as well as giving additional departmental information (for example, what is the questioner's usual political line? how will he attempt to score a political point in a supplementary? who else may join in?). The Minister reads the first (prepared) answer from his brief—very rarely he gets his answers in the wrong order.

The Supplementary is the Member's chief weapon against an unsatisfactory reply, or to take advantage of a supposed chink in the governmental armour. The Minister will find some support in his brief, but he will also need to know his business and to be quick in thinking on his feet as well as in repartee and judicious shots in the dark: however, if all this fails him, he can simply refuse to answer. In the last few years, Speakers have been generous in allowing Supplementaries, and sometimes 'mini-debates' have taken place. This is, however, at the expense of later Questions, and the House prudently decided in 1965 to try to cut down the time spent on Supplementaries.

The Member has another weapon in the somewhat restricted possibility of 'raising the matter on the Adjournment'—that is, in the half-hour debates that take place at 10 p.m. each evening, sometimes later, when the House adjourns. But this depends on securing a place by ballot. It is also open to a Member to move the immediate adjournment of the House under Standing Order No. 9 to 'discuss a specific and important matter that should have urgent consideration'. This depends on the Speaker's admitting the motion. Until recently Speakers have been strict in their interpretation of the stipulated conditions which formerly limited such debates to 'a definite matter of urgent public importance'. However, the House decided in 1967 to extend the scope for debate under Standing Order No. 9. Hence the new formula of the Standing Order. Moreover, the Speaker no longer gives reasons based on precedent, and since the change he has permitted debates which would have been unacceptable under the precedents (e.g., the debate of 5 December 1967 on the conditions attached to international 'stand-by' credits granted to Britain).

Most Members ask Questions occasionally, but comparatively few make regular and substantial use of Question Time. Opposition Members, as might be expected, ask more Questions than the Government side. Generally there is little difference between the parties, except for a slight tendency for Labour to ask more Questions than the Conservatives, and for the latter to oblige their own governments by asking only for written answers when the party holds office. One or two Members conduct long campaigns through Questions. Mr Gerald Nabarro, for example, mounted a marathon campaign against the anomalies of purchase tax. Some Questions, on the other hand, are inspired (i.e. arranged) by the Government.

Question Time is one of the more effective ways in which the backbencher may participate in the scrutiny and criticism of the Government. It is a moment in the parliamentary week when the rights of backbenchers are dominant. Questions do not have to be arranged 'through the usual channels' (i.e. through the Whips' office, although sometimes the Whips may intervene to plant or to block a question). Normally there is no party intervention at all, no Whips and no vote. Since there is no vote there is no decision—but then, if there were a vote, the Government would win. Here, as with Committees, the Commons must accept that the taking of divisions is not the essence of the parliamentary function.

Even without a vote, Questions make Ministers, and through them Departments, answerable in public over a wide range of their responsibilities; answerable, too, in conditions which attract publicity. For Question Time takes place conveniently for journalists; there is advance notice of topics, and the exchanges are comparatively short. Moreover, there is always the possibility of minor sensation, the revelation of maladministration, or a Minister caught out in ignorance, ineffectiveness or incompetence.

For all this, the effectiveness of Questions should not be exaggerated. Government policy is not often changed by a Question, though occasionally it may be pushed a little faster in a particular direction. A most striking example is the Guarantee to Poland, under which Britain went to war in 1939, which was first announced in answer to a Question. This is not to say that the Question provoked the policy, but only that it provided an opportunity to define and announce the policy, promulgation being an important operational aspect of the policy. More often, a Question uncovers some administrative discrepancy, inefficiency or injustice, and secures a remedy.

Governments do not rise or fall in Question Time, and Ministers rarely gain or lose in reputation. Their performance is part of a necessary relationship with the House, and most Ministers, having risen through the House, can cope satisfactorily with this modest test. For the few Ministers who have entered office without a parliamentary apprenticeship, it is perhaps the severest trial. The answers themselves usually present no problem: they are prepared by highly skilled civil servants, with all the resources of the Department at their call. Here the Private Member is at a disadvantage—as indicated by Barbara Castle in document 7 below. It is for reasons of this kind that an experienced Minister can go down to the House for Questions with a serene air and a jaunty step.

Illustrative material on Question Time is abundant and easily obtainable. The newspapers with full parliamentary reports usually include some account of Questions and answers. Copies of the daily or weekly Hansard, or of course the bound volumes, usually include Questions. The extracts in the following document give an indication of what you might look for.

....

DOCUMENT 4

SOME QUESTIONS IN THE HOUSE

(a) Sir W. Anstruther-Gray asked the Secretary of State for Scotland whether he is aware of the delay in the construction of the roundabout at Beltonford, near Dunbar; and what steps he is taking to speed up matters. (H.C. Deb., vol. 723, 31 January 1966, col. 166)

(b) Mr Turton asked the Secretary of State for Education and Science if he will give an estimate of the number of children receiving independent education in England and Wales who have parents living overseas. (H.C. Deb., vol. 723, 3 February 1966, col. 1281)

(c) Mr Higgins asked the First Secretary of State and Secretary of State for Economic Affairs what percentage increase his Department forecasts for the next six months in wages and salaries, prices and in gross national product. (H.C. Deb., vol. 723, 3 February 1966, col. 1269)

(d) Mr Dodds asked the Minister of Health what consideration has been given by his Department to the dangers which arise from the wide disparity in the size of teaspoons which are used for taking medicines, especially by children; and what advice and guidance is given to the public in this respect. (H.C. Deb., vol. 632, 12 December 1960, col. 17)

(e) Mr Awbery asked the Minister of Education in how many cases the requests by local authorities for new schools were reduced by his Department during the past three years; what was the estimated number required by the Bristol authority during each of these three years; and to what extent they were reduced each year. (H.C. Deb., vol. 631, 1 December 1960, col. 572)

(f) Mr Nabarro asked the Chancellor of the Exchequer why judo mats are subject to Purchase Tax at 25 per cent, whereas all other floor covering attracts Purchase Tax at $12\frac{1}{2}$ per cent; and, in view of the increasing number of violent crimes and the need for encouraging the art of self-defence against criminals by teaching judo, whether he will place judo mats on a $12\frac{1}{2}$ per cent rate of Purchase Tax only, along with all other floor covering. (H.C. Deb., vol. 635, 28 February 1961, col. 1356)

(g) Mr Symonds asked the Minister of Pensions and National Insurance why Mr. J. R. Thompson, of 43, George Street, Whitehaven, is not entitled to draw his pension from 15th December to 17th December 1960, having ceased to draw his unemployment benefit on 14th December 1960, and having been informed that pension was not payable until 19th December 1960. (H.C. Deb., vol. 635, 20 February 1961, col. 7)

....

EXERCISES
SOME QUESTIONS

11.1. In each case above, say whether the Question is:
(A) local or (B) national;
(A) of major importance or (B) comparatively trivial;
(A) straightforward or (B) with an 'ulterior motive' (i.e. to get at something else);
(A) based on special investigation or (B) general knowledge or local information;
(A) probably suggested by an outside body or (B) the Member's own work.

11.2. Why do you think the Member raised the case of Mr Thompson in a Question (g), when he could write to the Minister about it?

DOCUMENT 5

SOME QUESTIONS AND ANSWERS

(a) Mr Wyatt asked the Prime Minister whether he will recommend the appointment of a Royal Commission to inquire into the methods of operation and system of accountability of the nationalised industries.

The Prime Minister: No, Sir. I do not feel that a Royal Commission would be a suitable piece of machinery to help to solve this problem.

Mr Wyatt: As the Conservative Party have been running the Nationalised industries for nearly ten years, which is nearly three times as long as anyone else, will the Prime Minister now admit that if there is anything wrong with them, or anything which makes them unpopular, it is entirely the fault of the Conservative Party, and not the fault of the Labour Party? Will he start doing his duty by them, instead of using them to manipulate for party political purposes?

The Prime Minister: I have always tried to be a peacemaker, and I think that what the hon. Member has said may be a useful contribution to the difficult and delicate problem of Clause Four. (H.C. Deb., vol. 618, 23 February 1960, cols. 198–9)

(b) Mr Mapp asked the Minister without Portfolio whether he will refer to the Monopolies Commission or other suitable body for inquiry the scales of legal charges imposed by the legal profession in respect of house purchase.

The Minister without Portfolio (Sir Eric Fletcher): No, Sir. The scales of solicitors' charges for conveyancing business are prescribed by a committee set up under Section 56 of the Solicitors Act 1957, of which my noble Friend the Lord Chancellor is the chairman. My noble Friend has already initiated discussions with the Law Society with the object of reviewing the existing scales both for registered and unregistered land transactions. The Law Society has set up a sub-committee to consider these matters.

Mr Mapp: Is my hon. Friend aware that, in effect, the profession is both judge and jury in respect of these charges which are being demanded, in a monopoly sense, for what are private services? Will he say whether in these days we cannot have a disinterested and detached body to review the services, practices and charges of the profession?

Sir Eric Fletcher: I cannot accept what my hon. Friend says. The Lord Chancellor is perfectly impartial in the matter. As I have said, the matter of producing a reduction in the existing scales is under active consideration by a committee over which he is presiding.

Mr William Hamilton: What consumer interests are being consulted by the Lord Chancellor? . . .

Sir Eric Fletcher: I can assure my hon. Friend that the views and interests of consumers, as of the public generally, are being very carefully considered by my noble Friend.

Hon. Members: Where from?

Sir A. V. Harvey: Can the hon. Gentleman say why all these matters which affect the legal profession are always decided by the legal profession, even to his being at the Dispatch Box? Would it not be a good thing to have a quite impartial body and perhaps refer it to Mr Aubrey Jones of the Prices and Incomes Board?

Sir Eric Fletcher: The hon. Gentleman will be aware that this is a system which has operated for a very long time. (*Hon. Members:* Too long). I am well aware of the criticisms which have been expressed, and I can assure the hon. Gentleman that everything that has been said will be most carefully taken into consideration by my noble Friend.

Mr Mapp: On a point of order, Mr Speaker, in view of the unsatisfactory nature of the reply, I beg to give notice that I will raise the matter on the Adjournment. (H.C. Deb., vol. 724, 9 February 1966, cols. 400–2)

(c) Mr Alison asked the First Secretary of State and Secretary of State for Economic Affairs when the National Board for Prices and Incomes will complete its consideration of the proposal announced by brewers to increase the price of beer, which he has referred to the Board.

Mr George Brown: The Board has been asked to report by the end of March.

Mr Alison: Is the First Secretary of State aware that the Carlisle State Brewery put up the price of beer by a penny a pint as recently as last November without intervention by the Prices and Incomes Board? Will he cause the Carlisle State Brewery to reduce the price of beer by 1d. a pint pending the findings of the Board?

Mr Brown: All my visits to the Carlisle State Brewery experiment— despite the fact that geographically, although not electorally, my constituency includes Burton, lead me to say that I think that it is a very good experiment indeed.

Hon. Members: Answer the question.

Mr Alison: In view of the thoroughly unsatisfactory nature of the reply, I beg to give notice that I shall raise the matter on the Adjournment at the earliest possible moment. (H.C. Deb., vol. 723, 3 February 1966, cols. 1274–5)

....

EXERCISE

ANSWERING QUESTIONS

12. These answers illustrate the three main ways of avoiding a straight answer to a question:

(i) stonewalling;
(ii) evasion;
(iii) a party gibe.

Which method applies to which question?

DOCUMENT 6

QUESTION TIME OUT OF HAND

[Occasionally an exchange at Question Time blows up into a minor debate with the possibility of a political victory for the Opposition. This might be good for the Opposition's morale and bad for the Minister's reputation. Here is an example, in which at least the Members had fun. This is only about one sixth of the whole episode: Mr Gammans had thirteen questions altogether to answer. Mr Speaker intervened six times.]

Extract from H.C. Deb., vol. 532, 3 November 1954, cols. 369–71

Mr Hobson asked the Assistant Postmaster-General whether he will make alterations to the appropriate section of the Television Act regarding the formation of programme companies to ensure control by the Postmaster-General.

Mr Gammans: No, Sir.

Mr Hobson: Does not the Assistant Postmaster-General think that those people who have already been allocated programmes are not independent in any way, and that they are already powerful opinion-forming organisations? What step is he considering to rectify that, and to guarantee their independence?

Mr Gammans: The hon. Gentleman is, I think, by implication making a charge of political partiality against a statutory body set up by this House, and we are not prepared to alter the Act to effect what the hon. Gentleman wants.

Hon. Members: Resign.

Mr H. Morrison: Of course we are making a charge of political partiality (*Hon. Members:* Withdraw). The charge is against the Government and it may be the case that it is against the Television Authority. Can the hon. Gentleman say why these first contracts should be let to the proprietors of the Conservative newspapers? Is not that in line with the whole policy of the Government in public relations; that they are using public relations, and now commercial television, to further the political interests of their party?

Mr Gammans: I take it from what the right hon. Gentleman has said that he does make a charge of political partiality against the Independent Television Authority and he has suggested by implication that undue pressure has been put upon it by Her Majesty's Government. I deny any suggestions of that sort.

Mr Elliot: Is it not characteristic of hon. Gentlemen opposite, and the right hon. Gentleman in particular, that when they are dissatisfied with the verdict they try to bawl out the referee?

Mr Ness Edwards: To come back to the Question on the Order Paper, is not the hon. Gentleman aware that a financial tie-up has already occurred between two programme contractors? Is not that in contradiction of the undertaking given by the hon. Gentleman at that Dispatch Box, and is he going to do anything about it?

Hon. Members: Resign.

Mr Gammans: The hon. Member for Keighley (Mr Hobson) is asking whether I will make alterations in the Television Act to ensure control by the Postmaster-General. This matter was debated at great length by this House during consideration of the Television Bill, both on Second Reading and in the Committee Stage. The answer to the question is, 'No'.

Mr Ness Edwards: You have betrayed this House.

Hon. Members: Withdraw.

Mr Speaker: What did the right hon. Gentleman say? I did not hear: there was so much noise.

Mr Edwards: I am quite prepared to repeat what I said. The hon. Gentleman has betrayed his promise to this House.

Mr Speaker: Order. I do not think that the words were strictly un-Parliamentary, but I would ask the House to refrain from language of heat so far as possible.

....

DOCUMENT 7
QUESTION TIME INEFFECTIVE?

From Mrs Barbara Castle's speech, H.C. Deb., vol. 620, 31 March 1960, cols. 1538–9

Are we not setting our sights too low? Day in, day out we come here at Question Time and fire Questions at Ministers, at considerable public cost. I know because I run up as big a bill doing this as anybody in the House. A considerable amount of that money is wasted, because the Minister has resources for getting under the net which we have not got for following him under it. This is about the truth of it. It is all very well to have a parade about our great Question Hour. It may satisfy our egos, but are we doing the job of harrying the Executive, as it is our public duty to do? Are we able to track down an evasive Minister?

There are 24 main administrative Departments in Whitehall which we have to pursue at Question Time and in speeches. Every one of them has a huge library and huge research staff working overtime to give the Minister the wherewithal to pull the wool over our eyes. If any Minister wants to pull the wool over our eyes—and what Minister does not?—it is as easy for him to do it as taking pennies out of a blind man's hat.

The Board of Trade has a staff of 50 in its library and half a million books, periodicals, copies of Acts, and the rest, whilst we have in the Library four research workers—two statisticians and two non-statistical research workers—working night and day to dig up the little bits of information that we have apologetically to bother them about. But how can we do our job of scrutinising the Executive, with its massed phalanx of the Government's armoury, against the pathetic provisions that we have in this House?

....

EXERCISE

A MINISTER AND QUESTION-TIME

13. If you were a Minister, would you look forward to Question
Time
    with apprehension;
    with cautious pessimism;
    as a routine parliamentary chore of no great consequence;
    with cautious optimism;
    joyfully?
and why?

Adjournment Debates

Apart from infrequent adjournments under Standing Order No. 9,
there is regular provision for short Adjournment Debates. These
take place from Monday to Thursday each evening, either at the
end of business for the day, or at 10 p.m., interrupting other business. ('Exempted business', which includes some financial business
and any other business the Government asks to be exempted, is
not interrupted, so the Adjournment Debate takes place only when
the 'exempted business' is finished.) In either case the debate lasts
for half-an-hour, and the question of adjournment acts of course as
a procedural peg for more important subjects. Private Members,
selected by ballot, use the time for raising matters very similar to the
subjects of many Questions—ranging from local grievances to
neglected aspects of higher policy. The Member makes a short
speech and after a short debate a responsible (usually junior)
Minister replies. Here is a list of subjects raised 'on the adjournment' in part of a recent session.

DOCUMENT 8

SUBJECTS RAISED IN ADJOURNMENT DEBATES

1965: date and time	Subject
22 Nov. 11.45 p.m.	Slum clearance, Manchester
23 Nov. 2.45 a.m.	Staffordshire Medical Services Committee (child's death)
24 Nov. 1.31 a.m.	Dock and harbours, the Hartlepools
25 Nov. 10.47 p.m.	Timothy Evans, re-interment
29 Nov. 12.44 a.m.	Road communications, Hull
30 Nov. 11.30 p.m.	West Suffolk, town expansion programme

DOCUMENT 8 CONTINUED

1965: date and time	Subject
1 Dec. 11.31 p.m.	Railways, East Anglia
2 Dec. 1.55 a.m.	Prison, Nether Alderley
6 Dec. 11.34 p.m.	Fish vessel; building subsidies
7 Dec. 6.23 p.m.	War Disablement Pension (Mr Girdlestone)
and 6.52 p.m.	
to 10.29 p.m.	Rhodesia, oil embargo
8 Dec. 10.15 p.m.	Royal Infirmary, Glasgow
9 Dec. 11.00 p.m.	West Durham, regional planning and employment

The date given is that on which the sitting began.

EXERCISE

ADJOURNMENT DEBATES

14. On the above evidence, what kind of matter is most often raised in Adjournment Debates?

3 SELECTION AND TRAINING

An important function of Parliament is to be a great and prolonged training and selection school for future teams of Ministers (see chapter 3). Most Cabinet Ministers at the time of their appointment have had long experience of Parliament—fourteen years, on average, between 1916 and 1958, but a little less recently. Few will be chosen for preferment who have not put up at least a moderately good performance in Parliament: this is a minimum qualification. Some earn promotion by good parliamentary performances alone.

This means much more than making effective contributions to debate, and to the Committee work of the House. Each party has its own subject groups or committees, and these give a chance for Opposition members to work constructively in the shaping of party policy, in the drafting of policy statements and in the use of committees to secure agreement by discussion and compromise. Each party has, too, a dozen posts available as Whips, which will test a man's capacity to keep in touch with his colleagues, and keep his colleagues in line with the party leaders. Mr Heath, the Leader of the Conservative Party since 1965, spent over two years as Chief Whip before taking a high departmental office, but this is an unusual route to high office.

A government has at its disposal a range of posts in which promising talent may be tried out. The lowest rung, but one which many tread, is the office of Parliamentary Private Secretary (PPS), not to be confused with the junior ministerial post of Parliamentary Secretary. The PPS holds an unpaid appointment from a senior Minister: his job is to be the Minister's 'devil' (like a 'printer's devil'), keeping in touch with Members, listening and reporting back, conveying the Minister's line to the farthest corners of the tea-room. A PPS usually has a modest room in the Minister's Department, and sees at least the correspondence between his Minister and other Members. But, in exchange for this foothold in Whitehall, he gives up his right to speak in the House on his Department's business, and had best act circumspectly in other matters. It is a curious half-way job, and not well designed to encourage the exercise of talent. It also has the larger disadvantage that it adds to the number of Members who are restrained from criticism by their membership, however marginal, of the Government.

....

DOCUMENT 9

PARTICIPATION IN DEBATE

The following analysis of a Foreign Affairs Debate of 30 May 1960 shows yet one more application of that general rule of politics—as of life—that to him that hath shall be given. In major debates, front bench spokesmen of both sides take up a share of time which is certainly disproportionate to their numbers, possibly disproportionate to their importance and to the value of their speeches—and frustrating to the aspiring backbencher waiting for a chance to make his speech and his mark.

There were eighteen interjections recorded in $6\frac{1}{2}$ hours of debate—a little under three per hour.

There is an interesting difference between Government and Opposition speakers. The Government speakers are distinctly either front bench or back bench: there is no middle area of doubt. No one with a job on the Government side intervenes outside his own recognised field, and almost all the Members with a claim of some sort have a job of some kind. The Opposition speakers, on the other hand, are more difficult to classify. Some may be members of the Parliamentary Committee of the party (elected by the PLP), some are specially designated by the Leader as spokesmen on particular topics. They are mostly prominent men with some claim to office if their party were in power—front bench material, though not all of them actually got office in 1964. As part of their entry in the competition for office, they tend to speak frequently and over a wide field. Thus, on one

Front bench

Conservative	(min.)	Labour	(min.)	Other	(min.)
PM opens	40	Leader of Opp.	40		
Mr Nigel Birch	19	Mr Noel Baker	24		
				Mr J. Grimond	15
Foreign Secretary (Mr Selwyn Lloyd)	26	Mr D. Healey	27		
	85		91		15

Total: 191 min.

Back bench[1]

Conservative	(min.)	Labour[1]	(min.)
Col Tufton Beamish	25	Mr C. Mayhew	25
Mr P. Rawlinson	12	Mr J. Jones	15
Mr C. Fletcher-Cooke	13	Mr V. Yates	22
Viscount Lambton	8		
Mr G. Campbell	22	Mr A. Wedgwood Benn	23
Mr E. Gardner	6	Mr Stewart	24
	86		109

Total: 195 min.

[1] Ascription to back bench doubtful in some cases.

side there are ranks of able men silenced by their office, while on the other
there are ranks of able men stimulated into speech by the quest for office.

....

4 THE BACKBENCH MEMBER OF PARLIAMENT
AS CASE-WORKER

A good deal of evidence has now been set out to show what the
backbench Member of Parliament actually does. To complete the
picture, it is necessary to add one more area of his activity: he is a
case-worker on behalf of his constituents. They write to him, or see
him when he is in the constituency, to ask for help mainly on matters
in which the individual is involved with the Government—questions
of pensions or housing or military service, for example. The Member
may take up these grievances by an approach to the Minister,
privately or through a party committee, or openly in the House by
Question or Motion on the Adjournment. The publicity involved in
the open method is not always best for the settlement of a grievance.
It is unlikely that a problem which has to be solved in public will be
solved by abnormal principles and methods. This is unusual in
private, too, and would indeed be unfair. The Member's private
approach to the Minister, by correspondence, or more rarely in
person, secures a speedy answer at a higher level of the hierarchy
than a letter sent directly by a constituent to a Ministry: but the
answer is likely to be the same for both correspondents.

Dealing with the grievances of constituents takes up a good deal
of time for MPs and civil servants; more perhaps than its results
in practice justify. But it is important to keep open a channel of
protest which occasionally—and always potentially—is very effective
indeed.

....

DOCUMENT 10

THE MEMBER'S CORRESPONDENCE

(a) From a letter by Commander R. T. Bower, M.P., to the *Times*, 24 July
1957

The Member's voluminous correspondence can be dealt with during the
'long hours in the House from Monday to Friday in order to keep up his
voting record'. Half of it will require no more than a printed acknowledgement to the sender, whose letter is then forwarded to the appropriate Ministry with a printed slip requesting attention: after about a fortnight the

Minister's reply will arrive and in nine cases out of ten will be satisfactory and can be sent on to the complainant with a short covering letter. About a quarter goes into the wastepaper basket, leaving only a quarter needing serious personal attention.

[The quotations within the extract were taken by Commander Bower from a letter to the *Times* complaining of the difficulties of an MP's life. Commander Bower did not agree. He ends this paragraph of his letter: 'A secretary is for an MP a luxury, *not* a necessity.'

Compare chapter 5, documents 3 and 12. But it was later suggested that Commander Bower had known Parliament 'in the palmy days before 1945', and that Parliament has changed a good deal since then.]

(b) From a letter by Mr T. L. Iremonger, M.P., to the *Observer*, 28 May 1961 [Mr Iremonger set out the following order of priority and rules in dealing with correspondence:]

1. Personal letters from individual constituents or organisations in the constituency on particular problems or grievances—top priority and immediate action with the responsible Minister, including, if necessary, a personal visit to the constituent and/or the Minister.

2. Personal letters from constituents etc. on general political topics— immediate acknowledgement with invitation to come and discuss with me. (Discussion by correspondence is worse than useless: personal meetings are infinitely rewarding and educative) . . .

....

EXERCISE

THE FUNCTIONS OF THE BACKBENCH
MEMBER OF PARLIAMENT

15.1. Go back over chapters 5–7, and list all the activities in which a backbench MP might engage.

15.2. Which, in your view, are the most important of these functions?

5 THE ROLE OF THE BACKBENCHER: PARTNER OR REBEL?

Backbench rebellions

For much of the time, the backbench MP appears to be silent, docile and obedient. Is the backbencher really a 'dumb chum', mere lobby-fodder, or is he a 'pillar of democracy'? The answer is that, whatever his contribution to democracy, it is basically as a prop that he functions, and props cannot of their nature be free and independent. But they need not be dumb.

The absolute restrictions on a backbencher's actions show best on the very few occasions when he tries to rebel. Then the apparatus of party discipline, always in the background, is brought into operation. (See chapter 5, section 4, p. 173, on the Whips.)

Backbench rebellions do not happen often. Usually modification, adjustment and compromise go on behind the scenes. Dissident backbenchers may go no further than putting down an 'Early Day Motion'. In effect this means simply collecting signatures in support of a stated viewpoint. Open rebellion on the floor of the House and in the voting lobbies is a sign of the failure of this peaceful persuasion. The front bench naturally dislikes such rebellions, for they take up the time of already overburdened Ministers, weaken the morale of the party (causing strong resentments among the loyalists), and, above all, gravely damage the confidence of the electorate in the party. Disunity counts as a sign of weakness to an electorate favouring strong government.

But rebellion is perhaps an inappropriate word to use for occasional abstention or cross-voting by a few Members on minor issues. There were six of this kind involving Conservative Members in the session 1955–6: this is neither very frequent nor very damaging to the Government. But the disagreements over the British position in Suez from 1954 to 1956 were more dangerous, for they involved perhaps three-dozen Members, who were organised as a group (the Suez Group) and very persistent. The issue was, moreover, an important one: the dissidents' views could be regarded as in line with traditional Conservative principle, and the Prime Minister, Eden, was losing popularity. But the party rallied under a new Leader after the Suez crisis of 1956. Disaffection since then has been more sporadic, less organised. For example, some Conservative Members refused to follow the Whip over the deportation of Chief Enahoro in 1963, and again over the abolition of the Schedule A tax on property. Over the proposal to abolish Resale Price Maintenance (1963–4) there was widespread and vociferous opposition, which might have amounted to a rebellion if the Government had not made concessions in advance of the crucial votes in the Commons.

The Labour Party has suffered rather more in these years from major rebellions. There were thirteen between 1945 and 1955, with an average of nearly fifty participants. Nine of these occurred between 1946 and 1949, when the Labour Party was in power with a large majority. Mostly these were over foreign and defence policy—Russia, Palestine, conscription. Again, in the early 1960s, the party was acutely divided over nuclear armaments, both in and out of

Parliament. Over seventy MPs abstained in a vote in December 1960. Even with the party in power after the 1964 election with an overall majority of three, two Members threatened defiance over steel nationalisation. And within a few months of the major election victory of March 1966, some two-dozen Members refused to support the Government's economic policies. The Labour Party seems in fact to differ from the Conservative Party in the unsteadiness of its support for the leadership—according to your viewpoint, more volatile, less stable, and weak in loyalty, or more lively, less subservient, and strong in intelligence and principle.

The ultimate control on the backbencher is the fear that his own party will lose (or fail to gain) office. It may be expected therefore (in the 1960s as much as in the 1940s) that a government which appears to be comfortably in power will suffer from occasional rebellions.

The Labour rebellions in the early 1950s and 1960s arose from profound differences on questions of foreign policy—German rearmament and nuclear weapons. These rebellions divided front as well as back bench, and were thus transformed into struggles for the party leadership—with first Bevan and Attlee, then Gaitskell and Wilson as contenders. A scrutiny of recent political history shows that struggles of this kind are not due simply to the peculiar temperament of one party, or one political leader: they are frequent and important in both parties.

Rebellion from the narrower base of the back bench does not often seem to be successful. Indeed, the most notable backbench rebellion in recent history, that of May 1940 leading to the fall of the Chamberlain Government, suggests almost that the essential condition for successful backbench rebellion is frontbench support. Certainly, if the Cabinet were divided, strong backbench support for the policies of one section of the Cabinet would substantially strengthen the influence of that section.

The occasion illustrated here, the Suez Crisis of November–December 1956, emphasises the success of party discipline and loyalty in confining most rebellions to the embryo stage of discontent.

....

DOCUMENT 11

CONSERVATIVE DISSIDENTS DURING
THE SUEZ CRISIS, 1956

[The actual extent of opposition among Conservative backbenchers to the decision of Sir Anthony Eden's Government to intervene in the Suez Canal area is not known. It seems likely there was intense open disagreement among a comparatively few Members and almost none on the front bench. In consequence, unlike 1940, few of the dissidents expressed their disagreements openly, and nothing like a major revolt occurred. The Government emerged from this crisis intact, except for the loss of their leader and two Ministers. Nigel Nicolson's account shows the numerical weakness and lack of organisation of the rebels, also the intensity of feeling and the crisis atmosphere, which is an essential background for such defiance of authority. (See also chapter 9, p. 317, for 'the Bournemouth affair'.]

(a) From Nigel Nicolson, *People and Parliament*, Weidenfeld and Nicolson, 1958, pp. 133–4

I only knew for certain of a few other Conservatives in Parliament who felt in varying degrees as I did, although I have since heard of several more. We were still unorganised. Few of us knew of Anthony Nutting's or Sir Edward Boyle's impending resignations from the Government until they occurred, and neither of them attended our haphazard meetings. We met not more than twice as a group between the ultimatum and the cease-fire. We had never combined before and never combined afterwards. We let the Whips know of our attitude, but it remained in doubt until the last minute how many of us would actually abstain in the crucial vote of confidence on November 8th. In the event eight of us did so. They were Sir Robert Boothby, Anthony Nutting, Sir Edward Boyle, J. J. Astor, Sir Frank Medlicott, Colonel Banks, William Yates, and myself. From none of us was the whip withdrawn. But within a month, one had resigned his seat in Parliament, one had become an independent Member, one had previously announced his intention not to stand again, two had been ostracised by their constituency associations, and two were in deep disgrace with theirs. Only Sir Robert Boothby emerged relatively unscathed.

When the division was called, I went to the Library and read the *Illustrated London News*. Another Member, on his way to vote, paused to put his hand on the back of my chair. 'It looks to me', he said, 'as if you are doing something which may be either very right or very wrong. But whichever it is, you need never feel ashamed of having done it.' I looked up to see who it was, but by that time he had hurried out between Pugin's brass-encrusted doors. I do not know if it was a Conservative or Labour Member. It could have been either.

[The Government was also attacked on the other wing of the Conservative Party, by the Suez Group, for the opposite fault of not being aggressive enough in its dealings with President Nasser. In December 1956, some members of the group voted against the Government decision to withdraw from the Suez Canal area. Here is one comment on this revolt.]

(b) From the *Times*, 8 December 1956

Mr Patrick Maitland, M.P., said the Suez Group 'did pretty well to have 15 of our number daring to show themselves'. This was nearly three times what the Government Chief Whip had forecast and represented a good performance in view of the 'extraordinary and unexampled pressures, some of them altogether underhand, used to force the Tories into line'. These were pressures through 'the Westminster machine'.

[*The Times* itself commented in a leading article that members of the Suez Group 'were and are political lightweights'. The comment raises again the question whether all backbenchers, however able, however wise, and however skilled in politics are condemned by their position to be 'political lightweights'.]

....

DOCUMENT 12

OTHER RECENT EXAMPLES OF BACKBENCH REBELLION

Rebellion, in the context of British party politics, may be defined as a movement involving opposition on the floor of the House, including voting against the leadership, or abstention. Here are some recent examples of rebellion:

(a) *The Conservative Party*

Rent Bill, 1957–8. The Government's removal of rented houses from the protection of the Rent Acts led to widespread threats of eviction, and the Government subsequently amended its proposals. Backbench pressure was asserted mainly through private and party channels. The dissidents had the support of the press, and this, together with the imminence of a general election, probably helped sway the Government.

The Profumo case, 1963. There were twenty-seven Conservative abstentions in the debate on Macmillan's handling of the Profumo case. (Profumo, while Secretary for War in Macmillan's Government, had associated improperly with a woman who was a clear security risk, and he had in the first place denied the association.)

Resale Price Maintenance Bill, 1963–4. The Bill to abolish RPM was promoted by Mr Heath, backed by the new Prime Minister, Sir Alec Douglas-Home. The Bill met with intense opposition from within the Conservative Party. Almost fifty Members abstained or voted against the Government on the Second Reading. The Bill was amended by the Government in a way which seemed at the time to represent a considerable concession to the rebels. The Bill would probably not have been pressed but for Mr Heath's insistence and Sir Alec's need to establish himself as (in the cant word then gaining favour) a 'moderniser'.

(b) *The Labour Party*

The 'East of Suez' policy and the Vietnam war, 1966. Continuous hostility within the party to the Government's military commitments east of Suez and its failure to dissociate from the American war in Vietnam led to a stormy meeting of the PLP, and to the speech by Mr Wilson quoted in chapter 5, p. 172. Thereafter there were thirty-two abstentions in the House.

Prices and incomes policy, July 1966. The imposition of a wages freeze and other deflationary measures led to twenty-seven abstentions on the floor.

Defence policy, March 1967. Usually the Whips are made aware of impending rebellions in the voting lobbies, and numbers are kept within bounds by mutual agreement of the rebel leaders and the Whips. This rebellion, however, was not negotiated in the usual way: the party was momentarily out of control. In the event, the numbers abstaining were little higher than usual, but Mr Wilson reacted with his notorious 'dog-licence' speech, delivered to a meeting of the PLP, 2 March 1967: 'Every dog is entitled to at least one bite. But if the dog goes on biting continuously then it might well be that the question of the removal of the licence would have to be considered.'

....

EXERCISES

THE EFFECTIVENESS OF BACKBENCH REBELLION

16.1. In what conditions would you think backbench rebellions are likely to be successful?

16.2. What is the Cabinet's trump card against a rebellion?

The partnership of front and back bench

Discussion of the relations of front and back bench in terms of rebellions may well neglect the substantial and continuing influence of partnership in those relations. 'Rebellion' is not here the rising up of servant against master, of sheep against shepherd; rather it indicates the breakdown of a normal tie of partnership. Now the partnership is clearly an unequal one, the partners being senior and junior, leaders and led. All the same, the term is justified because there usually exist shared attitudes and common objectives. The relationship is one of communication and persuasion, reasonableness and goodwill. Rebellion signifies the breaking away from normal, discreet, private persuasion.

There are, indeed, many cases of governments making concessions to backbenchers before the angry state of rebellion has been reached. By their nature, most cases of persuasions privately made and agreed to do not come to light, but they seem to be fairly numerous. In other cases, backbenchers press hard and openly on the government, but still do not take their campaign as far as the division lobbies of

Parliament. Some examples of recent campaigns falling short of actual rebellion are set out in the following document.

....

DOCUMENT 13

BACKBENCH CAMPAIGNS SHORT OF REBELLION

(a) *The Conservative Party*

The Shops Bill, 1956–7. This Bill would have restricted the opening hours of shops, and was opposed by many Conservatives on the grounds that it limited competition and handicapped the small trader. The Bill had been introduced in the Lords, but was eventually dropped largely due to the pressure from backbenchers.

Nuclear weapons, 1960–3. Conservative Members were alarmed by the failure of the American missile, Skybolt, in 1960. Their pressure on the Minister of Defence amounted at times to high-level negotiation between equally powerful sides. They got their way—Macmillan was able to secure from President Kennedy the Nassau agreement providing for British Polaris missiles. Britain's position as an independent nuclear power was saved—by the President of the USA and the chairman of the Conservative backbenchers' Defence Committee.

(b) *The Labour Party*

Race Relations. The Race Relations Bill of 1964 was strengthened through backbench pressure, mainly but not wholly from the Government side. (The Government was by no means sure of itself in this matter.) Again, the deportation proposals of the White Paper of 1965 were dropped after discreet but effective pressure from the back bench. On the other hand, the Government whipped the Commonwealth Immigration Act of 1968 through all its stages in both Houses in less than a week. So much for the backbencher!

The nationalisation of iron and steel. This was proposed by the Labour Government in 1964 and finally carried through in 1967. Mainly this has been a concession to backbench opinion, though with the Cabinet itself somewhat divided.

....

Thus the Private Member of Parliament is not really in a position of servitude tempered by occasional rebellion. Rather, he has scope for continuous steady but slight influence and an occasional opportunity for digging in his heels with some hope of success. It is perhaps going too far to argue, as one recent commentator does, that parliamentary government involves a continuous striking of bargains between a Cabinet and its backbenchers. The position is probably more accurately indicated in the comment of a former Labour Chief Whip, Herbert Bowden (now Lord Aylestone):

> If the Chief Whip were to say to the Cabinet: if you do this [i.e. introduce this clause], there is likely to be a great deal of opposition from our own backbenchers, I am pretty sure that that influence of the backbenchers would be felt in the Cabinet and they would think twice about introducing a clause in legislation which would be likely to cause trouble for them on the floor of the House. (From a BBC transcript of 20 June 1963, quoted in R. Butt, *The Power of Parliament*, Constable, 1967, p. 185)

This is to concede to the backbencher a modest, but not wholly insignificant, influence. Most of the time the Cabinet will take into account the likely reactions of the backbenchers. If this be so, it follows too that the Cabinet is prepared to override its backbenchers all of the time, and sometimes without even 'taking them into account'.

GUIDE TO EXERCISES

The Select Financial Committees

1. (i) The question illustrates the difficulty of distinguishing between these three. Mainly it is a matter of financial administration, but it might be said that there is a general policy question involved in the principle of subsidising without detailed control.

1. (ii) This is a matter of judgement, but Mr Thornton presses his point well, despite an attempt by the Chairman (not given in the extract) to shield the officials somewhat. On party bias, perhaps a Labour MP is more likely to challenge subsidies going largely to assist private business.

1. (iii) Again a matter of judgement, and not a great deal of evidence to go on. The obvious and understandable tendency is to put the Department and its procedures in the best possible light—but in a rather general way, not usually amounting to vagueness or evasion. So the answer is perhaps 'efficiently but guardedly', but you need not agree.

1. (iv) An expert staff might have secured information on this point before the Committee hearing, so that the Committee could proceed on the basis of ascertained fact. This could prevent the element of evasiveness involved when the official admits to not knowing the answer in detail.

2. (i) Possibly the same kind of answer as for question 1.1. But these words do have different, if overlapping, meanings, and the question ought not to be evaded! So, insisting on an answer of some sort, the whole might be regarded as a matter of finance and administration.

2. (ii) This seems to be a searching and effective question: no party bias. (Mr Millan is in fact a Labour Member.)

2. (iii) It is difficult to appear open and efficient when faced with a damaging question. In the circumstances, the official's answer may be regarded as efficient and guarded.

3.1. The Committee commented on the overall increase in civil servants, which perhaps qualifies as policy. The matter of forecasting is purely administrative.

3.2. The Treasury carefully pass over the reference to overall increase in numbers, thus confining themselves to administration.

4. (i) Guardedly. They seem a little uneasy, and are quick to point out the limits of their own responsibility.

4. (ii) As long as the payment has been discovered, expert assistance is not needed. A lay committee challenging the administrators to justify themselves meets the situation well.

5. The PAC:

is smaller and does not divide into sub-committees;

has a leading member of the Opposition as chairman;

works on accounts of past expenditure, not estimates;

has the professional services of the Comptroller and his staff.

6.1. The defence contracts involve such a large expenditure of money that the matter enters the area of policy. The teaching hospital case may be regarded as financial administration.

6.2. It is possible that the rapid increase in the cost of guided missiles could be picked up by a vigilant member of the Committee. But the hospital matter is only likely to emerge from the professional scrutiny of the Comptroller's staff.

7. On the evidence here, the answer must be 'no'. It may be, of course, that the Committee had in fact succeeded in impressing their point on the Ministry, and that the Ministry's subsequent efforts had been of little avail. (The pharmaceutical industry is not after all a government-controlled industry, though the Government is its chief customer, and on a massive scale.)

8. In extract (e) (the Ferranti case), the questioning is very sharp. Mr Cledwyn Hughes pursues his quarry relentlessly, securing at Q.596 an admission of weakness. The responses of Sir Richard Way are however commendably brief and direct.

In extract (d) both question and answer are at a different level, more relaxed, and in the manner of laymen engaged in a random discussion. An impression of the general public is answered with a personal impression and a rather vague 'I am told . . .'

9.1. The two Financial Committees do rather similar work, despite the formal differences. The distinction between estimates and past accounts is not very important. The matters investigated by both Committees are equally important because they are part of the continuing operation of government; and the kind of investigation, in method and in purpose, is basically similar. The major difference arises from the work of the Comptroller and Auditor-General for the PAC. Hence, some reformers suggest the amalgamation of the two committees into one Committee on Expenditure.

The case rests in the first place on these considerations of tidy and logical organisation: if the functions are similar, the organisation should be uniform. But the case is linked with proposals for further reforms, and in particular with a division of the work of financial scrutiny by Departments. Thus, each Department or group of Departments would have attached to it a permanent sub-committee of the Expenditure Committee, charged with examining the financial implications of the Department's work, both in past accounts and future estimates.

Fundamental reform of this kind rests on the assumption that the existing arrangements are unsatisfactory. The illustrative documents provide some evidence to support this view. Thus, officials seem able to fend off or turn aside criticisms, or admit faults but make light of them. Recommendations may be ignored. The scrutiny is discontinuous. The Estimates Committee lacks expert advice. These weaknesses, it is suggested, might be diminished at least in a reorganised and amalgamated Expenditure Committee. Amalgamation itself would concentrate the resources of the House, the professional assistants, and the Departments themselves. It would also facilitate the simultaneous scrutiny of past expenditure and future estimates.

9.2. The advantage is that the Member of Parliament, coming into contact with civil servants, learns a good deal about the processes of administration and the way in which large decisions in Parliament have to be converted into administrative and financial procedures. The civil servant, for his part, has to face lay criticism which is not bound or blinded by the administrator's assumptions (for example that a policy is to be judged by its administrative implications).

One disadvantage is that the Members may become too engrossed in the pursuit of administrative detail to see the larger issues. Again, busy officials may be diverted from essential administrative tasks to meet the ill-informed questions of laymen.

Parliamentary Questions

10. The following would not be admitted:

(a) argumentative, not seeking information or pressing for action except in a very indirect manner; (d) on similar grounds; also (g) and (h).

The following would be admitted, and were actually asked:

(b), (e), (i) and (j).

The following would probably be admitted, but unless they were very serious or embarrassing, the Minister would probably claim that such matters were either beyond his responsibility, or beyond the area of his normal intervention:

(c) and (f).

11.1. (a) A B A B B

(b) B A B (to demonstrate one good argument for boarding schools) B B?

(c) B A B (to demonstrate the fallibility of economic forecasts and the National Plan) B B.

(d) B B A B B?

(e) A A A B A?

(f) B B B (to demonstrate the absurdity of a tax system including such anomalies.)

A B (It may look the kind of question an outside body would suggest, but in fact Mr Nabarro made the investigation of purchase tax anomalies something of a personal specialism).

(g) A B A B B

Note: It would be interesting to go on to draw conclusions from this analysis, but these few questions are not a sufficient sample. If you want to make such an analysis, take not less than two weeks of Questions.

11.2. Probably he had written to the Minister about it, and received an unsatisfactory or dilatory reply. A Question normally secures immediate attention at a higher level among officials, and of course the attention of the Minister himself. If the case has no special features, this procedure will not secure a different answer, only a quicker one. So Members would tend not to put down straightforward or routine cases as Questions.

12. (a) (iii)
    (b) (i)
    (c) (ii)

13. Perhaps a personal question which only you can answer. Clearly much would depend on the Minister's career-position and status, and the state of his Department's business. An experienced Minister, on top of his job and enjoying parliamentary combat, would perhaps admit to 'joyfully'. The text implies that no Minister worthy of his post would be pessimistic, still less apprehensive, about Questions.

14. Local and constituency matters.

15.1. Good cases can be made, on the evidence of the last three chapters, for:
    the Member in the Select Committees;
    the Member representing his constituency, its problems and grievances;
    the Member in the parliamentary party, helping to shape major policy.

Other cases are not ruled out, but it is perhaps best not to think of the MP as characteristically on his feet in the Chamber.

15.2. An answer to the question about important functions depends on one's view of the place of Parliament in the British system of government. See assessments below.

16.1. When the Cabinet is itself divided; when the rebellion is widespread and coherent (discipline is difficult to apply against large numbers, respect is weakened); when there is widespread support for the rebellion in the country, especially in the press and within the party (in this case the leadership will try to avoid the unfavourable publicity arising from a public 'row'); when, to be fair, the rebels seem to have a good case.

16.2. Making the issue one of confidence, i.e. if we are defeated on this, we resign. The most rebellious backbenchers of the majority side rarely want to bring their leaders down.

(a) *The purpose of Parliament*

(i) The following analysis by Walter Bagehot, writing in the 1860s, is acute. The first point is basically right according to one view of the British constitution, but out of date in detail. The third and fourth points are not easily distinguished; the fifth point is perhaps more important than Bagehot allows. (From W. Bagehot, *The British Constitution* (*1867*), Fontana, 1963, pp. 150-3.):

The House of Commons is an electoral chamber; it is the assembly which chooses our president ... our House of Commons is a real choosing body; it elects the people it likes. And it dismisses whom it likes too. No matter that a few months since it was chosen to support Lord Aberdeen or Lord Palmerston; upon a sudden occasion it ousts the statesmen to whom it at first adhered, and selects an opposite statesman whom it at first rejected. Doubtless in such cases there is a tacit reference to probable public opinion; but certainly also there is much free will in the judgement of the Commons. The House only goes where it thinks in the end the nation will follow; but it takes its chance of the nation following or not following; it assumes the initiative, and acts upon its discretion or caprice.

... because the House of Commons has the power of dismissal in addition to the power of election, its relations to the Premier are incessant. They guide him and he leads them. He is to them what they are to the nation. He only goes where he believes they will go after him. But he has to take the lead; he must choose his direction and begin the journey. ... (a Minister should say firmly), 'Parliament has maintained ME, and that was its greatest duty; Parliament has carried on what, in the language of traditional respect, we call the Queen's Government; it has maintained what wisely or unwisely it deemed the best executive of the English nation.'

The second function of the House of Commons is what I may call an expressive function. It is its office to express the mind of the English people on all matters which come before it ...

The third function of Parliament is what I may call ... the teaching function. A great and open council of considerable men cannot be placed in the middle of a society without altering that society. It ought to alter it for the better. It ought to teach the nation what it does not know ...

Fourthly, the House of Commons has what may be called an informing function—a function which though in its present form quite modern is singularly analogous to a mediaeval function. In old times one office of the House of Commons was to inform the sovereign what was wrong. It laid before the Crown the grievances and complaints of particular interests. Since the publication of the Parliamentary debates a corresponding office of Parliament is to lay these same grievances, these same complaints, before the nation, which is the present sovereign. The nation needs it quite as much as the king ever needed it.

Lastly, there is the function of legislation, of which of course it would be preposterous to deny the great importance, and which I only deny to be as important as the executive management of the whole state, or the political education given by Parliament to the whole nation. There are, I allow, seasons when legislation is more important than either of these.

(ii) Mr Wedgwood-Benn, in the following extract (H.C. Deb., vol. 620, 31 March 1960, cols. 1553–4) emphasises the importance of another function which is perhaps implied in Bagehot's first and second points, but without clarity or force.

At this time, we in this country need a strong Government and a strong Parliament, and I have never believed that the two are incompatible. I think that the House of Commons is greatly mistaken if it thinks that it can only be effective by trying to become the Government of the day through Committees. The House of Commons does its job well when it directs a barrage of informed criticism and questioning against the Government of the day. This has nothing to do with the relations between the Executive and the Legislature. What we are discussing is whether it is possible to make the Legislature more efficient . . .

(iii) Mr R. H. S. Crossman, in the following extract (H.C. Deb., vol. 738, 14 December 1966, cols. 479–80), gives a modern point of view. Mr Crossman was speaking as Leader of the House. His historical preface is perhaps a little overstated: the Cabinet has never really been 'merely the executive committee of the Commons'. But in other respects the analysis is an acute one:

Let me describe the central problem as I see it. The physical conditions under which we work and many of our main procedures are survivals from a period when parties were weak, when the making and unmaking of Ministries still rested with the House of Commons, not with an electorate based on universal suffrage, and when the Cabinet was merely the executive committee of the Commons. Procedurally, we still behave as though we were a sovereign body which really shared with the Government in the initiation of legislation, which exercised a real control not only of finance, but of the administration of the Departments. But, today, not only the House of Lords has been shorn of most of its authority. The House of Commons, too, has surrendered most of its effective powers to the Executive and has become in the main the passive forum in which the struggle is fought between the modern usurpers of parliamentary power, the great political machines.

In this transformation of the parliamentary scene the House of Commons has largely lost the three functions for which its procedures were evolved and to which they are relevant, the making of Ministries, initiation of legislation shared with the Cabinet, and the watchdog control of finance and administration.

The question the reformer has to ask himself is whether we should look backwards in an attempt to restore the pristine powers of this House to which our procedures are relevant or whether we should accept our present limited functions largely as they are and adapt our procedures to them. I know that there are some of my hon. Friends who dream of a time when the secret negotiations of the Government with outside interests which precede all modern legislation and the secret decisions in the Committee Room upstairs which largely determine party attitudes will be rendered insignificant because the House of Commons will once again become sovereign and make decisions for itself. I think they are crying for the moon.

It is no good trying to reform ourselves by harking back to ancient days. An effective reform must be an adaptation of obsolete procedures to modern conditions and to the functions we should fulfil in a modern highly industrialised community. Today, for example, it must be the electorate, not the Commons, who normally make and unmake Governments. It must be the Cabinet that runs the Executive and initiates and controls legislation, and it must be the party machines that manage most of our business, through the usual channels, as well as organising what was once a congeries of independent backbenchers into two disciplined political armies. Since this is the structure of modern political power, the task of the reformer is to adapt our institutions and procedures to make them efficient.

I believe that there are three questions by which the working of the House of Commons can be tested, both today and for future change: First, is the legislative process designed to enable policies to be translated into law at the speed required by the tempo of modern industrial change? Secondly, can our timetable, so long as the Finance Bill dominates our procedure, leave room for debating the great issues and especially for the topical debates on matters of current controversy which provide the main political education of a democracy? Thirdly, while accepting that legislation and administration must be firmly in the hands of the Government, does the House of Commons provide a continuous and detailed check on the work of the Executive and an effective defence of the individual against bureaucratic injustice and incompetence? It is by these three tests, I suggest, that we should try out both our existing procedures and the proposals for modifying them put forward by the various schools of Parliamentary reform.

(b) *The function of the backbench Member*

The following paper attempts to argue the case from what might be called a Morrisonian or (for those who know their *Candide*) a Panglossian point of view—everything is for the best in the best of possible worlds. This view is, of course, open to the charge of undue complacency, and there is plenty of evidence in the last three chapters to support an opposite case. Indeed, a professor of politics recently gone into Parliament has concluded that his previous lectures, which had stressed the weakness of the backbencher's position, had been far too moderate in their criticisms. After a few months as a Member, he took the 'dumb chum' view of the Private Member. So if you can refute the argument set out below, you will be in good company, and you may even be right!

(i) The function of Parliament is to sustain or break a Government. In practice, the majority party sustains the Government while the minority party fulfils the function of Opposition, that is, harrying the Government and offering an alternative policy. The job of the backbench Member is to support his party in all normal circumstances. This is a perfectly proper and useful job. It cannot adequately be done without the exercise of intelligence and judgement, for the discipline of a parliamentary party is not that of the barrack square. The Member is much more than mere 'lobby-fodder'.

Indeed, the marked decrease of political tension when Parliament is in recess is good evidence that the encounter between Government and Parliament is neither a sham nor a wholly unequal fight.

(ii) As a member of a parliamentary party, the backbench Member has many opportunities in committees and in meetings with party leaders to influence policy. This is especially true in the Opposition party, where there can obviously be more freedom of action for backbenchers. Moreover, parties in opposition prepare their policies for the time when they may be in power. A Member who can change the policy of the Opposition is changing the policy of a future government.

(iii) On the floor of the House, the influence of the backbencher is limited. In major debates, leading members of the front benches take up a large share of the time; and in any case parliamentary time is arranged by the Government to secure the transaction of its own business. There are occasions, however, for example, at Question Time, on Adjournment Motions, and on Private Members' Bills, when the backbench Member can speak. Question Time in particular is a valuable oppportunity for harassing a Minister, raising points of administrative detail (often very telling), and pursuing the grievances of constituents. Often of course, his speeches will not be reported as prominently as those of a front bench spokesman, but an adroit backbencher will sometimes hit the headlines.

(iv) In Committees, the backbencher does valuable if usually undramatic work. Standing Committees review Bills in detail, and often amend them extensively. It is not possible at this stage to challenge a Bill in principle, for this battle has been fought out on the floor of the House, but it is possible for both Government and Opposition backbenchers to secure amendments. Members who are experts on particular subjects are especially influential here.

In the major Select Committees (Estimates, Public Accounts, Nationalised Industries, and the new 'Specialist' Committees), the backbencher has an opportunity to examine and criticise the administrative aspects of government activity. Such Committees have the power to call for papers and to examine witnesses. Their power is limited, but a diligent and perceptive Member can here make close contact with the processes of government, and sometimes change them.

(v) The Member acts as a two-way channel of communication with his constituents. He is elected as a member of a political party, and it cannot now be maintained that his prime job is to represent the views of his constituents. Nevertheless, he cannot, and in practice does not, neglect their interests. He takes up their grievances and keeps in touch with their views and feelings. His job within the limits of the party system is to represent them at Westminster and to represent Westminster in his constituency. Perhaps this job is not done very well at present, but, if so, this is the fault of the public as much as of the Members of Parliament.

(vi) Finally, the backbench Member is a potential frontbencher. The House of Commons is both a training school and a continuing selection process for Ministers and leaders. Compared with the hit-or-miss methods of the USA, it works very well.

(vii) What ought the functions of the backbencher to be? It would seem from the above considerations that the backbencher is by no means useless and powerless. Moreover, given that the system is based on a powerful executive (Prime Minister and Cabinet) depending on disciplined party support, it is not easy to see how he could be given more power.

(c) *The uses of the Opposition*

Much of what has been said about the functions of Parliament and the role of the backbencher applies with most force to the majority party in the House. The majority party chooses and sustains a government, does its legislative work, defends it in the House and in the country, and may hope for the material and political rewards of power. Altogether, the work of the most humble backbencher on the Government side may be useful and satisfying, even if occasionally dull.

For the Opposition, the situation is different and even the frontbencher may feel at times that his daily work is largely without reward or purpose. This is not the case, however: opposition has its uses too.

(i) Criticism by the Opposition has some influence on government, especially in the same conditions in which rebellions have a hope of success, and when party principle or tradition or emotion are not at stake. Recent examples include legislation on immigration and housing.

(ii) Criticism by the Opposition makes an important contribution to the long slow process of public political education. In the Government's view, such criticism may seem both unrealistic and excessively partisan, but Opposition criticism has a special value just because it is lay criticism, divorced from the dampening, clogging effects of actual government responsibility.

(iii) The Opposition's part in public political education is also an appeal to the electorate. The Opposition has up to five years to show that it is a desirable alternative government. It may regard itself as involved in a continuous election campaign. This, it must be admitted, is a rather optimistic view of the influence of the Opposition on the electorate. It is extremely difficult to interest the electorate in general political issues, and equally difficult to look like a party capable of governing without actually being the Government.

(iv) An occasional period in opposition is essential if a party is to rethink its policies. In opposition it has the time, the incentive, and a necessary absence of immediate responsibilities. In this process backbench members of the party can contribute with the leadership on more equal terms than usual.

(v) Finally, Opposition Members of Parliament can participate in the undramatic work of the legislature, the parliamentary party and the constituency. In any large organisation, the number of persons able to take big decisions is necessarily small: they also serve who only sit and wait—for the next election.

(d) *The case for an extended Committee system*

There are three main schools of thought about Parliament:

(i) that it is doing pretty well and impious hands must not be laid on the ancient structure;

(ii) that it could be made much more effective by a development of the present system of Committees;

(iii) that it could be made much more effective by other reforms, especially of procedure on the Floor of the House.

The first view is not here examined. It seems clear from the evidence given above that Parliament is not a perfect political institution. It may be legitimate to conclude that it cannot be reformed, but not that it does not need reform. The second and third views are discussed briefly in this and the following sections.

The case for reform through the development of the system of Committees is as follows:

Parliament should accept that the electorate normally gives a party power to govern for four or five years, roughly according to a set of policies and a general approach. The function of Parliament must lie therefore much more in the detailed scrutiny of the Government's activities, not in futile attempts to change major policy. Such detailed scrutiny requires time and information which could best be secured in Committee, not on the Floor of the House. At present the Select Committees work in this way with modest success, and these should therefore be developed and made more effective.

A strengthened Committee system need not and perhaps could not be debarred from the discussion of policy at the preliminary stage of formulation and at the final stage of implementation. The Government's responsibility for the actual decisions would be preserved. But the range of information and argument on policy might be much improved, the Minister's position in relation to his Civil Service advisers might well be enhanced, and the advisers themselves might learn a good deal.

Specific proposals for making the Select Committees more effective are: first, that they should be larger, working more in specialised sub-committees; second, that they should have expert staff to advise and brief them; third, that their terms of reference should be widened to include the 'assumptions' and the 'implementation' of policy. Alternatively or in addition, it might be desirable to establish separate specialist Committees dealing with particular areas of the Government's operation, but not tied even formally to estimates or accounts.

Clearly, there is in proposals of this kind a readiness to extend the boundaries of a Committee's scrutiny as far at least as the margins of policy—the initiation and preparation of legislation, the formulation and administration of policies—thus challenging the normal division of functions between executive and legislature.

Recently, some specialist Committees have actually been established—Select Committees on Agriculture and on Science and Technology in the Session 1966–7, and on Education in 1967–8. The new Committees have scored a notable success by insisting on hearing evidence in public and summoning Ministers as witnesses, procedures now to be followed some of the time by the older Financial Committees. But the Government's attitude is still very cautious. The subject areas chosen (and those, like defence, still omitted) indicate a wariness about submitting major policy areas to the scrutiny of a Committee. The Select Committee on Agriculture soon ran into difficulties with the executive. The Foreign Office refused to show the Committee correspondence about strengthening the staff of the Agricultural Attaché to the EEC in Brussels, and was reluctant and dilatory in permitting the Committee to visit Brussels. This Committee was later wound up but others have since been established.

The executive has indeed good reason to believe that the extension of the Committee system through the existing Committees or by the establishment of new specialist Committees will raise delicate issues of demarcation. Many backbenchers would share this disquiet, though perhaps for different reasons.

The case against an extension of the Committees is that such a system is contrary to the British pattern of government, in which the function of Parliament is to support or criticise a government, but not itself to govern. The development of Committees derogates from the importance of Parliament as a centre of political confrontation, the 'Grand National Debate'. Committees—on major policy areas at least—are moreover likely to meet in secret, even if some of their hearings were open and most of their proceedings were published. Such Committees might plunge headlong into the sphere of policy, in which at present Committees tread only warily. This would immediately silence the circumspect, change the atmosphere and proceedings into a set party-battle, and raise difficult problems of relationships with the House as a whole. Members, it is argued, would be drawn away from the Chamber itself, would lose some of their effectiveness by becoming specialists, might even end up 'in the Minister's pocket'.

An important assumption of this kind of argument is that the Member is a layman, and that lay criticism is a perfectly proper and valid form of criticism. An argument can be right in general, even though wrong in detail—because being wrong in detail may mean only difficult in application. The danger in a specialist Committee, it is suggested, is that the lay Member might be overawed by the practical complexities and detailed difficulties of the problem, and capitulate too readily to conservative administrators, distrustful of change. In the end, the validity of arguments of this kind can only be assessed by experiment, and one safe conclusion in these matters is that the House should be more willing to try out new methods.

However, it may appear that the opponents of an extended Committee system are themselves unduly distrustful of change. Much depends on the interpretation of 'extension'. Horizontal extension to new subject areas is acceptable where vertical extension—towards policy—would not be accepted.

(e) *Other proposed reforms*

Most other proposed reforms start from the assumption that the Floor of the House is the arena that matters. Thus, Mr Michael Foot, from the left wing of the Labour Party but with the support of the Conservative Chief Whip, tried unsuccessfully to prevent the Select Committee on Procedure (1964–5) from reporting in favour of an extended Committee system. (Report of the Select Committee on Procedure, H.C. 303, 1964–5, p. xiv):

... the proliferation of parliamentary committees is not a cure but part of the disease ... a main purpose of parliamentary reform must be to restore the authority of the House of Commons chamber itself. For this purpose, measures should be taken to instil spontaneity and flexibility into its proceedings, and to enable debates to be held over a much wider range and at much shorter notice than is possible under present arthritic procedures ... the purpose of parliamentary reform should be to take more issues into politics, into Parliament, and above all, into Parliament's principal place of debate ...

Here is the voice of one of Parliament's most able backbenchers, who will have no truck with Committees and who sees his role as something quite apart from, set against, Ministers and the executive.

There are several reforms, mainly procedural, which might help to make the Chamber itself more effective. The removal of legislative debate into Committee after the Second Reading would save much time now expended in vain and repetitive demonstration that the Opposition do not approve of the Government's Bills. The continued broad interpretation of Standing Order No. 9 will allow many more immediate debates on urgent topics. Financial procedure could well be simplified, with much more provision for debating the Government's financial plans as a whole, the relation of proposed expenditure to resources, and the balance of various classes of expenditure (e.g., defence and social services). However, it is by no means certain that sufficient time can be made available without detracting seriously from the present activities of Parliament. Already there is a good deal of late-night sitting and some all-night sessions. No one pretends that this is an efficient or even a sensible way of doing business, but it is symptomatic of the acute shortage of time. (An experiment with morning sittings in the session 1966–7 proved unsuccessful and has not been continued.) Such considerations might drive reformers of the Foot kind back to a reluctant acceptance of further delegation to Committees.

Some other possible reforms are discussed elsewhere: the provision of professional facilities for Members (chapter 5); the televising of the Commons (chapter 6); electoral reform (chapter 12); the reconstitution of the Second Chamber (chapter 8). The possibility of devolving functions to regional parliaments raises questions about economic planning and local government which cannot be dealt with in this book. (See note in Part V, p.470.)

RECAPITULATION EXERCISES

THE FINANCIAL COMMITTEES

1. *True or False?* (Mark T or F)

(a) The Estimates Committee has thirty-six members and works in sub-committees.

(b) The Chairman of the Estimates Committee is the Chancellor of the Exchequer; and of the PAC, a Government backbencher.

(c) The Estimates Committee has no assistance at all from officials.

(d) Ministers do not attend meetings of the Estimates Committee either as members or as witnesses.

(e) The Estimates Committee's terms of reference do not include the examination of policy.

(f) When the Reports of the Committees are submitted to the relevant Departments, they are compelled to accept the Committees' recommendations.

(g) The Committee of Public Accounts bases its work on the Reports of the Comptroller and Auditor-General.

(h) Because the PAC is concerned only with past expenditure, its work is largely without influence.

(i) The Reports of these Committees are not considered in debate in the House of Commons.

(j) Questions are sometimes based on Reports of the Committees.

2. How does the work of the Committees have any effect on the Departments?

3. What is the case briefly for regarding the PAC as the more effective of the two Committees?

PARLIAMENTARY QUESTIONS

4. *True or False?* (mark T or F)

(a) Question Time takes place each day when Parliament is in session.

(b) Ministers choose whether to answer a Question orally or not.

(c) The Prime Minister never answers Questions.

(d) Members may ask Supplementary Questions arising from the original Question, but Ministers are not bound to reply.

(e) Answers to Questions are prepared by civil servants in the Minister's Department.

(f) Half-hour Adjournment Motions are often used to raise matters similar to those raised at Question Time.

5. If a Member is not satisfied by a reply, what procedures are open to him?

1. (a) T (b) F (c) F—clerks
   (d) T (e) T (f) F (g) T
   (h) F—It is concerned with operations which might be repeated
   and procedures which are continuous.
   (i) F (j) T

2. Through the appearance of officials to give evidence; the circulation of the Report in the Department; the pressure of the Treasury; the pressure of Parliament, which debates the Reports, exerted through the Minister; and general publicity.

3. It has more time; it has the help of the Comptroller and Auditor-General and his staff; it is dealing with finished business. (This does not add up to an overwhelming case; in particular the Estimates Committee has the advantage of being much larger and working in partially specialised sub-committees.)

4. (a) F (b) F (c) F (d) T (e) T (f) T

5. Asking a Supplementary Question, raising the matter 'on the Adjournment', or under Standing Order No. 9.

[8]
The House of Lords

1 INTRODUCTION

The House of Lords is the one part of the British political system which has been openly, deliberately and fundamentally changed in recent times. This gives it a special position in a State without a written constitution: there are statutes and official statements which fix its place in the constitution. So much the worse for the House of Lords—its place is, measured by power, a low one.

The traditional argument about the House of Lords is to do with the role of an hereditary peerage in a modern Parliament. On one hand, the Lords have been denounced as the last ditch of the Tory Party, from which, bloody but unbowed, the Tories would fight off the advancing hordes of Socialists, contriving to govern the country with or without a majority in the Commons. In this view the House was 'Mr Balfour's Poodle'—the great war cry of 1910, which still colours much discussion of the Lords' House. In a contrary view, the House provides a living demonstration of historical continuity, symbolising the nation, ordered society, service (and other rather doubtful attributes of Britain's past).

However, these are the outlooks of hardened campaigners on this dog-eared theme. The most common attitude towards the House of Lords is certainly one of indifference. Indeed, the sound and fury of battle over the privileges of a hereditary peerage and of the Conservative Party have obscured the serious political problem of the nature of a Second Chamber in a parliamentary system. In serious political discussion there is scope for disagreement on both the composition and the powers of such a Chamber. These are questions which cannot be settled outside the context of Parliament as a whole.

2 THE COMPOSITION AND POWERS OF THE HOUSE OF LORDS

Composition

There are about 900 hereditary peers and almost 150 life peers. Most of the 900 peers are of the first or second generation—there are very few 'fourteenth earls'—and about 100 who were themselves ennobled, and may be said to have earned their peerages. About half such peerages are awarded to politicians, and another quarter or so to distinguished businessmen. This does not mean that the Lords are representative of British society. Most of these ennobled peers are drawn from the upper strata of British society, so that although the House of Lords is not aristocratic in the ancient feudal sense, it is 'upper-class' in the sense in which Conservative Members of Parliament are 'upper-class' (see chapter 5, p. 162). But the ennobling of businessmen has declined since 1945, and it is now more usual to grant only life peerages.

An Act of 1963 permitted the renunciation of peerages, and the Lords have lost a few distinguished politicians in this way (including notably Mr Wedgwood-Benn, Mr Quintin Hogg and Sir Alec Douglas-Home). The Act is associated with two rather comic incidents. Parliament refused to allow Mr Wedgwood-Benn (Lord Stansgate) to take up the seat in the Commons to which he had been re-elected with a large majority, thus showing itself absurdly respectful of precedent. The Conservative Party had officially opposed Wedgwood-Benn, and only reluctantly promoted the Act permitting renunciation. But the Act enabled the Party to solve its leadership problem in the autumn of 1963, when it chose the Earl of Home as Leader. Lord Home quickly transformed himself into Sir Alec Douglas-Home and won a seat in the Commons. This was a once-for-all vanishing trick, since normally peers must renounce their peerages within a short period of their accession.

Life peerages were introduced by the Act of 1958. There are now almost 150 men and women life peers: the women are an important innovation in the House. Life peerages, like hereditary peerages, have been conferred on persons distinguished in public life, but distinction has been interpreted widely to include academics, writers, nonconformist ministers; many were Labour sympathisers and a few were women. Moreover, a life peerage has been regarded not simply as a reward for past service, but as an appointment to a legislative Chamber. The Lords now have a distinguished academic in Lord Annan, a distinguished journalist in Lord Francis Williams, a distinguished Labour Party woman in Baroness Gaitskell, a distinguished chairman of a public corporation in Lord Robens and a distinguished former Civil Servant in Lord Strang. These are the type of new person introduced into the Lords following the Life Peerages Act, but they are by no means representative of life peers, most of whom are in fact former politicians, who would earlier have been offered hereditary peerages.

EXERCISE

LIFE PEERAGES

1. Draw up a list of ten people whom you would recommend for a life peerage. Be bold!—but justify your choice.

Apart from the hereditary and life peers, the House includes two Archbishops and twenty-four Bishops of the Church of England and sixteen representatives of the Scottish peers (i.e. peerages dating from before the Union of 1707). The presence of the 'Lords Spiritual' is defensible insofar as an established State Church is defensible (not very far really in a country which has more active adherents of religion outside the Church of England than in it).

In addition there are the Law Lords, nine judges appointed to carry out the work of the Lords as a supreme Court of Appeal. They may be assisted in this by other peers with high legal experience. This function of the Lords is of course an indispensable part of the judicial system, but does not affect political arguments about the House of Lords. The judicial function is in practice a distinct activity and could be easily separated from the existing or a reformed Second Chamber.

....

DOCUMENT I

THE COMPOSITION OF A SECOND CHAMBER

From a letter from Viscount Bryce to the Prime Minister (Lloyd George), reporting the conclusions of the Conference on the Reform of the Second Chamber, Cmd. 9038, 1918, pp. 4–5

ELEMENTS THAT OUGHT TO FIND A PLACE IN THE SECOND CHAMBER
(1) Persons of experience in various forms of public work, . . .
(2) Persons who, while likely to serve efficiently in a Second Chamber, may not have the physical vigour needed to bear the increasing strain which candidacy for a seat in the House of Commons, and service in it, involve. . . .
(3) A certain proportion of persons who are not extreme partizans, but of a cast of mind which enables them to judge political questions with calmness and comparative freedom from prejudice or bias . . .

POSITION WHICH THE SECOND CHAMBER OUGHT TO HOLD . . .
All precautions that could be taken ought to be taken to secure that in a Reformed Second Chamber no one set of political opinions should be likely

to have a marked and permanent predominance and that the Chamber should be so composed as not to incur the charge of habitually acting under the influence of party motives . . .

....

COMPOSITION OF THE HOUSE OF LORDS

2. How far does the existing House (1968) conform to Bryce's criteria?

Few peers of any kind are very active in the House. The average daily attendance is in the 190s (April 1967)—rarely more than two-hundred. This figure is much higher than formerly: in the 1950s it was about a hundred. The difference has come about through the payment of an attendance fee of $4\frac{1}{2}$ guineas. The two-hundred is made up of a core of sixty or so regularly active politicians and a varying selection of peers drawn from about half the total membership. (In the session 1965-6, 177 peers attended fifty per cent of the sittings.) Most of the remainder attend rarely or never. (About three-hundred have not responded to the Royal Writ of Summons and may be formally deemed on 'leave of absence'.) Almost all the active politicians (active by speaking) are ennobled or life peers, but hereditary peers are prominent as attenders and voters. The famous 'backwoodsmen', flooding in from the shires to resist red revolution, have not in fact shown up since the (adverse) vote on abolishing the death penalty in 1956. The highest vote in recent years was the Rhodesia sanctions vote of June 1968 in which 377 peers took part. The Law Lords and the Lords Spiritual are not usually active except on matters within their special competence or concern. Thus, the working core of the House of Lords is a rather different body from that which parades in ermine at great State occasions like a Coronation.

Powers

The House of Lords lost its power in financial matters at the end of the seventeenth century, but it retained full power in legislation. Indeed, the centre of gravity of British political life lay in the Lords until the nineteenth century. Even the Cabinets continued to be drawn partly from the Lords, and Britain had a peer as Prime Minister as late as 1902. But by then the centre of gravity lay without doubt in the Commons, which could claim to represent the 'will of the people'. Liberal Governments in the years 1885 to 1914 met with effective opposition from the Lords, and were unable to carry major items of their legislative programme—on education and licensing for example. Finally the Lords overreached themselves and rejected the Budget of 1909 which contained formidable land tax proposals. There followed a long and bitter constitutional crisis which has made contempt for the House of Lords a fundamental tenet of radicalism ever since.

....

DOCUMENT 2

THE RADICAL DENUNCIATION OF THE LORDS, 1909

(a) *Lloyd George* (Chancellor of the Exchequer): The House of Lords has long ceased to be the watch-dog of the Constitution. It has become Mr Balfour's poodle. It barks for him; it fetches and carries for him; it bites anybody that he sets it on to.

[Balfour had said in 1906: 'Whether in power or in opposition, the great Unionist party will always control the destinies of this great Empire.']

(b) *Winston Churchill* (President of the Board of Trade in the Liberal Government), [described the Second Chamber as]: one-sided, hereditary, unpurged, unrepresentative, irresponsible, absentee . . . with all its anomalies, all its absurdities, and all its personal bias . . .

(c) *Churchill again*, in a speech at Birmingham in January 1909: [The Conservative Party in opposition] possesses a weapon, an instrument, a tool, a utensil—call it what you will—with which it can harass, vex, impede, affront, humiliate, and finally destroy the most serious labours of the other. When it is realised that the Party which possesses this prodigious and unfair advantage is in the main the Party of the rich against the poor, of the upper classes and their dependants against the masses, of the lucky, the wealthy, the happy, and the strong, against the left-out and the shut-out millions of the weak and the poor, you will see how serious the constitutional situation has become . . .

(d) *Lloyd George*: A fully-equipped duke costs as much to keep up as two Dreadnoughts.

(e) *Lloyd George*, in his famous Limehouse speech, July 1909: Who is going to rule the country? The King and the Peers? Or, the King and the People?

....

After two elections and the threat of creating three-hundred new peers, the Lords finally consented to the destruction of their powers.

By the Parliament Act, 1911, the power of the Lords over money Bills (narrowly defined and to be certified by the Speaker) was annulled; their power over all other Bills was reduced effectively to a power to delay a Bill for two years from the date of the Second Reading. Formally, the Lords reject the Bill, but the rejection is overridden after two years. The Lords also have the power to reject a Statutory Order. This is an anomaly: the growth of importance of such orders was not foreseen. In June 1968 the Lords rejected an Order providing for the intensification of sanctions against Rhodesia—a major aspect of the Government's foreign policy. However, this vote was of little practical significance, since the Order does not lapse immediately and may be maintained by re-submission with a single verbal change.

The Lords have rejected a few Bills, under the Parliament Act procedure, and in some cases delay itself has brought them modest victories. Thus, the Home Rule Bill of 1913 was delayed and finally suspended on the outbreak of war, and it was possible later on to salvage Ulster from Irish independence. The Labour Government's Education Bill was rejected in 1931 and the Government fell before it could become law. In 1949 another Parliament Act, restricting the Lords' delaying power to one year, was itself delayed, and this delay helped to frustrate the Government's nationalisation of the Iron and Steel Industry. During the Labour Parliament of 1945–50 the Lords acted with some restraint, but they made difficulties for the Government over some of the nationalisation Bills. On the Transport Bill, for example, forty-two separate amendments were moved in the Lords, and it took the Commons an all-night sitting to reject them. The Lords then carried three further amendments, one of which was accepted by the Government.

The influence of the Lords in this period cannot be measured solely by reference to their rejection (and hence delay) of Bills. The possibility of rejection or amendment has led to consultation and some negotiation, which has conceded to the Lords a modest influence. But this has been mainly with Conservative Governments who were predisposed to accord such influence. With the Labour Government of 1964, the Lords were in a weaker position, for they lived under a threat of fundamental reform. If they frustrated the Government even once, it might be their last serious political act. Indeed, even without such provocation, the Government in 1967 announced its intention of revising the powers and the composition of the House. The Rhodesia vote of June 1968 sharpened the reformers' appetites.

The place of the Lords in the political system depends now not on ultimate power in legislation but on the usefulness of their contribution to the political processes of central government. To be useful is to have influence—and that would be an honourable end for a House of Lords.

3 THE ORGANISATION AND FUNCTIONS OF THE HOUSE OF LORDS

Organisation

The Lords' Chamber is similar to that of the Commons—rectangular, small (it seats about 250), and imposing. Unlike the Commons, the Lords do not elect their own Speaker. The presiding officer is the Lord Chancellor, a member of the Cabinet (hence chosen by the Prime Minister), and the head of the legal system. The Lord Chancellor is the Government's chief spokesman in the Lords, so he is a playing captain as well as umpire. He sits upon the 'Woolsack', symbolic of Britain's medieval wealth and modern taste for tradition, however uncomfortable.

The Lord Chancellor's duties as umpire are not in practice onerous, since the House has few formal restrictions in its procedure. There is no distinction between Government and Private Members' time and no precedence for the Government. The Lord Chancellor has no battles to fight either as presiding officer or as Government spokesman and manager, for there is no pressure on time or tempers. Speeches are fewer and shorter than in the Commons, so everyone who wishes to speak can do so—and usually arranges a place in a timetable. Voting takes place, but its results are ignored because of the composition of the House. Governments do not feel the need to triumph in the Lords: Conservative Governments will win in any case, and Labour Governments lose. The tension and occasional disorder of the Commons are therefore almost unknown.

The House of Lords is nevertheless organised on party lines. Of those who can be accounted for, there are roughly 350 Conservatives, 100 Labour, 40 Liberal and about 100 Independents (figures given by the Lord Chancellor in 1967). In addition the Law Lords and the Lords Spiritual count as Independents. Each party has a Leader in the House, and Whips. The Conservative peers are represented in the National Union (the party's national organisation), and until 1965 assisted in the choice of the Leader of the party. Peers of all parties vote regularly for their party in the Lords. Cross-voting is rare: a few Conservative peers opposed their party on the Bill establishing commercial television (1953–4). In the Suez crisis of 1956, a suitable occasion it would seem for displaying political independence, the Conservative peers loyally supported their party.

Though the party battle is not regarded as seriously as that in the Commons, governments must be represented by Ministers in the House of Lords. The Lord Chancellor is perforce a member of the Lords and of the Cabinet. It is unusual now for any Minister of high office to sit in the Lords. Lord Halifax was Foreign Secretary 1937–40, and Lord Home held the same office from 1960 to 1963, but the appointment was criticised and it was necessary to appoint a junior Minister of some standing to answer for the Foreign Office in the Commons. Mr Churchill's Cabinet of 1952 included seven peers, among them the so-called 'overlords', the coordinating Ministers. Mr Macmillan also loved Lords—in 1961 his Cabinet had four peers. Mr Wilson, however, takes the traditional radical view and his Government has fewer peers than any previously (see chapter 3, p. 82). The Government still makes its case in the Lords and pilots its Bills; it uses the Upper House as a necessary, indeed useful, legislative instrument.

The Lords are concerned with three main kinds of business: Bills (including Private Bills); Questions; and general debates. The procedure for Bills is similar to that of the Commons, with First and Second Reading, Committee and Report Stage and Third Reading (see chapter 6, document 2). However, the Lords' power in financial matters is limited by custom, by resolutions dating from the seventeenth century and by the Parliament Act of 1911. Hence, the House does not make Money Resolutions and does not take Supply Bills through a Committee Stage. A second important difference between Lords and Commons procedure is that the House of Lords has no Standing Legislative Committees: the Committee Stage is conducted on the Floor of the House. Amendments of substance may also be moved at the Third Reading. When differences occur between the Houses, they are resolved by communication between the two. In practice, the House of Commons either agrees to accept a Lords amendment or proposes a compromise or insists on its original Bill— in which case the Lords perforce give way. If the Second Chamber were more powerful, then more formal procedures for the settlement of differences would be required.

Private Bills (e.g., Bills promoted by local authorities) are dealt with separately in a Select Committee.

Questions are very few compared with the Commons: peers have no constituents to pass on their complaints and to observe their representatives—and few Ministers answer questions. On average, there are one or two Questions a day, on general or trivial matters. There is no limit on Supplementaries, and sometimes little debates take place. But the tension, the cutting edge, of the Lower House is quite absent.

Motions 'calling for papers' are similar to Adjournment Debates in the Commons. A member raises a topic, again of general or of less importance, a few speeches are made, a Government peer replies, the motion is withdrawn and the House adjourns in time for dinner (or even tea).

The House also sits as a supreme Court of Appeal. But this is a separate operation in which only the Law Lords take an active part.

Functions

The desirable functions of a Second Chamber were set out by the Bryce Conference on Reform of the Second Chamber in 1918.

....

DOCUMENT 3

FUNCTIONS APPROPRIATE TO A SECOND CHAMBER

From a letter from Viscount Bryce to the Prime Minister, reporting the conclusions of the Conference on the Reform of the Second Chamber, op. cit., p. 4

FUNCTIONS APPROPRIATE TO A SECOND CHAMBER

(1) The examination and revision of Bills brought from the House of Commons, a function which has become more needed since, on many occasions during the last 30 years, the House of Commons has been obliged to act under special rules limiting debate.

(2) The initiation of Bills dealing with subjects of a comparatively non-controversial character which may have an easier passage through the House of Commons if they have been fully discussed and put into a well-considered shape before being submitted to it.

(3) The interposition of so much delay (and no more) in the passing of a Bill into law as may be needed to enable the opinion of the nation to be adequately expressed on it. This would be specially needed as regards Bills which affect the fundamentals of the Constitution or introduce new principles of legislation, or which raise issues whereon the opinion of the country may appear to be almost equally divided.

(4) Full and free discussion of large and important questions, such as those of foreign policy, at moments when the House of Commons may happen to be so much occupied that it cannot find sufficient time for them. Such discussions may often be all the more useful if conducted in an Assembly whose debates and divisions do not involve the fate of the Executive Government.

....

FUNCTIONS APPROPRIATE TO A SECOND CHAMBER

3. Do you agree with the above statement? Briefly justify yourself.

There is still general agreement on functions (1), (2) and (4), and the Lords continue to carry out these functions. Modern governments with heavy legislative programmes simply could not manage without the use of the House of Lords for the revision of contentious Bills and the (parliamentary) initiation of less controversial legislation. In the session 1966–7, for example, the Government introduced thirty-eight Bills in the Lords, eighty-nine in the Commons. The Lords' share included Bills on Hire Purchase Advertisements, Criminal Appeal, the Development of Inventions, Forestry, Public Health and the status of the Welsh language.

Discussions of 'large and important questions' do take place, but, equally useful, the Lords often examine and ventilate the unlikely minor subjects for which the Commons have no time. Occasionally, peers who are personally involved in these questions participate in debate, e.g., a former Governor of the Bank of England in a debate on devaluation, and two Trustees of the British Museum in a debate on the extension of the Museum. Debates of this kind, important or trivial, general or specialist, are obviously of some value. But a reading of the House of Lords Reports does not suggest that the level of debate in the Lords is consistently higher than that in the Commons.

The power to delay has not often been used, but on several occasions delay has led to destruction—e.g. the clauses to abolish the death penalty in 1948 and 1956. Under the Labour Government since 1964 the Lords have acted with enforced moderation. On three occasions recently the Conservative Opposition in the Lords has drawn back from rejections of Commons Bills: on the Burmah Oil Bill (a case of retrospective legislation); the London Government Bill (the postponement of London Borough Elections, allegedly for party advantage); and the Abortion Bill (in which issues of conscience were involved). In a fourth case, sanctions against Rhodesia, the Lords finally took the plunge, but managed a majority of nine only in a vote of 377.

But the House of Lords does not live in a continuous atmosphere of constitutional crisis. Most of the time it carries out Bryce's first, second and fourth functions effectively, but undramatically.

DOCUMENT 4

A WEEK IN THE LIFE OF THE HOUSE OF LORDS

Summary of the proceedings of the Lords, 27–30 November 1967

Tuesday, 27 November

The House met at 2.30 p.m.

There were four Questions, which with answers took up 29 minutes.

Two Statutory Orders (about mink and coypus) were passed in ten minutes.

There followed a debate of half-an-hour on the Committee Stage of a minor Bill. Then the House took up the Second Reading of the Expiring Laws Continuance Bill. The debate centred on immigration problems and unexpectedly took up nearly three hours. The announced business, the Committee Stage of the Consumer Protection Bill, was therefore postponed. (Incidentally, on this matter, Baroness Elliot said she was speaking for the Consumer Council.)

The House adjourned soon after 7 p.m.

Wednesday, 28 November

The House met at 2.30 p.m.

There were four Questions, including one on Oxford Railway Station and one on turnstiles in public lavatories.

During exchanges on boy entrants to the Army, Viscount Montgomery intervened: '. . . the more boys of 15 who join the Army the better . . . let them be taught some discipline . . . and let them get their hair cut.'

After 15 minutes of Questions, the Lords began a general debate on crime and the community, under the usual kind of motion 'calling attention to the problems and moving for papers'. This motion was withdrawn at the end of the debate, which had lasted six hours and included speeches from a former Home Secretary and a distinguished nonconformist minister (but no criminologist of course!).

Thursday, 30 November

The House met at 3 p.m.

Again a half-hour of Questions including one on the current outbreak of foot-and-mouth disease.

Two Bills initiated by the Lords came up. An Epping Forest (Waterworks Corner) Bill was read a third time. Lord Chorley introduced a Street Offences Bill. The postponed Committee Stage of the Consumer Protection Bill was then taken. (It was interrupted briefly for the reading of the Government's statement of international loans, just given in the Commons.) A number of Opposition amendments were moved, discussed and withdrawn.

The House adjourned for the week-end shortly after 9 p.m. (after a work week one day shorter than usual).

4 REFORM:
THE ARGUMENT ABOUT A SECOND CHAMBER

Constitutional reform inspires awe rather than enthusiasm. The sacred fabric must not be touched. But the House of Lords is something of an exception. Here the fabric is sacred, but in a lesser degree —reform is sinful, but it is an expected and therefore an excusable sin of radical governments. So, once again, in 1967, the Labour Government announced its intention to reform the House of Lords.

The existing situation was indeed uneasy. The Prime Minister had already decided not to create any more hereditary peerages. The tide of life peers was slowly gaining ground. The Lords accepted (perhaps too readily) that a Labour Government would allow them only 'one bite': once reject a Bill, and the minimal powers remaining to them would be taken away. Hence their recent retreats on a number of crucial issues. It seemed likely that the House of Lords, deprived of power because of its hereditary basis, was going to lose both power and hereditary basis.

Reform of the Lords was last discussed between the parties in 1947–8. These talks broke down on the question of the powers of the House of Lords but there was otherwise a large measure of agreement. This was embodied in a formal statement.

....

DOCUMENT 5

AREA OF AGREEMENT ON A SECOND CHAMBER, 1948

Agreed Statement on the Conclusion of the Conference of Party Leaders, February–April 1948, Parliament Bill, 1947, Cmd. 7380, 1948, p. 3

(1) The Second Chamber should be complementary to and not a rival to the Lower House and, with this end in view, the reform of the House of Lords should be based on a modification of its existing constitution as opposed to the construction of a Second Chamber of a completely new type based on some system of election.

(2) The revised constitution of the House of Lords should be such as to secure as far as practicable that a permanent majority is not assured for any one political party.

(3) The present right to attend and vote based solely on heredity should not constitute a qualification for admission to a reformed Second Chamber.

(4) Members of the Second Chamber should be styled 'Lords of Parliament' and would be appointed on grounds of personal distinction or public service. They might be drawn either from Hereditary Peers, or from commoners who would be created Life Peers.

(5) Women should be capable of being appointed Lords of Parliament in like manner as men.

(6) Provision should be made for inclusion in the Second Chamber of certain descendants of the Sovereign, certain Lords Spiritual and the Law Lords.

(7) In order that people without private means should not be excluded, some remuneration would be payable to members of the Second Chamber.

(8) Peers who were not Lords of Parliament should be entitled to stand for election to the House of Commons, and also to vote at elections in the same manner as other citizens.

(9) Some provision should be made for the disqualification of a member of the Second Chamber who neglects, or becomes no longer fitted to perform his duties as such.

[Twenty years later the disagreement over powers is as wide as ever, and more radical proposals on composition have breached the area of agreement mapped out in 1948.]

....

EXERCISES

THE AGREEMENT OF 1948

4.1. Which of these points have since been dealt with?

4.2. Does the agreement accept the right of hereditary peers to a place in a reformed Second Chamber?

The argument on composition

The Parliament Act of 1911 proclaimed the intention to substitute a popular for a hereditary basis, and for radicals heredity remains an unacceptable principle. They argue that it is more than simply nonsense: it helps to support the petty hierarchies and snobberies of British (or English) social life. Many Conservatives would say that the hereditary principle is not a bad one, and that it cannot be abandoned without weakening the monarchy. Some would argue that the principle does secure for the Lords a number of ordinary people, particularly young people, and these are a useful leaven in an assembly of distinguished public persons. This last is a good principle, but unfortunately young peers, however undistinguished, are rarely 'ordinary' in the important matters of social background and outlook. Thus there is a divergence of views. It seems likely that on one side heredity would be regarded as not counting as even part of a qualification, while Conservatives are inclined to accept a peer as having at least a partial claim on a seat in the Lords.

The appointment to the Lords of persons 'distinguished in public life' has been arranged through the operation of the Life Peerages Act. Such persons are generally accepted as proper and valuable members of a Second Chamber. Moreover, governments have to some extent avoided creating a life peerage composed of the elderly and retired. But it is difficult, in a system of virtually voluntary service, to get into the House a number of younger persons still active in public life, but ready to give substantial and regular service to the Lords. The House has the problems of local councils and the magistracy—how to avoid being overburdened with the retired and the leisured. In the long run, the present life peerage system cannot sustain a vigorous House.

Hence, schemes of election have been proposed—for example:

(a) election by the Commons for a twelve-year period, with one-third retiring every four years (thus evening out the swing of opinion over time);

(b) election by regions, either by popular ballot or by electoral colleges of local councillors (thus reinforcing the regional aspect of British local government);

(c) election by specified associations—Trade Unions, Industry, the Church, etc.

These schemes all assume that there should be a new class of politicians, full-time and paid, and that there would be enough candidates. There may be doubts about this. There are other objections to these schemes of election.

EXERCISE

SCHEMES OF ELECTION TO THE HOUSE OF LORDS

5. What objections do you see to the schemes mentioned?

The question of party representation is a difficult one. It was agreed in 1948 that ideally no party should have a permanent majority, but in practice this might be difficult to achieve. The question is also tied up with the problem of powers. If the House has virtually no powers, then it does not matter much how it votes. Yet a House reformed in composition and deprived of its remaining powers might acquire political *influence*, so that its voting counted with the public, if not in Parliament. This is why many Radicals still hesitate to reform the Lords at all: while its composition is absurd its influence is slight.

The argument on powers

The argument over powers turns now on the claim that the Lords should have the power to delay some legislation long enough for it to count. There is no serious claim that even a reformed Second Chamber should do more. Indeed, the British version of responsible government demands that government emerges from and is responsible to a popularly elected Chamber. There is, of course, a case for two-chamber government in federal systems, where the second cham er provides representation of the states or regions. But this would represent a revolution in the British constitution, which is hardly federal in character. The current argument is less fundamental, arises simply from the inadequacies of the existing House of Lords, and is concerned basically with a complementary or ancillary chamber.

The present period of delay, one year, is long enough to matter. It means an irksome delay in implementing legislation, and threatens a Labour Government with a veto in its last year of office. The following documents illustrate the argument for a power of delay.

....

DOCUMENT 6
THE ARGUMENT OVER THE POWER OF DELAY OF
THE HOUSE OF LORDS

(a) *The mandate argument*
From Agreed Statement, 1948 (op. cit.), p. 4

[The leaders of the official Opposition] hold that the purpose of the power of delay, which formed an integral part of the Parliament Act procedure, has never been to enable the Second Chamber to thwart the will of the People. It is an essential constitutional safeguard to ensure that, in the event of serious controversy between the two Houses of Parliament, on a measure on which the view of the electorate is doubtful, such a measure shall not pass into law until sufficient time has elapsed to enable the electorate to be properly informed of the issues involved and for public opinion to crystallise and express itself.

(b) *The constitutional argument*
From H. L. Deb., vol. 153, 27 January 1948, col. 652, Lord Salisbury

. . . What is essential, if a Parliamentary democracy is to succeed, is that both Parties should know that if a Government, either of the Left or of the Right—because it applies equally to both—with a temporary majority in the House of Commons, were to introduce really extreme measures, there is in existence a Second Chamber able to stop them. If that protection were to be removed, the defeated Party—and, as I say, it applies equally to the Right and the Left—frantic with anxiety, might well begin to flirt with unconstitutional practices. . . .

From H.L. Deb., vol. 280, 16 February 1967, col. 420, Lord Carrington

There could arise a matter of great constitutional and national importance, on which there was known to be a deep division of opinion in the country or perhaps on which the people's opinion was not known. In a case of this kind, it seems to me that the House of Lords has a right, and perhaps a duty, to use its powers, not to make a decision, but to afford the people of this country and Members of the House of Commons a period for reflection and time for views to be expressed.

(c) *The counter-argument*

From H.L. Deb., vol. 153, 27 January 1948, cols. 633–5, the Lord Privy Seal (Viscount Addison)

... The claim to decide whether a subject is or is not in accordance with the mandate of the people contains this implication that, if this House is of opinion that is not in the mandate, this House is at liberty to reject it; that is the deliberate and obvious implication. We challenge that implication from the very start. We claim that it is for the elected representatives of the people to decide whether an issue is or is not to be the subject of Parliamentary activity.... We do not accept, and we do not intend to accept, that this House, entirely unrepresentative, shall be the final arbiter as to what is and what is not the opinion of the people. There is the point of actual difference, and there can be no compromise on that. In our view, it must be the elected Chamber that has finally to decide these issues.

Let us examine this from another aspect. Of necessity in the life of any Parliament, a large number of issues must arise which were not foreseen or which were not in anybody's mind at the time of the Election.... But that does not in any way invalidate the claim or right of the representative House to introduce measures on these matters. There is no question of mandate at all ...

From H.L. Deb., vol. 280, 16 February 1967, col. 426, the Lord Privy Seal (Earl of Longford)

[Lord Carrington said that] in certain grave circumstances this House had a right to resist, at any rate for a time, the will of the House of Commons. For myself, I could never accept that this was part of the duty of the House of Lords. Legally they could do it within the terms of the Parliament Act. I am not going to offer any opinion as to what would happen if they did; I have not come here prepared to enter into that sort of discussion. I can only say, as someone who loves this House as much as the noble Lord does, and as much as anybody here does, that in my opinion it would be a bad day if the House of Lords ever sought to exercise that right. I hope that it never will, and I look to the noble Lord, Lord Carrington, to make sure that it never does.

The argument for a Lords' veto is indeed a thin one. It is quite certainly invalid given the present composition of the House, which is still overweighted in favour of the hereditary principle, and which gives a Conservative predominance both permanent and massive, so that the single-chamber government which Lord Salisbury abhors operates under Conservative Governments. However, even with a reformed composition, responsibility must surely lie with the elected chamber. This principle would be contradicted by a serious Lords' veto. Similarly, the devices which are sometimes proposed for over-coming disagreements between the Houses—conferences, or a referendum—equally contradict the basic principle of a government's responsibility to the Commons. There is thus much to be said for the reduction of the Lords' delaying power to a purely nominal three months as proposed by the Liberal, Lord Byers. This would deprive the veto of any practical effect: it would be a gesture not a veto.

The functions of a reformed Second Chamber

This eighty or perhaps 480-year-old argument has appealed to British constitutionalists, trained in the classics and history. But it has obscured the more important consideration of the functions of a Second Chamber in a modern Parliament. There is general agreement on three of the functions proposed by Bryce (document 3). In particular, the work of the Lords in revising and amending legislation has been indispensable to recent governments with heavy programmes of legislation. This, together with Bryce's functions of initiating Bills on non-controversial matters and holding general debates, forms a sufficient justification for an effective and rationally selected Second Chamber. Such a Chamber would be consistently useful and, for some work, essential.

A development of the functions of the House of Lords on these lines would not increase the constitutional power of the Lords, but it might increase their standing and their influence: above all, it would increase their usefulness. For these tasks, the rather leisurely procedure of the House would need to be overhauled—in particular, debate would have to be more strictly controlled to ensure relevance and save time.

It has been argued that the House could develop its role still further. In the discussion of the Commons it emerged that the House of Commons was finding an enhanced role for itself in the scrutiny of administration. This was in addition to the basic elective function of the Commons, and either in addition to or in place of the traditional contest on the Floor of the Chamber. A modernised Second Chamber, it is suggested, could contribute to this function of scrutiny through a system of Committees complementing those of the Commons. Further, a Second Chamber might take on a distinctive function as a kind of administrative Court of Appeal: here the Lords could supplement the work of the Commons' own Parliamentary Commissioner.

These are attractive suggestions, but they do involve difficulties, particularly in the function of scrutiny. This would duplicate work in the Commons, which the Commons with its 630 Members ought to be doing itself. The Departments under scrutiny would be justifiably displeased at the need to prepare material for, and spend time in, overlapping Committees. But the most serious difficulty is that the Second Chamber would require a much stronger force of full-time members than it has now. It is difficult to see how it could recruit such people. Ingenious suggestions for secondment from the professions (and the factories?) do not look viable. There are few serious jobs that can be done effectively by people on temporary leave from their life's work.

EXERCISES

REFORM OF THE HOUSE OF LORDS

6.1. Devise an ideal Second Chamber for Britain. (No answer is supplied!)

6.2. Devise a practical, politically acceptable scheme for a reform of the House of Lords by a Labour Government. (Acceptable means that the Opposition would accept it, even if they would not agree to it.)

Your answer may be compared with the actual proposals of the Labour Government, 1968 (document 7). These were embodied in a Bill, but opposition from both left and right, and shortage of time, led to the abandonment of the Bill.

....

DOCUMENT 7

HOUSE OF LORDS REFORM

From House of Lords Reform, Cmnd. 3799, November 1968, pp.28–29

The Government's proposals can be summarised as follows:

(a) The reformed House of Lords should be a two-tier structure comprising voting peers, with a right to speak and vote, and non-voting peers, with a right to speak.

(b) After the reform came into effect, succession to a hereditary peerage should no longer carry the right to a seat in the House of Lords but existing peers by succession would have the right to sit as non-voting members for their life-time.

(c) Voting members would be exclusively created peers, but some peers by succession would be created life peers and therefore become qualified to be voting peers.

(d) Non-voting peers would include created peers who do not meet the requirements of voting membership, and peers who at the time of the reform sit by right of succession.

(e) Peers who at the time of the reform sat by right of succession would have an opportunity to withdraw from the House if they wished to do so.

(f) Voting peers would be expected to play a full part in the work of the House and required to attend at least one-third of the sittings; they would be subject to an age of retirement.

(g) The voting House would initially consist of about 230 peers, distributed between the parties in a way which would give the government a small majority over the opposition parties, but not a majority of the House as a whole when those without party allegiance are included.

(h) Non-voting peers would be able to ask questions and move motions and also to serve in committee; but not to vote on the floor of the House or in any committee for the consideration of legislation.

(i) The reformed House should include a suitable number of peers able to speak with authority on the problems and wishes of Scotland, Wales, Northern Ireland and the regions of England.

(j) Voting peers should be paid at a rate which would reflect their responsibilities and duties, but the question should be referred to an independent committee.

(k) The reformed House should be able to impose a delay of six months on the passage of an ordinary public bill sent up from the Commons on which there is disagreement between the two Houses; it should then be possible to submit the bill for Royal Assent provided that a resolution to that effect had been passed in the House of Commons. The period of delay should be capable of running into a new session or into a new parliament.

(l) The reformed House should be able to require the House of Commons to reconsider an affirmative order, or to consider a negative order, to which the House of Lords disagreed, but its power of final rejection should be removed.

(m) There should be a place in the reformed House for law lords and bishops.

(n) All peers should in future be qualified to vote in parliamentary elections.

(o) Future peers by succession and existing peers by succession who choose to renounce their membership of the House of Lords should be enabled to sit in the House of Commons if elected.

(p) A review should be made of the functions and procedures of the two Houses once the main reform has come into effect.

(q) A committee should be established to review periodically the composition of the reformed House; it should have a chairman of national standing but without party political affiliations and its members would include representatives of the political parties and persons without party political affiliations.

....

GUIDE TO EXERCISES

1. Mainly you must assess your answer yourself, but see text p. 266. Compare your list with those of other people.

2. It certainly includes persons of experience in some forms of public work, but in fact only a limited range. For example, the following are absent or hardly represented—school-teachers, general medical practitioners, solicitors, junior officers of the armed services, municipal treasurers, hospital administrators, factory workers, salesmen, and so on.

There are certainly peers who simply would not undertake political work involving elections. There is a small band of 'independents', but most peers are partisans. They may not be extreme partisans in terms of position or attitude, but in practice this makes little difference to their activity in the Lords.

In consequence the House is dominated by one set of political opinions, though it does not always act under the influence of party motives.

3. The whole chapter provides a full answer. Briefly there is a good case for functions (1), (2) and (4), on the grounds: first, that these functions are essential in any system of government; second, that they cannot be completely fulfilled by the Commons; third, that they may gain from being carried out by a House composed differently from the Commons; fourth, that the carrying out of these functions need not derogate from the prime responsibility of the Commons.

4.1. (3); (5); (7); (8)—by renunciation; ?(9) the 'leave of absence' arrangement is voluntary, not a disqualification.

4.2. Points (1) and (3) hint that heredity might be acceptable, point (4) appears to leave the selection of 'Lords of Parliament' open, with no *rights* for hereditary peers. But this looks like a point of disagreement, with the Conservatives pressing for a definite allocation of seats to peers.

5. A radical objection is that an elected Second Chamber may rival the House of Commons. Some may see this as a positive advantage. There are objections to particular schemes of election, especially to (2) and (3): the regions do not yet have a political existence; local councillors ought not to be given national political influence, this is not their *raison d'être*; the associations already have considerable influence; how do you represent the unassociated?

6.1. No answer supplied.

6.2. The Government's answer in the 1968 proposals (document 7) was a skilful compromise but it still proved unacceptable. Radicals objected to its preservation of a hereditary element and legislative power; some Conservatives objected to the attenuation of the hereditary element. There was more general disquiet about the extension of the Prime Minister's patronage.

RECAPITULATION EXERCISES

1. To which of the following categories do these numbers apply? (Some of the figures are of course only approximate.): 26   60   900   190   100   150   100

number of peers
number of life peers
number of Lords Spiritual
average daily attendance in 1967
core of active peers
number of Labour peers
number of Independent peers

2. *True or false?* (mark T or F)

(a) Life peers are mainly politicians.

(b) The present power of the Lords to delay Bills is of no significance.

(c) The House of Lords rightly used its power of delay against the retrospective Bill on the Burmah Oil Company.

(d) The House of Lords is not organised on party lines.

(e) The 1948 talks between the parties on Lords reform broke down mainly over the question of powers.

(f) The Bryce Conference of 1918 accepted the principle of a delaying power.

3. What are the differences between Question Time in the Lords and in the Commons?

4. What are the main provisions of the Acts dealing with the Lords passed in 1911, 1949, 1958, and 1963?

KEY TO RECAPITULATION EXERCISES

1. The numbers should be in the order:
900   150   26   190   60   100   100

2. (a) T   (b) F—but you could argue about this.

  (c) F   (d) F   (e) T   (f) T

3. See text p. 272.

4. See text pp. 266, 270.

PART IV
Representation

[9]
Political parties

1 INTRODUCTION AND OUTLINE

Parties pervade the political system: there is no chapter in this book to which they have no relevance. There are two great areas of party activity—at the centre of Government, in Parliament and the Cabinet; and in the country, that is to say, in the exterior party. The party-in-Parliament and the party-in-Government have been studied in Parts II and III of this book. This chapter deals with the exterior party, which includes the leadership outside the relationships of Cabinet and Parliament, the constituency associations and, linking them, the regional and national organisations of the parties.

In the accepted model of Western democratic politics, political parties compete for political power in an election-based representative system. To do this they must recruit candidates, produce leaders, and develop a programme of policies. In the struggle for power, the party must engage in the 'market-place' activities (sometimes literally a market-place) of political communication and brokerage: discovering and assessing the needs, interests, prejudices, and levels of tolerance of people and of groups; identifying issues, developing and adjusting policies; finally, seeking support for candidates and a programme. In power, the party must continue with its market-place activity, but it will also be deeply concerned with the parliamentary activity of sustaining a government.

This wholesome democratic model depends for its working on the competition of two parties, preferably alternating in power. Britain had such a party system between roughly the 1860s and 1920, and since 1945. Many countries in Europe and around the world, where British influence has not been strong, have a single party or many parties, just as Britain did between the wars. It is an important question in political science how far a single-party system (as in Russia), or a multi-party system (as in France) can contribute to democratic politics. Such systems, with single-party or coalition governments, are generally regarded by their members, and in most cases by their citizens too, as democratic. The basic tasks of political communication and 'brokerage' can, indeed, be performed in such systems. But many political scientists regard the competitive, two-party, alternating system as superior because it gives the elector a choice and enforces on a party some responsibility for a programme and policies.

However, approval of the ideal model of the British party system must be qualified. The system has its disadvantages, for it sometimes encourages a false and damaging partisanship and an excessive concentration on electoral tactics. Moreover, study or experience of the party system at work shows that it falls far short in practice of the ideal engagement in democratic politics. The local party member or visitor to the Conservative club or Labour's Unity House may be puzzled to relate the activities he sees to the processes prescribed in the model. Inevitably, the local constituency association devotes much, possibly ill-organised, energy to the routine tasks of keeping the organisation going, collecting dues, and organising the Christmas social.

Political parties in a democratic system ought themselves to be democratic: membership should be high; the leaders should be responsible to the parliamentary party; both should be responsible at least to the membership; there should be an element of representation and consent in the relationship. Nevertheless, the leaders should not be mere puppets of the members. In practice, there seems little danger of this, and on the contrary rather more danger of a leadership unresponsive to the membership. The Labour Party seems to be more democratic than the Conservative Party: its Leader has less power than the Conservative Leader in relation to the Parliamentary Party, and to the central committee and conference of the exterior party. In office, however, the Labour Leader seems to be almost as powerful as the Conservative Leader, and experience of office has tended to transform permanently the Leader's power. Similarly, the autonomy of the Parliamentary Party in relation to the exterior party has been enhanced by periods of power.

There are two particularly important aspects of the work of the local party. First, the selection of candidates is equivalent in many constituencies to the selection of a Member of Parliament. The selection process may give due or undue influence to the national party, or in the Labour Party to Trade Union sponsorship, or it may simply be not a very effective process for selecting good Members of Parliament. Second, a constituency association with its candidate in Parliament may feel disposed at times to constrain its Member to follow a particular line of policy, in or out of accord with the party line. Such actions raise serious questions about the status of the Member of Parliament in the British system—individual conscience or party 'hack'? The tendency of this chapter is to discern democratic values in the maligned party hack.

A party line is the reaction of a particular group of people to a range of problems. But their reaction—and the party's line—is conditioned by the party's sources of support, by its image of itself, and, underlying this, its basic outlook and philosophy. Support comes not only from voters but from powerful interest groups aligned with or sympathetic towards the party. The Labour Party is backed by the Trade Unions, the Conservative Party by business and industrial interests. In both parties the relationship is close but not exclusive.

A consideration of the philosophies of the parties suggests deep and significant differences between them. These philosophical differences may not always be translated into different policies, but there remains some ground for believing that the struggle of the political parties in Britain is genuine and relevant, and that the voter is therefore presented with a meaningful choice.

2 PARTY SYSTEMS AND THE FUNCTIONS OF PARTIES

Britain's two-party system

Since 1945 Britain has had a two-party system. This has not always been the case. Until the 1860s political parties were only loosely organised: the great party split of 1846 over the Repeal of the Corn Laws was followed by the split of 1886 over Ireland, and then over Free Trade. Meanwhile the Irish Party had grown strong enough to modify politics by its alliances. Then the Labour Party weighed in and the Liberal Party began to decline. In the 1920s Britain had three major parties; in the 1930s it was reduced to one super party and two minor ones; only in 1945 was there a clear return to a system with two major parties competing for office and alternating in it. But nothing in politics is immutable; the two-party system was again in doubt until the election of 1964 ended a long run of Conservative power.

The alternation of parties is not accurately described as the swing of a pendulum, for the record shows a very odd pendulum, tending to stick to the right and with a period of triangular movement.

Even since 1945 Britain has had more than two parties. In that year there were eleven different party labels attached to Members of Parliament. Four of these (Liberal, Independent, Irish Nationalist and Communist) were not aligned with the two large parties, Conservative and Labour, and held between them thirty of the 640 seats. The Liberal Party has continued to challenge the giants, and attracted 2⅛ million votes in 1966, but it won only twelve seats.

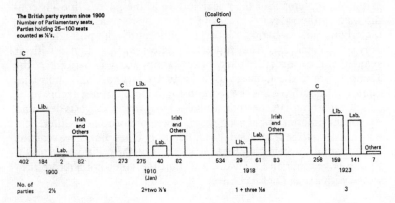

The British party system since 1900
Number of Parliamentary seats,
Parties holding 25–100 seats
counted as ¼'s.

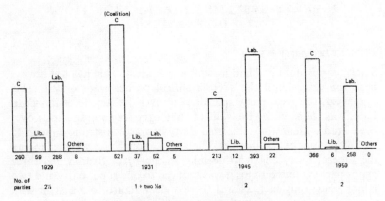

THE PARTY SYSTEM SINCE 1900

This is a clue to an explanation of the British two-party system. It is sustained by the electoral device of simple majority single ballot (see chapter 12). This is not to say that two parties are the inevitable consequence of the ballot method. Rather, a two-party system is the likely consequence of such a method, which not only undervalues third party votes but also discourages the casting of a vote for a third party.

Thus, the simple majority system at least reinforces the tendency of societies to divide into two: a lower- and an upper-class, employer and worker, town and country, Catholic and Protestant, private and public—and so on. There may be in all this a natural tendency to bi-polarity, easily convertible by electoral devices into a two-party system. But social conflict is usually more complex than bi-polarity allows, so the whole system is often under strain, with either the two-party system or the political expression of social cleavage imperfect—or a little of both.

Two-party systems are by no means normal throughout the world. France has a multi-party system, Russia a single party: the USA has mainly two parties, but with several of the states having one strong and one weak party (one-and-a-half parties, so to say). Most countries seem on the whole pleased with their party systems. Liberals obviously do not like the British system by which they lose so much. But Western political scientists are inclined to regard it with favour, seeing in competition and alternation between parties, and the coherence and responsibility of party-based governments, the best fulfilment of the democratic functions of a party system.

The functions of political parties

A party, simply defined, is an organised group seeking political power, at least partly through a representative system, and aiming to form or form part of a government. For the British system it might be tempting to add as a characteristic feature that the party is mainly a programmatic one, concerned to develop a programme in a process of two-way communication with the electorate, subsequently submitting the programme to the electorate at a general election, and, if elected, governing according to its main lines. But this is much too simple a view, and may give a misleading impression of party activity, which is in practice more varied, more diffuse, and less effective than this wholesome democratic model allows for.

First, it should already be clear from other chapters that the processes of policy formulation are more complex than the notion of a policy-making party suggests, and that policy is the product of more forces than are involved in the relationship between party and electorate. There is a historical measure for this—how far can the history of modern Britain be written in terms of party conferences, party programmes and general elections? Thus, 1906 and 1945 seem to be turning points based on elections and party programmes, although the election of 1906 hardly anticipated the great series of State welfare laws of 1908–12, which were rather the personal promotions of two energetic and skilful politicians, Lloyd George and Churchill. In many other cases, including 1964 and 1966, the relationship between election programme and actual policies seems to have been tenuous. Frequently, major changes in governments' policies have depended rather on economic and international trends and crises, slumps and wars, and overriding domestic political processes, and on changes of dominant generation among politicians.

Second, parties are not groups of people with identical ideas, interests and objectives. Even similarities are complicated by the existence of independents, factions and divergent tendencies. Political parties are by nature coalitions. Hence the internal processes by which policy is formulated are often as important and decisive as the party's public activity centred on elections.

Third, the simple description of the democratic political party neglects the range and complexity of a party's functions. These may be grouped as follows:

(a) keeping the organisation going:
recruiting members;
running essential committees and meetings;
arranging social functions to raise money and/or keep members happy.

(b) relating to the national organisation:
by correspondence;
by attending area or regional committees, and annual conference, or sending resolutions;
by liaison with the MP (if they have one).

(c) electoral:
selecting a candidate;
nursing the constituency;
campaigning and vote-getting.

(d) political communication and policy formulation:
keeping in touch with local opinion;
keeping in touch with local interests;
participating in the formulation of policy in this light;
promoting the party's programme.

(e) activities directed at local government under all of these headings.

EXERCISES

THE FUNCTIONS OF POLITICAL PARTIES

1.1. Which of these functions of political parties may contribute fundamentally to a democratic system of government? and why?

1.2. Do you see any ways in which:

(a) a single party system may be democratic?

(b) a multi-party system may be democratic?

(c) a two-party system may be more effectively democratic?

1.3. In the light of this account of their functions, is it desirable that political parties should have a substantial mass membership?

3 THE STRUCTURE OF PARTIES AND THE DISTRIBUTION OF POWER

The question of mass membership is essential to the discussion of the distribution of power within a party. The parties have many more supporters than members, but are formally concerned with supporters only at election times. Between elections and within the continuing structure of the party, the member is the party's first concern. The Conservative Party has about two-million members (out of six to nine-million supporters, i.e. regular voters). The Labour Party has about one-million individual members, but some five-million more are members by paying a political levy through an affiliated trade union. This is paid automatically unless the member specifically 'contracts out', so inevitably some Conservatives and many apathetics join the Labour Party in this way. The following discussion is concerned with only a part of the vital relationship—that between party and members, not party and supporters.

There are three main centres from which parties operate and in each, two kinds of person sharing power. Diagrammatically it looks like this:

Centres of operation	Parliament	Central Office or headquarters	Local
Power shared between:	Leaders/ Members	Elected officers and committees/ Appointed officials	Leaders/ Members

The structure of the parties is: (a) the way in which the operational centres are linked and the nature of the signals flowing along the links—information, advice, persuasion, command; and (b) the way in which power is shared between leaders, members and officials.

Analysis of the structure reveals the distribution of power. However, such an analysis is by no means easy, and it may assist judgement if the material is analysed in the light of two hypotheses. First, what *ought* to be the distribution of power in a democratic political party? It seems reasonable to argue that parties playing a serious role in a representative democracy should themselves attempt to be democratic, subject only to the limitations of responsibility and response.

The second hypothesis relates to the question, what is the distribution of power likely to be? Here an acceptable hypothesis is tha

Document 1 The structure of the parties
(a) *The basic structure*

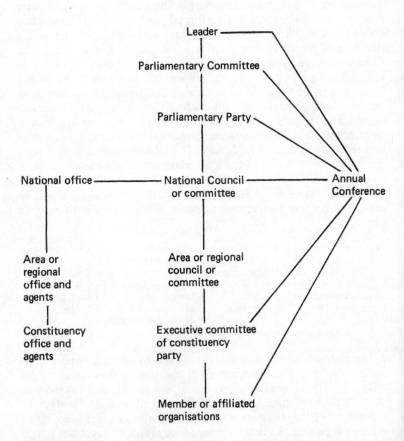

power tends to concentrate in the hands of a few. In the case of political parties, a German sociologist, Michels, formulated some fifty years ago an 'Iron Law of Oligarchy': power tends to concentrate in the hands of small groups of people in positions of authority, and this power is not and normally cannot be, subject to control by other members of the organisation.

The distribution of power within the parties may now be examined.

....

DOCUMENT I

THE STRUCTURE OF THE PARTIES

(a) *The basic structure*—see page 296

(Diagrams of this kind simplify highly complex relationships. The real problems are to discover and define the nature of the relationships indicated by the lines. These may be one- or two-way; neutral or weak relationships of communication and information, ranging up through advice and persuasion to the leadership relations of influence, pressure or command. At some points the line may indicate election or appointment, with their associated power relationships.)

(b) *The structure of the Conservative Party Leadership*

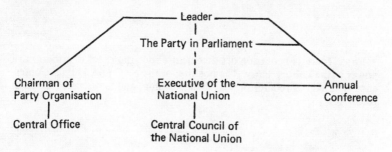

Note: Formally the Party in Parliament is separate from the National Union of Conservative and Unionist Associations. The 'Party Organisation' is separate again.

The Leader is (since 1965) elected by the Party in Parliament. He appoints the Chairman of the Party Organisation. Since 1965 he has attended the Annual Conference of the National Union.

Thus it would appear that the notion of the 'Conservative Party' as such is difficult to place.

(c) *The structure of the Labour Party leadership*

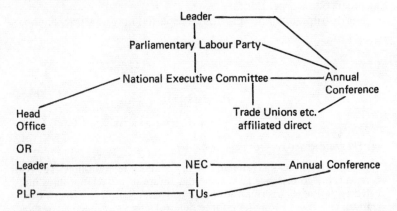

Head
Office

OR

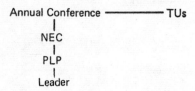

OR by one interpretation of constitution and tradition:

Annual Conference ———— TUs
|
NEC
|
PLP
|
Leader

Note: There is room for disagreement about the exact distribution of power in the Labour Party. The position of the NEC and Annual Conference is crucial in relationship to the leadership, and is discussed in detail below.

....

There are three main views about the distribution of power within the parties.

(a) *The views of Labour and Conservative propaganda.* The Labour Party believes itself to be a democratic party—a 'collective expression of democratic sentiment based on the working class movement and on the constituency organisations...' (Labour Party publication, 'Rise of the Labour Party', 1948, p. 14). The Annual Conference figures in this view as a 'Parliament of the movement'.

The traditional Conservative view of power in the Labour Party sees the democratic element as leading in practice to rule by cliques, bosses and the machine—the NEC and Transport House.

The Conservative Party, in its own regard, is genuinely representative, but accepts and respects strong leadership.

The Labour Party regards the leadership as excessively strong and unresponsive.

(b) *The views of Professor R. T. McKenzie and R. H. S. Crossman.* In a classic study of British political parties first published in 1955, Professor McKenzie set out a mass of evidence to support the thesis that the party views just described were in fact myths, only distantly related to the truth. The Labour Party was remarkably similar to the Conservative Party in the distribution of power. 'No major parliamentary party in the modern period has allowed itself to be relegated to the role of spokesman or servant of its mass organisation.' Within both parliamentary parties the Leader is a dominant force, formal differences in power notwithstanding. This was particularly true for the party in power, whose 'followers outside Parliament became little more than a highly organised pressure-group with a special channel of communication directly to the Leader, the Cabinet and the parliamentary party' (both quotations from R. T. McKenzie, *British Political Parties*, Heinemann Mercury Books, 1963, p. 642.) It was experience of office which had transformed the Labour Party from a mass movement to a party centred like the Conservative Party on the Cabinet and parliamentary system and above all, the Leader/Prime Minister.

R. H. S. Crossman took a similar view about the distribution of power in the Labour Party, but gives it a more Machiavellian background. Where McKenzie on the whole approved of a concentration of power at the top, Crossman deplored it.

....

DOCUMENT 2

MR CROSSMAN'S VIEWS ON THE
POWER STRUCTURE OF THE LABOUR PARTY

(a) From Introduction by R. H. S. Crossman to W. Bagehot, *The English Constitution (1867)*, Fontana, 1963, pp. 41–2

... In order to break down the walls of social oligarchy which surrounded Parliament, a battering ram was required and the Labour Party was created for this purpose. Its structure was determined by three conditions.

First it must have very large funds at its disposal; [hence the special relationship with the Trade Unions]... Secondly... the Labour Party required militants... But since these militants tended to be 'extremists', a constitution was needed which maintained their enthusiasm by apparently creating a full party democracy while excluding them from effective power. Hence the concession in principle of sovereign powers to the delegates at the Annual Conference, and the removal in practice of most of this sovereignty through the trade union block vote on the one hand, and the complete independence of the Parliamentary Labour Party on the other. Thirdly, since its avowed aim was social revolution, the Labour Party from the first accepted the semi-military discipline of democratic centralism, based on the enforcement of majority decision. Hence its intolerance of minority opinion.

(b) From R. H. S. Crossman, *Planning for Freedom*, Hamish Hamilton, 1965, pp. 132–3

Surely when it was faced with a tacitly hostile Establishment in Whitehall and an actively hostile press in Fleet Street, the Labour Government should have felt the need for a politically conscious and politically educated rank and file... after 1945 the party machine should have been instructed to organise a nation-wide crusade of workers' education so as to give the rank and file the feeling that they were needed by the leadership, not merely to man the electoral machine, but to create that pressure of active left-wing opinion required to combat Tory propaganda...

....

(c) *A middle view*. This rejects the extreme positions of party propaganda, and while not regarding any parliamentary party as controlled by its mass organisation, sees the mass organisation as having a more significant influence than McKenzie and Crossman would allow. This is especially true when the party is in opposition (and one of them always is): the period of opposition is important in the formation of future party policy. In this view, there are significant differences between the parties. In particular, the tradition and ethos of the Labour Party is regarded as important in restraining the ultimate power of the leadership.

The evidence of the following documents may now be used to assess the validity of these three views.

DOCUMENT 3

THE POSITION OF THE LEADER IN
THE CONSERVATIVE AND LABOUR PARTIES

	Conservative Party	Labour Party
Mode of election	Ballot of Conservative MPs replaced 1965 informal 'emergence' of Leader. No re-election required.	Ballot of PLP. Annual re-election which has once (1960) been contested. (When Labour is in office, the PLP elects a Chairman as well as a Leader—the Chairman is not a potential leader.)
	In ballot both parties require an absolute majority and use a second ballot.	
Choice of colleagues	Complete discretion.	Discretion when the Leader is Prime Minister; but in opposition the Parliamentary Committee ('Shadow Cabinet') is elected by the PLP. (The Leader may still designate others as 'spokesman'.)
Relations with Private Members of Parliament	As Prime Minister, he will occasionally attend meetings of the Parliamentary (1922) Committee. In opposition, he will attend more frequently, but is not constrained to do so.	As Prime Minister, he will attend meetings of the PLP, at his request or theirs, but not usually any other committees of the PLP. As Leader in opposition, he is Chairman of the Parliamentary Committee of the Labour Party—thus tied in to a committee system, which can however be *led*, if not dominated, by the elected Leader.
Relation to the national committee of the party	He is an important member both of the Executive Committee and of the Central Council of the National Union. Neither of these bodies has a major policy-forming role.	He is an *ex officio* member of the NEC and obviously an important one. Again the NEC is concerned with party management rather than policy.
Relation to Annual Conference	Mr Heath is the first Conservative Leader to attend the Conference, a fact which remains of some significance for the Leader's place in the Conference.	The Leader is compelled by constitution and tradition to exercise leadership, to win the support of Conference.

The place of the National Executive Committee in the Labour Party

The National Executive Committee of the Labour Party has twenty-eight members. The Leader and Deputy-Leader are members *ex officio*. The rest are elected at the Annual Conference to represent various groups in the party: twelve by and for the Trade Unions, seven by and for constituency parties, one by and for socialist and cooperative societies; and five women elected by the whole Conference. In addition, the Treasurer is elected by the whole Conference. The trade unionists virtually control the election of these last six members. Altogether they appear to make a formidable bloc, but in fact members of the General Council of the Trades Union Congress (top-ranking Trade Union leaders) may not stand for NEC, and several Trade Union members of NEC are always Members of Parliament (with overriding loyalties to the PLP).

The functions of the NEC are to do partly with the management of the exterior party, partly with policy. As party manager, the NEC is responsible for the work of the local parties, for research and propaganda, for party finances and for the formal machinery of discipline. Second, the NEC decides, jointly with the PLP, which items of the Party Programme shall be included in the Election Manifesto. Thus the NEC is concerned with policies and programme, including indirectly the implementation of the programme in Parliament. Altogether the NEC has a formidable set of functions and hence scope for considerable influence. In particular, it controls the financing and preparation of propaganda. In the case of serious disagreement with the Leader or the PLP, it can refuse to cooperate in propagating policies it disapproves of. Gaitskell was embarrassed by this kind of non-cooperation in 1960.

In practice, however, the influence of the NEC is quite limited. The PLP is a distinct body, both formally and in operation; it elects the Leader and provides Cabinet and Prime Minister. It shares in the constitutional powers of the State, from which the NEC is excluded. This does not normally mean that the NEC is a frustrated body spoiling for a power-struggle with the PLP. Most of the time it gets on happily with the work of party-management and liaison. It does not regularly challenge the Parliamentary Party because it shares the same objectives and usually has Members of Parliament making up half its membership.

The following document shows the NEC challenging the PLP—but with a lack of success which has served to reinforce the dominance of the Parliamentary Party.

DOCUMENT 4

THE PLACE OF THE NATIONAL EXECUTIVE COMMITTEE IN THE LABOUR PARTY: THE LASKI EPISODE

In 1945, the Chairman of the Labour Party's National Executive Committee was Harold Laski, a distinguished Professor of Political Science. Laski took the view that the Leader of the Party was responsible both to the PLP and to the National Executive Committee, and could not act in certain important matters without consulting those bodies.

In the war-time election of 1945 there was an abnormally long interval between voting and the declaration of the poll. Prime Minister Churchill therefore invited the Leader of the Opposition, Attlee, to attend the important Allied Conference at Potsdam, so that there would be continuity of major foreign policy if Labour were to win the Election. Laski, speaking as Chairman of the NEC, hastened to say that Attlee could attend only as an observer and could not commit the Labour Party to decisions on 'matters which have not been debated either in the Party Executive or at meetings of the Parliamentary Labour Party'. (Kingsley Martin, *Harold Laski*, Gollancz, 1953, pp. 169–70.)

Churchill seized on this curious statement and inflated it for electoral purposes. Attlee, thus challenged on his position as Leader, conceded only that he must consult the NEC. In his own version of the incident, Attlee comments that the Chairman of the NEC 'does not make authoritative pronouncements of this kind'.

A few weeks later, Attlee's position as Leader was again challenged. Laski and some of Attlee's parliamentary colleagues, including Morrison and Cripps, considered that Attlee could not accept the King's commission to form a Government until the new Parliamentary Party had met to elect a Leader.

This was not a wholly unreasonable view, since there had been no election for ten years, and the new Parliamentary Party of 1945 was markedly different from the tiny party which ten years previously had chosen Attlee as Leader. However, Attlee at once rejected the suggestion of a new election. Later he commented: 'If you're invited by the King to form a government you don't say you can't reply for forty-eight hours. You accept the commission and you either bring it off successfully or you don't, and if you don't, you go back and say you can't and advise the King to send for someone else . . .' (F. Williams, *A Prime Minister Remembers*, Heinemann, 1961, p. 4.)

Attlee's blunt and simple (possibly inappropriately simple) language conveys an important if old-fashioned interpretation of the working of the British constitution. The royal invitation to form a Government is regarded as the central procedure. Thus, Attlee asserted the primacy of the British constitution over the party's constitution.

POWER IN THE LABOUR PARTY: THE NEC

2.1. Which of the theories about the distribution of power (pp. 298–300 above) do these incidents support?

2.2. Do you see or know anything which would lead you to regard these episodes as uncharacteristic of the Labour Party, and therefore of less significance? (A little knowledge of the history of the period is really required here.)

The Conservative Party Conference and the making of policy

The Conference of the National Union of Conservative and Unionist Associations is, formally, as the title implies, a conference of only part of the Conservative Party. The mass-membership is inclined to accept the tradition that the Leader is the embodiment of the Party (as distinct from the National Union). Hence the place of the Conference in the making of policy is limited.

The evidence for this view is briefly:

(a) The importance and predominance of the Leader both formally and traditionally—see document 3.

(b) The record of the development of Conservative policy. There is very little evidence that an Annual Conference has ever fundamentally influenced party policy. Thus during the period in opposition (1945–51), new policies were largely the product of the inner councils of the Party, led by R. A. Butler. The Research Department of Central Office appears to have been the most important initiator of new policies. Nevertheless, there was a genuine attempt at this time (especially 1947–9) to submit new policies to the Party's mass organisation for discussion and amendment. The so-called Industrial and Agricultural Charters were subjected to a process called the two-way Movement of Ideas, a curious title (rather Chinese in flavour) but one whose intention was clear. In practice, only minor amendments were proposed. This was with the Party in opposition. It is not to be expected that policy development in office will be as much influenced by the mass Party.

(c) The record of Party Conferences. Generally these have been mass rallies rather than policy-making assemblies. However, there is some evidence of Conservative Conferences making, or at least trying to make, party policy. Some of this evidence is indicated in the next document.

DOCUMENT 5

THE CONSERVATIVE CONFERENCE AND
THE MAKING OF POLICY

(a) *The Conference of 1950*

The Conference was debating housing and had before it a rather vague resolution condemning Labour's record and calling for an increase in house-building. A delegate from the floor proposed a specific target— 300,000 houses a year under a Conservative Government. Support for this figure gathered like a wave. The platform, unwilling reasonably enough to give such an advance commitment, was embarrassed and hesitant. Finally, the Chairman, Lord Woolton, rose and conceded the point. In the event the target was reached in 1952, the second year of the Conservative administration. Thus Conference modified a major item of policy.

(b) *The Conference of 1965*

Rhodesia was on the brink of its 'Unilateral Declaration of Independence'. Lord Salisbury and a group of Conservative MPs were concerned that the interests of the European population should not be neglected by the British Government. The crisis developed rapidly at the time of the Conference. This made the issue at once more delicate but more pressing. Old colonial issues of this kind are very close to the heart of a certain old-fashioned Toryism. The scene was set for Lord Salisbury to demonstrate the power of the Conservative Conference.

But the platform beat him. The executive committee responsible for arranging the business of the Conference scheduled the debate on Rhodesia for late on Friday, the last full day. Lord Salisbury was not permitted to move a resolution of his own. Instead he proposed an amendment to a platform motion, but this had been toned down—'deeply deplore' instead of 'totally oppose' sanctions against Rhodesia.

Salisbury's seconder had scored some success with an emotional speech. ('Do you support the Socialist Party to transfer power to African Nationalist leaders—almost immediately?' 'No', the audience roared back. 'Then', cried Mr Wall, 'make your voice heard and you may yet change history.') A temperate speech criticising Salisbury's point of view was heckled and slow-handclapped. The atmosphere was highly charged, and the platform grew anxious. In desperation they finally invited Lord Salisbury to withdraw his amendment. He refused and appealed to Conference to decide whether there should be a vote. There was a resounding shout of 'No!', and the platform's day was saved; but it had been a very near thing.

THE INFLUENCE OF THE CONSERVATIVE CONFERENCE

3. Would you agree that Lord Salisbury's move failed in conditions that were unusually favourable?

The Labour Party Conference and the making of policy

The Annual Conference of the Labour Party has more influence than its Conservative equivalent. Formally, it has an important place in the constitution of the Party. Historically, it derives influence from the nature of the Party as a mass movement originating outside Parliament. Philosophically, the characteristic posture of the Party, its principles, slogans and myths, are democratic. However, the place and importance of the Conference are neither as definite nor as substantial as this would imply. In particular, when Labour has been in office (about fifteen of its first seventy years) the Conference has usually been docile, ready to accept the lead and the final responsibility of the Labour Cabinet. The range of possible influence is illustrated in the next document.

....

DOCUMENT 6

THE LABOUR CONFERENCE AND
THE MAKING OF POLICY (i)

(a) *The constitutional provision*

[Clause V of the Constitution of the Labour Party:]

The Party Conference shall decide from time to time what specific proposals of legislative, financial or administrative reform shall be included in the Party Programme.

No proposal shall be included in the Party Programme unless it has been adopted by the Party Conference by a majority of not less than two-thirds of the votes recorded on a card vote.

[The card or block vote system gives votes to conference-delegates in accordance with the numbers of members they represent. In consequence, the Trade Unions control roughly five-sixths of the total vote, and the six largest unions dispose of over half the votes.]

(b) *Some contradictory pronouncements*

[The Labour Party Conference] lays down the policy of the Party and issues instructions which must be carried out by the Executive, the affiliated organisations and its representatives in Parliament and on local authorities ... The Labour Party Conference is in fact a parliament of the movement.
(C. R. Attlee, *The Labour Party in Perspective*, Gollancz, 1937, p. 93.)

I want to point out why the Executive cannot accept the resolution ... It contains an instruction to the Parliamentary Party. (J. Walker, M.P., replying for the NEC at the Labour Party Annual Conference, 1937. Report pp. 209–10, quoted in McKenzie, op. cit., p. 427.)

It is quite impossible for a conference of 1,100 people, even if it were constitutionally proper, to determine the order in which the Parliamentary Labour Party and the Government introduces legislation into the House of Commons. It is for the Conference to lay down the policies of the Parliamentary Party, and for the Parliamentary Party to interpret those policies in the light of the Parliamentary system. (Aneurin Bevan, Annual Conference, 1947, quoted in McKenzie, op. cit., p. 516.)

... constitutionally it would be monstrous to have MPs dictated to by an outside body; ... because the Parliamentary Labour Party reflected public opinion far more accurately than the Conference. (Christopher Mayhew, in an interview about nuclear disarmament, in particular the Conference decision of 1960, reported in the *Listener*, 23 March 1967, p. 386.)

....

EXERCISE

THE LABOUR CONFERENCE AND
THE MAKING OF POLICY

4. Does Bevan's view agree with any of the other quotations?

....

DOCUMENT 7

THE LABOUR CONFERENCE AND
THE MAKING OF POLICY (ii)

(a) *The Conference of 1959*

The Leader of the Party, Hugh Gaitskell, opened a debate on the lessons of the Party's defeat in the general election of 1959, and urged reconsideration of the famous Clause IV of the Party's Constitution. This clause seems to commit the Party to nationalisation ('the common ownership of the means of production, distribution and exchange').

Gaitskell's apparently ill-prepared attack on a hallowed principle of the Party met with a good deal of criticism at the Conference and was firmly rejected by the NEC a few months later. Gaitskell perhaps intended only to introduce the idea into discussion, to ventilate it: but the Conference proved quite the wrong place to do so. Clause IV lay next to the old-fashioned heart of the Party and, as with the Conservatives, it is the old-fashioned heart that is worn by many conference delegates.

(b) *The Conference of 1960*

Next year Gaitskell was again in trouble. The Party was divided over Britain's possession of nuclear armaments. The PLP and the leadership, including the NEC, accepted their necessity: many of the delegates, especially from the larger Trade Unions, favoured their abandonment by Britain ('unilateral nuclear disarmament'). The extent of the constitutional authority and actual power of the Conference was crucial, and was also fought over. Thus a delegate from Nottingham, speaking in support of a resolution that '... Labour policy is decided by the Party Conference, which is the final authority', declared: 'There will be those who say we are seeking to tie our Parliamentary members hand and foot. Yes, that is exactly what we do want.' The motion was carried.

Gaitskell, aware that the vote on nuclear arms might be won by the disarmers, stated his intention not to accept the decision of Conference as final:

... It is not the end of the problem because Labour Members of Parliament will have to consider what they do in the House of Commons ... what do you expect them to do? Change their minds overnight? ... Do you think we can simply accept a decision of this kind? ... there are some of us ... who will fight and fight and fight again to save the Party we love ...

Gaitskell did lose the vote, but by comparatively small margins, none more than 407,000 in a total vote of 6–6½-millions. The voting included of course the block votes of the Unions. In this case, the decision of Conference was determined by Mr Cousins, the 'unilateralist' who led the giant Transport and General Workers Union. Cousins and his executive controlled over 800,000 votes at the Conference, and it was their decision to support the unilateral policy which swung the Conference decision. Thus arguments based on the superior democratic rights of Conference obviously have their weakness.

(c) *The Conference of 1961*

Gaitskell and his supporters did fight back with a highly organised intra-party campaign, the so-called Campaign for Democratic Socialism. Gaitskell himself survived a challenge to his leadership by Harold Wilson (the first time the annual re-election of a leader had been contested). Several large unions abandoned the cause of nuclear disarmament. The 1961 Conference reversed the unilateral decision of the previous year. Conference resolved nevertheless that the American Polaris base in Scotland should be removed, but this was ignored by Gaitskell and later, with Labour in power, by Wilson.

EXERCISE

THE INFLUENCE OF THE LABOUR PARTY CONFERENCE

5. R. H. S. Crossman considered that the events of 1960 and 1961 demonstrated the supremacy of Conference. Do you agree?

THE LABOUR PARTY CONFERENCE AND THE
NATIONALISATION OF THE IRON AND STEEL INDUSTRY, 1945

Clause IV of the Party's Constitution contains a commitment to nationalisation:

IV. To secure for the workers by hand or by brain the full fruits of their industry and the most equitable distribution thereof that may be possible, upon the basis of the common ownership of the means of production, distribution and exchange, and the best obtainable system of popular administration and control of each industry or service.

The 'Mikardo amendment', calling for the inclusion in the Election Manifesto of a list of industries to be nationalised, was passed overwhelmingly by the Party Conference of December, 1944. The NEC had asked Mikardo not to press his amendment, but Mikardo ignored the request. Thus Conference had defeated the NEC.

But did it make any difference to the Party's policy? The answer is, some, but not very much.

First, Mikardo's list was much larger than that later included in the Manifesto. Mikardo's list was: 'land, large-scale building, heavy industry, and all forms of banking, transport and fuel and power'. 'Heavy industry' was understood to mean iron and steel. In the event, the Election Manifesto omitted mention of land, building and banking (apart from the Bank of England). So the Conference motion appears to have had only partial success.

Second, the Manifesto's emphatic commitment to nationalise iron and steel was not simply the outcome of Mikardo's Conference amendment. The nationalisation of iron and steel was in fact a time-honoured element in Labour orthodoxy. Conference was here swimming with a strong tide. This suggests one possible rule for Conference influence on policy: Conference is most likely to press a point of policy, and most likely to succeed in doing so, when the point is one of respected orthodoxy.

Third, there is further evidence from Dalton's account of the work of the Committee drawing up the Election Manifesto. Dalton was then a leading member of the Labour Party, and President of the Board of Trade in the Coalition Government. In 1945 he became Chancellor of the Exchequer in the Labour government.

From Hugh Dalton, *The Fateful Years*, Muller, 1957, pp. 432–3:

[In April] we had a row. Morrison proposed, supported by Greenwood, to back down on iron and steel, and leave it out of the Policy Declaration. . . . I strongly resisted this, and won. I said that, if iron and steel was dropped, I should refuse to speak in support of the Policy Declaration at Conference, and then Morrison and Greenwood could explain to the delegates why this item, which had been enthusiastically adopted by Conference only last December, had now vanished.

THE LABOUR PARTY AND THE
NATIONALISATION OF IRON AND STEEL

6. What is the significance of the above extract in assessing the power of the Labour Party Conference?

....

DOCUMENT 9

RECENT CHANGES IN THE CONSERVATIVE PARTY

(a) *The importance of the Annual Conference*

Until 1965, the Conservative Leader did not attend the Party's Conference, but addressed a mass rally after the close of the Conference proper. Baldwin often omitted even that. Since 1965, Mr Heath has attended the Conference and taken part in its debates.

(b) *The selection of the Leader*

Until 1965, Conservative leaders 'emerged'—that is to say, somewhere within the higher circles of the Party, general agreement developed about a successor. Nomination and unanimous, uncontested election followed in a special meeting of MPs, peers, prospective candidates and representatives of the National Union.

In the disputed election of 1957, a genuine attempt was made informally to arrange a census of Conservative parliamentary opinion (including the peers). In the more highly disputed succession of 1963, some sounding of opinion was attempted but haste and the profusion of candidates made an expected and therefore accepted decision impossible. The choice of Sir Alec Douglas-Home secured the full confidence neither of the Party nor, it seems, of the electorate.

The Party therefore established in 1965 a straightforward system of election of the Leader by ballot of Conservative Members of Parliament only. Under this system, Mr Heath was elected in July 1965, defeating Mr Maudling and Mr Enoch Powell.

....

EXERCISES

POWER IN THE CONSERVATIVE PARTY

7. What do these examples show of the recent trends in the distribution of power in the Conservative Party?

8.1. In the light of the evidence and discussion so far, what overall assessment would you make of the influence of Annual Conferences (of both parties) in the formulation of party policy?

In general, is it:

decisive?
considerable?
moderate?
slight?
insignificant?
wholly without significance?

Is it greater in opposition than in power?
Is it greater in the Labour Party than in the Conservative Party?
Is it greater on some kinds of issue than on others?
Is there anything in the nature of very large meetings which affects the issue?
Is there anything in voting or other procedures which affects the issue?
Is there anything in the selection of delegates which affects the issue?

8.2. Does it seem desirable to you that the Conferences should be influential?

(*Note*: As this is one of the most important questions arising in this chapter, the suggested answers appear as an assessment, p. 334.)

4 THE PARTIES AT WORK

Most of this chapter so far, like much recent discussion of political parties, has been concerned with the distribution of power. This is, indeed, an important question, but there remain other equally important aspects to be studied. Pressures and programmes will be dealt with in the next two sections. First, though, it is worth considering what local constituency parties actually do, for the day-to-day job of keeping an organisation going often obscures for the harassed practitioner the nicer problems of power, and hence modifies the struggle for power.

Thus, the local party committee may well be more concerned about the attendance at the next meeting, or the weather for the garden fête, than about their own influence on the development of policy. The business of keeping the organisation going is, in fact, a prime task of the local activists. There are meetings to call, minutes to write up, subscriptions to collect, someone to be coaxed into taking on the treasurer's job next year. This round of activity is the dynamic centre of any voluntary organisation, producing its own experts, its own sense of group endeavour and its own justification. Its ethos is corporate loyalty, not intellectual wrath and insurgency. From all this, the national party may hope to gain faithful toil or, as second best, cosy loyalty, or, a not uncommon third, ineffectual bumbling.

One of the most important jobs of the local party is to gain and hold members, the source of support, funds, help in constituency work, and a small pool of candidates for office. None of the major parties has an individual membership of more than a fraction of the voters who regularly turn out on their behalf at elections. The Conservative Party has had in recent years between two and three million members; the Labour Party about one million directly, excluding members of the politically affiliated trade unions. Thus a political party outside Parliament has four sections: supporters, members, elected officers, professionals. Supporters range from habitual voters to those who feel more deeply committed without actually joining.

The major parties employ full-time professional agents in the constituencies, the Conservatives having an agent in most constituencies, Labour in about a third. On their broad if sometimes threadbare shoulders fall the routine chores of organisation. They are particularly important in maintaining communication with area and national parties, where the professional element is much stronger. The party with the sitting MP has an advantage in the possession of further professional support, and a figure of some prestige and importance to address meetings, open the garden fête, attend to grievances and generally to give the impression of serving all constituents of whatever party.

But the life of the party locally is not confined to routine chores and social events. Elections happen just often enough to keep activists active. Again, there is an immense amount of routine work—writing out envelopes for election literature, arranging meetings, canvassing, radiating confidence. In marginal seats the excitement keeps the parties going. Where, as in two out of three constituencies, the result is fairly certain, the parties fight on, believing logically enough that no seat is won or lost until 10 p.m. on polling day.

Local government also provides stirring work. In local elections some seats are not contested, and, especially in county areas, the contest is not overtly between the national parties. But in the big cities, where nearly four-fifths of the population live, local elections are hotly contested under national party labels, with the party organisation fully engaged. There is some evidence, notably for 1967 and 1968, that such local elections are in practice decided by the electorate's judgement on national issues and the national government. Hence they count as a kind of referendum on a government's performance. The Government's hold on Parliament is not of course affected by the result, but in some policy areas—education and local broadcasting for example—the local implementation of its policies may be checked or hindered. Hence the local party organisation is likely to regard the local elections as an important battleground.

Little of this round of activity has a direct place in the development of policy. The local party will of course receive information about the national party's policy, and will endeavour to promote that policy, especially at election times. The processes of communication are in theory two-way. Ideally, the party members will be aware of, or will inform themselves about, local interests and points of view, and will discuss party policy and pass on their thoughts. A strongly held viewpoint could be formulated as a resolution to an area or national conference. In practice, the processes of communication are more haphazard—a chance discussion with a local shopkeeper, a question to the visiting speaker, a resolution proposed by an articulate stranger and cheerfully passed on because it is nice to have a resolution down. These are the processes of democracy, operated, as they must be, by mostly ordinary people.

Of these processes of party activity two are now examined in more detail: the selection of candidates, and the relations of Members of Parliament with their constituency associations.

The selection of candidates

Two-thirds of parliamentary seats are safe over long periods for one party or the other. In these constituencies, selecting the candidate means selecting a Member of Parliament. The processes of selection are therefore of great importance. The formal processes are analysed in the following document.

DOCUMENT 10

THE PROCEDURES FOR THE SELECTION OF PARLIAMENTARY
CANDIDATES IN THE LABOUR AND CONSERVATIVE PARTIES

	Labour	*Conservative*
Nomination	By ward, or executive committee, or affiliated organisation (not by individuals). Local nominations must be approved by NEC which may also submit nominations.	By the constituency association or its committees, by individuals, including the candidate himself. Local nominations must be approved by the national Standing Advisory Committee on Candidates. The Central Office may also submit names. (The Chairman of the constituency association usually visits Central Office for discussions at the beginning of the process.)
Selection	Short-list of candidates drawn up by the Executive Committee. The NEC has the right (exercised occasionally) to add to the short-list. Candidates then appear before a meeting of the General Management Committee. Both committees are attended by the Regional Organiser. After speeches and questions, choice is made by ballot.	Short-list of candidates drawn up by a small selection committee appears before Executive Council. After speeches and questions, choice is by ballot.
Ratification	The candidate is not introduced to the public until approved by the NEC.	By a general meeting of the constituency association.
Financial considerations	Sponsoring organisations (i.e. trade unions) may contribute up to eighty per cent of maximum permitted campaign expenditure and up to £420 p.a. to funds. (Trade Union sponsorship is not limited to a Union's own members and officials exclusively.)	Since the Maxwell Fyfe Report of 1948, candidates are not asked about their financial standing, and are limited in their contributions to party funds—£100 maximum to electoral campaigns, £25 p.a. maximum to funds, or £50 p.a. if a Member of Parliament.

9.1. At what points in the selection procedure can pressures from the national party be applied?

9.2. Is there any significant difference between the two parties in the matter of selection?

9.3. What effect would you expect the Labour Party's financial arrangements to have in a selection contest between one Trade Union-sponsored and three unsponsored candidates?

The study of formal procedures does not yield much evidence about selection. The study of the results of the procedures—who was selected and who failed—throws more light.

(a) Direct and open veto by the national party is rare in the Conservative Party and infrequent in the Labour Party. Since 1945 there is one known case in the Conservative Party and ten in the Labour Party (mainly concerning Communist or near-Communist candidates).

(b) Party headquarters do not find it easy to secure seats for Ministers, ex-Ministers and others. The local association may be flattered to receive a well-known or distinguished person—Sir Alec Douglas-Home in Kinross, Perthshire, in 1963, Mr Cousins at Nuneaton in 1964. But they may well prefer their own favourite son. For example, Leyton was reluctant to part with its sitting member of many years' standing to accommodate the new Foreign Secretary, Mr Gordon Walker, who had been defeated at Smethwick in 1964—so reluctant that Gordon Walker lost the by-election.

(c) Party efforts to promote particular kinds of candidate, are not very successful. The Conservative Central Office has asked in vain for more trade unionists and more women to be adopted, in place of peers, landowners and brigadiers.

(d) The importance of the local constituency association in the selection of parliamentary candidates does not mean that local candidates are preferred. A large majority of candidatures go to non-locals. There is no hidden 'locality rule' as in the USA, restricting candidature to natives and residents of the locality. Thus, there is no restriction by selection procedures of the opportunity to embark on a political career. A Londoner may seek a seat in Lancashire or Devon, and not expect his geographical connections to count much against him.

(e) To sum up, there is naturally a potential conflict between the central party and the local association. But both sides have equally naturally a common objective—to secure able and attractive candidates, loyal to the party. These qualities may of course be assessed differently at the centre and locally by, say, a retired colonel or a miner, but tact and skill from the professionals normally solve the differences. Dictation from the centre may be impossible, but defiant revolt by the constituency association is also rare.

It is sometimes argued that selection of parliamentary candidates is too important a function in a democracy to be left to quite small groups of party officers and committee-men—a 'selectorate' which it is alleged is not representative in any way of the electorate. There is indeed a problem here. One solution lies in much more vigorous political parties with large and actively participating memberships. Another is the primary election, discussed in chapter 12 below.

The continuing relationship of candidate and constituency

In hopeless seats, candidates move on as soon as they decently can to more fruitful pastures, and the problems of a continuing relationship are thus avoided. But a constituency is stuck for some years at least with its sitting Member, and the relationship between him and his party constituency association is of some importance. The normal relationship is no doubt an easy one, shaped by party solidarity and dominated by the Member, descending from Westminster at week-ends, full of prestige and half-disclosed inside information. But such normal relationships are always shaped to some extent by the possibilities of abnormality. What happens when tensions and disagreements arise?

The constituency association's influence then depends on its ultimate weapon, a refusal, or a serious threat of refusal, to re-adopt the Member as their candidate for the next election. This has happened occasionally—eighteen times in the Conservative Party between 1945 and 1964; sixteen in the Labour Party. Here are some illustrations.

....

DOCUMENT 11

THE MEMBER AND THE CONSTITUENCY ASSOCIATION—
THE THREAT TO REFUSE READOPTION

These and many other cases are described and analysed in A. Ranney, *Pathways to Parliament*, Macmillan, 1965

(a) *Viscount Hinchingbrooke and South Dorset, 1952*

Lord Hinchingbrooke was the Conservative Member for South Dorset. In 1952 he publicly opposed the Government's policy of rearming Germany, thus siding with the Bevanite rebels in the Labour Party. The officers and committee of the Constituency Association remonstrated with him, but Hinchingbrooke asserted his right to 'express and act on his own opinions'. Further, he insisted on putting his case to the whole Association, and before 1300 people won a resounding vote of confidence. The officers of the Constituency Association resigned, and Lord Hinchingbrooke returned in triumph to Westminster, a triumph entirely of his own making.

But Lord Hinchingbrooke was not a good party man. Ten years later, as a peer, he supported an independent candidate campaigning against the Common Market, and the seat was won by Labour (1962–4). Perhaps it is not surprising that Lord Hinchingbrooke (after renouncing his peerage) has been unsuccessful in securing a Conservative nomination in the neighbouring Dorset constituency.

(b) *Miss Burton and Coventry South, 1955*

In this case, the Member won with the backing of the Labour Party's national organisation.

Miss Burton refused to follow the instructions of the Coventry Central Labour Party to cast her vote in the Parliamentary Party against the Leader's motion to withdraw the Whip from Aneurin Bevan and seven of his followers. Miss Burton stated firmly that the issue was one of loyalty to the Leader. The Management Committee of the Coventry Central Labour Party responded with a massive vote of no confidence in Miss Burton. Then the national Party stepped in to indicate that Miss Burton had the full support of the National Executive Committee. The matter was dropped and Miss Burton secured re-adoption for the election of 1955 a few weeks later.

(c) *Nigel Nicolson and Bournemouth East, 1956–9*

In this case, the Member was beaten in a long-drawn-out fight with the Constituency Association and lost his seat. As is usual in the Conservative Party, the national Party was reluctant to intervene (openly and directly at least) in disputes between a Member or candidate and his local association. Local autonomy counts for a great deal. There is of course no guarantee that what is decided locally will be wise and tolerant, any more than that national intervention is bound to be the opposite.

Nicolson opposed the Eden Government's intervention in Suez (October 1956) and abstained in crucial votes in the Commons. He was censured by his Constituency Association and a new candidate was adopted. There was no election, however, and Nicolson remained in Parliament. At the end of 1958 the new prospective candidate resigned his candidature and Nicolson was able to re-enter the fight. He asked for a poll of all party members in the constituency and this was done. Members voted by post for or against Nicolson's readoption. By a few hundred votes in several thousands, Nicolson lost. This was as near as Britain has been to a primary election. (See also chapter 7, p. 247.)

In the Conservative Party, it would seem that deviation to the right is tolerated more easily than deviation to the left. Four of the seven rebels opposed to the attack on Egypt were not re-adopted. A few months later, another set of rebels, this time in the other direction, opposed the resumption of the use of the Suez Canal. None of them experienced much trouble with his constituency association. In the Labour Party, tolerance seems to extend to the left in the constituencies, but the NEC backs loyalists not rebels.

The business of re-adoption is crucial to party coherence and discipline. It is virtually impossible in Britain now to win an election as an Independent, without the financial and organising help and the label/cue to voters which the major parties alone can provide. To be refused re-adoption is equivalent to being dismissed from the profession of politics. In the Labour Party, expulsion by the NEC has the same effect, making re-adoption unconstitutional: the guillotine then falls in the constituency. (It is possible that Mr Desmond Donnelly will prove an exception to this rule in the Pembrokeshire constituency.)

This discussion brings us to the points raised in chapter 5 on the House of Commons. See especially p. 170. There is in this connection a famous pronouncement by Burke condemning 'authoritative instructions':

DOCUMENT 12
BURKE ON 'AUTHORITATIVE INSTRUCTIONS'

From E. Burke, *Speech to the Electors of Bristol*, 1774, in *Speeches and Letters on American Affairs*, Dent, 1908, p. 73

Your representative owes you not his industry only, but his judgement; and he betrays instead of serving you if he sacrifices it to your opinion . . . authoritative instructions arise from a fundamental mistake of the whole order and tenor of our constitution. Parliament is not a congress of ambassadors from different and hostile interests . . . [it] is a deliberative assembly of one nation, with one interest, that of the whole . . . You choose a member indeed; but when you have chosen him, he is not a member of Bristol, but he is a member of Parliament.

EXERCISE
THE DUTY OF AN MP TO HIS CONSTITUENCY

10. Consider the above quotation, and attempt to justify the action of the Bournemouth East Constituency Association in virtually dismissing Nicolson.

5 THE POLITICAL PARTIES AND PRESSURE GROUPS

In the British political system, groups with interests or ideas to promote work mainly in direct relation with the executive, and to a lesser extent with Members of Parliament (see chapter 10). These direct approaches to governing circles seem more effective than approaches to the political parties for pressing specific policy changes or administrative action, revising legislation, or obtaining an increased subsidy. But political parties can have some influence in these matters, participating at an earlier stage in the formulation of policy, and occasionally modifying government action by last-minute protest. So the parties are not neglected by the pressure groups.

Of course, relations with MPs provide good channels of communication to the party, and for most groups this suffices. The parties are clearly somewhat unwieldy instruments for the promotion of specific causes. However, two massive interest groups press continuously on the political parties. The Labour Party has the Trade Unions as a permanent built-in force, and the Conservative Party has close if less formal links with industry.

The Trade Unions and the Labour Party

The Trade Unions are the basis of the Labour Party. Historically they created it in the famous decision of 1900 to set up a Labour Representation Committee. (It is true that much was due to the vision and initiative of Keir Hardie of the Independent Labour Party, and some Trade Union leaders were happy to go on bargaining with the existing parties. But the Party could not have been viable without Union support.) Constitutionally, through political affiliation, the Unions provide the bulk of the membership, a great majority in Conference and almost half of the NEC. Further, they sponsor about forty per cent of Labour's Members of Parliament.

The Trade Unions are just as closely tied to the Labour Party financially. Politics is an expensive activity. The political parties are spared the cost of buying broadcasting time, and the costs of election campaigns are limited by law to something like half-a-million pounds for each party. But the continuing costs of maintaining the organisation are high: propaganda between elections (which is not subject to limitations) is probably necessary and is certainly expensive. The Conservative Party was estimated to have spent over £1 million on propaganda in the period May 1963 to September 1964. Professor Richard Rose has recently assessed the annual cost of running a national party at about £3½-millions (Richard Rose, *Influencing*

Voters, Faber, 1967, p. 58). So a party needs money, even if only to keep up with the other party.

The Trade Unions contribute to the finances of the Labour Party through the 'political levy' paid by all members of affiliated Unions who do not specifically 'contract out'. The total annual contribution amounted in 1967 and 1968 to about three-quarters of the Party's central income. Thus the Labour Party depends on the Trade Unions for finance.

In the light of the historical, constitutional and financial position of the Unions in the Labour Party, is the Party the prisoner of the Unions? Their influence at the Annual Conference has been discussed above. Their influence on the deliberations and voting of Conference is significant, but the Conference itself is not in practice a sovereign body. When the Unions had seemed to gain a victory in 1960, Gaitskell fought back and won. In office, Labour Governments have been able to pursue policies contrary to the interests and principles of the Unions, notably in the case of the incomes policy of the Wilson Government in 1966–8. The powerful Trade Union leader, Mr Cousins, unable to have his way, resigned from the Cabinet and lost influence. Labour Cabinets always include some Trade Unionist Members of Parliament, but they have usually been outnumbered by the university-educated, middle-class professionals and intellectuals.

It is doubtful in any case whether a great party, once in office, can respond exclusively to any one pressure upon it. The collective strength of the Cabinet, the corporate force of the Civil Service, as well as the nature of the problems, force a Government to a viewpoint which is necessarily wider than that of any single element in the political world. This is not to say that the Trade Unions are of little account in the shaping of Labour's programme and policies. Clearly, Union interests and aspirations count a great deal and are pressed continuously on the Government by the Unions themselves, Ministers and Members, by the NEC and privately by the General Council of the Trades Union Congress. The Labour Party needs the support of the Unions, and cannot oppose them too openly or too long. (Significantly, legislation which would have restricted the right to strike was withdrawn by the Government in 1969, in face of opposition from the Trade Unions.)

EXERCISES

THE TRADE UNIONS AND THE LABOUR PARTY

11.1. Should Trade Unions avoid 'getting mixed up in politics'?

11.2. What is the case for accepting that the Trade Unions should have a considerable influence in the Labour Party?

11.3. Do you see any justification for the view that the Labour Party leadership in its relations with the Unions 'gets the worst of both worlds'?

Industry and the Conservative Party

The Conservative Party has no formal links with industry equivalent to the Labour Party's relationship with the Trade Unions. Nevertheless, there is a strong informal connection. Conservative policies and principles are clearly more sympathetic to the needs and desires of industry, more precisely to the owners and managers of industry and business. Many Conservative Members of Parliament have a business background and continue to hold directorships and other positions in industry (see chapter 5). Conservative Cabinets usually include one or two members with strong business or industrial experience.

There is no doubt, moreover, that industrial interests provide a good deal of financial support for the Party, directly by contributions, or indirectly through propaganda organisations like Aims of Industry and the Economic League. Groups of this kind spent nearly £1½m. on anti-nationalisation propaganda before the 1959 election, and almost £2m. in the period before the 1964 election. Such propaganda was inevitably pro-Conservative. There is very little public information about the finances of the Conservative Party, which did not publish any detailed accounts until 1968. For the year 1967, the Party had an estimated income of over £800,000 and spent over £1-million. It is known, moreover, that Conservative appeals for funds have met with a good response: in 1947 Lord Woolton asked for £1m. and got it, and an appeal in 1967 was equally successful. Regular contributions by business firms may amount to about one third of central income. This is high absolutely but much less than the Unions' contribution to the Labour Party. The Conservative Party is certainly able to afford a much larger professional staff than any other. In 1963 it had 677 members on its full-time administrative staff, to Labour's 286, and the Liberals' 89. The Conservative Party is, comparatively, a wealthy one.

But this is not to say that the Party is the slave of industrial or any other wealthy interests. There is, indeed, much evidence to the contrary. Thus, there are Conservatives who are not connected with industry, and who may not feel an identity of interest with big business—farmers and small businessmen for example. The Conservative leadership includes academics, lawyers and writers, who may be regarded in this context as independent of the industrial interest groups. There is usually little evidence of such interests at the Party's

Conference, but of course this indicates that these groups operate more discreetly than the Trade Unions in the Labour Party, rather than that they do not operate at all.

There are occasions when the policies of the Conservative Party have not served, or have even gone against, the interests of industry. This was true, for example, of the legislation on Resale Price Maintenance in 1963–4, which was pushed through by the Cabinet (with some concessions, it is true) against the vociferous opposition of the business interests both inside and outside the Party. Again, the 'Industrial Charter' of 1947 was developed within the Research Department and among a small group of leaders centred on Mr Butler. The Conservative Party in office is bound by the same political and constitutional constraints as Labour. It must work within the framework of Cabinet and Civil Service, and secure support from a mass electorate. On the other hand, for both parties these major interests are so closely bound in with the party that they will not always be seen as external forces. Hence, following such interests may seem perfectly natural, and not a concession to a pressure group at all. Gross concession to abnormal pressure is therefore somewhat inhibited.

EXERCISES

BUSINESS INTERESTS AND THE CONSERVATIVE PARTY

12.1. Should business stay out of politics?

12.2. Suppose we construct a scale to indicate the closeness or strength of the relationship of a party to a pressure group:

> captivity
> close alignment
> loose alignment
> bias in favour
> high receptivity to suggestions
> low receptivity to suggestions
> sympathy

Where on this scale would you place the Labour Party in relation to the Trade Unions, and the Conservative Party in relation to business and industry? (Of course, if you care to construct a scale of your own, please do so.)

6 PROGRAMMES AND PRINCIPLES

What the parties stand for

Parties seek support for programmes and principles, ideas and faith. These are what the struggle for influence in the exterior party is about and these—the basic ideology of the party—may bar or modify the pressures of interest groups.

There are four levels at which the parties reveal 'what they stand for'. At a literary and philosophical level there are expositions of party principles. In political speeches, particularly during elections, there emerges a more general image, a highly favourable one for your own side, and on the reverse a caricature of the other side in various unsavoury disguises. At the same time, a party will put forward a more specific programme. And if it gets into power its principles may be inferred (subject to some qualification) from its performance.

At all levels, however, a rough bipolarity tends to arise. Partly this is natural—one is for or against, right or left, good or bad—but the movement to opposite poles is reinforced in Britain by the electoral system.

The philosophical level. There is no single, simple guide to the philosophies of the great parties, for each is in reality a coalition (cynics would say a ragbag) of ideas and policies, based on a philosophy which is eclectic and pragmatic, picking up ideas here and there, and dropping them if they do not work or do not appeal. Thus, the Conservative Party is not devoted merely to avoiding change; the Labour Party caters for interests wider than those of labour, and leaves its opponents to call it socialist; the Liberal Party is not sure of the ways in which it is liberal (free trade?—free enterprise?—freedom from want?).

With this reservation, here are some extracts which may convey at least the tendency and the flavour of the Conservative and Labour Parties.

....

DOCUMENT 13

THE PHILOSOPHY OF THE CONSERVATIVE PARTY

From Quintin Hogg, *The Case for Conservatism*, Penguin, 1947, pp. 10, 11, 13, 14, 97

(a) Conservatives do not believe that political struggle is the most important thing in life ... The simplest among them prefer fox-hunting—the wisest religion.

(b) The Conservative does not believe that the power of politics to put things right in this world is unlimited.

(c) Conservatism is not so much a philosophy as an attitude . . . Indeed history records no example of a fixed political theory, however successful, which does not appear wrong, and even ridiculous, in the eye of succeeding generations.

(d) . . . private property is to the interest of the community since the desire to obtain it provides an incentive for work which is morally legitimate, and at the same time sufficiently material to operate on natures which in most of us contain certain elements not entirely spiritual or unselfseeking . . . private property—including some large fortunes—is the natural bulwark of liberty because it ensures that economic power is not entirely in the hands of the State.

....

DOCUMENT 14

THE PHILOSOPHY OF THE LABOUR PARTY

(a) C. A. R. Crosland, formerly a Fellow of Trinity College, Oxford, has been a member of the Labour Government since 1964, and a Cabinet Minister since 1965. This is a brief summary of part of the main argument of chapters VI–X of *The Future of Socialism*, Cape, 1964, dealing with the idea of social equality:

Crosland argues that the economic welfare argument for equality no longer applies with much force: 'to make the rich less rich would not make the poor significantly less poor'. The case for equality rests now rather on 'certain value or ethical judgements of a non-economic character'. These are:

the need to diminish social antagonism ('collective resentments');

the achievement of social justice—equitable rewards for ability and effort; and the diffusion of power;

the avoidance of social waste (barriers to mobility).

Thus far, Crosland's ideal society is one of equality of opportunity, and social mobility. But he accepts that this must be modified to avoid the replacement of the old élite of birth and wealth by a formidable new élite of brains and examination distinctions (meritocracy, as it has sometimes been called).

(b) From R. H. Tawney, *Equality*, Allen & Unwin, 4th edn., 1952, p. 49

So to criticise inequality and to desire equality is not, as is sometimes suggested, to cherish the romantic illusion that men are equal in character and intelligence. It is to hold that, while their natural endowments differ profoundly, it is the mark of a civilised society to aim at eliminating such inequalities as have their source, not in individual differences, but in its own organisation, and that individual differences, which are a source of social energy, are more likely to ripen and find expression if social inequalities are, as far as practicable, diminished. And the obstacle to the progress of equality . . . is the habit of mind which thinks it, not regrettable, but natural and desirable, that different sections of a community should be distinguished from each other by sharp differences of economic status, of environment, of education and culture and habit of life. It is the temper which regards with approval the social institutions and economic arrangements by which such differences are emphasised and enhanced, and feels distrust and apprehension at all attempts to diminish them.

(c) From a Statement of the National Executive Committee, March 1960 Labour Aims. The British Labour Party is a democratic socialist party. Its central ideal is the brotherhood of man. Its purpose is to make this ideal a reality everywhere.

(i) It stands for social justice, for a society in which the claims of those in hardship or distress come first; where the wealth produced by all is fairly shared among all; where difference in rewards depend not upon birth or inheritance but on the effort, skill and creative energy contributed to the common good; and where equal opportunities exist for all to live a full and varied life.

(ii) Regarding the pursuit of material wealth by and for itself as empty and barren, it rejects the selfish, acquisitive doctrines of capitalism, and strives to create instead a socialist community based on fellowship, co-operation and service in which all can share fully in our cultural heritage.

(iii) Its aim is a classless society from which all class barriers and false social values have been eliminated. . . .

....

EXERCISE

THE USES OF PHILOSOPHY

13. It may be thought that ideas of the kind put forward in documents 13 and 14 are lofty, vague and of no relevance or application in practical politics. In order to test this, list the three most important problems facing the present Government and say how, if at all, these ideas might help in the solution of the problems.

The level of public political struggle. This is the level of slogans, sly propaganda and image-making. Here are two examples.

....

DOCUMENT 15

PARTY PROPAGANDA

(a) From F. Marquis, *Memoirs of the Earl of Woolton*, Cassell, 1959, pp. 334–5

The word 'Conservative' was certainly not a political asset when compared with the Socialist word 'Labour'. The man who first called the Socialist Party the 'Labour Party' was a political genius, for indeed the word 'labour' implied the party that would look after the best interests of 'labour': this word 'labour' had nothing to do with the Socialist conception that all labour should be employed by the State. . . .

I made up my mind that we would call the Government the 'Socialist Party'. This was their true description; it was on the dogma of [nationalisation that they had been elected]. I would have liked to call the Conservative Party the 'Union Party'. That, indeed, is its proper title, representing the unity of the Empire, the essential unity between the Crown, the Government, and the people . . .

(b) From Labour Party pamphlet, 'The future Labour offers you', 1959

. . . Unlike Socialists, the Tories still believe that, in the age of automation and atomic power, the economic future of fifty million people packed on a small island can—and should—be shaped decisively by a free-for-all scramble with private profits as the prize.

They believe that the major economic and political decisions should be taken by the rich and the powerful—government by 'top people'.

They believe that they have some inherent imperial right to impose their will by force. We are still paying for their reckless and futile Suez campaign. [Propaganda of this kind contains the key words which characterise party attitudes. Conservatives tend to use: freedom, opportunity, unity of the British people, the nation. Labour tends to use: fair shares, social justice, equal opportunity, the classless society.]

....

Programmes and performance. When it comes down to party programmes, there is a good deal of common ground between the parties. All are in favour of peace, prosperity, more and better roads, schools, hospitals, pensions (and the cynic might fail to see any firm and practicable proposals for achieving these desirable goods).

A novelist and former Member of Parliament has neatly caught the situation:

....

DOCUMENT 16

THE CANDIDATE'S DILEMMA—
IN WHAT DOES HIS PARTY DIFFER?

From David Walder, *The Short List*, Hutchinson, 1964, p. 166

[The (fictional) Conservative candidate sits in his hotel room, towards the end of his campaign, and contemplates the three election addresses:]

'The Labour Party is in favour of social justice.' No Party campaigned against it. 'The Conservative Party favours freedom.' The reverse was, to say the least, unlikely. 'The Liberal Party wants a modern Britain.' On the face of it there seemed to be no argument.

Education bulked large. 'Expanding', said the Tories. 'Expansive', said the Liberals. 'Extending', said the Socialists. Each Party hammered home the care of the young and the elderly, as if its rivals stood for child labour and compulsory euthanasia at sixty . . .

....

For all this, if the evidence of performance in office is considered alongside principles and programmes, important differences between the parties emerge. Even party cant (which, alas, the system produces in good measure) has its different styles.

....

DOCUMENT 17

THE BASIC DIFFERENCES BETWEEN
THE CONSERVATIVE AND LABOUR PARTIES

	Conservative Party	Labour Party
Economy	For private property and free enterprise: hence outright opposition to nationalisation and a lack of enthusiasm for planning.	For common ownership, planning—enthusiastic planners.
Taxation	High taxation regarded as discouraging enterprise.	'Robin Hoods' (robbing the rich to feed the poor).
Welfare	Perhaps unenthusiastic, especially about 'universal' welfare schemes i.e., irrespective of need; aims to work welfare state efficiently.	Enthusiasm for 'fair shares', helping the weak, concern for a national minimum.
Social equality	Favours private education and (in the recent past at any rate) selective grammar schools: hence sees the ideal society as based on distinctions of merit and wealth, a society in which there must be leaders and led.	Against both private and selective schools. This is one of the sharpest distinctions now between right and left, and is related to fundamental ideas about social equality, as against Conservative notions of a society which is necessarily unequal to some extent, because this reflects natural inequalities and encourages enterprise through competition and rewards.
Foreign policy and defence	Strongly patriotic, favouring a world role for Britain; willingly high spenders on defence; suspicious of UNO.	Tendency to split on this, particularly when the Party is in power. Strong tendencies to 'Little Englander' policies, colonial withdrawal, distrust of NATO and nuclear weapons and Germany. Consistently enthusiastic support for UNO.

....

Overlap between the parties. Clearly there are important differences between the parties. Nevertheless, on many matters they do not sit around opposite poles, and at many points the differences lie in degrees of enthusiasm or reluctance, no more. There is much common ground.

EXERCISE

PARTY OVERLAP

14. Does this overlap between the parties matter? Would you prefer:

(a) to choose between two parties clearly opposed over a wide range of policies; or,

(b) to choose between two parties which overlap so much that it will not make so much difference who gets a majority?

Sources of support for the parties. The major parties share, then, a large area of common ground. But despite converging programmes they still draw support from sociologically different sections of the community. Very roughly, the Labour Party draws ten-million voters from the manual wage-earning class, and two-million from the middle class. The Conservatives draw roughly six million from each class. These differences are not haphazard: there are clearly elements in each party's programme, attitudes and history which make one mainly a working-class party, the other something of a middle-class party. It seems likely, therefore, that the parties will converge in programmes insofar as social classes converge in outlook. And insofar as social divisions tend to persist, then differences between the parties will tend to persist.

GUIDE TO EXERCISES

1.1. All except (a), and that is of course essential for the carrying out of other functions.

Why?—because all of these functions are to do with representation, and with the political communication, education, persuasion and control that go with democracy.

1.2. (a), (b) and (c). All of these functions, so valuable for democratic politics, can be carried out in single and multi-party systems. The special merit of a two-party system lies in the competition, the clear choice, and the possibility of alternation. By comparison, the single party restricts choice, and many parties complicate it. But a two-party system may impose an unnatural pattern of choice.

1.3. Desirable for what end? If for good or democratic government, the answer would seem to be, yes: representation, communication and so on are democratic insofar as they involve a substantial proportion of the people. This leaves the problem of what constitutes a substantial proportion. It cannot be expected that all, or nearly all, the people will wish to belong to, and take an active part in political parties—and the theory of democracy does not require this. The present membership of the parties, counting all affiliated Trade Unionists, is about nine-million. This is a quarter of the electorate, and is perhaps rather low from the idealistic point of view of this exercise.

2.1. The third, or perhaps the second view. Attlee managed to assert a view of the leadership similar to that of Professor Mackenzie, with the Leader of the Party predominant especially when transformed into Prime Minister. On the other hand, the fact that Attlee was challenged is itself significant.

2.2. The lapse of time—ten years—since Attlee was elected; the absence of normal party politics during the war; the circumstances of Attlee's election in 1935, when the PLP was very small; his rather modest methods of leadership; the peculiar abilities and prestige of Professor Laski—all these matters detract from the significance of these incidents of 1945.

3. It failed at the time, but registered a point of view which had much sympathy and has had at least some influence on Conservative policy since then. This was not absolute failure, therefore. But conditions were certainly favourable for success: there was a crisis; the issue was important to party philosophy and to party interests; Salisbury was of high, even though by then waning, prestige; the party was in opposition and not therefore cramped by practical considerations; and the platform had shown little positive leadership.

4. Bevan's view seems to fit none of them exactly, for he lays down a division of function which accords major powers to Conference (the making of policy), but large if obscure powers to the PLP too (interpreting those policies in the light of the parliamentary system). Thus Bevan tries to preserve Conference sovereignty, without making the PLP the slave of the Conference. In theory these are incompatible, in practice the relationship is left open for persuasion and pressure.

5. No: Gaitskell quite openly and specifically rejected the decision of the 1960 Conference. The presumption is that, in office, he would not have acted upon the decision, leaving his critics to unseat him if they could. (But, as he well knew, the leadership is a matter for the PLP; so the ultimate power lies there and not in Conference.)

On the other hand, the fight to rescind the decision implied a certain respect for the authority of Conference.

Note that the Polaris decision of 1961 went unheeded.

The incidents of 1960 and 1961 show well the power of small groups of activists working through the machinery of mass democracy. This may affect the ultimate judgement on whether a Conference decision is more 'democratic' than a decision of, say, the PLP.

6. The Conference resolution was not simply an assertion of the floor against the platform. At least one influential senior member of the Party strongly sympathised with the resolution. In consequence, he was able to use the Conference as a stick to beat his faint-hearted colleagues. Without this, perhaps, the Conference resolution would have had much less effect. Even conceding this, however, the Conference resolution was a factor of some significance in the ultimate policy decision.

7. The new arrangements for the election of the Leader are clearly an attempt to make the Party's procedures more obviously open, democratic and efficient. Formally, at least, power has shifted in this matter towards the Party in Parliament, away from the influence of peers, candidates and constituency representatives, all of whom had previously had at least a formal part in the Leader's election. But that election had always been little more than a formal ratification. In the real choice, made in the process of 'emergence', influence had lain with the Party's leaders in Parliament, and with Conservative Members of Parliament, but also with 'elder statesmen' and Party establishment figures (like Churchill and Salisbury in 1957). If this was so, then the movement of power in 1965 was from the inner circle of leaders to the Party in Parliament, with the mass Party not involved.

In the case of the Conference changes, however, the intention, and the achievement, was to involve the mass Party in communication with the Leader.

8.1. and 2. The answers to these exercises appear as an assessment (p. 334).

9.1. Formally, the points of influence are: at the nominating stage in the submission and approval of names; at the selection stage in the presence of a regional organiser in the case of the Labour Party; and at the ratification stage in the case of the Labour Party.

But formal procedures do not tell the whole story. It is possible for the party headquarters to apply pressure behind the scenes, tactically the sooner the better.

9.2. Formally, the NEC has slightly more influence than any central body of the Conservative Party. It is, indeed, usual to regard national influence as predominant in the Labour Party. If this is so, it is due to the nature of the Party, with a tradition of 'democratic centralism', a vigorous mass-movement, but one closely controlled to prevent factionalism. Also Labour's constituency officers have not the high local prestige of some

Conservative officers, and are readier therefore, it is assumed, to concur with pressures from the centre.

However, hard and precise evidence on selection procedures is not available.

9.3. There is a tendency for sponsored candidates to be preferred because of the money they can bring with them. But this is far from being always the case—it still depends on the quality of the candidates. (It is perhaps fair to point out that a Conservative selection committee may well be attracted by a candidate with spare time for political work, and also by one who is willing to buy a house in the constituency.)

10. There are two possible lines of argument. (a) Burke is wrong, at least for the twentieth century. Party is a fundamental principle of organisation. The electorate votes for a party, rather than a candidate, and the winning party may reasonably expect conformity to party principle. Individual conscience may properly be subordinated to the higher principle (in this context) of party solidarity. (b) While Burke is in general acceptable, his principle does not apply to this particular case, for Nicolson was either clearly wrong, or just as clearly in conflict with basic Conservative principle, or both. This is to imply that the constituency association is a proper judge of the scope of individual conscience.

It is important to separate the political/constitutional argument from the argument about Middle East policy. It might be that the constituency association was mistaken in its views on foreign policy, but correct about its own constitutional position.

11.1. They are 'mixed up in politics', whether they like it or not, for they are organised specifically to press views and interests where there is certain to be disagreement and conflict. But it does not follow that they should ally themselves with one political party.

11.2. But why not have such influence? There can be no objection in political morality unless the result were gravely to distort the processes of representation. Now trade unionists and their wives make up about half of the electorate, and their interests are of great importance in the community. Hence, even if they exercised considerable influence in the Labour Party, this would not amount to 'grave distortion'.

Of course, the Labour Party ought to represent other interests as well as those of the Trade Unions—for example the interests of the professions and of consumers, which might be in conflict with those of the Unions. If it were consistently prevented from doing so, then distortion might occur. The Constitution of the Labour Party, by giving weight to the Trade Unions, seems always in danger of permitting distortion. (There are equivalent dangers arising from less formal liaisons in the Conservative Party.) In practice, distortion does not occur continuously. If it did, the remedy (one remedy at least) would lie in the ballot-box.

11.3. In this question the argument changes from considerations of morality and propriety to considerations of political tactics. The Party gets a great deal from the Unions—particularly money, sympathy, support. But, of course, the support is not guaranteed: no votes are delivered, and Trade Unions have been known to wreck a Labour Government's policies. Their influence sharply restricts a Labour Government's freedom of action. For all this, however, the credit balance is still massive: the Trade Unions are still the rock on which the Labour Party is raised. So the brief answer is: No!

12.1. No: in a modern industrial state, business, like the Unions, forms one of the great interests involved in society. Of course, it will certainly be in conflict with other groups and with society as a whole. But such conflicts are the agenda of politics, and business has a right to engage in political activity. Moreover, since these conflicts are among the most important in any modern society, a political party may properly seek to defend or promote the interests of one side. But we should expect this to be done with a reasonable regard for other interests, and the need of a party for mass support normally ensures this.

12.2. There is room for disagreement here! But it seems reasonable to put both in one or other of the alignment categories. This may be justified by reference to Labour's constitution, its philosophy and history, its personnel, and to some extent its policies. In the case of the Conservative Party, all of these, except the constitution, would seem to apply.

13. In broad terms, the major problems facing any modern British Government are: (a) economic efficiency and prosperity, (b) social justice, (c) security. The parties might place these in a different order, and give varying interpretations to these terms.

It is notably difficult to translate the philosophies into hard policies, except in relation to social justice. This might well be because the few extracts offered on party philosophy are not truly representative. But the case perhaps is that the characteristic beliefs and attitudes which divide the parties are about social justice, rather than economics or foreign policy. This is perhaps a surprising conclusion. But it helps to explain why governments seem most of the time to be pursuing policies very similar to those of the opposing parties. Social justice tends for all governments to be lower in priority than security and prosperity (which might be regarded as preconditions of social justice). Indeed, some governments have to struggle so hard with the preconditions that they have neither time, scope, nor energy to tackle the matters on which they have distinctive policies.

14. This is a matter of taste; more precisely a matter of judgement, depending on both one's personal view of the nature of politics, and the range and nature of the problems the system has to grapple with. Thus, in the Depression of the early 1930s, it was a pity that a choice of economic policies was not available. When problems are less severe, it may seem beneficial that a large measure of agreement be maintained. Politics, it may be argued, should not disturb the minimum basic cohesion of society. On the other hand, this may seem a rather static view of society, evading the tensions which promote necessary change. However, in practice, given the nature of society, it seems likely that it will suffer more from excessive divisions than from an excess of consensus. Overlap between the parties contributes to a continuity of policy and administration which is efficient and comfortable—as long as it does not obscure relevant and important differences.

ASSESSMENTS

(a) *The influence of the exterior party: general*

Exterior parties in Britain do not have a substantial or decisive influence. There are good general reasons for this. First, it is in the nature of the political system that government is the initiating force: it is responsible to, but not directly controlled by, the people. The Opposition, as an alternative government, tends to operate in the same way. This fundamental aspect of the system is reinforced by the practical possibilities. The parliamentary leadership is in a decision-making position: it has information, a national viewpoint, and the requisite machinery. The local parties are better equipped to gather votes than to formulate policy. Hence, a division of labour exists and is perpetuated by traditions and institutions. Finally, all parties accept in practice a form of 'democratic centralism'. Democracy is not contradicted by discipline and central control: rather these are necessary props of an effective democratic movement.

However, this is not the whole of the matter. Exterior parties do have some influence, and for good reasons. First, the parties need the constituency associations. They depend on the local party loyalist for essential electoral work. Second, being, or at least looking, democratic ensures a certain approval—the reverse leads to murmurs, and headlines about dictatorship. This is true for both parties. If the Labour tradition of democracy is strong, it is modified by the embattled revolutionary tradition of democratic centralism. And if the Conservative tradition of democracy is weaker, it draws force from the social strength and independence of its constituency associations.

There is another consideration. The party out of office is much less of a central decision-taking machine, much more open to pressure from below. Compared with the governing party, the parliamentary party in opposition is a weak administrative machine, and may well be rivalled by the central organs of the exterior party. Periods out of office promote intra-party democracy.

All this is the argument in specifically political terms. It is well to remember that the relationship will be determined for much of the time by more human considerations—respect for the leaders, loyalty to the party, ignorance and some bewilderment among the ordinary members—but crossed and modified occasionally by notions of independence and assertiveness, illumined by bright ideas, and strengthened by sturdy if sometimes cantankerous principle. These human considerations appear to reinforce the verdict of political reasoning: the influence of exterior parties is weak, uneven, discontinuous, but rarely negligible, and occasionally of some significance. Michels' 'Iron Law' is not wholly acceptable in this context.

(b) *The influence of the exterior party: the Annual Conference*

(This assessment is also an answer to exercise **8.** p. 311.)

The first assessment sought to determine the influence of exterior parties by reasoning about their nature, the nature of the leadership, and the relations of the two. It is also important, as has been attempted within limits in the text, to examine the historical record of the relationship. This assessment tries to sum up the record for one important aspect of the record, the Annual Conference.

The influence of party conferences is slight but uneven, ranging perhaps from insignificance to occasional moderate importance. This last would be a formulation of the maximum, and may overstate the case.

The influence of conferences is normally greater when a party is in opposition, for the leadership is not confined by its responsibility, and bound to its government-centred bureaucracy. Moreover, the leaders are likely to be seeking new policy ideas, and have more time as well as more reason to listen to the voice of the exterior party.

The Labour Party is more open to influence from its exterior organisation than the Conservatives, though the difference is not great. The crucial factors are the position of the Trade Unions, and the constitutional position of the National Executive Committee. The Labour Party Conference has been on balance more effectively awkward than the Conservative Conference, notably in 1959 and 1960. This is not to deny that the leadership usually wins such conflicts in the end; that the NEC is usually effectively penetrated by the Parliamentary Party; that the constituency parties have less independence that the Conservative associations; and that the tradition of a mass-movement is overlaid by a tradition of democratic centralism, and a growing awareness of the traditions of British Cabinet government. The point here is not that the Labour Conference is powerful, but that it is slightly more influential than the Conservative Conference.

For both parties, the influence of Conference is greatest on issues where the leaders are divided or unsure, and where the party's own previous attitude has been well-defined and touched a little with emotion—the issues near the old-fashioned heart of the party. In the Conservative Party, this includes old colonial and free enterprise issues; in the Labour Party it includes nationalisation, the welfare state and colonial withdrawal.

Conferences are mass meetings, and by their nature can only proceed under a substantial measure of platform management. Initiative from the floor requires great skill as well as courage. On the other hand, such meetings are open to waves of crowd emotion which can sometimes endanger both platform and party. The card-voting system used by the Labour Conference facilitates control, as long as the leadership and the major Unions are in line. There are obvious possibilities of a major breakdown here: but the record shows that this has been avoided, narrowly, through the moderation, good sense, conservatism, malleability and internal divisions of the Trade Unions.

There is little evidence to suggest that the people who go to conferences are especially radical or loyalist in their attitudes. They are distinguished mainly by having both the time and the enthusiasm to attend.

There is a certain unreality about Party Conferences. David Walder's fictional candidate said conference was like a visit to brigade headquarters after a week on continuous military exercises—it hardly seemed to be the same army. Again there is some truth, applicable to all parties, in Aubrey Jones' view of the Conservative Conference of 1946: there was, he said, 'much facile revolt and much aimless candour, a cry that the party should march somewhere, though few could suggest where.'

Clearly the main business of conferences is not the formulation of policy. Conferences are mass rallies and necessary rituals, something like a speech day crossed with a meeting of the students' representative council. At the end of the day, the headmaster is still in office, and that is what counts most.

This leaves the question of what is the desirable relationship between the leadership and the exterior party. It seems reasonable that party leaders should have to *report* to a representative meeting of the membership, and hear comment, both approving and critical. It seems reasonable again that Conference should be able to *propose* new or modified policies. In the longer range and within wider limits, it seems reasonable that Conference should even *prescribe the outlines* of party policy. 'Reasonable' here means fair and just by democratic standards, and practicable.

To go beyond this towards close direction of the party by Conference seems unlikely to be either efficient or truly representative. But these cautious considerations of power should not lead us to accept a passive, even apathetic exterior party. Democracy gains from a high level of political interest, information and participation. There is much virtue in Mr Crossman's vision of a pervasive, dynamic exterior party (document 2 (b)).

(c) *Political parties and democracy*

Political parties perform functions which are essential to a democratic system of government. This was argued in the introduction (p. 289) and in exercise 1. (see p. 294).

On this theme of democracy two further questions arise. First, are the British political parties carrying out their democratic functions effectively? Clearly more could be done! Neither party is a really satisfactory instrument of political education either for the masses, or more narrowly, for its own members. Neither makes full use of the membership for comment, criticism and ideas. Neither can be described as dynamic or creative; they are simply useful for getting out the vote. However, anyone with experience of a large voluntary organisation will know the difficulties of securing and maintaining momentum. It depends on the most difficult kind of leadership, leadership from among rather than from above or in front of the led.

The second question relates to the wider study of comparative politics. Does the British evidence suggest that political parties, more specifically a two-party system, are essential to democracy? The answer was indicated in the introduction and in exercise 1. It is quite possible for the functions of representation and political communication to be carried out within a single party, but the two-party system confers the advantages of choice and competition. Democratic politics without any kind of political party at all is possible—it happens in British local government in some rural areas. But if non-party Councillor Smith is to behave democratically, he must spend a good deal of time and energy in finding out what his constituents want. In larger and more complex political communities, the organisation of groups for electoral, representative and governmental purposes is a necessary condition of effective democracy.

Of course, this is not to say that the two-party system is without disadvantages. If it confers a genuine choice between two sides (or points of view, or sets of attitudes), at the same time it restricts choice virtually to just those two sides, leaving many other viewpoints without adequate representation. Again, parties are necessarily partisan, but often, in a two-party system, excessively so. Issues and policies are seen as black and white, sometimes with a degree of deliberation and hypocrisy. One distinguished Labour MP, and former (resigned) Minister, Christopher Mayhew, has recently complained of the difficulties of being at once partisan and honest: 'A certain degree of humbug is inevitable in politics, but the amount required of us now to keep the party system going is becoming excessive.' The fault is one to which the system easily runs, but it is avoidable. There is a responsibility on the partisans themselves to restrain their partisanship well this side of dishonesty and hypocrisy.

RECAPITULATION EXERCISES

1. *True or false?* (mark T or F)

(a) Britain has had a two-party system since 1900.

(b) The Leaders of both major parties are elected by their Members in the House of Commons.

(c) The Leader of the Conservative Party does not attend his party's Annual Conference.

(d) The Leader of the Labour Party is an *ex officio* member of the National Executive Committee.

(e) In the Conservative Party, the selection of candidates is a purely local affair.

2. What in general terms are the major functions of political parties?

3. Why would you say the Leader of the Labour Party has slightly less power than the Conservative Leader?

4. Indicate briefly the distinctive attitudes of the major parties.

5. Why in general is neither party the 'slave' simply of a major interest group?

KEY TO RECAPITULATION EXERCISES

1. (a) F   (b) T   (c) F   (d) T   (e) F

2. At its simplest: developing a programme; recruiting candidates; securing support, including votes for programme and candidate. A party is involved in a two-way communication and brokerage operation.

3. Because of constitutional differences—the system of election, the relation to the National Executive Committee and the Conference. Also because of the different tradition, ethos or nature of the Party— especially the Party as a radical democratic mass movement.

4. See document 17.

5. Because each has to take account of other possibly competing interests within the Party; each must gather the support of almost half a mass electorate; and because government itself (Civil Service and Cabinet) provides built-in barriers.

[10]
Pressure groups

1 OUTLINE

Definitions

Pressure groups are groups which seek to change government policy, in its fundamental or in its administrative aspects, by various forms of persuasion, and without themselves taking over government power.

'Changes in government policy' are sought because the group has an interest to protect and foster, an idea to promote—or something of both. The group might be concerned with fundamental government policy, e.g., the nationalisation of steel; or with an administrative detail, e.g., the application of a lower rate of purchase tax to domestic pots and pans. 'Persuasion' includes methods ranging from rational argument in a pamphlet or a restaurant to a threat of withdrawal from the Health Service or a parade of taxis blocking Parliament Square. Pressure groups do not want to take over government themselves: if so, they would be political parties.

The term 'pressure group' may be regarded as unsatisfactory because 'pressure' is a loaded word. We should all be happy to persuade but not to bully—pressure may always seem undue. Another objection to the word 'pressure' is that it might imply a continuous activity, and thus not cover the many organisations which simply keep an eye on government, in case pressure may be needed. The best alternative, 'interest group', has the same kind of defect, and omits the group which has an idea or an attitude to promote. The use of the term 'lobby' is also misleading, for the lobbies of Parliament are not so much frequented by serious pressure-groupers, and 'lobby' is not a neutral word for Americans. It seems that any term we use will at best be a shorthand expression requiring definition if it is to be useful.

Examples

(a) Groups which seek to protect and foster interests, or 'spokesmen of sectional interests':

(i) Manufacturing, commercial and business interests: e.g., the Confederation of British Industries, the Association of British Chambers of Commerce, the Champagne Association.

339

(ii) Employers, professional men and employees: e.g., the National Federation of Building Trades Employers, British Medical Association, National Union of Mineworkers.

(b) Groups with an idea, ideal or cause to promote: e.g., the Lord's Day Observance Society, Electrical Association for Women, Howard League for Penal Reform, Campaign for Nuclear Disarmament.

(c) Other groups having interests or ideals which may suffer from or benefit by government action: e.g., Country Landowners Association, Income Tax Payers Society, National Federation of Women's Institutes, British Legion; associations representing the Churches, ethnic groups, sport and many more.

These lists could be very long indeed: there are very few activities which are not the subject of 'pressure' of some kind.

....

DOCUMENT I

ILLUSTRATIONS OF PRESSURE GROUP ACTIVITY

(a) The Consumers' Association. Extract from Seventh Annual Report, July 1964

Although representation of the consumer is not CA's main function, we do submit evidence to official bodies where our experience of comparative testing suggests possible improvements in legislation or in voluntary standards. For example, a memorandum on the revision of Hire Purchase legislation was submitted to the Board of Trade. We were very pleased to see that the subsequent Parliamentary Bill on this subject not only dealt with our recommendation that any declared or advertised hire purchase charge should be expressed in terms of a true rate of interest, but also adopted the formula we had suggested for calculating the true rate of interest. We also made various detailed suggestions arising from the results of our tests to Government departments and the British Standards Institution.

(b) The British Plastics Federation. Extract from *Industrial Trade Associations, Activities and Organisation*, PEP, 1957, p. 87

The British Plastics Federation is in regular contact with the Board of Trade, the industry's sponsoring department, over export matters and statistics, with the Ministry of Works on matters concerning plastic fitments for housing, and with the Engineering Industries Division of the Board of Trade on plastics working machinery.... From time to time the Federation has made representations on specific issues: it was instrumental in securing a reduction in purchase tax on certain plastic articles, in reducing freight rates for a number of plastic materials after negotiations with the railway and shipping authorities, and, after approaches to the Inland Revenue, in obtaining more favourable wear-and-tear allowances for [processing machinery].

(c) Lord Morrison of Lambeth and the Association of Municipal Corporations. Extract from H.L. Deb., vol. 224, 28 June 1960, cols. 657 and 664

[In the House of Lords on 28 June 1960, Lord Morrison moved an amendment to the Public Bodies (Admission to Meetings) Bill. At one point he said:] I have been asked to move this amendment on behalf of the Association of Municipal Corporations. [A few minutes later the following dialogue took place:]

Lord Rea: Before the noble Lord withdraws his amendment may I make one small point? If I understand him aright, at one point he said he was moving this Amendment on behalf of some body. I think that that was probably a slip of the tongue and he meant with the support of, or at the request of. A member of this House does not put forward anything on behalf of some body. This is just for the record.

Lord Morrison: That is a new one on me. The noble Lord has been here longer than I have, and, on the assumption that he is right, I will say 'at the request of'. I happen to be President of the Association of Municipal Corporations and it was natural that they should approach me in the matter. It is not so bad as I have heard in another place when I once heard an honourable member say 'Mr Speaker, speaking on behalf of the railway company which I represent in this House.' I followed him and condemned his phrasing as impudence, whereupon I was ruled out of order by Mr Speaker, who said, 'Such language must not be used in the House . . .'. I nearly fell through the floor . . .

(d) The Government invites 'interested organisations' to offer their views, in this case, on Town and Country Planning. Extract from Town and Country Planning, Cmnd. 3333, 1967, p. 10

They [i.e. the Government] are now anxious to receive the views of interested organisations (including the local authority associations and the Council of Tribunals) on how these aims can best be achieved, within the framework proposed in this White Paper.

....

The mode of operation of pressure groups

To gain their objectives, pressure groups must influence governments. Generally the more direct methods are the best, so the most powerful groups do their work in Whitehall, i.e., in the Departments and with Ministers. Thus pressure groups endeavour to influence decisions at the point at which they are taken. But Parliament and public are not neglected by the powerful, for it would be tactically unwise to allow hostile opinion to develop. Less important and less powerful groups may find Whitehall less accessible, and for them Parliament and public may be the only targets for their activity. Here are some illustrations of pressure group activity:

sitting on standing joint official committees;

regular formal contact with officials, in meetings and by correspondence;

informal contacts with Ministers, ranging from private interviews and telephone conversations to dinners and golf;

delegations to see the Minister and his senior officials (a touch of desperation about this: other means of persuasion have failed);

regular representation through Members of Parliament;

occasional attempts to secure the support of Members, through meetings, dinners, written material;

public campaigns to draw attention and win support, including advertising, feeding material to the press, and demonstrations: e.g., parade of farmers on tractors; unemployed lying down in the middle of Oxford Street at rush-hour; all London taxi-cabs converging on the Houses of Parliament, causing a traffic jam in Parliament Square; carrying a coffin to the Ministry (the coffin symbolising the Ministry's alleged destruction of something or other and containing either a petition or the bearers' packed lunches).

EXERCISE

CURRENT ACTIVITY BY PRESSURE GROUPS

1. Go through not more than three issues of a daily paper and note cases of the current activities of pressure groups.

Analyse, as far as your information permits, under the following heads:

(a) *Object:*

1. an interest to protect or foster;

2. an idea, ideal or cause to promote.

(b) *Methods:*

1. discreet, e.g., contact with a Government Department; or,

2. open, e.g., through Parliament, press or a public campaign.

(c) *Effectiveness:* Is there any evidence to suggest (or would you judge) that the group:

1. will get its way?

2. will have a substantial influence?

3. will have its point of view taken into account?

4. will have virtually no effect?

(d) *Concern for the general interest:*

    1. exclusively self-interested;

    2. self-interested but responsible;

    3. some concern for the public interest some of the time;

    4. strong concern for the public interest most of the time.

2 CASE STUDIES ON PRESSURE GROUPS

Education

Education is an active field for pressure groups, because it matters a great deal to people, because there is vast scope for passionate disagreement, and because its loose organisational structure permits effective pressure. Active groups include:

(a) professional bodies, notably the National Union of Teachers, who have both an economic interest and certain ideals to promote. This group includes associations of headmasters, headmistresses, principals and even deputy principals.

(b) the Churches, especially the Church of England and the Roman Catholic Church, who can promote their faith by securing financial assistance for the provision of schools, or favourable treatment of religious worship and instruction. (The Act of 1944 includes a requirement (sect. 25) that the school day begin with collective worship—a triumph for the Churches in a predominantly non-Christian country.)

(c) the local authorities, represented by their officials.

(d) the local authorities, represented by their associations (Association of Education Committees, County Council Associations, Association of Municipal Corporations).

(e) the institutions themselves in the case of private and independent schools and universities.

(f) advisory bodies, which have no special interests, but exist to offer advice (e.g., Central Advisory Council, the Schools Council, Advisory Centre for Education).

(g) groups with ideas or ideals to promote (e.g., the Council for Educational Advance, the Workers' Educational Association, the Classical Association).

(h) recently parents have begun to organise themselves, mainly for or against comprehensive reorganisation. Besides the National Organisation of Parent–Teacher Associations, there is a Council for the Advancement of State Education, a Comprehensive Schools Committee, and a National Education Association. None of these last has more than a few thousand members.

In consequence, almost any change in the system of education is the product of many pressures and counter-pressures. The Acts of 1902 and 1944 both represent the Government's ideas, moderated and moulded by pressure (and who knows where the Government got its ideas in the first place?) Several major issues have recently been in play in this complex process of corporative consultation and compromise: for example, the proposal to change the system of selective secondary schools; the proposal to introduce auxiliaries into primary schools; and the question of the future of the 'private sector' schools.

EXERCISE
A MINISTER'S RIGHT TO IMPOSE HIS POLICY

2. The Labour Party campaigned openly for comprehensive education in the general elections of 1964 and 1966. The Party received majorities in both elections, a large one in 1966. Does the Secretary for Education and Science thus have a right to impose the reorganisation of education on comprehensive lines, no matter what representations are made to him by any of the bodies indicated above? (Note that this question is concerned with the political aspects of the issue; your answer cannot derive simply from the assertion, with or without proof, that comprehensive schools are good or bad.)

Agriculture

The relationship of the Government and the National Farmers' Union is very close—'unique in its range and intensity' (P. Self and H. J. Storing, *The State and the Farmer*, Allen and Unwin, 1962, p. 230). The Government pays farmers well over £250-million each year in grants and subsidies, a very large sum for a privately-owned and controlled industry. The amount of money and the manner of its distribution are the subject each year of negotiations between the Government and NFU. These usually, but not always, result in an agreed award. In 1965, the NFU did not agree to the settlement, which was 'imposed' by the Government. Note that the NFU's use of the term 'imposed' implies a right to settlement by consent. There followed a public campaign to denounce the Government for its dealings with the farmers, but the settlement remained settled.

This annual Price Review is part of a close and continuing process of consultation between Government and NFU. The Union's representatives frequent the Ministry of Agriculture—and not merely its corridors. They sit on committees, they inform, advise, persuade, stand firm; they are adamant. The Minister and his officials normally attempt to secure agreement before acting. The official description of this relationship is 'partnership': some political scientists call it 'symbiosis', or living together.

There are two ways of assessing this 'symbiosis': by its economic and social results, and by its political method. In both cases, some balance has to be struck between the private and the public interest, between the interests of farmers and the interests of consumers.

An assessment of the first kind, social and economic, is not a special concern of this book, but it clearly has some relevance. It would seem that since 1939 the close partnership between Government and NFU has brought about a great increase in the productivity and prosperity of the countryside (both were lacking previously and highly desirable for the community at large as well as for the farmers and farmworkers). But these gains have been at the expense of heavy State subsidies, which have in some cases bolstered ('feather-bedded') inefficiency. The balance has perhaps been unduly favourable to the farmers.

Whatever the social and economic results, the political methodology would still be open to judgement. Here are some possible conclusions:

(a) The Government has in the NFU a source of information and advice; it has also an instrument (a channel of communication at least), through which it might influence the industry, for example to greater efficiency.

(b) The farmers have an instrument too, for communicating with and influencing the Government. They have virtually exclusive rights. There is some advantage in this for the Government, in that it has only one body to deal with, and that body must itself effect compromise between the sectional interests of its own members. Moreover, the Union, having got itself into a privileged position, has much to lose by recalcitrance. But, if the arrangement saves the Government some diplomatic labours, it precludes some diplomatic manoeuvres, and concedes the NFU the strength of a monopoly.

(c) The Government has the ultimate power to grant or withhold public finance. This is altogether a greater power than the Union's ability to withdraw cooperation, and a power which is immediately available and practicable.

(d) The recent history of the partnership suggests that the farmers have had their way most of the time. When they have been deeply dissatisfied, concessions have often followed: for example, the dissatisfaction of the Union in 1956 was followed by the Agriculture

Act of 1957. The NFU's efforts on behalf of hill dairy-farmers in the Hill Farming Bill of 1956 were, however, unavailing; and the disappointing Price Review of 1965 was not fully compensated for in 1966.

At times of dispute, the Union seems to have been granted a right of appeal to the Chancellor of the Exchequer or even to the Prime Minister. The Government has never been willing to win by simple refusal to fight.

Summarising these points, it would seem that the NFU may have acquired an undue influence, the Government has restrained itself from full and brutal use of its advantage in ultimate power. There are three explanations for the Government's restraint:

First, State support to agriculture developed during World War II, after a long period of depression in the countryside, and when the production of food was a vital national necessity. The Minister of Agriculture in the post-war Labour Government continued and developed the policy, so that by the 1950s financial aid to farming depended on government inertia in the face of established interests, rather than on a continuing assessment of national needs.

Second, farming has been well represented in Parliament. There have never been less than thirty to forty MPs (mostly Conservative) describing their occupation as farmer. In the House of Lords, agriculture is also well represented, though many peers are members of the not wholly coincident interest-group, the Country Landowners' Association. Naturally some members of government have been farmers, and others have had a stake in farming through landownership. This is not to suggest that Members of Parliament or Ministers have improperly advanced their own interests; but it is to suggest that close personal involvement in an activity makes for understanding and sympathy, insight and perception, a greater facility for seeing a point of view and adjusting action to it.

Apart from parliamentary representation, the NFU has been well represented in Whitehall itself, in committees and in office in the Ministry itself. Thus the traditional representation of the farming interest at Westminster is matched by a carefully built-in partnership in Whitehall. This is a most effective foundation for a successful pressure group.

Third, Governments have regarded the support of agriculture as a proper policy anyway, on social and economic grounds. This is to imply that Cabinets still have some choice in the matter, and have not merely capitulated to a vociferous pressure group. The effect of a pressure group in a case like this seems to be to increase the pace and intensity of the Government's pursuit of a policy, and to make it more difficult for the Government to slow down, turn aside, or stop.

If you were the Minister concerned with a particular interest group:

3.1. Would you be concerned to discover whether the group you were dealing with was genuinely representative of the interest it claimed to represent? If so, how would you do this?

3.2. How would you distinguish between consulting with the group, and negotiating with it? Would you regard negotiation as improper or not?—and why?

The steel industry, 1950

The British Iron and Steel Federation was a loose organisation of the iron and steel industry, born in 1934, during 'the Slump', to ensure the protection of the industry from imports and perhaps to promote efficiency. It was naturally opposed to the nationalisation of the industry, and entered into negotiations with the post-war Labour Government to seek a compromise arrangement, tempering private ownership with a measure of public supervision. The negotiations failed. The Government passed its nationalisation Bill, but was forced by the House of Lords to delay its operation until the first day of October 1950—by which time a general election would have to be held. The Federation undertook reluctantly to cooperate in nationalisation as long as the Government obtained a 'clear majority' in the election.

The steel industry, led by the BISF, along with other industries threatened with nationalisation (notably sugar), and assisted by the educational and propaganda organisation, Aims of Industry, then plunged into a long, loud and expensive campaign against nationalisation. In the election of February 1950, the Government's overall majority was reduced to eight. Thus the Iron and Steel Act was bound to come into effect, but in political conditions which encouraged non-cooperation or even obstruction.

In the House of Commons (9 March 1950), Mr Oliver Lyttelton warned the Government: '... no Government depending upon so exiguous a majority had any right to put into force an Act so far reaching that it would once and for all put an end to private enterprise ... do not let the Government underrate the forces which would come to our aid.' The Conservatives adduced the supposedly democratic argument that, since the Labour Party had polled less than fifty per cent of the votes cast in the election, they had no 'mandate' to continue with the nationalisation of steel. This doctrine of the mandate is discussed below (chapter 12, p. 408). The question of right is a difficult one, and is usually submitted to the simple pragmatic test: will the House of Commons stand for it? Of course there are problems of morality and conscience where the writ of the House would not be thought to run. But the nationalisation of the steel industry was not one of these. By most theories of parliamentary democracy, the Government had both right and power, through control of the House of Commons, to enact the nationalisation of steel. They also had the right, but not the power, to coerce the iron and steel industry. Moreover, coercion would not suffice; for the effective execution of the Act, they needed the positive cooperation of the industry.

With the Government's term of office so insecure, the BISF decided not to cooperate. The Federation began by refusing to suggest members for the new Iron and Steel Corporation, and announced that anyone who joined would 'forfeit the respect of the industry'. This boycott was effective. The Government managed to find some eminent and able men to serve, but no one could pretend that the Board as constituted could run a steel industry. The Minister of Supply described the boycott as ' . . . concerted action by a number of people for the specific purpose of sabotaging an Act of Parliament'. The Corporation gradually won some cooperation from individual firms, but the Federation continued to withhold its cooperation. Little had been done to change the industry before the election of 1951 drove Labour from office. Three weeks later the new Conservative Government directed the Corporation to make no fundamental changes in the industry. A denationalisation Bill was introduced the following year, and enacted in 1953.

EXERCISES

THE NATIONALISATION OF STEEL

4.1. Do the powers of government in your view extend to the nationalisation of industry?

4.2. Did the British Iron and Steel Federation commit 'sabotage'?

4.3. Would you, instead or as well, put some blame on the Government? Why?

3   PRESSURE GROUPS AND PARLIAMENT

Pressure groups and the voter

Most pressure groups are not large enough, either in the nation or in a constituency, to deliver a vote of a significant size. There are three cases in which this might be possible:

(a) The Trade Unions. It is true that most Trade Unions and all the large ones officially support the Labour Party. However, they are not able to control, and hence 'deliver', the votes of their members, though they do exercise a very general influence. Some Trade Unions do not try very hard as party agents, and it is clear from surveys that many trade unionists vote Conservative.

(b) The farming vote. Calculations by Self and Storing (op. cit., p. 202), show that in 1955 the agricultural vote (including farmers, workers and wives) was more than ten per cent of the electorate in 126 constituencies. Even allowing for a slow diminution of the farming population, this may still seem a significant total; but of course farmers and farmworkers do not vote as a block for the same party. Still, if all those who voted for one party moved into abstention or voting for the other side, the effect in marginal constituencies could be startling. In practice, however, this is unlikely. Voters do not desert their traditional allegiances so easily; and the Farmers' and Agricultural Workers' Unions would be reluctant (and rightly so) to call on their members to switch from their natural party loyalties. Unions have to respect their members' sensibilities, and keep open the possibility of good relations with all political parties.

(c) The National Union of Mineworkers is very strong in some mining constituencies. Its power to deliver or withhold the miners' vote is not normally exercised: it is simply assumed, and the Union attains power within the Constituency Labour Party. For example, in the summer of 1965, Union representatives in the Bosworth, Leicestershire, Constituency Labour Party led an attack on their Member of Parliament, Mr Woodrow Wyatt. It seemed possible that the Party would choose another candidate for the next election, but not that the Mineworkers would, or could transfer their vote to another party. This is the situation now. Before the development of the Labour Party, branches of the Miners' Federation were inclined to interview both Liberal and Conservative candidates and support the man whose views on mining questions best fitted theirs. The present arrangement probably gives the miners more power.

Pressure groups and the MP

Members of Parliament are naturally sympathetic towards some groups (mainly occupational) because they belong, or formerly belonged, to those groups (see chapter 5 for the occupational backgrounds of MPs). But many Members acquire more formal connections with pressure groups.

....

DOCUMENT 2
THE RELATIONS OF PRESSURE GROUPS AND MPS

(a) From a booklet published by the Institute of Directors (1967)

Over 250 Members of both Houses of Parliament are Fellows of the Institute. They can be counted on to see that the views of directors are adequately voiced in Parliament and their interests protected whenever the occasion demands it.

(b) From the Report of the Transport and General Workers' Union, 1956, section dealing with the work of the Parliamentary Group. Quoted in Allen Potter, *Organised Groups in British National Politics*, Faber, 1961, p. 285

When [the Road Traffic Bill] was first introduced (in 1955) the Group set up a Working Party of three to meet officers of the Union, deal with the matter in the Transport Committee of the Parliamentary Labour Party, speak on it in the general debates in the House, and become members of the Standing Committee which was to consider it in detail.

(c) From Annual Conference Report of the United Commercial Travellers' Association, 1949. Quoted in J. D. Stewart, *British Pressure Groups*, Oxford University Press, 1958, p. 157

Mr Lipson [MP for Cheltenham and President of the local branch of the Association] is available at any time that I like to get in touch with him either by letter or by phone, and he always listens respectfully to what I have to say to him, and he also pays me the compliment that whenever I want a question put in the House he asks me actually to draft the question. I cannot expect more than that from a Member of Parliament.

(d) The Association of the British Pharmaceutical Industry has been concerned to defend the industry from allegations of overcharging (e.g., by the Public Accounts Committee). In 1966 the ABPI increased its annual budget from £54,000 to £71,000 and secured the services of a Conservative MP as acting parliamentary adviser. The ABPI sought actively 'to expand

and strengthen our contacts with Parliament'. Several Members of Parliament were in fact already directors of major drug firms.

(e) From leading article in the *Times*, 1 August 1966

(i) [On the Selective Employment Taxation Bill]: . . . Owing to the convention of secrecy surrounding all budgetary matters before a Budget is opened, the usual legislative preliminaries of behind-the-scenes discussion and adjustment with affected interests did not take place. It might have been possible to repair that omission at the committee stage by open discussion in which many MPs could be expected to argue on behalf of particular sections of employers. Instead a strict timetable was placed on the progress of the Bill . . .

(ii) [On this Bill and the tabling of major amendments to the Prices and Incomes Bill at the Committee Stage]: . . . The rights of the official Opposition and of private members of Parliament are conferred for good reason: to protect the liberties of the people from arbitrary government and to allow the varied interests in the state to be heard . . .

(f) From a speech by Anthony Wedgwood-Benn, M.P. (H. C. Deb., vol. 484, 22 July 1951, cols. 1553–4)

[A problem in the work of Members] is the pressures under which we work in the modern age. The power of the modern pressure groups in this country is increasingly being achieved by persuasion. People do not any longer use the big stick to get their way. They employ the public relations officer and the research agencies. Like every hon. Member, I am bombarded with statistics and glossy publications designed to convince me that I want to adopt a particular attitude towards the roads lobby, towards the licensed trade or this or that. I do not object to them bringing pressure or seeking to bring pressure on me, because that is their job as the pressure group. But it is my job to have the equipment behind me to assess whether their claims are just, whether their figures are accurate and whether what they ask is in the public interest. It is only in Parliament that people are represented as people—as consumers. We are the only representatives of the nation as a whole. That is why it is vital that we should do our job properly.

....

The above quotations illustrate the sort of connection a pressure group may have with Parliament. In some cases, a Member is 'sponsored' by the group, receiving some financial assistance for his election campaign and for his subsequent activities, and being expected to look to the interests of the group. The National Union of Mineworkers sponsored twenty-eight MPs in this way in the election of 1964. In other cases, the connection is more tenuous. A Member may take a part-time salaried post as an adviser to a group and thus naturally come to brief himself on its work and problems. Again, a Member may be invited to take honorary office in an association, as a vice-president or as a co-opted member of the managing body, for example, and thus, by taking an interest, come to support that interest. Or a number of MPs may form a parliamentary group, having links with an outside body. Such relationships are very common. It is possible broadly to take three views about such relationships:

(a) The traditional view: that a Member's first duty is to his judgement and conscience, or to his constituents, or to his party. These variations might be combined by saying that a Member's duty is to Parliament. Formal relationships with other bodies inhibit the Member in the discharge of his parliamentary duty, and are therefore undesirable, indeed, improper.

(b) The opposite view: that the purpose of Parliament is to represent the community and this representation may be done through associations as well as through the constituency and the party.

(c) A middle view: that outside relationships may be valuable in bringing relevant information and opinion to the notice of Parliament, and in communicating parliamentary opinion to the outside world. The danger that the Member may be unduly influenced is much exaggerated. It would be unnatural if the individual MP did not sometimes have his judgement influenced by his outside connections; but if we are to say that his judgement is thus 'distorted', we assume that in the first place his mind is either blank or completely shut off from outside influences. In any case, the special views of a few Members will be more than balanced by the others, and on important matters party discipline overrides sectional allegiance.

The latter view is not necessarily the correct one. Some general criticisms which apply to all pressure group activity apply to that in the House of Commons. Too much is, if not secret, then hardly acknowledged; too little voice and weight is given to unorganised causes and unassociated people.

....

DOCUMENT 3

THE CASE OF W. J. BROWN, M.P.

(a) Mr Brown had been General Secretary of the Civil Service Clerical Association since 1923. In 1942 he was elected Independent MP for Rugby, and the Association, adjusting itself to the situation, changed Mr Brown's title to Parliamentary General Secretary. As such, he was to continue to receive a salary. An agreement was drawn up which endeavoured to reconcile the independence thought proper for a Member of Parliament with the services to the Association properly to be expected from one of its most important officials. In 1946 the matter was referred to the Commons Select Committee on Privileges.

(b) From Additional Agreement made between W. J. Brown and the Civil Service Clerical Association, 1943 (H.C. 118, 1946–7, cols. 59–60. The Agreement is printed as Appendix C of J. D. Stewart, *British Pressure Groups*, Oxford University Press, 1958)

... 3. The said William John Brown shall be entitled to engage in his political activities with complete freedom.

4. The said William John Brown shall deal with all questions arising in the work of the Association which requires parliamentary or political action and shall advise the Association from time to time on such matters. [He] shall further confer and consult with the Association on all problems requiring his assistance and advice thereon if and when so required by the Association.

5. The said William John Brown shall hold the appointment of Parliamentary General Secretary for so long as he shall remain a member of the House of Commons and so long beyond this period as his Executive Committee of the Association shall decide in general meeting and at the termination of the Parliamentary General Secretaryship, [he] if he so desires shall be entitled to resume the appointment of General Secretary.

6. Nothing herein contained shall entitle the said William John Brown in his political and parliamentary activities to purport to represent the political views of the Association (if any) and shall only represent the Association in so far as Civil Service questions are concerned.

(c) From evidence given before the Select Committee on Privileges, H.C. 118, 1946–7. The President and Vice-President of the CSCA took this view of the agreement:

Q.378. Was Mr Brown bound to carry out the wishes of the Civil Service Association in Civil Service matters?—That was our understanding and expectation of the arrangement between us.

(d) At one point at least, Mr Brown himself took a rather different view. From Mr Brown's answer to Q.130:

... I am denying that I was a mandated delegate, and I am saying that I only represented the interests of the Association in the same way as ... any one of a dozen types of Labour Members of Parliament in this House would have tried to do his best for the people he knew best ... If I were asked to take action, as I not infrequently was, which I thought was not the right action, I would say; 'No that cannot be done' or 'It cannot be done in that way.'

I.T.B.P.—M

EXERCISES

MPS AND OUTSIDE BODIES—
THE CASE OF MR W. J. BROWN

5.1. Which view, that of Mr Brown or that of the officers of the Association, as indicated in the extracts, is most nearly in line with the terms of the Agreement?

5.2. Is the view of the officers of the Association improper, or undemocratic?

5.3. Is Mr Brown's view unrealistic?

....

DOCUMENT 4

THE VIEWS OF THE COMMITTEE ON PRIVILEGES
AND OF THE HOUSE

(a) From the report of the Committee, op. cit., p. xii

The relationship between a Member and an outside body with which he is in contractual relationship and from which he receives financial payments is, however, one of great difficulty and delicacy in which there must often be a danger that the rules of privilege may be infringed. Thus it would certainly be improper for a Member to enter into any arrangement fettering his complete independence as a Member of Parliament by undertaking to press some particular point of view on behalf of an outside interest, whether for reward or not.

(b) Motion subsequently approved by the Commons, H.C. Deb., vol. 440, 15 July 1947, cols. 284–5

That this House agrees with the Report of the Committee on Privileges, and in particular declares that it is inconsistent with the dignity of the House, with the duty of a Member to his constituents, and with the maintenance of the privilege of freedom of speech, for any Member of the House to enter into any contractual agreement with an outside body, controlling or limiting the Member's complete independence and freedom of action in Parliament or stipulating that he shall act in any way as the representative of such outside body in regard to any matters to be transacted in Parliament; the duty of a member being to his constituents and to the country as a whole, rather than to any particular section thereof.

....

The above pronouncements may appear to be based on the assumption that an MP is a remote judicial person, whose only contact is with his constituents (all 50,000 of them). Of course, this view is unrealistic: a modern MP is no more set apart from his own background and experience than an eighteenth-century Knight of the Shire. Now there is no reason why the background and experience represented in the House should be limited to that already available to Members themselves. Indeed, if this were so it would be quite unfair that the composition of the House should be as biased as it is (see chapter 5). The representation of other outside organisations is quite proper; indeed, such organisations are often more meaningful than the territorial constituency. There is, in short, no objection in principle to such representation.

The problem lies in the form of the representation, and in the case cited here Parliament was fully justified in registering concern. The representation of interests ought to go on only under certain conditions. First, there should be no contractual obligation on the part of the Member to put forward a sectional view, whether or not he approves it. Second, a contract should be terminable without notice by the MP. Third, any relationship, whether contractual or informal, should be publicly avowed. Finally, the salary of MPs should be high enough to make the rewards of representation (or 'advising') insignificant—not so much to discourage the Member as to leave him independent.

There is still a good deal to be said for the maintenance of the traditional view of Parliament as a collection of independent judicial individuals. Though out-of-date and unrealistic, the continuing assertion of an ideal that never was helps to achieve a balance between independence and outside control. The case of Mr Cousins (1966) illustrates the point. Mr Cousins was granted leave from his post of General Secretary of the Transport and General Workers' Union when he joined the Labour Government in 1964 as Minister of Technology. He resigned from his post in July 1966, because he disagreed with the Government's proposals for legislation on prices and incomes. His Union then, it seems, restored him to his post, but on condition that he shortly gave up his seat in the Commons; that while there he opposed the Government's Bill on prices and incomes; and that a part of his MP's salary should meanwhile be paid to the Union. Thus, while Mr Cousins' continuance in the House was hardly objectionable (except that he held another full-time job), his continuance on these terms was to imply that his seat was the property of the Union, and he their servant in Parliament. 'I am in the position', said Mr Cousins, 'that I shall do the job the Union wants me to do.' In this matter there is much to be said for observing the proprieties.

THE PROPER RELATIONS OF AN MP WITH
AN OUTSIDE BODY

6. Draft an agreement between an outside body and an MP, in the light of the foregoing discussion.

4 PRESSURE GROUPS AND THE PARTIES

The relations of pressure groups and parties are important but in the main, informal (formless) and difficult to discern, because pressure groups and parties are not wholly separable, overlapping and inter-penetrating one another. Thus, a chemist and a mechanic may join the local Conservative and Labour Parties respectively. They are individuals, but they are also members, respectively, of the British Pharmaceutical Society and the Amalgamated Engineering Union. It is likely, to say the least, that some of their views will be coloured by their membership of those organisations. If they are party activists, still more if they are candidates, or Members of Parliament, their political work will contribute to the promotion of the interests of their groups. But no pressures will be openly applied.

Just as the case of Mr Brown is simply an open and formalised expression of many unavowed relationships of groups and Parliament, so the relations of groups and parties are not wholly represented by those links which are publicly declared or obvious.

Of the open relationships, the most notable is that of the Trade Unions and the Labour Party. By the Party's constitution, the Unions are a constituent part of the Party: the two bodies are not wholly distinct. In a rather special way, therefore, pressures flow from the Trade Unions to the Party (and also back again). There is no similar relationship in the Conservative Party. Broadly, the Party represents the interests of commerce and industry (and other partly contradictory interests too) but there is no identifiable formal link. Thus, the Confederation of British Industries or the Institute of Directors do not have votes at the Party's Conference, or seats on the Central Council or sponsored Members in Parliament. Nevertheless the CBI and the Directors are well, even heavily, represented at all levels in the Party.

The relations of the Trade Unions to the Labour Party and of industry to the Conservative Party are further discussed in chapter 9, p. 319.

5 CAMPAIGNS ON A SINGLE ISSUE

In the areas of public life discussed above, pressure groups are more or less permanently organised and continuously active. In addition, pressure groups arise from time to time to fight for or against some new direction of government policy or intention, and lapse when the struggle is decisively won or lost.

The best example of such a campaign is also an early one, the Anti-Corn Law League, active from the late 1830s to its triumph in the Repeal of the Corn Laws in 1846. The League drew on the energies and finances of the new manufacturers, and mounted a massive public and parliamentary campaign. This was planned as deliberately and even as skilfully as any contemporary campaign mounted by public relations experts. Victory came when the Prime Minister himself, Sir Robert Peel, confessed himself convinced by the League's arguments, and introduced the Bill to repeal the Corn Laws.

The only recent campaign of any importance which can claim equal success is the campaign for commercial television (see document 5 (c)). Here are some examples of recent campaigns on a single issue. A feature of such campaigns is their concentration on parliamentary and public activity: there is no time, and usually no basis, for the development of close relations with a Department.

....

DOCUMENT 5

EXAMPLES OF CAMPAIGNS ON A SINGLE ISSUE

(a) *The Campaign for Nuclear Disarmament*

The Campaign for Nuclear Disarmament began in 1957 and declined in the mid-sixties. The Campaign was a protest against the possession by Britain of nuclear weapons, and, for a section of the movement, against all nuclear weapons. The first protest aimed at 'unilateral nuclear disarmament' (i.e. by Britain), the second at a British withdrawal from NATO, hence from defence policies associated with the American nuclear armoury. The Campaign was not simply a gesture of protest, but a positive attempt to persuade the Labour Party (hopefully the next Government) to modify its defence policies.

The characteristic method of the Campaign was the mass public demonstration—above all, the Easter marches from Aldermaston in Berkshire (where there was an atomic weapons establishment) to Trafalgar Square in London. There was some disagreement on methods within the movement. One section of the Campaign, the so-called Committee of 100, advocated non-violent civil disobedience (e.g. sitting on pavements)—rather like

Gandhi's Independence movement in India in the 1930s, and deliberately eschewing the violence of the suffragette movement (1910–14).

At its peak, in 1961 and 1962, CND's major annual demonstration was supported by perhaps 100,000 people, counting those attending the final rally. Many fewer, of course, took part in the marching, but these orderly, good-humoured pilgrimages were impressive alike for their numbers and their organisation.

The impact on the public was considerable. The campaigners got into the news, and almost everyone heard about them, their badge and their banner—and their cause. Merely to hear about was far from being persuaded of the rightness of the cause: all the same, CND won many converts and one notable victory. In the spring of 1960, a gallup poll showed a third of the adult population prepared (when asked) to agree that 'Britain should give up nuclear weapons entirely' and another quarter or more ready for Britain to give up independent nuclear weapons and pool hers with NATO. However, this remarkable conversion of the British people was due perhaps rather more to the concurrent collapse of the British Government's 'Blue Streak' missile programme. Events have a greater influence than arguments. The demonstration that Britain might meet economic and technical difficulties in retaining her own nuclear weapons obviously enhanced the Campaign's moral and strategic case for abandoning them.

The notable victory was the unilateralist vote at the Labour Party's Annual Conference at Scarborough in 1960 (see chapter 9). The interpretation of this is open to doubt. A cynic might say that CND had simply converted the General Secretary of the TGWU; but to be fair the majority vote in support of Mr Cousins was perhaps made possible by the efforts of the Campaign.

The Scarborough resolution was ambiguous: unilateralist, but not clearly against a British commitment to the nuclear-armed NATO. The following year, the Labour Conference rejected the unilateralist position, but called for the removal of the American Polaris base in Scotland (a favourite target of CND demonstrators). CND had not yet lost its struggle, and Labour fought the 1964 election on a defence policy which renounced the independent national control, but not the possession, of nuclear weapons. These were distinctions not easily to be appreciated by the uninitiated; still, it seemed that the Campaign had won half a victory.

However, even that victory was short-lived. China exploded an atomic device the day after the poll. Other factors combined to defeat the unilateralist cause: the lack of progress on preventing nuclear proliferation; the fact that Britain's Polaris nuclear-armed submarines were already being built; the need to retain American goodwill and sustain the NATO alliance. In February 1967 the wife of Labour's Defence Secretary herself launched Britain's latest Polaris submarine. The Campaign for Nuclear Disarmament had failed in its main objective. But it was not without achievements. It had brought about a prolonged and widespread argument about nuclear armaments and defence policy; and, perhaps in the long run more important, it had crystallised for a while the moral seriousness and the seeking for commitment of a generation.

(b) *The campaign for and against the Abortion Bill, 1966–7*

The Medical Termination of Pregnancy Bill was introduced by a Private Member, Mr David Steel, in 1966. Its purpose was to extend the permitted grounds of abortion to include, in particular, cases in which there was a possibility that the child if born would be deformed, or would place an intolerable burden on the mother. (These were the rough intentions; the precise wording was obviously a matter of the most acute difficulty.) The objectives of the Bill were not a matter of party controversy, but they were both supported and opposed by strong convictions, touched with emotion. In the end the Government, without adopting the Bill, gave assistance with drafting and an indispensable portion of its own parliamentary time. The Government thus held the ring and ensured a contest between two rival private armies.

The Bill was sponsored and actively supported by an all-party group, including several doctors, and one or two frontbenchers—over two-hundred MPs in all. The parliamentary group was supported by a specially created 'Association for Abortion Law Reform', described by one of its opponents as 'rich and professionally organised'.

The opposition was led by Mr St John-Stevas, M.P., and included a hundred or so Members of Parliament, with again a few doctors, a few frontbenchers, and most of the Roman Catholic MPs. Mr St John-Stevas, himself a distinguished Catholic and a regular contributor to the *Catholic Herald*, was able to mobilise the Catholic opposition in the country. The British Medical Association and the Royal College of Gynaecologists were also brought into the battle. A 'Society for the Protection of Unborn Children' was organised to counter the 'Association for Abortion Law Reform'. Half a million signatures to a petition were collected.

Such public campaigning was relevant only insofar as it affected the struggle in Parliament, which was the decisive battleground. There, it turned out that the Bill's sponsors had a clear majority behind them. The opposition to the Bill had two weapons left. The first was the procedural one of using up the slender resources of time available to the promoters. The Bill was thirty-three hours in Committee where, by general consent, it was much improved, not least by its opponents. At the Report Stage, on the night of 29–30 June 1967, the Bill's opponents mounted a further campaign of obstruction. The debate went on for 11 hours and 41 minutes, and included some deliberately time-wasting procedures, slow movement through the voting lobbies, and prolonged, repetitive and irrelevant speeches. These were the techniques of the filibuster, and their employment, in Britain as in the USA, on behalf of a minority viewpoint is at least questionable.

This filibuster was successful for the time being, but was frustrated when the Government provided further time for the passage of the Bill in the

Commons. The second and last weapon for the Bill's opponents lay in the Lords. But the peers finally drew back, refusing to press their amendments against the Commons. Their constitutional position was too insecure for such an action: this was not the last ditch to die in.

(c) *The establishment of commercial (independent) television in Britain, 1951–4*

(The history of this campaign is set out and analysed in H. H. Wilson, *Pressure Group*, Secker and Warburg, 1961)

The Television Act of 1954 established television broadcasting separate from the British Broadcasting Corporation and financed by advertising. All broadcasting previously had been conducted by the BBC as a monopoly public corporation, financed by license fees, and based on a concept of public service. The system inaugurated by the Act of 1954, breaking the BBC's longstanding monopoly and based on the commercial concept of attracting large audiences for advertisers, represented a fundamental change in British public life. It was directly contrary to the majority recommendations of the Beveridge Committee on Broadcasting (1947–49); it was not mentioned in the Conservative Party's election campaign in 1951; only a few members of the Cabinet (perhaps three) were positively in favour; the Prime Minister was not interested, and neither was the public; many 'influential' people were opposed. How then did it happen?

The answer would seem to be that the Cabinet gave way to pressure from (or were persuaded by) a vigorous campaign organised by backbench MPs and interested persons from the radio industry and advertising. But if it were as simple as that, then the conclusion would be that any interest group which could capture the support of a handful of Conservative backbenchers, would have captured a Conservative Government. This is clearly unlikely.

Consider the history of the case.

(i) Selwyn Lloyd, M.P., as a member of the Beveridge Committee on Broadcasting, wrote a minority report, criticising the BBC on the grounds that all monopolies were undesirable, and one in the field of information, comment and culture was deplorable (see chapter 11, p. 397). This is an argument within the tradition of the Conservative philosophy of freedom of opinion and freedom for enterprise and competition. At the end of 1951 the Conservative 1922 Committee expressed its emphatic view that the BBC monopoly must be broken.

(ii) A few Conservative backbenchers were associated in a committee with members of the radio and advertising industries. The committee was for some of the time an official Party committee. In July 1953 it was the Party's Radio and Television Committee, but had previously been an informal study-group, and before that a Broadcasting Policy Committee. The committee or group had as members or associates at some time one or two MPs as well as outsiders who were connected with the radio and advertising industries. For example, Anthony Fell, M.P., was connected with the Pye company; F. Bishop, M.P., with Broadcast Relay Services and later with Morphy-Richards Ltd; Lady Tweedsmuir, M.P. was connected with advertising. The Chairman of Pye, Mr C. O. Stanley was himself a member of (or associated with) the committee/group; so was Mr I. Harvey, an advertising agent.

(iii) A prominent member of the Conservative Central Office, Mr Mark Chapman-Walker, at one time in charge of propaganda, favoured the introduction of commercial television, and has himself attributed some of the success to the party professionals.

(iv) Some 'influential' people from the radio and television industry supported the establishment of commercial television. Among these was Sir Robert Renwick, holder of fourteen directorships in the electrical industry, well-connected in finance, in the Institute of Directors and in the Conservative Party; also Mr Norman Collins, ex-BBC, an able and dedicated man who had the necessary (and sometimes overlooked) capacity to organise an independent television company.

But there were 'influential' people (in this general sense) on the other side—including most of the Conservative peers, among them Lord Hailsham.

(v) Outside Westminster there was much activity. Interested groups were not unanimous, and one large electrical manufacturer was thought to be against commercial television. Some advertisers claimed to be disinterested. Cinema, theatre and newspaper interests were mostly opposed, but some began to move into the not-quite-existent independent television industry.

In June 1953, the opponents, led by a Labour MP, Christopher Mayhew, promoted a National Television Council. The other side, spurred on by signs of a Government wavering, established a Popular Television Association (July 1953). According to Lord Woolton, this body was created 'ex Central Office' (the 'ex' is unfortunately a little obscure). The Popular Television Association quickly raised £20,000 and produced a national publicity campaign, including inspired news stories, letters to newspapers, articles under the names of well-known people (cricketers, comedians, historians and the like), pamphlets and lectures.

(vi) But the Cabinet was the crucial body: without its acquiescence, as a minimum, there could have been no Television Act. In 1951 they were not very interested. They were theoretically opposed to the BBC's monopoly, but Cabinets are theoretically opposed to a good many things they leave alone. Some of them, it seems, disliked the idea of programmes 'sponsored' by advertisers. As late as 1953, the Government announced a White Paper in the autumn to discuss the possibilities. However, the following year, the Television Act received the Royal Assent.

The passing of the Act could be explained simply in terms of the pressures indicated above: but this is to degrade the Cabinet's role in British government. The Cabinet seems, in fact, to have exercised some positive choice in the matter. First, a few members of the Cabinet (Lords Kilmuir and Woolton, Mr Stuart) favoured the introduction of 'independent' television. Second, there was no pressure of other matters for legislation.

Third, there was a slackening of positive leadership on the part of the now elderly Prime Minister, Mr Churchill. Fourth, the proposal broadly fitted Conservative theory and ceased to offend in detail when it was shown that direct sponsorship of programmes could be avoided. Indeed, the device of a public authority exercising a mild supervision of private enterprise fitted some earlier Conservative proposals for the electricity industry: it had a 'Conservative ancestry'.

Thus it would be too simple to conclude that the Government capitulated to a commercial pressure group; or, alternatively, reacted with commendable flexibility to a reasoned case reasonably presented. The truth appears to be something between these poles of political action. The lesson for pressure groups is the same as for backbench MPs and party members: the support of at least one or two Cabinet Ministers is a condition of success. The lesson for democrats is that it is the pressure groups most closely related to government which need checking. But one element of government is missing from this assessment and the foregoing account of the Television Lobby—the Civil Service. What part, if any, did the permanent advisers play? It would seem that they played a small part. In this situation, with a powerful pressure group infiltrating the Cabinet, the Department's usual braking force is perhaps least effective. This follows, for better or for worse, from the nature of British government.

....

GUIDE TO EXERCISES

1. You must do this for yourself. Here is an example: *The Guardian*, 4 July 1966:

(i) The National Coal Board in *Coal News* reports that some of its pits were producing natural gas—a counter-blast to the companies hoping to get gas from the North Sea. Analysis:

(a) 1.; (b) 2.—but 1. not excluded;

(c) 3.—at least; (d) 2.—at least.

(ii) Aims of Industry have published a study of the steel industry, opposing nationalisation.

(a) 1.; (b) 2.;

(c) 4. ?3.; (d) 2.

(iii) The Fabian Society has published a pamphlet on estate agents, a counter to the agents themselves and some sympathetic MPs who have promoted a Private Bill.

(a) 2.; (b) 2.;

(c) 3.; (d) 4.

(iv) Durham County Local History Society has advocated an integrated archives service.

(a) 2., ?1.; (b) 2.;

(c) 4., ?3.; (d) ?4.—4. and 1. would be regarded as identical.

(v) Shrewsbury Town Council were to meet the West Midland Study Group to argue the case for a substantial increase in population in the town.

(a) 1.; (b) 2.—but 1. not excluded;

(c) 3.; (d) 4. and 1. would be regarded as identical.

(vi) The Advisory Council on Public Sanitation, with women's organisations in the north-west, and the Council of Sanitary Ware Manufacturers, and the Association of Public Health Inspectors were all concerned to promote the introduction of foot-operated lavatories in public buildings. The women's organisations (unspecified) were to try to persuade local authorities.

(a) 2., but 1. for the manufacturers; (b) 1., and 2.;

(c) 3.; (d) 4.—but this might not apply to the manufacturers.

Other groups mentioned include the Methodists, the old boys of Malvern College, the York and East Yorkshire Architectural Society, the vocational services committee of Leeds Rotary Club.

These are all good examples of the multitude of minor groups at work trying to persuade or press the Government. Very little of this activity is highly self-interested and a good deal of it is done by voluntary workers. In some cases it is difficult to distinguish between ideals and interest. Press publicity through news items is a frequently used method, cheap but not very effective.

This happy glimpse of archaeological societies and north-western women having their say should not of course obscure our understanding of the giant groups going about their more effective persuading labours.

2. 'Right' is a difficult and dangerous word, for it encourages mere assertion and inhibits cool analysis. A Government would be justified in initiating reorganisation on comprehensive lines: (a) if this had been proposed and assented to at a general election; (b) if it had been widely discussed in both educational and other circles and had not met massive or unanimous opposition; (c) if some substantial and reliable expert and lay opinion approved; (d) if a substantial number of local authorities were agreeable, or at least, had no good reason for opposing the change; and (e) if parents and teachers were willing to offer minimal cooperation.

In the last resort, the judgement on these questions must lie with the Government, who are entitled constitutionally to ignore all the conditions. The first one, in particular, is frequently ignored, e.g. in the passing of the Act of 1944. A Government can always justify its actions by pointing to its final answerability at the next election.

In the case of education there is, however, one strong line of counter-argument—that decisions should be taken by the local authorities.

3.1. Yes, of course, it is reasonable to ask a body like the NFU for details of its membership.

3.2. Consulting means asking for advice, and implies a readiness to listen to that advice. Negotiation implies discussion between two bodies, both of whom must consent to the outcome. Usually the bodies are nearly equal in power: otherwise the more powerful will tend to impose a settlement.

'Improper' is another difficult and dangerous word. All government is in the last resort by consent of the governed, but we cannot live all the time in conditions of last resort. Governments need the cooperation or goodwill of some important groups within the community. Is it improper for you to refuse to help with the washing-up? No, but it may be destructive of the conditions of family life, and therefore open to objection—and over-ruling by established authority.

4.1. It is difficult in cases like this to see the constitutional position clearly, and unaffected by our economic and social judgement of the Government's action. We tend to concede the Government's constitutional right to take actions we approve of, and denounce as unconstitutional any action we dislike.

Leaving aside this particular kind of pre-judgement, there is an arguable constitutional theory that nationalisation is *ultra vires*, beyond the proper limits of power for any government. (This theory would certainly have wide support in the USA, but none in the USSR!) If you take this view of government, then your view of the case of the steel industry (questions 4.2. and 4.3. below) will be clear and uncompromising. So these questions are prefaced by this difficult but important question about your political philosophy. Wrestle with it! It is too big a question to be answered fully in this book, but some awareness of the problem is essential.

Briefly, these are the questions and considerations you have to assess. If it could be shown that nationalisation of a particular industry would (a) promote economic efficiency; (b) serve consumers better; and, (c) provide a better deal for workers—would nationalisation be justified? To put it another way, if nationalisation is demonstrably of advantage to the nation economically, are there any constitutional grounds for not nationalising? The answer must be that if the House of Commons can manage to enact it, then it is constitutional. That is the nature of the British constitution. If we then ask, but is it wise politically?—we must have some regard for the arguments about the inviolability of property, about the dangers of concentrating too much power in the Government's hands, and about the need for the Government to secure a minimum of consent from those directly affected by its actions.

4.2. 'Sabotage' is an emotive word, and better avoided. In any case, it implies positive destructive activity, not just passive non-cooperation. But here non-cooperation means the quite serious business of failing to carry out a statute enacted by Parliament, with the intention of nullifying that statute. It would seem that the action of the BISF was open to strong objection on constitutional grounds, but use of the word 'sabotage' is not perhaps justified.

4.3. Some blame ought to be put on the Government for enacting highly controversial legislation, involving the fundamental reorganisation of a major industry and much consequent disturbance to owners and workers, in the last years of the Parliament. They had a 'right' to do so, but 'right' as we have indicated, is a dangerous word. It was perhaps imprudent of them.

Yet we must avoid the notion that a Parliament in its last two years ought not to enact controversial legislation. There is already a tendency to shape policy in the last two years for its electoral appeal, and governments should not be discouraged further by dubious constitutional arguments from doing what it judges best for the nation.

5.1. The Agreement is ambiguous. Clause 3 gives Brown 'complete freedom'; clause 4 says he must 'confer and consult' with the Association. The answer is 'neither', or perhaps 'Mr Brown's version' (favouring freedom).

5.2. Improper, in that Mr Brown's place in the House of Commons was within the gift of the electors of his constituency. They had put him there to follow his own views, or theirs or both (Brown was an Independent Member). He was not therefore entitled to give up his rights in some matters to another association.

In democratic theory, both the electors of Rugby and the CSCA might be entitled to have their views heard. However, in the British version of the theory, Parliament is the only representative institution, and it represents the general public, arranged in territorial constituencies. Hence the view of the officers of the Association is undemocratic (in contemporary Britain).

We could of course change the theory, and some of the argument put forward here suggests we should. But in that case the CSCA might well be over-represented by one MP.

5.3. If you accept the views just stated, the answer is 'no'. But having regard to the fact that Mr Brown was paid a salary and accorded a title by the CSCA, it seems unrealistic to believe he was meant to have complete freedom on Civil Service matters.

6. The relevant points are made in the text (p. 355). The first two points could be covered in a contract (no obligation to speak or take any action on behalf of the retaining association; the contract terminable without notice). Public avowal would require a register of such relationships. High salaries are a matter for Parliament itself.

Note: The question of Members' Interests arose again early in 1969 (case of Mr G. Bagier) and there was a statement by the Prime Minister on 26th March, 1969. A select Committee was set up to consider the matter.

ASSESSMENTS

(1) *The case for pressure groups*

(a) Pressure groups are both natural and necessary. It is arguable that individuals have very few political needs which cannot be expressed and moderated through representative groups. Indeed, it is likely that there is no other way in a large community of meeting the demands of the individual. In this way, as Allen Potter writes, pressure groups 'supplement the constitutional conditions of legitimacy' (*Organised Groups in British National Politics*, Faber, 1961).

(b) The organisation of a group imposes some discipline on the members of the group: they must reach compromise among themselves. Thus, government, by dealing with a group, ensures a measure of self-discipline within the group; also, a unified source of information and centre for consultation.

(c) Pressure groups do not operate as an irresistible force in a vacuum, without friction, hindrance or check. Other pressure groups provide countervailing power. Government itself, while not an immovable object, has inner and outer defences against assault and infiltration:

(i) The Civil Service will not normally give way to obvious unreason or naked self-interest. It will try to apply tests of reasonableness and public interest to the proposals of interested groups. But these tests are not always easy to apply: there is no equivalent of the chemist's litmus paper. Where there is doubt and confusion, it may sometimes seem unreasonable *not* to concede a case pressed with vigour and intelligence.

(ii) The Cabinet will have to approve of major changes of policy. With its overall political responsibility, the claims of national interest will not be overlooked, though they will be subject to interpretation. The average Cabinet Minister does not stand outside or above the battle. He is not an Umpire Buller, prepared to no-ball the home team's crack bowler; nor is he the visiting captain, playing for victory. No games metaphor quite covers the case. The Cabinet Minister is at once a player on both sides, also an umpire and rather wanting everyone (including himself) to win so that all may have prizes. His Cabinet colleagues will also be playing and not necessarily on the same side. Out of this complicated conflict, only a Cabinet which has a collective mind, and knows it, can consistently control the pressure group.

(iii) Some major changes of policy will stand as planks in the party's platform, and neither group nor Minister can act freely on these matters, once decided. Partly, this merely changes the point at which pressure is applied—before the formation of party policy and (for it is not immutable) when it is open for modification. No party, however, is absolutely the prisoner of any one pressure group.

(d) The agreed assumptions of British politics moderate the self-interest of pressure groups. The last point (c) dealt with the institutions of government as if they formed a castle or defensive system, threatened by invading pressure groups. One of the Government's weapons, it was suggested, was the ideological one of 'public interest'. Now this picture requires modification: although there is often a battle, a sharp opposition of interests and profound conflict, yet both sides share some common assumptions and aspirations. The pressure groups do not like to think of themselves as nakedly self-interested; they too appreciate, and indeed serve, the commonweal. If it comes to a battle they fight, most of the time at least, under a Geneva Convention of political warfare; it is not a conflict with no holds barred. Thus they are ready to listen to arguments about the public interest, and they do not resort to undue pressure except under what they would consider gross provocation.

(e) The above is the outlook of the pressure groups: no doubt it exaggerates their altruism (an altruistic interest group would be an absurdity). But it may not exaggerate their good sense. For it is sensible of them to play the game according to some rules, for fear that the game will otherwise be called off. Most pressure groups act with this kind of consideration of enlightened self-interest. The most powerful have the most to lose by the breaking of their established links with the Government. The less powerful have less to lose, but then they also lack the means of 'undue pressure'. The tendency for 'pressure' to be in the hands of the officials, not the members of the group, strengthens this sense of playing according to the rules. The official is a professional player of the game, with an interest in keeping the game going.

All this is to justify pressure groups as necessary and wholesome, or at least difficult to do without, mostly useful and not often actually harmful. But there are some grounds for concern: all is not for the best in this area of politics.

(2) *The case for concern about pressure groups*

(a) In this free-for-all conflict between groups and government, some groups have too big a voice and too much power. In particular, the interests of producers are over-represented, because they can be easily organised and have the money. Meanwhile, the interests of consumers, old people, children, all of whom are difficult to organise and comparatively poor, may go unheeded. For the same kind of reason, the British Travel and Holiday Association gets more financial support from the Government than the Council for the Preservation of Rural England.

In this sphere, as in many other aspects of British public life, the advantages of wealth and size for political propaganda are partly neutralised by the character of the broadcasting organisations. Broadcasting time cannot be bought, and the Aylesbury Consumers' Association is as likely as the Buckinghamshire Branch of the National Farmers' Union to get three minutes of television time.

(b) The activities of pressure groups go on mostly in private—in the corridors of Whitehall. Some of their public activity, as in Parliament, and in the feeding of news and opinion to the press, is not open and avowed. They seldom operate openly, and then only when they are not getting their own way. Thus an innocent observer might conclude that pressure groups were underdogs in politics, hastily banding together to tell the Government how ill it was treating them. This is not the case, and there is much to be said for Professor Finer's conclusion: 'through this secrecy', he wrote, the lobbies become 'faceless, voiceless, unidentifiable; in brief, anonymous' (*Anonymous Empire*, 2nd edn., Pall Mall, 1966, p. 145).

(c) A third cause for disquiet is that the scope for 'sabotage and blackmail' (Professor Finer's phrase) which necessarily exists in a civilised community may be exploited. This kind of activity is most often seen in industry, where groups like transport workers, dockers or doctors sometimes use their power to damage the whole community by striking, or threatening to strike, in order to wrest increases in income or other advantages.

Now, industry is not blessed with representative institutions, and this baronial or jungle lack of restraint is perhaps to be expected where power is ill-balanced, and the rewards of negotiation from strength are substantial. It may even be sanctified as a *free* system of collective bargaining. But its results are often damaging to the interests of the community, and are therefore of political concern.

There are other matters of much closer and more direct concern to government in which pressure groups may frustrate the intentions of Parliament by resistance or refusal to cooperate. The case of the iron and steel industry has been discussed above. The British Medical Association might be cited as by no means consistently willing to help sustain the National Health Service. Mr Enoch Powell was suggesting in 1965 that there was no obligation on managers or workers to cooperate with the (Labour) Government.

The problem here is to balance the 'right' of private property, including the ownership of a professional or working skill, against the 'right' of the community. Each case has to be assessed on its merits, within a framework of political principle. Such questions as these have to be answered:

(i) Is it proper to regard Parliament as the only judge of community and individual interests, subject to the right of others to offer their views?

(ii) Or is Parliament only one among the groups whose combined views and pressures should determine social policy?

(iii) Has an individual or a group the right to resist or withhold his cooperation from a scheme he disapproves of?

(iv) Does this scheme balance fairly the interests of the community and the interests including the freedom of the individual?

At times there is no doubt that such difficult questions are brushed aside, and the matter is decided by political or industrial *force majeure*.

(3) *Fitting pressure groups into democracy*

In the light of the above arguments, it seems clear that pressure groups are useful, even indispensable, and that there already exist defences and moderating influences in the political system. There are cases, however, of decisions being taken which appear unduly to neglect the public interest, and too often the decision-making is hidden from the public view.

Bringing the operation of pressure groups into the open would encourage a greater concern for the public interest. But British politics go on very largely in secret, and it is not easy to open the central processes to public scrutiny. Something might be achieved by the extension of the Parliamentary Committee system as an administrative inquisition (see chapter 7, p. 260). It is only by fundamental reform of this kind that the pressure of private groups may be civilised.

RECAPITULATION EXERCISES

1. Define a pressure group.
2. Give examples of pressure groups in education.
3. List the methods of persuasion used by the National Farmers' Union.
4. Briefly, how would you justify pressure group activity?

KEY TO RECAPITULATION EXERCISES

1. See text, p. 339. Note that the term includes groups with ideas as well as groups with interests.
2. See text, p. 343.
3. Mainly the methods implied in the term 'symbiosis'—see text, pp. 344–5—working in close partnership in committees, in consultation and negotiation. But public campaigns are also used, especially when private methods have not produced the desired result.
4. See text, p. 365.

[11]
Political communication: public opinion and the mass media

1 INTRODUCTION

There are many oversimplified and misleading theories about the place of public opinion and the mass media in a democracy. It is often held that governments should be responsive, and do in fact respond, to public opinion; but that, unfortunately, public opinion is distorted by the operations of the mass media, and notably by the press. A major difficulty about this theory is to identify and define public opinion; a further difficulty is to find a method of assessment of the relations of the mass media to public opinion. Guesses and impressions are common but unsatisfactory.

However, some aspects of the subject are easier to establish. The mass media are certainly massive, measured by their audiences and by their ownership and control. Newspapers are not primarily concerned to inform and educate their readers: they are mostly devoted to entertainment and 'human interest', and their political content is selective, partisan, often distorted and misleading. Broadcasting, on the other hand, is still dominated by the public service objectives and tradition of the British Broadcasting Corporation, and its presentation of political news and comment is balanced, fair and not insubstantial.

The influence of the media on public and government—and of public and government on the media—is much less certain. It seems plausible to argue, both on general grounds and with some empirical evidence, that the media have small but not insignificant long-term effects on public opinion; and that governments are at least sensitive to such movements of opinion. Sensitivity here implies a reaction ranging from 'aware of' to 'responsive to'.

But government is not a passive target for public and the media. Rather, British Governments defend themselves from the curiosity of the media: bluntly, they are secretive. At the same time they try hard to influence the media by constitutionally proper means, that is, by briefings, leaks, emphasis and de-emphasis. Nor is the public a completely passive receptacle for the messages of the media: the public resists pressures contrary to its deep convictions or firm desires.

This picture of government, public and the media is only part of the whole process of political communication. This is a complex process involving the entire political system, and especially the political parties and electoral activity. The media, and what we have been calling public opinion, are only a part of this, and not an autonomous independent part.

Political communication is, then, a central part of the political system. It is a crucial process in a democracy, for the notion of consent in a democracy implies at least effective communication between government and governed.

Thus the loose and ill-defined term 'public opinion' has to bear a considerable weight of practical and philosophical meaning. Some attempt at a usable definition is therefore vital.

2 WHAT IS 'PUBLIC OPINION'?

'Public opinion' is a term frequently employed, not least by politicians. Thus Herbert Morrison wrote:

....

DOCUMENT I

HERBERT MORRISON ON PUBLIC OPINION

From Lord Morrison, *Government and Parliament*, Oxford University Press, 1964, p. 180

One of the duties of the Government—and it is not always an easy one to discharge—is to estimate the reaction of public opinion to proposals under consideration and the extent to which those reactions should influence Government policy. We are a democracy and there is clearly an obligation on Ministers to take public opinion into account. A wise Government would not wish to bring itself into sharp conflict with predominant public opinion or, unless the public interest really required otherwise, with informed bodies of opinion entitled to respect and consideration. Such estimates of public opinion may be right or wrong. Some politicians have a valuable 'hunch' as to what the British people are or will be thinking about a given matter. Others are failures in this respect and a liability to their party as a consequence. More than once a policy has been changed after it was announced as a result of extensive public criticism, and certainly the ministerial estimate of what the public will or will not stand is a factor in the shaping of policy.

The art of judging public opinion is not an easy one. The most desirable requisite is an extensive knowledge of the outlook of the people in various walks of life and an understanding of how their minds work. It is important to have a respect and not a contempt for the general body of good citizens.

....

This is a firm expression of respect for public opinion, which would be accepted by most British politicians. They believe and expect that public opinion ought to influence their behaviour. The conclusion stands and may be significant, even if in practice it seems unrealistic.

Further analysis does, however, suggest that public opinion is too loose a term to bear the weight of Lord Morrison's pronouncement. The term implies that fairly precise views are quite widely held. If we define 'quite widely held' as 'held by more than sixty per cent of the adult population', then we should probably find that:

(a) The 'views' held are attitudes rather than precisely formulated opinions.

(b) Such attitudes are concerned with long-standing social traditions—e.g., in matters such as cruelty to animals, Sunday observance, loyalty to the Royal Family or to a wartime leader like Churchill, harsh punishment of criminals, mistrust of foreigners— rather than with matters of immediate political controversy.

(c) There would appear to be fluctuating widely-held attitudes to- wards governments, especially between elections, when party loyal- ties are weaker. These attitudes involve very general approval or dis- approval, affecting what is referred to as the 'standing' of the government.

(d) Where views are widely-held, precise and political, they are likely to arise from the prejudices of the pocket (e.g., objections to rates, taxes, rents) or a crisis involving national security and war (e.g., Munich, Suez). In the 1930s there seems to have been a widespread popular attitude of revulsion from war, inculcated by the casualties and horror of 1914–18. Here was public opinion, general, profound, influential, but also unique, the product of a bloody four-year lesson in pacifism. At other times, there have been great waves of opinion, commonly intolerant and puritanical—against 'Popery', drink, denominational education, prostitution, the mass media—all rather vague and emotive.

This is to attempt a definition of public opinion in the sense of 'widely-held attitudes'. But there is another more readily identifiable meaning: public opinion, as the articulated opinions of many small 'publics'. These include:

(i) individuals (writers, academics, directors, bishops, retired generals, writers of letters to the *Times*, and many others who are articulate and may claim public attention);

(ii) groups (i.e. pressure groups, all of which by definition have views to press on government);

(iii) the mass media (press, radio, television, putting forward their own views but also those of individuals and groups). It is misleading to term these opinions 'public'; really they are private opinions made public (i.e. articulated).

The opinions of these small publics may have some influence on general public opinion and perhaps the reverse too. Government, meanwhile, is not a passive receptacle for the views of others; both by just being 'the Government' and more deliberately through official information and political propaganda the Government influences public attitudes and the opinions of the publics. Thus, there is a movement, a process: flow, circulation, interaction.

3 THE PLACE OF THE MASS MEDIA IN POLITICAL COMMUNICATION

Mass and monopoly

The mass media of the mid-twentieth century are, above all else, massive. In the nineteenth century, journalism was dominated by the *Times* with a circulation of 50,000. In 1896, Lord Northcliffe (Alfred Harmsworth) published the *Daily Mail*; by 1900 it was selling nearly one-million copies at $\frac{1}{2}d$. a copy. By 1947, both the *Daily Mirror* and the *Daily Express* were selling nearly four-million copies each. By the mid-1960s the *Mirror* had topped five-million. The Sunday *News of the World* had almost sixteen-million readers, a world record outside the USSR—one of the few which Britain now holds.

Such massive circulations have been built up at the cost of destroying many small newspapers. In 1921, Britain had twelve national morning newspapers; by 1964 there were eight left (excluding the Scottish *Daily Record* and the specialised *Financial Times*). Meanwhile the forty-one provincial morning papers of 1921 had been reduced to a modest nineteen (1961). The ownership of the press—which is connected with its control—is even more restricted. Lord Rothermere, at the height of his career owned three national dailies, two provincial morning papers, three evening and five Sundays, as well as a hundred or so periodicals and an interest in three other national papers.

DOCUMENT 2

OWNERSHIP AND READERSHIP OF NEWSPAPERS

(a) *The concentration of readership*

From Institute of Practitioners in Advertising, National Readership Surveys, 1966, table 1A

Total Readership of British National newspapers, 1966			
	millions		*millions*
Daily Mirror	15.5	News of the World	16(15.974)
Daily Express	11.2	The People	15.4
Daily Mail	6.1	Sunday Mirror	14.5
Sun	4.5	Sunday Express	10.2
Daily Telegraph	3.4	Sunday Post	4.3
Daily Sketch	3.1	Sunday Times	3.6
Daily Record	1.4	The Observer	2.4
Guardian	0.8	Sunday Mail	2.0
The Times	0.8	Sunday Telegraph	1.8
The Financial Times	0.4	Sunday Citizen	0.6

(b) *The concentration of ownership*

Table from the Report of the Royal Commission on the Press, 1961–2 (Cmd. 1811, 1962, p. 15)

A few newspaper undertakings owning several newspapers control substantial portions of the total circulation of newspapers.

All daily newspapers			
1948	Per cent of circulation	*1961*	Per cent of circulation
Beaverbrook Newspapers	17	Daily Mirror Group	24
Associated Newspapers	15	Associated Newspapers	23
Daily Mirror group	13	Beaverbrook Newspapers	20

[The same three undertakings also own Sunday newspapers. Altogether, they controlled sixty-five per cent of the daily and Sunday press in 1961 (ibid. p. 16). Such multiple ownership compounds the effect of the concentration of readership, so that the British press has a tendency to monopoly.]

This lack of diversity in the British press is without parallel in any other Western democracy. It would be cause for concern if the press were not itself subject to keen and effective competition from the other mass media, radio and television. Wireless broadcasting began in 1922, and in 1927 the British Broadcasting Corporation was established as a public corporation with a monopoly of broadcasting. By 1945 almost ten-million wireless sets were licensed annually. But in the 1950s television rapidly became a rival to radio for public attention. In 1958 the number of licences for television and radio surpassed those for radio alone. By 1967 there were over fourteen-million combined licences, and only 2½-million for wireless only. By then, over ninety per cent of the British people had access to a television set.

The Coronation of 1953 played to an audience of over twenty-million. This figure was easily surpassed by the World Cup Final of July 1966, which was seen by twenty-six-million people in Britain (and an estimated four-hundred-million in the whole world). Some entertainment programmes are viewed regularly by audiences of seven to eight-million. Programmes of news and political information and commentary are of course less popular, but a few serious programmes of this kind regularly reach three-million or more people. The election broadcasts of 1966 had audiences of up to thirty per cent of the viewing population (over five years of age).

Only the very high circulation newspapers can match these figures. Moreover, broadcasting is even less diversified than the press. The BBC's monopoly in television was broken in 1954 with the establishment of commercial television under the Independent Television Authority. But the fourteen companies cooperate in what is for some of the time a national network. In radio, the BBC retained its hold unchallenged. The experimental local radio stations established in a few large cities in 1967–8 were still sponsored by the BBC.

Broadcasting, especially by television, is now the most important source of political information and opinion for most people. In terms of massiveness and monopoly it has far outdone the press. But it has been largely spared the criticism which afflicts the press.

The media and the inaccessibility of British government

The influence of the media in the British political system is substantially modified by the inaccessibility and secretiveness of British government. The convention of party solidarity, collective responsibility, and Civil Service anonymity combine to form almost impenetrable barriers around the centres of power. Thus an attempt by a national newspaper to introduce a correspondent into Whitehall (as distinct from the established parliamentary lobby in Westminster) failed: he was frozen out and withdrew, complaining bitterly of the secret power of 'the twin state of Whitehall'. Another example: in 1955 the Government established the '14-day rule' (now defunct), by which the broadcasting organisations were forbidden to arrange a discussion on a topic debated in Parliament within fourteen days of the debate. Local government, imitating the vices of central government, has gone to great lengths to exclude the press and public. Meetings of committees of the whole local council must now be open to the public; to evade this, such committees are sometimes arranged as committees of the whole council, less one.

The secretiveness of government is reinforced by the reticence of the press. Partly this derives from a prudent regard for the Official Secrets Act and the laws of libel. These can be particularly severe, and there is no understanding (as in the USA) that libel hardly applies to politicians. Reticence also derives from the voluntary restraint of the press. This has been demonstrated most notably over the Abdication crisis of 1936 and in the early stages of the Profumo affair in 1962; in both cases British newspapers refrained from publishing information 'in the public interest'. These were, of course, unusual cases, and the monarchy might be regarded as a very special case. In other respects, voluntary reticence is perhaps breaking down. Arising from the case of H. Philby, the Russian spy who became head of the Russian section of the British security services, the *Sunday Times* published, in 1967, details of the security services sufficient at least to embarrass the Government.

The Government's defence against the press involves management of the news as well as secretiveness. Information officers, official briefings and press conferences all provide formal channels from Government to newsmen. The parliamentary 'lobby' (journalists attached to Parliament) has privileged access to Ministers as well as to Private Members. Ministers try to win friends among the press, exchanging exclusive information for the promise of sympathetic treatment: the press as a whole may resent, but individual pressmen cannot always resist, such blandishments. The arranged 'leak' is a product of this system. Thus, Mr Randolph Churchill claimed to have seen a Cabinet document setting out Prime Minister Macmillan's arrangements for the choice of a successor. The *Sunday Times* of 29 October 1967 gave details of the Government's proposal to reform the House of Lords—still to be announced in the (supposedly secret) Queen's Speech.

It is not surprising, therefore, that the press and broadcasters in Britain are not well informed about the course of British politics. 'Scoops' are rare, and at vital moments the press seems as much in the dark as the public. Thus, a few days before Eden's resignation in January 1957 one newspaper confidently reported that the Prime Minister had recovered his health and was extending his responsibilities in government. Most newspapers seemed unaware of the Conservative Party's emerging preference for Macmillan rather than Butler. Traditionally the press has often been cast as lackey or watchdog of government. The British press is neither.

4 THE PRESS: NATURE AND INFLUENCE

The nature of a newspaper

The press is a commercial enterprise, and exists to make a profit; indeed, it cannot exist for long without making a profit. Its costs, especially in newsprint and labour, are high; hence it needs a high circulation to bring in the pennies of the millions and the pounds of the advertisers. To secure a high circulation, the press must cater for the tastes of the masses, 'giving the public what it wants'.

....

DOCUMENT 3

EDITORS AIM AT THE MASSES

(a) Extract from National Union of Teachers, 'Popular culture and personal responsibility' (verbatim report of a conference held in October 1960). Speech by Mr Cecil King, chairman of the *Daily Mirror*, p. 253

Of course you have got to give the public what it wants, otherwise you go out of business as we have seen recently in the case of two or three newspapers. You try and raise its standards as well. The trouble is the critics imagine the great British public is as educated as themselves and their friends . . . In point of fact it is only the people who conduct newspapers and other similar organisations who have any idea quite how indifferent, quite how stupid, quite how uninterested in education of any kind the great bulk of the British public are . . .

(b) Arthur Christiansen, former Editor of the *Daily Express*, quoted in F. Williams, *Dangerous Estate*, Arrow Books, 1959, p. 191

I journeyed from Rhyl to Prestatyn on Sunday past lines of boarding houses, caravans, wooden huts, shacks, tents and heaven knows what else. In every one of them there were newspaper readers. Happy citizens, worthy, fine people but not in the least like the reader Fleet Street seems to be writing for. These people are not interested in Glyndebourne or vintage claret or opera or the Sitwells or dry-as-dust economics or tough politics. It is our job to interest them in everything. It requires the highest degree of skill and ingenuity.

....

Like most commercial organisations, newspapers are controlled by a few men at the top, especially the chairman of the board and the editor. Some newspaper proprietors, such as Lord Beaverbrook, have notoriously directed the editorial policy of their papers; others, such as Lord Thomson, have granted considerable discretion to the editor. But a free editor does not necessarily mean freedom for the editorial staff. Thus, in the 1930s, the *Times* rewrote or suppressed despatches from its Berlin correspondent criticising Hitler's régime in Germany. On the other hand, some writers have been permitted to write in a sense opposed to the policy of their paper. In October 1967, the *Daily Mirror* published a leading article criticising one of its own feature writers; and for many years Vicky, the brilliant left-wing cartoonist, worked for the Conservative London *Evening Standard*. Still, in general, newspapermen, like the rest of us, work for bosses and do not have a free hand. This is not to say that newspaper offices are battlegrounds or prisons. As in other organisations, the staff tends to include like-minded people, who do not need to be dragooned by the editor. Such organisations acquire civilised relationships and traditions which discourage (while not precluding) dictatorial direction.

Newspapers sell news—a highly perishable commodity. The best news is the newest; for a morning paper this means the news that happened too late for either the evening papers or the evening television bulletins. Hence, newspapers are produced at speed, reports may be written by people with inadequate information, sub-edited and headlined by people with no relevant information at all. Little wonder then that the standard of accuracy is not high. The editor of a national Sunday paper admitted to the Royal Commission of 1947-9: 'I do not wish to be hypercritical, but the plain fact is—and we all know it to be true—that whenever we see a story in a newspaper concerning something we know about, it is more often wrong than right.' The Commission in its Report considered this statement 'extreme' but also 'in our experience it has a substantial element of truth.' This situation is not the fault of the newspapermen; it is a consequence of the conditions of their work. Indeed, the competition of television in hard news is so intense that some newspapers have become magazines, looking for stories of 'human interest', not national concern.

Newspapers are politically partisan, and news is normally reported, selected and presented with a bias intended to secure approval for the paper's favoured party. This includes selection of favourable and suppression of unfavourable news, headlining and treatment. News and comment are inevitably mixed. The tendency of newspapers to become magazines rather than political journals has perhaps modified partisanship somewhat; but on major political events like the devaluation of November 1967, most national newspapers are predictably, and in some cases shrilly, partisan. The political line-up is as follows:

....

DOCUMENT 4

PARTISANSHIP OF THE BRITISH PRESS
(NATIONAL DAILIES)

Partisan Conservative	Moderate Independent		Partisan Labour
	Right	*Left*	
Daily Telegraph	The Times	Guardian	Daily Mirror
Daily Mail			Sun (to 1969)
Daily Express			Daily Record
Daily Sketch			
The Financial Times			

....

EXERCISE

PARTISANSHIP AND READERSHIP

1. Transfer the figures for readership given in document 2 (p. 375), and add up in the partisanship columns above. What conclusions do you draw?

According to a National Opinion Poll survey taken in July 1967 and published in the *Sunday Times* of 17 September 1967:

the paper with the highest proportion of Labour sympathisers among its readers was the *Sun* with sixty-nine per cent;

the papers with the highest proportion of Conservative sympathisers were the *Financial Times*, seventy per cent, and the *Daily Telegraph*, sixty-seven per cent;

the *Mirror* had fifty-three per cent Labour sympathisers, the *Express* forty-seven per cent Conservative sympathisers;

the *Guardian* has a claim to the most diverse readership: thirty per cent Conservatives, thirty-six per cent Labour, nineteen per cent Liberal.

There is a tendency for the political alignment of readers with their newspapers to diminish. This is seen as 'either a consequence or a cause' of the movement of the papers themselves to be politically independent or simply non-political. Further, many readers 'see' more than one paper, in some cases with differing political attitudes. Thus, for example, about one-fifth of the *Mirror's* readers also see the *Express* (1967).

In the case of the *Times* and the *Guardian*, there is an element of independence of party, with sympathies towards the right and left respectively. In the case of the *Express* and the *Mirror*, the support of a party is sometimes modified by peculiar enthusiasms or antipathies (e.g., the *Express* detests the Common Market).

DOCUMENT 5

DISTRIBUTION OF NEWSPAPER READERSHIP BY SOCIAL CLASS (NATIONAL DAILIES, 1966)

From Institute of Practitioners in Advertising, National Readership Survey, 1966. (The figures represent percentages of each class reading the newspaper.)

Social grade	Middle class	Lower middle class	Skilled working class	Unskilled and very poor	Total
% of population	AB (10%)	C1 (19%)	C2 (39%)	DE (31%)	
Mirror	14	28	49	42	39
Express	29	32	29	24	28
Mail	24	20	13	12	15
Sun	3	8	14	13	11
Telegraph	29	15	4	2	8
Sketch	5	6	9	8	8
Record	1	2	4	5	3
Guardian	8	3	1	1	2
Times	9	2	1	—	2
Financial Times	5	2	—	—	1

....

DOCUMENT 6

DISTRIBUTION OF READERSHIP BY TERMINAL EDUCATION AGE
(NATIONAL DAILIES, YEAR ENDING JULY 1964)

From M. Abrams, 'Education, social class and reading of newspapers and magazines', I.P.A. Booklets, no. 5, 1966

Terminal education age	19 or more	16–18	15 or less	All
Telegraph	35	27	4	9
Express	30	38	32	33
Mail	21	24	16	17
Times	18	7	1	2
Guardian	15	6	1	2
Mirror	9	23	42	38
Financial Times	7	6	1	2
Herald	3	6	14	12
Sketch	3	6	9	8

....

EXERCISE

THE 'QUALITY' PRESS

2. In the light of figures of circulation (document 2, p. 375) and social class and readership (documents 5 and 6, above), what can you say about the existence of a 'quality press' and a popular press?

Finally, it must be said that writing for the popular press calls for communicating skills of a very high level. It is facile to criticise the views expressed in document 3 (p. 378); the fact remains that the mass circulation papers are attempting to provide reading for people with little reading skill and virtually no interest in serious public affairs. Research into the reception and understanding of quite simple messages demonstrates the difficulties of communicating anything at all. (Consider the communication failures of the classroom!) The popular dailies for the most part accept a five per cent responsibility (so to speak) for raising the level of their readers' tastes and appreciation; and they have some success in inducing their readers occasionally to attend to serious public affairs. The *Daily Mirror*, for example, rightly boasts that its leading article is read by a greater proportion of its readers than the *Times*' leading article (by *Times* readers). Such readability is secured sometimes at a heavy cost in bias, sensationalism, or trivialisation. But the alternative may be no article on a serious theme at all. Writing of this kind is extremely difficult, as the following exercise may show.

WRITING FOR THE *Daily Mirror*

3. This is your chance to find out whether you would make a good reporter or sub-editor on the *Daily Mirror*. Decide on a treatment and devise a headline for a leading article based on the following story: the wife of a Church of England vicar (herself happily married and mother of two children) refused to join the Mothers' Union, because the Union does not accept divorced women as members. Do not spend too long on this: just a few minutes, and then look up the guide to exercises (p. 399).

Content and style of a newspaper

ANALYSIS OF A NEWSPAPER

4. The analysis of newspapers by content and style is a useful piece of research which may be easily organised. (There are good examples of such analyses in, e.g., the Report of the Royal Commission on the Press, 1949, and in R. Williams, *Communications*, Penguin, 1962.) A study of these will give you a good idea of what can be usefully done.

Here are some general points: decide which kinds of newspaper you wish to study—dailies, Sundays, national, local—and whether you wish to examine all the papers on one day or on several days; or whether you will compare two or three papers.

A little time (but not too much) may usefully be spent in measuring the amount of space devoted to news, comment, features, pictures and advertisements. What are the proportions of political and other serious matter compared with human interest and trivia?

Analyse lead stories—which have been chosen, and how they are presented (length, detail, headline, slant, comment). Compare the choice and treatment of other matter. How are parliamentary proceedings reported? And so on.

The influence of the press

Enough has been said about the nature of newspapers to suggest the following hypothesis: it is not desirable in a democracy that newspapers should have a substantial, profound and continuous influence on political opinion and activity. But does the press have such an influence? Here are some case studies:

....

DOCUMENT 7
THE INFLUENCE OF THE PRESS

(a) *The Suez crisis, 1956*

The press generally followed the party it normally supported, Conservative papers for intervention, Labour and Liberal against it.

The *Daily Mirror* criticised the Prime Minister with all the customary force and brilliance of its front page. But it did not carry along all its readers —circulation dropped by 70,000. The *Mirror* then trimmed its policy slightly, and confused the political issue with admiration of the British soldier. 'Heads high', it wrote. 'The British Army could have wiped out the Egyptians within forty-eight hours. Everybody knows this, including Colonel Nasser and all the other Egyptians.' A historian of the *Mirror*, Maurice Edelman, comments: 'It was an editorial which skilfully reflected the changing mood of the British public . . .' (*The Mirror, A Political History*, Hamish Hamilton, 1966, p. 163.)

Thus, it seems the *Mirror* did not lead its readers, it followed them. But too much should not be made of this one incident. On war as such (not foreign policy), the public knows its mind, thus restricting the influence of the press.

(b) *The Common Market, 1961–3*

The first attempt to negotiate British entry into the Common Market began in the summer of 1961 and ended with President de Gaulle's veto in January 1963. The issue was a new one, and had not been raised during the election of 1959. It was a complex issue, over which the experts were divided and the public, almost certainly (and justifiably) ignorant and undecided.

Of the two great mass circulation dailies, the *Mirror* came out strongly in favour of joining the Common Market, the *Express*, with equal strength and stridency, was opposed. These positions probably represented the personal views of the men at the top: Cecil King, the *Mirror's* chairman, and Lord Beaverbrook, the proprietor of the *Express*.

According to Woodrow Wyatt, M.P., the *Mirror's* campaign was admitted by two members of the Government to be 'the tip-over factor . . . if they had the *Daily Mirror* behind them, well, then they would probably be all right.' (Quoted in Lord Windlesham, *Communication and Government Policy*, Jonathan Cape, 1966, p. 57.) This is good evidence of a newspaper's actually influencing government policy—confirming it in a course it was inclined to follow, at the least giving it confidence.

But the Government was prepared to shrug off the anti-Market campaign of the *Express*. This campaign, according to one expert observer, 'made it publicly known that no one unhappy about the Market need ever feel alone . . . in preventing defections and fortifying the anti-Marketeers, more than in occasional conversions, the *Daily Express* can claim to have had some influence on popular opinion in this period.' (Lord Windlesham, op. cit., pp. 160–3.) This view cannot, in fact, be proved, but it seems a reasonable assessment.

Thus it seems the Government almost decided on its policies (virtually without reference to party or electorate); then looked around for some support; was glad to have one popular newspaper behind it, but not unduly worried about the direct and vigorous opposition of another.

(c) *The Cabinet changes of 1962*

In July 1962, Mr Macmillan reconstructed his Government, making thirty-six changes altogether, including the dismissal of seven Cabinet Ministers. The press had no doubt made a modest unspecific contribution to this 'purge' (by reporting and interpreting unfavourably a series of by-election reverses), thus reflecting a 'mood' or 'climate' of general disaffection with the Government. The press also seems to have had a quite specific effect on the timing of the operation. The *Daily Mail* 'scooped' the Prime Minister by predicting the changes with some accurate detail four or five days before the changes were due to take place. Macmillan, embarrassed by the speculation, carried out his reconstruction the day following the *Mail's* revelations and four days before he had intended. The operation looked, and was, in consequence clumsy and brutal, with some of the ex-Ministers bewildered and antagonised. What should have been a major reconstruction was dubbed a purge; and this was a direct consequence of press reporting. This is a specific but somewhat unusual example of the influence of the press.

(d) *Spot checks for drinking drivers*

In 1965 the Minister of Transport proposed random or 'spot' checks of motorists to test the amount of alcohol in their breath. This proposal was subsequently withdrawn and replaced by a more limited proposal for breath-tests when the motorist had been involved in an accident or was thought to have been drinking or to have committed a motoring offence. The Minister, on withdrawing her proposal, said she must 'bow to public opinion', which was generally hostile to the proposal.

The press was certainly involved in the hostility, along with the motoring and civil liberties organisations and a good majority of the public as revealed in Gallup and other polls. But this example, even more than the previous one, does not argue a general influence of newspapers on policy. Clearly, in the relations of police and public and in a matter involving direct interference with the 'liberties of the citizen' a government must be more than usually sensitive to public reactions.

I.T.B.P.—N

(e) *The press as champion of the oppressed individual*

A concern for individual freedom is one of the British citizen's most creditable 'rooted notions'.[1] The press has occasionally taken up the case of some individual apparently oppressed by a 'tyrannical and bureaucratic' State— the victim of a planning decision, an immigrant about to be deported, the colonel's batman set to paint the colonel's private house. These heart-warming crusades (which may well be unfair to the officials concerned) often have some success, especially if they are taken up in Parliament. Indeed, they play much the same part as the Parliamentary Question or the Adjournment Motion. They are concerned with maladministration, not major policy.

(f) *A new airport at Stansted*

The 'Stansted affair', 1967–8, is likely to remain a notorious case in British politics, illustrating the deficiencies of the Civil Service and the Cabinet in face of a difficult technical issue. But it is also an example of a government's changing its mind in response to pressures from Parliament and public. Briefly, the Government decided in 1967, after some years of inquiry, that a third London Airport should be sited at Stansted in Essex. Vociferous protests, public and private, were followed by the withdrawal of the decision and the establishment of a new Inquiry. It is difficult to say which was the most important pressure: from its own backbenchers in Parliament; from the Opposition; from the organised interests, local authorities, residents, the Council for the Preservation of Rural England; or from the press and television. All these pressures are the more urgent because they are reported in the mass media and thus may affect the standing of the Government, so there is some justification for including the Stansted affair at this point. It is an example, if you like, of the operation of public opinion as an effective check on government; but an example which shows that the term public opinion is meaningful only when it is analysed into 'little publics'.

(g) *The press in general elections*

See chapter 12, sections 4 and 5 (pp. 416 and 427).

....

In the light of the above case-studies, it appears that the political influence of the press is modest and limited, varying with the issues, with the pressures and counter-pressures of other sources of opinion

---

[1]Bagehot: 'The English people do not easily change their rooted notions, but they have many unrooted notions'. (*The British Constitution* (1867), Fontana, 1963, p. 194.)

and with the general tendency of public attitudes. Newspapers provide an agenda for discussion, cues for latent opinions, reinforcement for weak, half-formulated attitudes. As Cecil King said, 'A newspaper can dramatise an interesting new movement but when there is no interesting new movement a newspaper cannot create it.' On the other hand, major events provide the press (and broadcasting) with a public profoundly hungry for information and comment. In the devaluation crisis of November 1967 the circulation of the *Times* increased for a while by 20,000 copies a day. This is a situation ripe for exploitation—for good or ill.

It is easy, indeed, to underestimate the influence of the press. 'Reinforcement of existing tendencies' may after all represent considerable influence. Consider, for example, the political situation of autumn 1967. The Government was in considerable difficulties with its economic policies and unemployment was high (higher than at any time since the Slump between the wars). A series of statements —by the Governor of the Bank of England, by the Chancellor of the Exchequer and by the Chairman of the National Coal Board— seemed to emphasise the Government's intention to accept unemployment as part of the overall strategy of regional economic planning and modernisation. These statements were seized on by the press and presented in a way which associated Government policies with unemployment in a negative way. The Government suffered severe setbacks in by-elections at the time. Clearly it would have preferred a more sympathetic press. Still, the press could hardly be accused of *gross* distortion: the facts and statements which formed the basis of their reporting were provided by the Government, not invented. But the question here is the influence of the press: and it seems unreasonable, until proof is provided to the contrary, to assume that the press had *no* influence on the formation of opinion hostile to the Government.

It seems possible, moreover, that the press can exert some influence not simply in reinforcement of existing tendencies but in situations of neutrality, or the absence of any positive tendency, as long as there is no prejudice or sentiment to the contrary. This is almost equivalent to the manufacture of opinion.

No politician can afford to ignore and neglect the press. Many leading politicians seem rather to be avid readers of newspapers. The influence of the press does not depend simply on the movement of public opinion. A prudent politician must recognise that the press *may* have some influence on opinion. Moreover, leaving aside any such possible influence, a prudent politician reads newspapers with attention and even respect. He reads and values comment and criticism; the press is a component of the diverse public opinions of which he must at least take notice.

This is of course a much more limited conclusion than that suggested in the hypothesis proposed at the beginning of this section. The press does not have 'a substantial, profound and continuous influence' on politics. So its imperfections as a medium of political information and education may be forgiven.

5 BROADCASTING: NATURE AND INFLUENCE

The nature of political broadcasting

The press is basically competitive and partisan, organised and operating for the most part like a commercial venture in a market-place. Broadcasting is quite different in style, working with some sense of public service and cultural responsibility, and within a long tradition of political impartiality. These qualities derive from the history of broadcasting and from its statutory obligations.

Broadcasting was from 1922 until 1954 a monopoly of the British Broadcasting Corporation, which began as a company licensed by the Postmaster-General but was established as a public corporation in 1926. The BBC's Charter underlines its responsibility as a public service, and the Corporation's first Director-General, Sir John Reith, gave it a tradition of high morality, propriety and political impartiality. Possibly Reith, a Scots Presbyterian, went too far. In his day, newsreaders wore evening dress, Sunday was entirely given over to serious, mainly religious, programmes; on days of thin or trivial news, no news bulletins were given at all. Still, Reith's achievement was substantial: he founded and sustained one of the most distinctive (and widely admired) features of mid-century Britain, public service broadcasting.

Radio has remained a BBC monopoly, moderated slightly by foreign stations like Radio Luxemburg and 'pirate' stations. In television, the monopoly was broken in 1954 with the establishment of commercial companies, financed by advertising but operating under the supervision of the Independent Television Authority. Thereafter, the BBC and the commercial companies competed for viewers, rather as newspapers compete for readers, and with similar effects. But the BBC can still afford to ignore viewing figures; its long-standing traditions have not crumbled, and have even had some influence on commercial broadcasting. Moreover, in the political field, the Independent Television Act has laid down standards of impartiality.

The historical and statutory basis of the public service tradition in broadcasting is illustrated in the following document.

....

DOCUMENT 8

THE PUBLIC SERVICE TRADITION IN BROADCASTING

(a) *The BBC'S Charter and Licence*

Under the terms of the Charter and Licence of the British Broadcasting Corporation:

the Broadcasting Service is recognised as 'a means of information, education and entertainment';

the Corporation is charged with the duty of broadcasting each day an impartial account of the proceedings of Parliament, and announcements by Government Departments;

the Corporation is not permitted to broadcast its own opinion on matters of controversy, i.e., unlike a newspaper, it has no editorial policy.

(b) *Relations of BBC and Government*

The Corporation must comply with the directions of the Postmaster-General, and the Postmaster-General specifically has the right (still unused) to 'require the Corporation to refrain from' broadcasting particular matter. In practice, the Postmaster-General normally refuses to answer for or intervene in matters of content and style of programmes. The independence of the BBC is genuine. During the Suez crisis of 1956, the BBC stood up to strong pressure from the Government, insisting on broadcasting criticisms of Government policy in its external services and permitting the Leader of the Opposition to reply to the Prime Minister's broadcast.

(c) *Lord Reith on the influence of broadcasting*

The tradition established by the first Director-General, Sir John (later Lord) Reith was strongly one of public service. Two extracts from Reith's Memorandum to the Broadcasting Committee of 1949 convey the flavour and the fervour:

Objective
The exploitation and development of Broadcasting were (haply) under control from the outset; and in the public interest; without prejudice to entertainment functions, under a feeling of moral responsibility, moral in the broadest sense—intellectual and ethical; with determination that the greatest benefit possible would accrue from its output.
Conclusion
... It is in terms of moral effect that the influence of Broadcasting will eventually be judged ...

[Reith regarded listening figures with some disdain.]

(d) *The Television Act, 1954*

Independent television inherited the tradition of the BBC, but is also guided by the provisions of the Television Act, 1954. Section 3 of the Act requires *inter alia*:

'that nothing is included in the programmes which offends against good taste or decency or is likely to encourage or incite to crime or to lead to disorder or to be offensive to public feeling . . .';

that news is 'presented with due accuracy and impartiality';

that 'due impartiality is preserved on the part of the persons providing the programmes' on matters of political controversy;

that programmes might include 'properly balanced discussions or debates';

Broadcasting time cannot be purchased for political purposes. The political parties are allocated time on both BBC and ITV (simultaneously) for 'party political broadcasts'.

....

Thus, in television political broadcasting, there is not the concern for circulation, the high sensationalism and acute partisanship of the popular press; nor is there a division in television between 'quality' broadcasting for an educated and attentive minority, and mass broadcasting.

All the same, television has some features which detract from its qualities as a source of political information and education in a democracy. There is an element of competition for viewers; low figures for the BBC would affect its prestige and its chances of increasing the licence fee. Mostly the BBC is in 'show-business': political and current affairs programmes are a small part of a vast entertainment operation. If the press had its overly powerful barons in Northcliffe and Beaverbrook, broadcasting had its authoritarian knight, Sir John Reith. Now, possibly, excessive power lies in the hands of a few performers. The star interviewers can at their best—like the press— help to secure the answerability of politicians, but at their worst they can cast suspicion on an honest statement. Television seems much more than the press to give rise to a spurious, superficial air of concern and omniscience. It suffers like the press from the necessity for speed and brevity; but, dealing in pictures, not the printed word, it can exaggerate and distort simply by illustrating rather than narrating or analysing.

Still, for all its imperfections, the BBC has raised the level of political information and understanding; television has probably extended information and understanding to a wider audience than ever before: and fairness, balance, impartiality have been maintained.

ANALYSIS OF TELEVISION

There are obvious practical difficulties in the analysis of content and style of television. With television, you have to be there when it happens; newspapers can await your leisure. A tape-recorder and a stop-watch would obviously help, but are not indispensable. Answers should be sought to some of the folllowing questions:

5.1. *News Programmes.* Do BBC and ITV tend to treat the same items at roughly the same length? Are there variations in the selection of the lead story? What use is made of film and interviews? Is the report just a report, or a comment, or a judgement? Is the presentation easy to understand, moderately difficult or suitable only for comparatively well-informed people? How does the treatment compare with that of the newspapers?

5.2. *Other current affairs programmes.* Similar questions.

Also, what is the effect of interviews?—to elucidate or to obscure? to press the person interviewed hard or not? fairly or not?

Viewing figures and make-up of programmes

Figures for the proportion of news and other programmes in the whole output are conveniently available from the BBC, the ITA and the companies. So too are viewing figures for individual programmes. In this respect, there is more information available on broadcasting than on the press. (There is no regular source of information on the readership of *particular sections* of the newspaper.)

....

DOCUMENT 9

TELEVISION PROGRAMME OUTPUT

(a) *Estimated weekly average in London, October–December 1966*

	%
News and news magazines	7 }16
Documentaries and news features	9
Adult education (incl. repeats)	4
School programmes (incl. repeats)	9
Children's programmes	8
Plays, drama, series and serials, films, entertainment	45
Sport	13

(From ITA, *ITV1968*, p. 16. BBC figures not notably dissimilar.)

(b) Per head of population, viewing amounted in 1966–7 to about 13.34 hours per week (BBC Annual Report, 1966–7).

(c) In the fifteen-million homes with a choice of service, the TV set is on average switched on for 4½ hours a day, varying with the time of the year. (ITA, *ITV 1968*)

(d) 'Between 7.30 and 10.30 p.m. in September 1966 an average of almost 13-million people were viewing ITV programmes. Audiences for the most popular programme often reach about 20-million.' (ITA, *ITV 1967*, p. 23)

(e) Viewing figures, BBC 1966–7:
    Till Death Us Do Part—average audience 15–20 million
    Cathy Come Home—seen by 19 million viewers
  Listening figures, BBC 1966–7:
    The Dales—average 4½–6 million
    The Archers—4–4½ million (in 17th year)
    Housewives' Choice—8 million
    The Ken Dodd Show—10 million
(From BBC Annual Report, 1966–7)

(f) TV election broadcasts 1966. About 30% of the population aged five and over on average viewed each of the programmes of the major parties; slightly more than 1964 (24–27%) and more again than for 1959 (21–23%).

....

The influence of television

It was suggested at the beginning of the section on the influence of the press (p. 383) that it might be undesirable for the press to have considerable influence in politics. The assessment of television has been a little more favourable, but it would again seem a reasonable working hypothesis that television should not be a dominant influence in politics.

Television, like newspapers, could influence politics in two ways: by direct influence on Ministers and Governments, and by influencing 'public opinion' and hence indirectly acting on Governments.

....

DOCUMENT 10

THE POLITICAL INFLUENCE OF TELEVISION

Little is known with any precision or certainty about the influence of television. Here are some indications:

(a) The general conclusion of a survey of two Leeds constituencies in the 1959 election, conducted by J. Trenaman and D. McQuail, is quoted in chapter 12, p, 436. Notice that the conclusion is for the short term of the campaign only. It is a negative conclusion. Yet there remains a suspicion that a medium that can increase information may also modify attitudes—information is never neutral.

(b) There is an impression, and some evidence, that in the general election of 1964 Sir Alec Douglas-Home was less effective as a television performer than either of his chief opponents. A National Opinion Polls survey showed that only 47% of intending Conservative voters regarded Home as the most impressive leader on TV, while 41% regarded either Wilson or Grimond, the Labour and Liberal Leaders, as the most impressive. Intending Labour voters, on the other hand, were 75% for Wilson as most impressive (NOP survey quoted in D. Butler and A. King, *The British General Election of 1964*, Macmillan, 1965, p. 162 n.l.).

Sir Alec's lack of impressiveness seems to have been due mainly to superficial matters—voice and style of speaking, 'half-moon' spectacles—but perhaps also to an evident lack of grasp and 'bite' on economic matters.

(c) Television has superseded the press, and is now widely accepted and relied on as a primary, general source of information and comment on public affairs. (ITA, *ITV 1967*, refers this conclusion to 'specially commissioned audience research'.)

(d) The impartiality of television ensures that the viewer is exposed to the persuasion and arguments of the other side. (Up to half the audience for party political broadcasts belongs to the other party.) Newspapers and meetings do not attract such politically diverse audiences. The ultimate effect of this is not known. Further, the impartiality of television evens out the partisan tendencies of the press.

(e) The nature of the medium. It is generally and easily available in the home, and, by its use of pictures as well as words, catches the attention and impresses the viewer. Of course, there is also much casual viewing and many ineffective pictures.

(f) The long-term effects are likely to be more profound than the short-term, but are difficult to measure. A Conservative politician once surmised that television was 'putting over the middle-class ideas' and thus 'destroying the working class'. This is plausible. Again, the approach of television to politics and politicians, though balanced and impartial, is critical rather than adulatory, and may contribute to a distrust of politicians. The showing of domestic political instability, especially street demonstrations, may encourage further demonstrations, as it did in the USA in 1967. The television coverage of wars and famine brings disaster and suffering directly to the homes of people, as never before; this may shock and horrify or make people hard and insensitive; or it may make no deep or lasting impact at all.

All these points are speculative: we do not know how television will influence politics in the long term.

6 THE PROCESSES OF POLITICAL COMMUNICATION

The complexity of the process

Political communication, if considered as all the communication which is politically significant, involves much more than the press and broadcasting. The social environment in which politics takes place includes elements which communicate, inform, mould—family, work, church, and so on. These are powerful in the formation of social and political attitudes, but the processes are unspecific, long-term, dealing in attitudes rather than information. They are referred to, therefore, as 'political socialisation' rather than 'political communication'.

The more specific processes of political communication are, however, the concern of political parties. General elections provide opportunities for sustained and intensive communication. Pressure groups join in, endeavouring to create favourable public attitudes, as well as working on the more serious business of direct persuasion of the executive. Some pressure groups are indeed mainly concerned with propagation of public attitudes, for the good reason that they have no other access to government. The best recent example is the Campaign for Nuclear Disarmament, but organisations promoting or opposed to British entry to the Common Market and Abortion Law Reform have devoted energy, skill and money to the modification of public attitudes. Parliament itself is, of course, engaged most of the time in political communication. These aspects of political communication are dealt with in other chapters, especially those on parties, elections and pressure groups.

There is another aspect of political communication which may be neglected just because it does not fit neatly into the simple categories by which we think about government. Government and people listen to a diverse collection of 'public advisers', academics, publicists and, in corporate form, institutes, committees and commissions. The influence of academics has grown as universities have developed studies of immediate contemporary significance—economics, the social sciences, atomic physics. Lord Keynes, one of the most influential academics ever, wrote:

....

DOCUMENT 11

KEYNES ON THE POWER OF IDEAS

From J. M. Keynes, *The General Theory of Employment Interest and Money*, Macmillan, 1951, p. 383

... the ideas of economists and political philosophers, both when they are right and when they are wrong, are more powerful than is commonly understood. Indeed the world is ruled by little else. Practical men, who believe themselves to be quite exempt from any intellectual influences, are usually the slaves of some defunct economist. Madmen in authority, who hear voices in the air, are distilling their frenzy from some academic scribbler of a few years back. I am sure that the power of vested interests is vastly exaggerated compared with the gradual encroachment of ideas.

....

Academic scribblers are as busy as ever and, in popularised manifestations, not without influence. In a few cases, this kind of academic advising has a corporate form, as in the Royal Institute of International Affairs, or the Institute of Strategic Studies. In the 1930s, All Souls College, Oxford, served informally as an exchange mart for (top) academics and politicians; and it is arguable that it contributed to the policy of appeasement.

Another main source of 'public advice' is the Royal Commission, or Advisory Committee appointed by the Government to investigate and report on particular problems. This is a peculiarly British device. Some reports have had considerable effect on popular opinion and on Government policy—for example, the Beveridge Report of 1943 on Social Insurance and the Robbins Report of 1963 on Higher Education. Others, like the Buchanan Report on Traffic in Towns (1963) have contributed notably to public discussion without having substantial influence on policies. Still others have sunk without trace, serving only to facilitate the shelving of a problem without embarrassment.

Thus the agencies of political communication are many and diverse. The process of communication is also complex. Simply analysed, the actual, physical operation of communication consists of a transmitter, a message and a receiver. But this simple analysis hides great variations in the nature of the process. Consider the complexities of the spreading of a rumour through a school or a village. The sinuosities of the grapevine may give a more accurate image than the radio transmitter!

Again, simply analysed, the public is 'ignorant and irrational'. 'The lower orders, the middle orders,' wrote Bagehot in 1867, 'are still, when tried by what is the standard of the educated "ten thousand", narrow-minded, unintelligent, incurious. It is useless to pile up abstract words. Those who doubt should go out into their kitchens' (Bagehot, *The English Constitution*, p. 63). Of course Bagehot expected to find his domestic servants, not his wife, in the kitchen!

Most people hear only what they want to hear, will receive only the political message which fits their prejudices. However, this analysis does not account for the slow changes and great swings in popular attitudes. The people, for all their ignorance and gullibility, seem occasionally to make up or change their minds in senses contrary to prevailing prejudice and the urgings of the persuaders. The rise and fall of ideas like free trade, the decline of the Liberal Party over the last fifty years, and the recent success of nationalist parties are sufficient evidence that popular opinion has an independent and unpredictable potential in British politics.

Political communication and democratic theory

The theorist of democracy (and all its well-wishers too) is faced with some difficult problems in the field of political communication, particularly in regard to the notion of 'public opinion':

(a) How far is there a general popular opinion as distinct from the opinions of many 'little publics'? And how is such a general opinion identified?

(b) To what extent is such a popular opinion based on ignorance or prejudice?—and to what extent is it the creation of the mass persuaders (press, broadcasting, politicians, advertisers)?

(c) Is it worthy of respect? How far should a government follow public opinion?

(d) How should the mass media be organised to serve best the needs and interests of a democracy?

Some answers to these fundamental questions are indicated in the assessments (p. 400). Meanwhile here are two problems:

....

DOCUMENT 12

HOW FAR SHOULD GOVERNMENTS DEFER TO PUBLIC OPINION?

From H.C. Deb., vol. 317, 12 November 1936, col. 1101

[In the 1930s, public opinion (in this case a widespread popular attitude) was strongly pacifist—after the horror of 1914–18, was was unthinkable. Historians have argued that the rise of Hitler in Germany threatened war and necessitated a programme of rearmament in Britain. The Prime Minister, Baldwin, once said in the Commons—in an unguarded moment—of the 1935 election:]

. . . I have stated that a democracy is always two years behind the dictator. I believe that to be true. It has been true in this case . . . You will remember at that time there was probably a stronger pacifist feeling running through this country than at any time since the war. . . . You will remember the election at Fulham in the autumn of 1933, when a seat which the National Government held was lost by about 7,000 votes on no issue but the pacifist. . . . My position as a leader of a great party was not altogether a comfortable one. I asked myself what chance was there—when that feeling that was given expression to in Fulham was common throughout the country— what chance was there within the next year or two of that feeling being so changed that the country would give a mandate for rearmament? Supposing I had gone to the country and said that Germany was rearming, and that we must rearm, does anybody think that this pacific democracy would have rallied to that cry at that moment? I cannot think of anything that would have made the loss of the election from my point of view more certain.

....

EXERCISE

GOVERNMENTS AND PUBLIC OPINION

6. Churchill, in the index to his book, *The Gathering Storm* (Cassell, 1948), refers to this incident as: '[Baldwin] confesses putting party before country.' In the text itself he was kinder: there is indeed a defence of Baldwin. What is it?

....

DOCUMENT 13

COMPETITION AND MONOPOLY AS PRINCIPLES OF ORGANISATION OF THE MASS MEDIA

(a) The Report of the Broadcasting Committee, 1949. From Minority Report by Mr Selwyn Lloyd (Cmd. 8116, pp. 202–3)

. . . I will refer to four of the principal evils inherent in monopoly:

(a) *Size and unwieldiness.* . . .

(b) *Hindrance of development.* It is also unavoidable that monopoly should lead to complacency and rigidity. Throughout the whole organisation there must be a fear of taking risks and of making mistakes . . .

(c) *Only one employer.*

(d) *Excessive power.* Fourthly and most important, there is the danger of abuse of power. It is true as suggested above that a public monopoly may be so timid of making mistakes that it divests itself of initiative and purpose. On the other hand, there is no knowing when it may swing to the other extreme and exercise its power excessively and so as to abuse it. The BBC state in effect in their evidence that it is the BBC's duty to decide what is good for people to hear or to see, and that the BBC must elevate the public taste and constantly be ahead of public opinion and public wishes in their programmes. It is just as though a British Press Corporation were to be set up with a monopoly of publishing newspapers, and were to decide what choice of newspapers people were to have and what it was good for them to read in them. Again, we might have a British Publishing Corporation with a monopoly of publishing books, deciding what books should be published; or a British Theatre Corporation with a monopoly of producing stage plays deciding what plays it was good for people to see. These national Corporations might all be staffed by good and worthy people, animated by the loftiest principles, but it would be the negation of freedom and democracy to vest in them such powers. The argument that ordinary people cannot be trusted to make wise decisions for themselves is the stock argument of dictators . . .

(b) From Evidence of Sir Robert Watson-Watt and Mr Geoffrey Crowther (Appendix H of the Report, p. 341)

. . . a monopoly of broadcasting . . . is a most definite and potent force in creating that uniformity of society that can so quickly and easily turn into totalitarianism. The only ultimate safeguard of liberty lies in diversity. It is not enough that the individual should have an abstract right to be different. He should, in fact, be different and should be encouraged to be different. But if there is safety only in diversity, how can diversity itself be safe, with the most powerful organ of publicity and of propaganda in one centralised control? . . .

(c) From Evidence of Lord Reith (ibid., p. 364)

. . . It was the brute force of monopoly that enabled the BBC to become what it did; and to do what it did; that made it possible for a policy of moral responsibility to be followed. If there is to be competition it will be of cheapness not of goodness. The usual disadvantages and dangers of monopoly do not apply to Broadcasting; it is in fact a potent incentive . . .

....

EXERCISES

COMPETITION AND MONOPOLY IN THE MASS MEDIA

7.1. In the above extracts, the arguments against monopoly are set out more explicitly (and more convincingly) than those for monopoly. Can you develop and make more explicit Lord Reith's powerful affirmation of faith?

7.2. Do the arguments against monopoly amount to an argument for the introduction of 'commercial' broadcasting (i.e. produced by companies seeking a profit through the sale of advertising time)?

GUIDE TO EXERCISES

1. First, the partisanship of the press is roughly balanced by its readership, but with a five per cent or so advantage to the Conservatives. Second, the Labour Party depends on the *Daily Mirror* to give it a reasonable share of a favourable press. But the *Mirror* is an independent or wayward supporter of Labour, and its relations with the Labour Government in 1966–7 were far from harmonious. In May 1968, the *Mirror's* chairman, Cecil King, published a front-page article calling for Mr Wilson's resignation—under the banner headline, 'Enough is enough.' A few weeks later Mr King was dismissed. It seems likely that the *Mirror* will now be less wayward in its support of Labour.

[Note: After a change of proprietor in 1969 the *Sun* ceased to be 'Partisan Labour']

2. The existence of a 'quality' press depends on judgements about quality of content as well as 'quality' of readership. In fact, the papers which would generally be regarded as making the most demands on a reader's intellect, do circulate among the higher social classes. But the popular press is one of the great classless bonds of British society.

3. The *Mirror's* editorial was headed: MESSAGE FROM ST PAUL.

The text referred to 'faith, hope and charity . . . and the greatest of these is charity'.

Clever?

4. and 5. These you must do for yourself.

6. Mainly that, as Churchill said, 'if the Socialists came into power even less would be done than [Baldwin's] Government intended.' It is fair to add that Baldwin's Government had begun to rearm, and his own statement put his policies in the worst possible light. Baldwin to his credit accepted that in a democracy a government must retain the allegiance of the people —because that is democratic and efficient, not simply in order to stay in power. But Baldwin neglects the duty of a government to lead public opinion and if necessary to defy it. The passage has, of course, been given undue prominence by Churchill and others.

7.1. Reith clearly has in mind Gresham's Law—the bad drives out the good (the original law referred to coinage). The best way to win in competition between broadcasting concerns would be to appeal to lower rather than higher tastes, a quick and cheap attractiveness rather than 'deeper' and 'more worthy' satisfactions. This is not to set up as an arbiter of public taste, offering the public what you think is good for them; it is to offer the public what it 'really' wants, what it can be taught to want, instead of debauching it.

This is, of course, a vulnerable argument and can easily be turned into an argument of dictatorship against 'freedom'. In practice, most civilised states, accepting the standards implied by 'civilisation', attempt to encourage what they see as the best, without too much restriction of the individual's freedom to choose the worst if he wishes. Hence, for example, regulation of night clubs and subsidies to the opera. Reith perhaps erred on the side of restriction—but also of high standards, *as he saw them*. His argument that, 'the usual disadvantages and dangers of monopoly do not apply to Broadcasting' is unsupported and difficult to support. Altogether, in this matter, the affirmation of faith is a good deal simpler than the making of a case.

N.B.: In the case of children there is usually less hesitation: restrictions outweigh freedoms and many adults do not appear to be concerned about democracy for children!

7.2. No. But Mr Selwyn Lloyd did go on to make a case for commercial broadcasting (i.e. broadcasting financed by advertising). Briefly, he argued that the profit motive involved in seeking high audiences for advertising would necessarily lead to the provision of a service appreciated by a large audience. Other kinds of non-commercial competition would not provide this incentive to wide public appeal. (Mr Lloyd accepted that there should be a non-profit-making service alongside a commercial one.)

ASSESSMENTS

(a) *Government and public opinion*

Democratic government is government by consent of the governed, so it is proper that governments should have regard to the wishes of the people. This condition is enforced insofar as the system of elections provides that a government which grossly offends popular wishes will lose power.

The 'wishes of the people' may be regarded quite loosely as including both general, widely-spread attitudes and the views of the 'little publics', articulate groups, 'public advisers' and the like. A government may identify the general opinion by reference to polls and by-elections, and by the hunches of the politician week-ending in his constituency. The views of the little publics are made articulate, but a government has some obligation to consult and elicit views. There are many indications that British governments do 'have regard to' public opinion as here defined.

The more difficult question is to place a precise meaning on 'have regard to'. Given that the system provides a quinquennial accounting to the public, there is really no further requirement in democratic theory that governments should continuously follow or defer to public opinion. They ought clearly to weigh public opinion when devising their policies, but they may go against it if this is in accordance with their better judgement. However, there is one qualification: defiance of public opinion might be difficult if the government's policies require positive cooperation from the public. In this case, a government ought not to provoke defiance of the law, for fear of the collapse of the whole fabric of social discipline. The need for positive cooperation from the public applies notably to those acts of government which interfere directly and profoundly with the citizen's daily life—for example, taxation, conscription for military service, control of incomes, licensing, motoring offences. Notice that existing severe restrictions (as on licensing hours) may be resented. But in cases where few people are directly involved—as in the reform of the laws on capital punishment or homosexual acts—then governments have been able to defy a public opinion which, according to surveys, was quite substantially against them.

Thus the problems of defining, identifying and assessing public opinion are left in government hands. Academic study offers few golden rules to help governments in their task. It would seem that:

on issues by which the public is not immediately and directly affected, it is unlikely that there will be a majority of the public with clear and profound convictions of any kind;

on other issues governments must act with prudence, avoiding public resentment intense enough to lead to non-cooperation and resistance;

the mass media are of some importance, and a wise government will try to ensure that its projection by the mass media is not consistently and continuously unfavourable;

in the short term, the views of the 'little publics' must be taken into account without being allowed to dominate decisions in their own field of interest;

in the long term, the judgement of the electors is the one that counts;

in both the short term and the long term, there is a responsibility upon a government to stand by its own judgement against what it regards as public folly, to lead and educate public opinion (in the last resort, to lose power, rather than submit to popular opinion, but in practice, with five-year parliaments, this dramatic martyrdom can be avoided).

These views accord public opinion an important role in a democratic political system. Public participation in the political system provides government with a wider range of ideas and criticism, from a highly relevant source—which knows 'where the shoe pinches'. Participation also generates energy, an atmosphere, a sense of belonging, which may well be important in achieving harmonious and productive community life. This last is perhaps an arguable point, and a matter of personal preference. Some people like active political life, involving all citizens; others think that life is about religion, family, music and so on, a private affair to which politics is largely irrelevant. One side therefore likes participation, the other political apathy. In schools, it is usual to regard participation in the life of the community as a positive good; hence you are encouraged or even compelled to stand and watch the first XV on wet November afternoons. Good for the soul?—but is that really 'participation'?

Still, in national politics, the first argument for participation—to improve government by offering criticism and ideas—is sufficient: hence the problem of how to secure participation, and how to improve the quality of public opinion, so that its influence may be most beneficial. Mostly, the answers lie with governments and their choice and presentation of policy, and with the political institutions of Parliament and party, which clearly have substantial functions in political communication. (These have been discussed in other chapters.) Beyond these, both the public educational system and the mass media have a responsibility for public political education. In both, there is some reluctance to accept the responsibility. Schools have other responsibilities and fear to be accused of 'bias' in teaching contemporary studies. The mass media are concerned with sales and crippled as educators by their partisan tradition. The problems of the mass media are less tractable, and some of their problems of organisation are discussed below.

(b) *The organisation of the mass media*

In Western democracies there is no disagreement about the freedom of the press and broadcasting. It is accepted that these means of public communication should be largely free of influence or intervention by a government. But how to secure such freedom? One view is that of Mr Selwyn Lloyd, quoted in document 13 (p. 397 above): that the only guarantee of freedom lies in the private ownership of competing companies.

There are, however, grave defects in this argument. Commercial companies may themselves acquire excessive power. The contribution to democracy of the great press barons—Harmsworth, Northcliffe, Beaverbrook—is by no means indisputable. In the days of their potency, one of them, Lord Northcliffe, gave Stanley Baldwin instructions about the composition of his Cabinet. The Prime Minister defied Northcliffe, accusing the press lords in a famous phrase of seeking 'power without responsibility—the prerogative of the harlot throughout the ages'. Moreover, the pursuit of commercial success may lead (has led) to a disastrous decline in standards: triviality and sensationalism in place of serious news responsibly treated. Again, the commercial organisation of the press has led to the building-up of a few massive newspapers, in some cases linked in chains with others; the decline of the provincial press; and the slow reduction in the number of national dailies. Freedom of the press secured by commercial competition now means that a daily paper with a circulation of over a million copies can hardly survive.

In this curious situation, two of Britain's eight national dailies, the *Times* and the *Sun*, survive mainly because they are subsidised by their proprietors from profits made by other newspapers. It is clear that freedom through commercial organisation is a chancy affair. The alternative is government subsidy. This is hotly resisted on the grounds that subsidy would bring influence. But there are in fact many precedents and strong traditions in British public life suggesting that a subsidy could be administered by a semi-independent body without fear or favour. The BBC is a good example, though this has its own tax-revenue in the licence fee.

Broadcasting has had a rather different history and has a different organisation (see document 8, p. 389). There is the public service tradition of the BBC, still very powerful, with its public service organisation and monopoly in radio broadcasting. Commercial television, which modifies the BBC's monopoly, is itself checked by the existence of the Corporation, and by the supervisory Independent Television Authority. Like all good compromises, the system appears to give the best of both worlds.

(c) *The Press Council*

It seems clear enough that the standards of a free, commercially competitive press tend to decline. Yet to maintain standards by government regulation (as in factories and shops for example) is an unacceptable and dangerous diminution of the independence of the press. The solution offered by the Royal Commission of 1949 was the establishment of a non-government regulatory board, composed of representatives of industry and some independent members. Four years later (1953) the Press Council was established—but without any lay members, meeting in private and with a tiny budget. The recommendation for lay members and a lay chairman was repeated by the 1962 Royal Commission, and the composition of the Council was subsequently modified, Lord Devlin being appointed as independent chairman.

Mainly, the Council has been concerned with the misdeeds of the press in such matters as intrusion into privacy and the exploitation of criminal notoriety and of sex. In cases of this kind it has begun to establish standards. The press is perhaps becoming more acutely aware of the bounds of truth and the boundary between fact and comment. Moreover, newspapers have been persuaded to offer corrections of fact and to publish the Council's adjudications on their own behaviour. Of course, the press has certainly not changed its essential nature. It is still partisan, selective, biased, sometimes downright unfair; but its grosser misdeeds are subject to some check.

Just as important, the independence of the press has been protected and reaffirmed, in a period when governments have become unduly sensitive to press criticism. The relations of the press and the Labour Government during 1967 were particularly bad. Apparently this was due to breaches of security (the Philby and D Notice affairs), but there was perhaps also more general resentment of the anti-Labour prejudices of the Conservative newspapers. In this situation, Lord Devlin and the Press Council have been a useful reserve line of defence. Thus the Press Council may yet solve the problem of providing regulation in the public interest, within a private independent system. It is 'a classic demonstration of the British genius for imposing moral sanctions by voluntary means. The Council is a toothless watchdog, but its bark has been enough' (Clive Irving, *The Times*, 23 November 1967).

RECAPITULATION EXERCISES

1. How would you define public opinion?

2. In what ways are the mass media massive?

3. In what ways does broadcasting differ from the press as an agent of political communication?

KEY TO RECAPITULATION EXERCISES

1. See section 2 (p. 372) and Assessment (a) (p. 400).

2. In audience, ownership, and control.

3. In form of ownership and control; in statutory requirements of balance and impartiality; in the tradition of public service; also in the nature of the output, i.e. the differences between a television programme and a newspaper article.

[12]
Elections

1 OUTLINE

There are significantly few chapters of this book without some reference to elections. General elections are the source of the House of Commons' power, and hence of the Prime Minister's. They are the core of the life and work of political parties.

Elections provide for the political system a substantial element of representativeness and responsibility (which is the essence of British democracy). This is not to say that elections are the only element of that kind. Governments maintain a continuing relationship with public, press, interest groups and interested persons. In this perspective, general elections form a one-month incident in a fifty- or sixty-month-long process. However, elections are distinguished by their intensity, their involvement of a mass electorate and their capacity to make or unmake governments.

The existing electoral system is comparatively new. The mass adult electorate dates only from 1928. All seats were contested at one election for the first time only in 1945 and two-member constituencies and extra votes were not abolished until 1948. Polls of public opinion had some influence on the system from the 1950s on. Since 1959, television has transformed the election campaign, possibly without affecting the result.

The British electoral system is notoriously unfair, especially to minority parties, but is retained on the grounds that it makes for stable government. The character of the electoral campaign is determined nationally, and much of the most publicised electioneering is done by party leaders to a national audience. In the constituencies, the candidates and party activists work away at meetings, addresses, and getting the vote out on polling day. Both politicians and mass media resort to stunts, sensationalism and appeals to prejudice and emotion, and use skilled commercial advertising techniques for manipulating opinion. Still, election campaigns are comparatively remarkable for being concerned with politics, quite incorrupt, and for the most part well above the heads of the mass electorate.

There is abundant evidence that most voters are not much affected in their voting by the electoral campaign. The average voter's reception of politics is in terms of fairly crude notions about the general character of the parties—'the party for people like me'; 'out for the nation as a whole'; 'has no clear policy'. Such notions include assessments of a party's fitness to govern, and its relation to the social class to which the voter belongs or aspires. Nevertheless, the voter's choice is both political and complex.

2 THE POLITICAL FUNCTION OF ELECTIONS

Elections and politics

A general election is part of the whole, complex, continuing process of political communication and adjustment, in which government, parties, pressure groups, the mass media and the public are all engaged. It is an important, but not, on its own, a decisive factor in this process. Its importance lies in the making and unmaking of governments, though this occurs at other times too (e.g., 1916, 1931, 1940). A general election determines which party shall have power. The leadership of the party is already chosen, and policy in detail and in practice has still to be determined. But the name of the party, and hence of the Prime Minister, emerges from the election.

The importance of general elections is increased by the regard, even fear, which politicians have for them. This is understandable enough, since the electorate is in a sense the politician's employer— a somewhat capricious and stern one at that. The politicians do not fully understand what behaviour alters the judgement of the electorate, so, taking no chances, they assume a politically conscious and censorious electorate, and play to it so far as they can. This process of assuming perceptive and critical judgements has been called the 'law of anticipated reactions'. It accounts for the playing down of nationalisation in Labour propaganda, and the Conservative Party's abandonment of its Leader, Sir Alec Douglas-Home, in 1965. Both were regarded as electoral liabilities. In this way, assumptions about the likely relations of political decisions to electoral support endow a general election with very considerable influence.

The politicians are certainly right that the general election is for them a kind of employees review board. They may be right too that the board (i.e. the electorate) makes a highly political judgement, based on a closely remembered and well understood record of political performance. There is a good deal of evidence against this view (see section 5, p. 427), but, after all, *some* political matters influence electors' opinions. In any case, general elections are major public events, well-reported, impinging on the lives of most adults, raising a certain excitement as with a major sporting event, and ending with massive broadcast programmes going on for half the night. The public perception of politics is thus raised and enhanced.

The scale and intensity of activity during a general election gives the process a further significance. Its outcome is accepted without question and the resulting government gains legitimation and a certain allegiance. In this way, an election is a major political ritual, equivalent to the coronation of the monarch.

The process and the ritual get their intensity from the competition and conflict of an election. This is genuine: important matters are at stake, and partisanship may be sharp and bitter. But the contest takes place against a background of stability, cohesion and calm, in which the intentions of the other side are seen as not wholly disastrous. Hence the decision of the polls is accepted, and life goes on. Politics takes place, as it were, in a fenced-off arena, not in the High Street or in Laburnum Grove, the streets where we live.

The frequency and extent of elections

Elections are not as frequent or as extensive in Britain as in, for example, the USA or even France. The proper frequency of elections is a matter of nice judgement. The five year limit to the duration of a parliament was laid down in the Parliament Act of 1911. This shortened the interval between elections by two years to compensate for the reduction in the powers of the House of Lords over the Commons. (The people must replace the peers as the guardians of the constitution—so ran the argument.) In practice, many parliaments have lasted for much less than five years, and the average interval is less than four years. But many decisions of government, for example on defence and on major public investment, are long-term, and work themselves out over years. Clearly, a government needs time to prove itself, time to govern without undue concern for temporary popularity; time, too, simply to govern. For the object is good government, not continuous answerability to the electorate. The answerability must be frequent enough to be effective: an interval in practice of four years seems about right.

For central government, elections are held for membership of the legislature only. There are no direct elections for the executive, as in the presidential elections of USA and France, and there are no primary elections within parties to decide on candidates.

The first point is a fundamental one in the British system. A Prime Minister has no national constituency of his own, like an American

President, and no route to, or source of, power outside the House of Commons. This situation is slightly modified by the nature of general elections, with the party leaders prominent in drawing support to their party (see section 5, p. 433).

Primary elections for party candidates are in theory democratic, giving a greater measure of consumer choice, and eliciting more vigorous party activity. Their introduction would treble the volume of national electoral activity, with consequences which cannot be precisely foreseen. There might be a decline in interest on the part of candidates and public, or a great renaissance of 'grass roots' political activity; or something in between.

The doctrine of the mandate

The doctrine of the mandate is the strongest form of the notion that a government draws a fairly precise set of instructions from a general election. A programme, both general and particular, has been submitted to the electorate, and winning a majority of at least moderate size indicates popular approval for carrying the programme out. This is the mandate, which includes an element of command and a weaker element of trust. Governments may justify unpopular policies by reference to the 'mandate', and oppositions complain of 'broken promises' and novel policies; or, in the case of a government with a small majority, say that it has no mandate at all. The democratic theory (British version) is in outline fairly clear. A general election would be meaningless if it included no presentation of policies. What takes place is in a crude way equal to conversation or dialogue: the elector is intended to have the opportunity to acquaint himself with party policies before casting his vote. The difficulty lies in delimiting the process. Should a party present its policies in practical detail? (Too little means an ill-informed elector, too much an over-committed party.) Should the party feel bound in all circumstances by its campaign presentations? (Again the dilemma of meaningless choice or over-commitment.) If a major issue arises after the election (e.g., the Common Market), is a government morally bound to hold an election before executing a policy? (Crises requiring urgent action are excepted.)

In theory, the status of the mandate would seem to be this: some relationship between party programme and government action is necessary, but a close and detailed mandate is not essential for democratic politics. The mandate may lead to mistaken policies through commitment of a party prior to its confrontation with the problem as a government. On the other hand, most policies gain from subjection to extensive and critical discussion.

This rather limited view of the mandate is supported by some practical considerations. The electorate as a whole is not really sophisticated enough to give a reasonable judgement on, say, the devaluation of the pound or British nuclear strategy; nor could it be enlightened in the course of one election campaign. Political parties cannot foresee in detail which (if any) of their policies will be practicable or even appropriate. The movement of events and ideas abroad as well as at home, and the activities of individuals and of masses, seem to determine a large part of government policy. There are many historical examples of this. The Welfare State owes a good deal to Lloyd George, Winston Churchill and two wars—not to a party with a programme. Current ideas on the management of the economy arose mainly from reaction to the continuing failures of the British economy. Educational policy in the mid-1960s is largely determined by the decisions of parents to have children and of the children to stay on at school after the age of fifteen. For these reasons it is probably impractical as well as undesirable that a political party should feel bound closely to every item of a detailed mandate.

The question of the mandate is linked with that of the referendum: both involve the popular determination of detailed policies. There is a brief discussion of the referendum in the assessments (p. 441). Meanwhile, to focus your views on the mandate, here is an exercise.

EXERCISE

THE DOCTRINE OF THE MANDATE

1. Say whether you agree with any of the following statements:

(a) The Conservative Government had no right to introduce the Act of 1954 establishing commercial (independent) television, as it was not part of their programme presented in the election of 1951.

(b) The Labour Government had no right to introduce the statutory control of prices and incomes in 1966, as it was not part of their programme presented in the elections of 1964 and 1966.

(c) Neither Conservative nor Labour Government had the right to apply for membership of the Common Market (1962, 1967), since this was not presented in their election programmes.

The alternation of parties

General elections bring about changes of the party in power. Roughly this is an alternation, but the common description of it as a 'swing of the pendulum' is inaccurate.

DOCUMENT I

PARTIES IN POWER IN BRITAIN SINCE 1900

The horizontal lines indicate a change in the party in power. Dates after name of Prime Minister are dates of formation of the Government.

General election	Party in power	Prime Minister
Oct. 1900	Con.	Salisbury (June 1895) Balfour (July 1902)
Jan. 1906	Lib.	Campbell-Bannermann (Dec. 1905) Asquith (May 1908)
Jan. 1910 Dec. 1910		
	Coalition	Asquith (May 1915) Lloyd George (Dec. 1916)
Dec. 1918		Lloyd George (Jan. 1919)
Nov. 1922	Con.	Bonar Law (Oct. 1922)
Dec. 1923	Lab.	Baldwin (May 1923) MacDonald (Jan. 1924)
Aug. 1924	Con.	Baldwin (Nov. 1924)
May 1929 Oct. 1931 Nov. 1935	Lab. Coalition	MacDonald (June 1929) MacDonald (Aug. 1931) Baldwin (June 1935)
	Con.	Baldwin (Nov. 1935) Chamberlain (May 1937)
	Coalition Con. ('Caretaker')	Churchill (May 1940) Churchill (May 1945)
July 1945 Feb. 1950	Lab.	Attlee (Aug. 1945) Attlee (Mar. 1950)
Oct. 1951 May 1955 Oct. 1959	Con.	Churchill (Oct. 1951) Eden (April 1955) Macmillan (Jan. 1957) Douglas-Home (Oct. 1963)
Oct. 1964 Feb. 1966	Lab.	Wilson (Oct. 1964)

2. What is wrong with the idea of a pendulum?

3   THE ELECTORAL SYSTEM

Dissolution of Parliament

The decision to hold an election is taken by the Prime Minister subject only to the five year limit on Parliaments. He may of course consult whom he pleases, but recently Prime Ministers have tended to keep this matter to themselves. The decision will be formulated as advice to the Queen to dissolve Parliament. This is not advice which the monarch can normally refuse to accept; nor can she insist on a dissolution. Such action on the part of the Queen would amount to partisan intervention in politics, and is incompatible with the convention of non-involvement (see note on monarchy, p. 447).

Since political parties have had to face a mass and virtually incorruptible electorate, the timing of a dissolution has been a difficult tactical exercise. Prime Ministers have naturally been concerned for the electoral prospects of their party. Since the 1950s, the calculation of the prospects has been made moderately accurate by the application of survey technique to the forecasting of election results. The 'polls' of the forecasters have given Prime Ministers a notable advantage in the electoral contest. Given the see-sawing of popular support for the two major parties, the one in power has simply to choose the right date for an election to ensure remaining in power. For example, it seems probable that an election held at most times in 1962, 1963 or early 1964 would have given Labour a clear majority; an election in the summer of 1965 and again in the summer of 1966 and 1967 would have returned the Conservatives. The elections of 1955, 1959 and 1966 were nicely calculated to secure the sitting tenants. In 1951 Attlee seems to have dissolved without regard for the prospects; in October 1964, Sir Alec Douglas-Home had run out of time. Observation of the polls now reinforces the tendency of the swinging pendulum to stick on one side.

3. The introduction of fixed terms for Parliament would eliminate the majority party's advantage in choosing the time of the election. Clearly it is not a reform likely to appeal to those in power. But there are advantages in the present system. What are these?

The franchise

The franchise (the right to vote) formerly inhered in property, not in persons. By a series of Reform Acts in the nineteenth century, the vote was given to householders, but the electorate in 1910 numbered under eight-million, little more than one quarter of the adult population. The Representation of the People Act of 1918 extended the vote to all men on the principle of residence, and to women over thirty on the principle of occupation of land or premises worth at least five pounds annually (or being married to such an occupier). Occupation implied payment of rates on property and is of course more limiting than residence—apart from campers and tramps we all reside. This reform almost trebled the electorate—to over twenty-one-million at one stroke, about three-quarters of the adult population. In 1928 the franchise for women was assimilated to that for men—being over twenty-one[1], and 'residence'.

However the franchise was still not quite equivalent to the old Chartist cry of the 1830s 'One man, one vote!' Until 1948, two classes of person had an extra vote: university graduates and occupiers of business premises. The graduates voted by post in special constituencies for twelve seats. Most university MPs were somewhat independent Conservatives, with, notably in 1945, a number of genuine Independents. A few, like A. P. Herbert, made a distinguished contribution to the work of the Commons. There were no Labour university MPs.

EXERCISES

'FANCY' FRANCHISES

4.1. What justification do you see for university and business votes? Is your justification sufficient?

4.2. Would you regard any other 'fancy' franchises as justified?

The ballot system

The ballot system employs simple plurality in single-member constituencies. This is the first-past-the-post system, in which the contestant with the most votes wins the seat. It is the simplest of all electoral systems—and some would say the crudest. In two-member constituencies (common until 1885: a remaining fifteen abolished in 1948), the crudity of the system was modified because two votes gave the elector a greater range of choice—he could vote for both parties if he wanted. In practice he was often deprived of any choice at all by agreement between the parties to share the seats and avoid an

[1] Reduced to eighteen in 1969.

election altogether. Since 1945, virtually all seats have been contested and the elector has had a choice—if a crude one.

The effect of the ballot system is normally to over-represent, in terms of seats won, what may be quite small majorities in votes, and seriously to under-represent minority votes. Thus in a constituency of 60,000 with 50,000 voting and two candidates, a vote of 25,001 secures the seat, and 24,999 votes are left unrepresented. With three candidates it is theoretically possible for a vote of one-third of the electors, plus one, to secure the seat, and winning on a minority vote is not uncommon—73 cases in 1959, 183 cases in 1966 (over two-thirds of the latter were won by Conservatives).

The effect may be seen in the election results of 1966:

	Seats	% of seats	Votes (m)	% of votes
Conservative	253	40	11.4	41.9
Labour	363	58	13.1	47.9
Liberal	12	2	2.3	8.5
Other	2	—		
	630			

This shows clearly the exaggeration of a majority and the under-representation of a minority party. However, a proportional distri-bution of seats, based on this voting, would have made the Liberals the masters of a coalition—hardly a democratic result.

The results for the Liberal Party have been consistently adverse since the 1920s. In 1964, they won nine seats in return for over three-million votes (11.2 per cent) and in 1950, nine seats for 2.6-million votes. The distortions for the major parties have sometimes also been serious. In 1945, the Conservatives retained only a third of the seats in the Commons in return for forty per cent of the votes. The 'land-slide' was not a landslide in votes, for Labour had only 48.5 per cent of votes for their sixty-two per cent share of the seats. In 1931, the Conservatives took three-quarters of the seats for fifty-five per cent of the votes, while Labour got 8.5 per cent of the seats for thirty per cent of the votes.

However the system does not often change the overall result of the election; it simply hands out bigger prizes to the winners, and bigger penalties to the losers. The election of 1951 was exceptional in that its overall result in seats was due to the system and the quirks of the distribution of votes within it, and not to a massive movement of opinion on the part of the British people. The figures for the 1951 election were:

	% of vote	No. of seats
Conservatives	48.0	321
Labour	48.8	295
Liberal	2.5	6

The defects of the system are significant enough to give rise to a persistent movement for electoral reform. The system, it is argued, needs to be proportionately representative; and various schemes for proportional representation (PR) have been proposed. This movement is strongest, for obvious reasons, in the Liberal Party, but has been supported by an all-party Speaker's Conference in 1918 and by a vote of the House of Commons in 1918 and again in 1931. Occasionally the leaders of the major parties nod in the right direction (for example, Mr Churchill in 1950 and Labour's Chief Whip in 1965), but those who hope to gain by the existing system have little incentive for changing it.

A completely proportional system would require a national list of candidates, to be elected in a prescribed order for a certain quota of votes. Such a system would destroy the territorial constituency system, and pose difficult problems in drawing up the lists; it would also mean that any party or group which could collect say 50,000 votes out of the whole of the country would secure a seat in Parliament. This prospect frightens some people and delights others.

However, there are ballot systems which secure a measure of proportional representation within a constituency system. These involve preferential voting and either eliminative counting (the alternative vote) or quota counting (single transferable vote—STV). In the alternative vote system, votes for candidates at the bottom of the poll are redistributed according to the second or subsequent preferences. In the STV system a five- or seven-member constituency is used and candidates are elected as they reach a minimum quota of votes.

EXERCISES

PROPORTIONAL REPRESENTATION

5.1. It helps the appreciation of the problems and possibilities of PR to organise and take part in an election on these lines—as the

House of Commons did once in an unwonted enthusiasm for experiment. You can vote in this way for a students' representative body, or for the most (or the three most) popular television programmes or what you will. The ballot form must provide for voting in order of preference, 1,2,3, etc. In counting, eliminate the candidate with the least number of first choices and redistribute the vote according to next preferences. Alternatively, where several places are to be filled, first determine the quota:

$$\frac{\text{no. of electors}}{\text{no. of places}+1} \quad +1$$

Then in counting, redistribute surplus votes (votes above the quota) according to the second preference of *all* the votes for that candidate —and so on until all places are filled by candidates reaching the quota. (If you are in doubt about these methods, consult J. F. S. Ross, *Elections and Electors*, Eyre and Spottiswoode, 1955, especially chapter 8; or E. Lakeman and J. D. Lambert, *Voting in Democracies*, Faber, 1959.)

Compare the results with those obtained by counting first preferences on a simple majority basis. Note that a different ballot system may elicit different electoral behaviour. For a true comparison it is therefore necessary to hold a completely new election by the other ballot system.

5.2. What do you see as the main advantages and disadvantages of proportional representation?

The boundaries of constituencies

Under the single ballot simple plurality system the drawing of the boundaries of the constituency is crucial. The inclusion of, say, a rural area with part of a city can swing a seat from Labour; the addition of a city centre to a residential suburb can move a seat from the Conservatives. In a highly stable system in which two-thirds of the seats are safe for one party, the redrawing of boundaries is a major element of instability and an alarming professional hazard for the MP.

However, the old Chartist ideal of 'equal electoral districts' has been accepted in principle since 1885. With continuing rapid social change, notably the recent growth of suburbs, regular and radical redistribution is essential. Thus, for example, the constituency of Billericay in Essex contained under 60,000 electors in 1955 and over 100,000 in 1966. This was almost four times the size of some constituencies in the centre of large cities: e.g., Manchester Exchange, 26,400 in 1966. The remote parts of Scotland and Wales, e.g., the Western Isles and Merioneth, are also over-represented, for practical and for policy reasons.

Under legislation of 1944 and 1958, redistribution is carried out by four Boundary Commissioners for each of the countries of Great Britain. These consist of the Registrar-General, the Director of the Ordnance Survey, and two senior officials, chaired by the Speaker. Redistribution normally occurs at intervals of ten to fifteen years. A generous allowance of seats is provided for Scotland and Wales, and a few for Northern Ireland (which has its own Parliament for home affairs at Stormont). The Commission aims to keep the number of electors in each constituency as near as possible to the quota. Local government boundaries are respected where possible.

The Commissioners have a difficult task, and have not escaped accusations of gerrymandering, that is, shaping constituencies with an eye to political advantage. This is not the case, and their work is a remarkable illustration of the capacity of British public life for incorruptibility. By contrast, gerrymandering is a normal part of American political life.

Note: The force of this last point has to be modified in the light of the Government's rejection (1969) of most of the Commission's recommendations. The justification offered was the pending reform of local government boundaries.

4 THE NATURE OF THE CAMPAIGN

This section is mainly concerned with the way in which a political appeal is made to the elector; the next section, on electoral behaviour, deals with the voter's response to the appeal.

Most voters do not make up their minds how to vote at the end of the election campaign; they knew before the campaign started. In general elections, perhaps three-quarters of the electorate vote for the party they have always supported. So the campaign is a brief incident in a continuing process of political presentation and appeal to the people. But an election campaign involves high intensification of the political appeal. It is important for providing political information, arousing interest, and encouraging voters to vote, as well as for determining the vote of a small but significant minority. Election campaigns also contribute to the long-term processes of political education and choice: the most habitual, unaware and unthinking voter derives his habit in part from a reaction to politics and political appeals.

The election campaign proper runs from the announcement of dissolution to polling day, though the expectation of an election may give an electoral atmosphere to much longer periods—for example, from the autumn of 1963 through the indecisive election of October 1964, to March 1966.

Some of the most significant electioneering goes on at national level. Each party produces a manifesto which presents its outlook and policies in vague but attractive language. These documents represent as firm a commitment to a programme as may reasonably be expected, while still being beyond the interests and understanding of most electors. (The manifestoes are printed in full in *The Times Guide to the House of Commons* to which you should refer to test these statements.)

If the manifestoes have little direct impact, they provide an agenda for the rest of the campaign. In this the national leaders play the biggest part. Their speeches up and down the country are well reported; further material is fed to press and broadcasters through specially arranged press-conferences. In addition, party leaders figure prominently in the special party political broadcasts. The voter in the constituencies is much more likely to hear a party leader for a few minutes on television than to hear his own local candidates; though there is a good chance that he will read at least one of the election addresses sent out by the candidates. The candidates do indeed prosecute vigorous campaigns in the constituencies, addressing meetings, speaking on street corners and outside factory gates, calling on voters, encouraging the party workers. All this is very impressive, considering that two-thirds of candidates have no chance of success at all; of the rest, about two-thirds will win anyway, and for the last third the result is unlikely to depend on the local campaign.

So why does it go on? The rational answer is that no election is won or lost until the votes are cast, and *getting the vote out* is in part a local, street-by-street job. But it is also important that there is a strong tradition of the hustings in British life. Heckling is a characteristic British activity, and the confrontation and conflict of the hustings is evidently satisfying for the participants. At the least it reinforces the partisans in their faith, encourages interest in politics, and perhaps even disseminates a little political information.

In the nineteenth century, elections were notoriously corrupt, voters were bribed and intimidated and huge sums were spent on securing a seat. The average sum spent in each constituency by the Conservative Party in the 1880s seems to have been £2–3,000, equivalent now to perhaps £10,000. Expenditure on this scale, and the corruption that went with it, has now been eliminated. All kinds of undue influence are illegal, and a candidate must avoid even casually buying a meal or a drink for a voter not actually working for him. Expenditure is restricted under the Act of 1948 to £750 plus 2*d*. per elector in county constituencies or plus 1½*d*. per elector in boroughs. This amounts to about £1200 in counties and £1150 in boroughs. The candidate is also entitled to spend £100 on his personal expenses. These are very severe limits. They are generally observed, though skilled management and accountancy make for some latitude.

These limitations apply only to the campaign period, thus excluding the much larger sums spent by the national parties on poster and other advertising in between elections; and by prospective candidates. In that way, financial resources still have some influence on the conduct of elections, and possibly on their outcome. It may be too that the resources of party supporters—cars, typewriters, leisure—count for a little. On the other hand, broadcasting is shared between the parties without regard for money. British elections are not now corrupt in the nineteenth-century sense, but undue influences may arise from the operations of the mass media. Such possibilities are discussed below.

Aspects of the campaign

The studies of general elections sponsored by Nuffield College and published by Macmillan give excellent full accounts of elections since 1945. The volumes for 1964 and 1966 are by D. Butler and A. King. These provide complete case studies of election campaigns. It is well to begin with an assumption of values: it is assumed that a general election *ought* to be concerned with a reasonable presentation of serious political argument. This assumption can be challenged, but only on the grounds that other methods of representation (pressure groups, political parties, 'public opinion') are more effective, and that general elections have mainly a legitimising function. However, these views seem to underestimate the importance of elections in choosing a government, and, indeed, to reduce an election to something of a confidence trick.

(a) *The presentation of policies.* A general election elicits a great flood of propaganda for the parties—the manifestoes and major speeches of the national party leaders, the addresses and speeches of the candidates, broadcasts and articles, leaflets and posters. It is impossible easily to encompass this mass of material in formal analysis, though the election surveys attempt to do this for parts of the material (manifestoes, addresses, broadcasts, posters). A general impression of the material may be obtained by reading one or more of the surveys, or better, by experiencing a general election 'live'.

There are two significant questions for which such an impression may provide answers. First, does serious political material (dealing with issues, policies and differences between the parties) form a sufficient part of the outpouring? Here the answer must surely be affirmative. Despite the evidence that much of this material does not pass the voters' barriers of interest and perception, the parties go on producing it. They see themselves as involved in political encounter, and insist, to their credit, on a political debate. The second question is more difficult to answer. Is this material relevant to the main national problems and reasonable in content, approach and style? Here too the answer might be affirmative, if you can once accept the proviso that party A's production will be entirely and unreservedly favourable to party A. This is of course a major proviso of irrationality which some democrats find difficult to swallow.

(b) *Stunts*. 'Stunt' is a word from the hustings, not from political science, and at its simplest refers to a bit of the other side's electioneering which your side does not like. More precisely, a stunt involves a gross distortion of issues, policies or events for the purpose of making a sensational and unfair appeal to the electorate.

Stunts in the modern sense began when politicians were first compelled to appeal to a mass electorate open to such approaches. For example, Gladstone's Midlothian campaign of 1880 was possibly a stunt: it distorted, inflated and vulgarised the issues involved. In the election of 1906, the treatment of free trade in terms of large and small loaves was possibly a stunt. But in both these cases, the 'stunts' could as well be judged brilliant popular electioneering. Mere vulgarisation is not reprehensible; gross distortion is.

The classic stunt of modern times was the so-called 'Red Letter scare' of 1924 (the Zinoviev Letter). MacDonald's Labour Government of 1924 went to the country after less than a year in office, in an attempt to improve its minority position. Just before polling day, *The Times* published a letter said to be in the possession of the Foreign Office, and containing instructions from the International Communist organisation to the Communist Party of Great Britain. The instructions provided in detail for a Communist take-over of Britain. The Government fumbled the issue badly, and after a delay admitted the existence of the letter. The whole truth of the matter has never emerged, but two points seem clear: first, the letter was certainly a forgery, produced for electoral purposes. Second, a letter of this kind may have indicated the aims and activities of international communism, but there was nothing except fear and prejudice to link

MacDonald's moderate Government with Red Revolution. Nevertheless (and despite an increased vote overall), MacDonald's Government fell, the victim of a wave of opinion which had perhaps been strengthened by the Red Letter scare.

This classic stunt provides a criterion of measurement: a stunt involves distortion and sensationalism, not simply inflation and vulgarisation.

EXERCISE

ELECTION STUNTS

6. Accepting the above definition, which of the following election episodes would you regard as 'stunts'—and why? (If you know about, or can look up, the historical background, that will help, but otherwise make a rough commonsense judgement.)

(a) 1931: Savings Bank scare. It was suggested that a Labour Government would use Post Office Savings Bank deposits to pay for the dole.

(b) 1945: Gestapo speech. Churchill in his ringing, wartime anti-Nazi style, assured the electors that a Labour Government would soon establish a Gestapo, secret police system.

(c) 1950: Summit talks. In mid-campaign, Churchill proposed talks at the highest level to settle the differences between Britain, the USA and Russia.

(d) 1951: Warmonger campaign. Churchill was denounced as a warmonger, likely to lead Britain into war again to settle Middle Eastern problems.

(e) 1955: Anti-Bevan campaign. A Labour Government would be dominated by Aneurin Bevan, who was an extremist, a fellow-traveller.

(f) 1964: Sir Alec's 'donation'. The Prime Minister in an unguarded moment talked of making a 'donation' to old-age pensioners. This phrase was seized on by Labour leaders and proclaimed as typical of the Conservatives' nineteenth-century charity attitude to the Welfare State.

Stunting at elections seems to be a declining sport. There are possibly two reasons for this. Accusations of stunting seemed to cancel out any possible gain from the stunt itself. Gaitskell found in 1959 that the promise late in the campaign of a pension increase (planned long before) caused a hostile reaction, and possibly lost votes. Second, the incursion of television into elections inflates even modest election gambits far beyond the control of the electioneers themselves. Politicians have no need to produce stunts themselves: they are likely to have stunts thrust upon them.

(c) *Incidents and events.* Actual events can have a powerful effect on election campaigns, and perhaps on their outcome. For the politician, they are an unpredictable hazard which may be turned to advantage. For the public, they are like case studies or exercises, in which the politicians must demonstrate their skills.

In recent elections, the most significant incursion of events was in 1951, when a crisis arose over Persian oil. The Anglo-Iranian Oil Company had been nationalised by Dr Mossadeq's Persian Government, and after fruitless negotiation the last group of technicians was withdrawn from the refinery at Abadan at the beginning of October. Shortly afterwards, the Egyptian Government denounced the Treaty with Britain regulating the British use of the Suez Canal Zone. The Labour Government clearly faced serious setbacks in its foreign policy. The Opposition tried to exploit the situation, but was out-flanked by Labour's counter-attack—the 'warmonger' campaign referred to above. The electoral result was probably a draw, with some slight gain in public political education.

In the 1955 election, the Foreign Secretary contrived to be nego-tiating in Paris during the election; and—another example of clever stage-management—in 1959 Macmillan managed to appear on tele-vision with the visiting President Eisenhower. But events did not match these promotions of personality. In 1964, the election provided ironic examples of events happening too late to benefit the Govern-ment. On polling day itself the Russian leader, Khruschev, fell from power: next day China exploded an atom bomb. The effect of crises relating to national security is normally to rally support to the govern-ment of the day, of whatever party. Thus the Conservative Govern-ment was possibly deprived of power by this failure of events to match its needs.

(d) *Advertising.* All political campaigning is advertising, but it is customary to distinguish between legitimate political appeals and improper advertising. For some people all advertising is undesirable. Here it is assumed simply that there are degrees of propriety in advertising, ranging from the perfectly acceptable to the deplorable. The criteria of legitimacy and impropriety must clearly relate to the methods as well as the political content and reasonableness of the appeal. The nature of the criteria, and the difficulty of defining and applying them, may appear from the following exercises.

LEGITIMATE POLITICAL CAMPAIGN OR IMPROPER MANIPULATION?

7.1. Is the hiring of a commercial public relations firm to manage a party's election campaign:

improper in itself;

likely to lead to improper advertising;

a serious diminution of the political nature of the campaign;

a sensible attempt to improve the party's propaganda?

7.2. There are illustrations of election posters in the Nuffield election surveys, published by Macmillan; also in R. Rose, *Influencing Voters*, Faber, 1967. There may be a poster campaign on now. Consider some examples of political posters and say whether you regard any of them as making an improper appeal.

7.3. Do you regard as improper Macmillan's famous slogan of the 1959 election 'You never had it so good!'?

7.4. Do you regard as improper the Labour Party's use in 1964 of the phrase 'Thirteen wasted years'?

DOCUMENT 2

AN ATTACK ON ADVERTISING IN POLITICS

From a speech by Miss Alice Bacon, in a debate on the control of public expenditure, H.C. Deb., vol. 627, 21 July 1960, cols. 788–9

... The Representation of the People Act lays down the maximum amount that can be spent by Parliamentary candidates. During the election every single penny has to be scrupulously accounted for, and woe betide the election agent who is even a shilling or two out in his accounts. What a farce all this is if, three weeks before the election campaign has begun, the election has already been won by unlimited expenditure on nation-wide advertising campaigns.

As we have heard today, the Conservative Party placed itself in the hands of an advertising agency, which produced the so-called image of the Tory Party by advertising methods. I believe that in doing this it introduced something into our political life which is alien to our British democracy. Do we want our politics run like this? Do we want British politics to become like a battle between two Madison Avenue advertising agencies? I believe that we do not, and I should like to quote something from something written by Henry Fairlie in the *Daily Mail* of Thursday, 9th June. ... Henry Fairlie says:

The Conservatives at the last election treated the electors as conditioned morons, who could be won by the methods used by commercial advertisers on TV. ...

This was my first criticism of the Conservatives at the last election. My second was that they had introduced into British politics a professionalism which should be automatically rejected by anyone who cares for the health of a free society.

....

EXERCISES

ADVERTISING AND POLITICS

8.1. If you were to make a speech in support of Miss Bacon, what points would you make?

8.2. If you were replying to those speeches (yours and Miss Bacon's) what points would you make?

(e) *Financial resources for political campaigning.* One of the more important arguments about the propriety of political advertising is that it raises the costs of politics, and so may give electoral advantages to the wealthiest groups. The Conservative Party draws on the support of individuals and groups controlling more wealth than the Trade Unions which are the principal financial supporters of the Labour Party (see chapter 9, section 5, p. 319).

Labour has a more regular source of finance, but there is little doubt that the Conservatives can from time to time tap greater wealth. This advantage has been heavily reinforced in recent years by the propaganda activities of industries and related bodies mainly concerned with opposing nationalisation. It has been calculated that the iron and steel industry (individual firms and the British Iron and Steel Federation) spent about £1¼-million in their campaign prior to the 1964 election. Expenditure for similar purposes by the education and propaganda organisation, Aims of Industry, raised the total to well over £1½-million. In the period, May 1963 to September 1964, the Conservative Party had spent about £1-million and the Labour Party about a third-of-a-million on propaganda (figures from R. Rose, *Influencing Voters*, Faber, 1967).

The anti-nationalisation campaign included massive newspaper advertising aimed at securing votes for the Conservative Party. A poll of views on nationalisation was conducted in marginal constituencies, where holding the poll might have some propaganda effect. But there was no evasion of the technical arguments about nationalisation; it was assumed that votes could be influenced, even in the short term, by serious economic and political argument.

This kind of political advertising poses problems for a democracy. Clearly the industries threatened with nationalisation have a right to defend themselves, as do, say, grammar schools threatened (if that is the word) with comprehensive reorganisation. But in the case of industry, elephantine financial resources might appear to make the debate rather one-sided. A democracy devoted to this kind and scale of political advertising would ensure only the survival of the richest. However, there is no evidence that the vast expenditures of the anti-nationalisers were effective. They failed to secure Conservative victories in 1964 and 1966. It would seem, too, from survey evidence, that the public was not especially interested in the issue, and was, if anything, slightly more favourable to nationalisation at the end of the campaign than at the start. The assumptions of the anti-nationalisers about the capacity of a rational electorate to respond to highly technical argument were highly creditable to both sides, but quite erroneous. Danger in the future may lie in the employment of massive financial resources for cruder kinds of persuasion. It is important in this connection that broadcasting time cannot be purchased for political purposes. It is not directly available to pressure groups at all, and the time available to the parties is strictly and fairly shared. There is a sharp contrast here with the USA, where broadcasting time is for sale and elections cost fantastically high sums of money.

(f) *The role of the mass media in elections.* (Note: For the mass media generally, see chapter 11 on political communication.) The parties rely on broadcasting and the press to spread their message. These mass media count their audience in millions (fifteen-million readers for the *Daily Mirror*, and about the same number of viewers for some election broadcasts on television). In terms of mass meetings, even a whole year of the most massive of mass meetings simply does not compete.

The press is characterised by high circulation and immoderate partisanship. Figures showing the political line-up of the British press are given in chapter 11. Their partisanship is illustrated in the following document.

....

DOCUMENT 3

PARTISAN ELECTIONEERING BY BRITISH NEWSPAPERS

(a) *The 'warmonger' campaign of 1951*

The *Daily Mirror* took a leading part in the warmonger campaign arising from the Persian Oil crisis. The campaign aimed to suggest that the crisis was likely to lead to the outbreak of war if it were handled by a Conservative Government under Mr Churchill. At the peak of the campaign the *Mirror* ran a banner headline: WHOSE FINGER ON THE TRIGGER?

(b) *Summit talks in 1950*

Churchill proposed 'summit' talks with President Truman and Stalin to settle international problems. Some newspapers interpreted the responses of Truman and Stalin according to their party allegiances. Thus, in headlines:

STALIN ANSWERS CHURCHILL (*Mail*)

STALIN TURNS DOWN WINSTON (*Herald*)

TRUMAN OPENS WAY TO NEW ATOM TALK (*Graphic*)

NO SHAM AGREEMENTS ON ATOMIC CONTROL FOR ME, SAYS TRUMAN (*Mirror*)

(c) *The* Express *makes a headline in the election of 1945*
From Arthur Christiansen, *Headlines All My Life*, Heinemann, 1961, p. 240

One night when I got back from supper, Brian Chapman, a Socialist who as Assistant Managing Editor was in charge of production that evening, handed me a headline which he had held out of the first edition for my consideration. 'This is pretty thick,' he said, 'but you can use it if you like.' The headline was:

THE NATIONAL SOCIALISTS

This, of course, was the official title of the German Nazi Party and the smearing implications of the headline were obvious. I gleefully gave the O.K. to print the headline. Weeks later Chapman resigned and joined the *Daily Herald*.

[Christiansen was Editor of the *Express*. The paper was criticising (or exploiting) the position of Harold Laski as Chairman of the NEC of the Labour Party (see p. 302).]

(d) *The power of the* Express *in the election of 1945*
From Christiansen, op. cit., p. 241

When the Tory defeat had been recorded and the paper put to bed, I went home exhausted. From his penthouse Lord Beaverbrook telephoned me for the latest news. As I told him, I broke down. I was suffering from acute shock. I had believed that the *Daily Express* campaign would swing the election for the Conservatives. I had thought that my Press propaganda machine was invincible. I had been proved wrong and hurt where it hurt most—in my professional pride. It was not pity for Winston Churchill and his party that made me weep, but pity for myself at having failed to justify my faith in the power of the *Express*.

(e) *Treatment of Aneurin Bevan 1955*

The *Express* and the *Mail* attempted to build up Bevan as a bogeyman in British politics, a fellow-traveller at the least, and a power in the Labour Party. This campaign was particularly noticeable in the cartoons. In fact Bevan was not a fellow-traveller, i.e. a near-communist, and such accusations have some of the hysteria of the 'red scare'; nor was he so powerful by then in the Labour Party. Bevan was a fiery radical and an emotional orator; these are hardly discreditable qualities in a politician of the left.

....

Since 1955, television has transformed electioneering. In the election of 1959, both the BBC and commercial television began broadcasting news reports of electioneering, press conferences, interviews and discussions, as well as the special broadcasts allocated to the parties themselves. The coverage was intensive and was broadcast to a high proportion of the electorate. In 1966, when over ninety per cent of homes had television sets, eighty-five per cent of the electorate claimed to have seen at least one of the party television broadcasts. By then television seemed to have replaced the press as the major source of political information and opinion. Indeed, the study of two Leeds constituencies in 1959 (J. Trenaman and D. McQuail, *Television and the Political Image*, Methuen, 1961) showed that within the period of the campaign neither television nor press had any influence on the opinions of the electors; television but not the press contributed to the political information of the electors.

This conclusion is highly significant because television operates in this field under quite different rules from that of the press. Newspapers are commercial enterprises involved in severe competition for readers (as the demise of some major newspapers has shown) and following a tradition of political partisanship. Television, on the other hand, is much less competitive (there being only two contestants) and observes statutory rules of fairness and non-partisanship, and a tradition of impartiality and integrity (see chapter 11, p. 389). Broadcasting time on television or radio is not open to purchase, but some time is allocated to the parties (in proportions determined by the votes received at the previous election) for party political broadcasts. In consequence the background and style of a British general election no longer derive from the screaming headlines of the popular dailies, but rather from the comparative reasonableness of the television screen and studio. This is true even of the parties' own 'party political broadcasts' which are rather dull for the most part.

The balance between the two major parties is thus reasonably fair. The rationing of time according to votes received may however work to the disadvantage of a minor party; the broadcasting arrangements, like the ballot system itself, tend to confirm the dominance of the two big parties. Of course, this formal rationing applies only to the special 'party political broadcasts'. Programmes of news, comment and discussions are designed under the more flexible rules of fairness and balance. These are in general fair for the parties, but they may be unfair for particular candidates. Strictly, if one candidate is given time, his opponents must also be shown, and this is usually arranged. The status of broadcasting under the Representation of the People Act 1949 is obscure. According to the Act, any presentation of the candidate or his views is chargeable to the candidate's election expenses. Newspapers were specifically excepted from this provision. The Act has not been amended to take account of broadcasting, but it has not been interpreted to restrict the national coverage of 'national' politicians. So a party leader appearing on television is not regarded under the Act as promoting his candidature in his own constituency: hard luck on his opponent!

These then are aspects of the election campaign seen from the transmitting end. The campaign must now be observed from the electors' point of view: how is it received? and what is its impact?

5 ELECTORAL BEHAVIOUR—
THE NATURE OF A VOTER'S CHOICE

Between a half and three-quarters of the electorate votes at general elections for the same party over long periods of time—possibly over a lifetime, but this depends on the endurance of parties as well as of voters! Thus, voting is an habitual act, and the choices in policy it may appear to register were in fact made, prejudged, before the issues were apparent. For most people, voting choice is not based on a perceptive appreciation of issues and a high political awareness. In the main, it is based on the dim discernment of hazy outlines, an 'image', the elements of which carry with them feelings of approval for the side you are choosing, disapproval for the other side. It is possible, therefore, for a voter's specific opinions to fluctuate while his voting behaviour remains solid.

....

DOCUMENT 4

ELEMENTS IN THE VOTER'S IMAGE OF THE PARTIES (1959)

Derived from J. Trenaman and D. McQuail, *Television and the Political Image*, Methuen, 1961, pp. 42–8.

(a) *Conservative Party image*

(i) among its supporters:
national ('out for the nation as a whole');
strength (clear policy, keeps promises, no squabbling);
individualism (opportunity, prosperity).

(ii) among Labour supporters:
national ('out for the nation as a whole');
upper-class party;
prosperity.

(b) *Labour Party image*

(i) among its supporters:
betterment of the common people;
a divided party;
the nation ('out for the nation as a whole').

(ii) among Conservative supporters:
weakness (e.g., absence of a clear policy);
not national (e.g., identified with the working class).

(Note that these images contain judgements about capacity to govern as well as assessments of policy; also, Labour supporters had some favourable views of the other party.)

....

These images of the parties are accompanied by a subjective image of the self. Thus, the voter sees a kind of party as suited to a kind of person: 'the X party is the party for people like me.' This is a fairly complex political judgement.

Interpretation of voting in terms of comparatively crude images does not apply evenly throughout the electorate. Roughly a quarter of the electorate is interested in politics, and perhaps one-tenth quite knowledgeable: at the other end of the scale, one-third knows virtually nothing about politics. In between are voters who perceive politics mainly in terms of benefits for themselves or their groups.

However crude the process, voters do not acquire their images of the parties accidentally or at random. There are explanations, if not wholly rational ones, for their voting behaviour.

Social class

Voting is related to social class; that is to say, voting is related to a large number of social and economic characteristics which are lumped together under the label 'social class.' These characteristics include education, occupation, income, residence and social habits. Voting is not absolutely determined by these characteristics, for none of the tables shows complete correlation. But the evidence of association is strong enough to suggest that the characteristics of social class have a profound influence on voting. An example of the survey evidence is given in the following document.

....

DOCUMENT 5

SOCIAL CHARACTERISTICS AND VOTING BEHAVIOUR

From NOP table in D. E. Butler and A. King, *The British General Election of 1964*, Macmillan, 1965, p. 296 (this table gives figures for a fairly evenly divided election):

		Middle-class AB (10%) %	Lower middle-class C1 (19%) %	Skilled working-class C2 (39%) %	Unskilled 'very poor' DE (31%) %
	All %				
Con.	42.9	74.7	60.7	33.9	30.9
Lab.	44.8	8.9	24.8	54.4	59.1
Lib.	11.4	14.9	13.7	10.9	9.1
Other	0.9	1.5	0.8	0.8	0.9

Note: Survey evidence suggests that these results are similar to those of 1945, when Labour acquired a large majority. At elections between these dates a higher proportion of all social classes except the lowest voted for the Conservatives.

....

EXERCISE

SOCIAL CHARACTERISTICS AND VOTING BEHAVIOUR

9. Would you say these figures justified describing British politics as 'class-ridden'?

These figures about social class give a clue to the sources of electoral behaviour. Social class derives from family background, education, occupation and income. These are therefore important influences on voting. Survey evidence thus confirms that people tend to vote as their parents did; that the longer your education the more likely you are to vote Conservative; the higher your job in status and pay, the more likely you are to vote Conservative—and vice versa. These are matters of general background and influence, not of specific persuasion to vote one way or the other. Parents do not (we suppose) command their children to vote for X Party; nor do schoolmasters persuade their pupils towards a particular vote. But adult employment may provide more specific influences: your mates on the factory floor or your fellow executives in the board room will certainly discuss, or at least indicate their attitude to, politics, and there will be indirect pressures on your voting. This is particularly true if you come under the influence of Trade Union officials in a large factory or working place. This is the nearest any British party gets to a cadre of opinion-leaders set among the population.

DOCUMENT 6

TRADE UNION MEMBERSHIP AND VOTING

Voting	Member of TU	Not a member of TU
Con.	27.7%	48.1%
Lab.	62.2%	38.8%
Lib.	8.8%	12.3%
Other	1.3%	0.8%

From NOP tables in Butler and King, op. cit., p. 296

EXERCISE

TRADE UNION MEMBERSHIP AND VOTING

10. Do these figures suggest that the Trade Unions have a disproportionate and unfair political influence?

Other social characteristics influencing voting behaviour

Social class represents a whole cluster of characteristics, and these are evidently related to electoral behaviour. There are a few other characteristics which seem to be similarly related. Age makes some difference, both because of different social needs and different political experience. But there is little evidence of a marked and continuing tendency, e.g., for the young to vote Labour and their elders

Conservative. Voting is not usually spread evenly through the age-groups in the proportions of the overall vote, but the deviations are not substantial and not consistent from one election to another. Similarly, analysis of the vote by sex shows minor deviations from an absolutely proportionate distribution: here the deviations have tended to persist. More women than men vote Conservative, and vice versa. The explanation probably lies in the closer involvement of men with work and Trade Unions.

Religious affiliation appears to have a slight connection with voting. Nonconformists and Catholics tend to vote Labour more often than adherents of the Church of England. This might be expected on grounds of social class; also because of the historical and psychological connection between religious nonconformity and political radicalism. But the influence is not marked, and difficult to separate from the stronger push of social and other factors. Of course, there is in Britain nothing like the 'confessional politics' of France or Germany, with Catholic political parties and strong anti-clerical opinion.

Nor are there any regional differences in voting strong enough to override the national swing of opinion and votes to and from the parties. This is not to say that voting is absolutely uniform throughout the country—in 1959 two large areas, Clydeside and South-East Lancashire, voted against the national trend. There are certainly differences in political outlook between town and country, and between small towns and large conurbations. This may make a difference in the few remote areas where countryside is unrelieved by town. Even so, the change (swing) in voting, as distinct from continuing differences, tends to be the same in these areas as elsewhere. However, in Wales and Scotland, nationalist feelings are politically significant; but just how significant is not clear, for these areas have traditionally supported the Liberal Party. It seems that strong nationalist sentiment does not normally lead to substantial support for nationalist parties in general elections. By-elections produce exceptional behaviour. In a by-election in 1966, Carmarthenshire elected a Welsh National candidate; in 1967, Hamilton elected a Scottish Nationalist. Northern Ireland is another exception, indeed an anomaly. For historical reasons its twelve MPs are normally committed to the Unionist (Conservative) Party. Nevertheless, the possibility of regional voting patterns exists, and may develop if regions grow in importance and self-confidence as economic planning and administrative units.

The political content of voting

So far, voting may appear to be a socially determined rather than a political act. This is a misleading formulation. Voting is certainly determined by long-term social environment and experience; also, probably to a less extent, by the activities of politicians seeking support, especially during election campaigns. But there is no need to label the social factors as non-political, as if they should have no part in the true citizen's political judgement. Thus, social class is perfectly relevant to politics. The voter who identifies his position in society, relates this to the appeals of the party, and then casts a vote, has carried through a complex political judgement. This is so even if the voter were unable to explain his vote, or demonstrate his acquaintance with party policies.

Of course, some voting is even less politically informed than this. At the lowest, the voter simply votes; this is his only participation in the system, and his social awareness and political information are negligible. At the next level, the voter is aware of at least some aspects of his place in society, and of the nature of the parties. Above this, the appeal of the parties enters more clearly into the process, and the voter's reaction becomes more specifically political. At this point, a vote may be said to have a substantial and specific political content, and the electoral campaign becomes more relevant. Here are some indications of the nature of the political content of voting behaviour.

(a) *Interest and information.* There is much survey evidence to show that a high proportion of electors are neither interested in, nor knowledgeable about, politics. For example, in 1959 a fifth of all voters were unable to name even one party leader (survey reported in M. Abrams, 'Social trends and electoral behaviour', in *British Journal of Sociology*, vol. xiii, no. 3, 1962, reprinted in R. Rose, *Studies in British Politics*, 1st edn, Macmillan 1966). Some people in a Birmingham survey of 1966 thought George Brown, the Deputy Prime Minister, was a Birmingham City Councillor. (You can easily devise a poll of your own with passers-by or parents, to demonstrate the same things.) Roughly one person in ten is reasonably well informed about politics, and one in three quite ignorant. All the same, a high proportion (about seventy-five to eighty per cent) of British voters turn out to vote—a positive, if isolated, sign of political interest and commitment.

(b) *The ranking of issues.* Voters tend to regard 'peace and prosperity' as the most important issues in an election. Their own vote, however, appears to be much more influenced by the issue of prosperity, and considerations of general fitness to govern.

(c) *Party commitment*. There is a persistent liking for coalition (non-party) governments. In a survey published in the *Economist* in January 1966—at a time, it must be admitted, of uneasy government based on an overall majority of three—forty-one per cent of respondents agreed with the statement: 'What this country needs is a coalition government.'

Even consistent voters do not consistently support all of the policies of their chosen party. Some cannot identify many of their party's policies. In a survey of 1960 (quoted in M. Abrams and R. Rose, *Must Labour Lose?*, Penguin, 1960), only thirty-two per cent of Labour voters and sixty-two per cent of Conservative voters agreed with their party on seven items or more out of ten.

(d) *The appeal of party leaders*. General elections sometimes appear to be fought as contests between two leaders rather than two parties. The prominence of the Prime Minister in modern British government, and of the party leaders in the television campaign, has contributed to this impression. But is the impression correct?

It is certainly true to some extent. A few unusually good or unusually bad local candidates seem to win or lose votes beyond the national swing—but rarely more than a few hundred votes. Party leaders count for a little more than this. In 1874 the Conservative Leader, Disraeli, did not campaign outside his own constituency of Buckinghamshire. Today a party leader spends hardly any time in his constituency; instead he stumps the country, holds press conferences, broadcasts. In consequence, party leaders are better known than any other politician. Insofar as the electoral judgement is about capacity to govern, it is a judgement above all about potential Prime Ministers. However, the study made in Leeds in 1959 suggests that attitudes to leaders were still a comparatively small element in voting decision. (It has to be borne in mind that television has taken a larger part in elections since then.)

....

DOCUMENT 7

ANALYSIS OF THE IMAGE OF A POLITICAL LEADER

From J. Trenaman and D. McQuail, *Television and the Political Image*, Methuen, 1961, p. 160

If one wanted to partial out the influence of the several factors, one might roughly estimate that the leader image is compounded of nearly one-half traditional-versus-radical feelings, about a quarter projections of other elements in the party image, and about a quarter personal attributes. These proportions are necessarily reduced by any unreliability in the tests.

....

(e) *Political memory*. Political memory is notoriously short and highly selective. The Labour Party used pictures of unemployed marchers of the 1930s as late as 1950, but with little effect. The mantle of Winston Churchill was not a very useful garment for the Conservatives by 1959. The association of the Labour Party with food-rationing was meaningless by 1964 for most voters. 'Thirteen wasted years' was an effective slogan in 1964 to focus feelings about 'time for a change'. But within a few years the reference becomes obscure.

The political record of a government counts, but only in the short term and against a background of prior allegiance to one party. In politics, as in everyday life, people *choose* what they remember.

EXERCISES

VOTING AND SOCIAL CLASS

In the light of this account of the sources of voting, can you explain:

11.1. Why about a third of the manual wage-earning class votes Conservative?

11.2. Why about a fifth of the middle class votes Labour?

11.3. Why some people in all classes vote Liberal?

Target voters and the swing

Election campaigns were once particularly aimed to convert 'floating voters' from their former allegiances. It was assumed that elections were decided by the movement of voters from one party to another, and that such 'floaters' were politically interested and informed, able therefore to respond to a reasonable political case.

Elections are indeed about floating voters, but it is now clear that electoral movement is a complicated process involving movement between three (or more) parties, and from each of these positions to abstention, and from abstention towards one of the parties. In addition, movement out and back again (wavering) may occur. (The mathematically minded may compute how many different movements are possible.)

On top of this, there are the changes arising from death at one end and the accession of new voters at the other. The movement of voters finally registered at the polls is called the 'swing'; this is the percentage of voters who appear to have moved from one party to another. The swing is a figure for overall change, and does not indicate movements which cancel out.

This complicated ballet of movement takes place among a comparatively limited section of the electorate, ranging from about a quarter to a half or more, depending on the length of the interval between elections, and on political circumstances. According to some evidence, slightly more than half the moving takes place between elections, and just under a half within the period of the campaign. Well-corroborated evidence shows that electoral mobility is most common among the least informed and the least politically aware.

Since electoral mobility (floating) decides elections, these movers are the target voters for the politicians. The object is to gain the most movers, while retaining the votes of steady supporters. Movement is of course most fruitful in terms of seats in the marginal constituencies, and it is there that the game is played hardest. Britain is governed by the party which succeeds in this game.

The impact of the mass media

During an election the elector faces a barrage of material from the mass media, intended to influence him, and in some cases carefully and skilfully designed for the purpose. He does not fall victim easily, for he is protected:

by the competition and self-cancelling of the persuaders;

by the rooted pre-judgements derived from his background and environment;

by qualities which might be called either personal integrity or deep suspicion of strangers—the resistance to being 'got at'.

This conclusion would appear to contradict the implications of much commercial advertising. Commercially it pays to advertise. Political propaganda through the mass media is a different matter. There is a different kind of product to sell, and different needs to meet; different conventional rules, and different conventional responses. Thus, selling a brand of petrol involves selling a product which every motorist has to buy and which can be promoted in fairly direct and easily understood terms of speed, power, engine-wear, etc., by advertisements exploiting sex or social prestige. And the customers do not have built-in notions and principles about petrol anyway.

Selling a political party poses quite different problems, and certain approaches are ruled out—so far (for example, associating Conservative voting with social or sexual success; or Labour voting with manly beer-drinking, rugger players—any other suggestions?). This is not to say that all political propaganda is ineffective. For example, before the 1959 election, the Conservatives discovered by market research that their party was associated with privilege. An advertising campaign, mainly in newspapers, concentrated on displaying working-class people who voted Conservative. After the campaign, further market research showed a drop of seven to eight per cent in the association of the Conservative Party with privilege. This demonstrates, not the simple proposition that political advertising pays, but that in circumstances of rising prosperity advertising could help to formulate political attitudes to that prosperity—in this case, to persuade newly prosperous working-class people to identify themselves with the Conservative Party.

....

DOCUMENT 8

THE LIMITED INFLUENCE OF POLITICAL CAMPAIGNING

From J. Trenaman, 'The Politician's Platform', *The Guardian*, 2 November 1961

[Dr Trenaman's conclusions were based on his study of two Leeds constituencies in the general election of 1959. He is here referring to the influence of television within the limits of the election campaign, that is, in the short term.]

At the last general election no part of the political campaign, nor any combination of parts, either on television or through other media, was found to have any direct bearing on changes of voting decision or even of attitudes towards the parties, according to our Leeds study. People picked up quite a lot of information from the campaign; they became more familiar with the party policies, and the issues which were being placed before them, but they managed to screen themselves completely from direct persuasion. They made up their minds independently, working from general impressions of the party as a whole, and not because of any item of policy or any manoeuvre in the campaign.

....

It should be clear from the foregoing sections that voting is a complicated action. A vote is a product of the interaction of an individual with his home and work background and his life history, with a series of political principles, attitudes and policies, formulated and promoted by a complex organism called a political party, and modified in their significance by events.

Democracy depends on this process being at least a little reasonable and relevant. One critic has called general elections a 'ramshackle and haphazard procedure'. Another calls them 'a blunt instrument'. The fundamental question of the reasonableness and relevance of election campaigns is examined in the assessments (p. 440).

GUIDE TO EXERCISES

1. The answers to all these questions depend on the view you are prepared to take of the mandate; also—and especially if you take a strong view of the mandate—on an examination of the election programmes of the parties. (Remember 'right' is a powerful word.)

Case (b) might be regarded as a reaction to a crisis, and thus exempt from the limits of the mandate.

In case (a), the Government's right might be regarded as doubtful, since there had been very little public discussion of the issue: a Royal Commission had reported in the contrary sense; and the case was being pressed by a powerful lobby representative mainly of producers.

Case (c) might again be regarded as one where some kind of mandate was necessary, since joining the Common Market would be not only a fundamental but an irreversible step. The issue was not raised in the 1959 election. In the elections of 1964 and 1966 it was raised, but Labour pronouncements were cool and non-committal.

However, in both cases (a) and (c) it is arguable that a government has the right, even the duty, to govern as it thinks fit, subject only to the nation's judgement at a general election. Of course, this view somewhat downgrades the electoral process.

2. The pendulum swings unevenly, tending to stick on one side. For some parts of the twentieth century, the pendulum would have to swing three ways—a very odd clock. Further, the metaphor implies an alternation in opinion and in policy and obscures the substantial continuity in both.

3. The freedom to dissolve gives the Prime Minister a useful flexibility: for example, in 1955 Eden was able to dissolve soon after his appointment, thus securing popular confirmation. In 1966, Mr Wilson was able to extricate the country (and himself, of course) from the bare majority of 1964. In the development of its policy, a government can play to its own timetable, with time for unpopular measures if need be. Generally, it may be thought, a government deserves some advantage in the electoral game (but it already has the advantage in publicity and public appeal just by being a government).

Dissolution was once regarded as a disciplinary weapon in the hands of the Prime Minister (appealing to the electors against Parliament), but party organisation has rendered this invalid.

4.1. For university votes, the superior political judgement of graduates— but this is plainly absurd, whatever the subject of graduation.

For business premises, having a stake in another constituency—but many other people work in another constituency: should they have an extra vote too?

4.2. There is a case for giving additional votes to those with superior political judgement, but it is impossible to define or detect this rather vague quality. In any case, it is consistent with the theory of democracy to regard a vote as representing a person, his interests, emotions and prejudices, *not* his political wisdom.

5.1. This you do for yourself.

5.2. The advantages lie in the equity of a more proportionate system; and equity would appear to be the logical end of a representative system. This applies particularly to the representation of minorities, who get a very unfair deal out of the present system.

The STV system would work particularly well in large cities where results in seats depend on the drawing of constituency boundaries, which is likely to be arbitrary: e.g., in Leicester in 1959 the Conservatives had an overall majority of votes in the four city constituencies but only secured one seat.

PR systems are not strange and untried devices. They are used in other countries (e.g., Australia, Sweden, Holland) without disaster; also in some Trade Unions.

The disadvantages lie in the very life and influence which the system might give to small parties. It is argued that this would not contribute to effective representation and might lead to a situation in which a small party held the balance of power, hence to coalition government, in which decisions are made by inter-party bargaining, bearing little relationship to popular representation. PR systems cannot provide effective responsible government, it is said, because they upset the two-party system. It is also objected that PR systems are complicated (but the voter does not have to do the counting).

There is, too, more to be said positively for the existing ballot-system. Once it is working, it registers shifts of opinion. It preserves the territorial constituency (though some people doubt whether it is worth preserving). It provides a form of representation which may be defended by the sturdy assertion that democracy does not depend on mere arithmetic. (But, again, this is a tricky argument: representation involving majorities and minorities is bound to involve arithmetic.)

Altogether, on ballot systems, unease persists.

6. Judgements on these incidents are necessarily subjective: you may disagree if you wish.

(a) Quite unjustified; the Labour Government had been orthodox in their use of POSB deposits. But the point was not a major feature of the campaign. Still, it merits the description of a stunt.

(b) An absurd and insulting accusation: Churchill could not escape from his wartime character. Any speech of Churchill's counted in the campaign, so this was a stunt, but probably not a successful one.

(c) The difficulty here lay in Churchill's enormous prestige. A proposal by him was more than a mere suggestion by an Opposition Leader; it was a vigorous push to British foreign policy. Perhaps Churchill might have spoken more cautiously, but at least his intervention secured public discussion of foreign policy, which is normally most difficult to bring about. In fact, not a stunt.

(d) Churchill was a good war leader and no doubt enjoyed the role; but to imply that he sought war for its own sake was untrue and absurd, and (as Churchill proved later in court) libellous. The warmonger campaign was a stunt, though one promoted mainly by the press.

(e) The campaign against Bevan went too far. He was not a 'fellow-traveller' (i.e. a sympathiser of communism), and he was not the leader of the Labour Party. At least something of a stunt, but such exaggeration is likely to go with popular politics.

(f) Similarly for this one. Quite unfair electioneering; something of a stunt.

7.1. The last, but with some danger of the alternatives ranging down to impropriety. The advertiser is trained to sell, and is interested only in the marketability of the product. The politician is expected to have some concern for the quality of the product, even if it damages sales. There is a conflict of objective here, which the politician may not be able to control.

7.2. Remember that posters only permit brief cryptic statements. It seems, then, legitimate to link the Conservative Party of 1959 with prosperity, and the Labour Party of 1964 with drive, modernisation, etc. Opponents might not accept these sweeping claims, but they do not represent gross distortion of the intentions of the parties. It may not be improper, therefore, to use a poster which, briefly and pictorially, conveys these points.

7.3. A vulgar formulation of the prosperity theme, but surely not improper?—except to those who believed either that Britain was not uniformly prosperous in the 1950s, or that prosperity was a fortuitous result of the state of the world economy, and had little to do with the efforts of the Government.

7.4. Again, not improper as a slogan, though with the defects of all slogans, that truth may be obscured rather than illuminated.

8.1. That the use of market research and advertising techniques in the way she alleges reduces the political content of electioneering below the level of which the public is capable; that it wastes the possibilities of popular political education; that it subordinates political principles to the needs of salesmanship; that it gives advantages to the wealthiest party.

8.2. That the use of specialists in market research and advertising is no more than the utilisation of newly available professional techniques in a field in which politicians had previously blundered somewhat blindly. It is a specialisation of customary processes.

Anyway, don't overrate the power of advertisers or advertising. Politicians can still control the whole operation; advertisers always need a good product to advertise; the public is not so easily gullible.

9. 'Class-ridden' is an imprecise and emotional term: its use is hardly justified in an academic context at all. Obviously, class plays a large part in the determination of voting; but only one class, the highest but the smallest, can be regarded as solidly committed to one party. For the rest, there are strong tendencies but no absolute commitment.

The term 'class-ridden' implies disapproval: social class is, however, a perfectly relevant ground for voting, though one may still disapprove of a class-divided society.

10. The Trade Unions have a right to seek to influence votes, of course. The strength of their position in factories can easily be exaggerated. Less than half of all manual workers belong to Trade Unions (though non-membership does not necessarily exclude influence). The workers' vote cannot be 'delivered': six-million or so manual wage earners consistently vote Conservative.

What influence the Trade Unions have might be regarded as some compensation for the lower political awareness of the class to which they appeal.

11.1. Surmise and survey evidence suggest:

that many manual wage earners do not see themselves as working-class, and aspire to be middle-class;

that they do not see the Conservative Party as an inappropriate party for working people (why should they? a Conservative will say);

that many British people are deferential and accept the right and ability of the old upper class to govern (and see the Conservative Party as the representatives of that class).

In the light of the analysis in the text it will not do simply to say that the working classes judge the Conservatives to have the better policies.

11.2. This is a difficult one, on which there is still not very much evidence. Some of these middle-class voters have risen from the lower classes, and retain strong working-class sympathies. Others are adherents of the intellectual tradition of the left, making well-informed, highly political (but not necessarily correct) judgements.

11.3. The safest answer is no, not really! The Liberal Party is a kind of in-between party, neither one thing nor the other. It seems to attract people who wish to dissociate from their own social class, people who wish to opt out of bi-polar politics. Put more positively, this is a protest vote.

Of course, there are also Liberal voters with Liberal convictions, but as with the other parties, such informed adherents of an ideology are a minority.

ASSESSMENTS

Most of the major problems have been assessed in the course of this chapter. Here are some final judgements.

(a) *General elections a 'ramshackle and haphazard procedure'?* General elections are an *effective* procedure for deciding at least one great question: which party shall form the government for the next four years or so.

The ballot-system by which this decision is made is undoubtedly rather rough and unfair, but the quirks of the system do not normally affect the overall result of the election.

A good deal of the election campaign is about politics, and relevant. But, of course, some electioneering is exaggerated, distorted and sensational, and appeals in ways which are not politically relevant.

The voter may be said to make a meaningful political choice in a manner which is not entirely irrational. The images of the parties are caricatures but have some basis in political truth.

Democracy requires a low minimum of rationality from the electorate. It does not require a high level of information or interest or participation. Popular apathy does not render a democracy undemocratic. Capacity to express political attitudes in words is not required; literacy helps but is not essential. Dropping a stone in a box, as the Greeks did, is therefore a good image of an elector in a democracy. The elector's judgement is simple, even crude. The instrument is blunt, but the job does not require a sharp cutting edge.

(b) *The referendum.* The case for the referendum (voting on specific questions) is the basic democratic case: government by consent of the governed. Genuine popular decisions are arrived at, and in the process a good deal of political education goes on.

But it is clear from the discussion above that specific questions of policy are too fine a task for the blunt instrument of a mass electorate. Moreover, the theory of democracy requires representative and responsible government, but not direct popular government. Indeed, there are times when a responsible government quite properly defies popular opinion, or gives a lead where popular opinion is silent. There is evidence from countries where it is used that the referendum is rarely on the side of change, and may often be on the side of reaction. For example, in Britain today a referendum would almost certainly favour the re-introduction of the death penalty— against all the evidence that it has virtually no deterrent effect.

There is no case for a consultative referendum, since the Government can always discover opinion by commissioning a survey.

There is a case for referenda on minor local matters, and these do take place. For example, electors in a single parish have voted on whether they want a village hall or not; city electors have decided whether they want to subsidise bus fares for old people. These are matters on which the elector certainly knows best and where political leadership is not really called for.

It has been argued that entry to the Common Market is an issue on which a referendum should be held, because entry will be irreversible and involves profound political and economic change. But the issues involved are of formidable complexity. In any case such a referendum could not commit future Parliaments.

(c) *Long-term movements in electoral attitudes.* In the middle of the nineteenth century, Karl Marx predicted that the introduction of universal suffrage in England would bring about the political supremacy of the working-class. Similar prophecies were heard after the Labour victory of 1945; but Labour lost power in 1951.

By the end of the 1950s, a new prophecy was in vogue. Rising prosperity was making us all middle-class; there would soon be no old-fashioned working-class left. Two social scientists wrote a book called *Must Labour Lose?*; a leading Labour politician argued that after all, political power did not matter to the Labour movement. An American political scientist boldly speculated about the prospect of one-party politics in Britain. In 1964 the Labour Party regained power, and it consolidated its position in 1966.

Prophecy is obviously unwise, explanation difficult. Politicians fight for the allegiance of the middling voter, without ideological preferences or strong class allegiance. In consequence, the Conservative Party has succeeded in winning substantial support from Karl Marx's proletariat; and the Labour Party has modified its Marxism to gain the votes of aspiring upper working-class people, and some middle-class people too.

The parties which face one another at the end of the 1960s are descendants—wayward children—of the parties of 1945; grandchildren of the parties of 1924. Their great-grandparents would not recognise them, and might well disown them. Political evolution of this kind demonstrates—for better or for worse— the power of the ballot-box.

RECAPITULATION EXERCISES

1. *True or false?* (mark T or F)

(a) Governments never change except after a general election.

(b) The Prime Minister chooses the date of a general election.

(c) The principle of 'one man (or one woman) one vote', or universal adult suffrage, was fully achieved by 1928.

(d) Highly partisan newspapers dominate electioneering in Britain.

(e) The less you earn, the more likely you are to vote Labour.

(f) A substantial proportion of trade unionists vote Conservative.

2. Define and assess the doctrine of the mandate.

3. What is the case against (a) 'stunts' and (b) political advertising?

4. Has the average vote a political content?

KEY TO RECAPITULATION EXERCISES

1. (a) F (b) T (c) F (d) F (e) T (f) T (if a quarter equals a substantial proportion).

2. See section 2, p. 408.

3. See section 4, pp. 419 and 421.

4. See sections 1, 2 and 5, pp. 405, 406, 427. (Remember that image and social background are not non-political.)

PART V
General Notes

General notes

1 THE MONARCHY

The monarchy no longer has any substantial political power, but is not without political significance. The hereditary theory (though not the sentiment) which supported it has collapsed; changing political conditions and the growth of parliamentary and popular responsibility have deprived it of power. Yet the memory and the sentiment linger on, indeed grow stronger.

Sixty years ago, in 1909, Lord Esher said:

Our system of government—Constitutional Monarchy—is a happy blending of the personal influence of an hereditary rule with the organised expression of popular opinion. The will of the majority is the decisive factor, but it is subject to the indirect guidance of a monarchical sentiment acting and reacting through the person of the sovereign.

More recently, in a sudden access of 'coronation fever' (the year was 1953), a Conservative newspaper wrote:

In an imaginary crisis, only the royal prerogative—affirming and supported by law—stands as a bastion against dominance by a clique or individual in a single Chamber. The Queen may still reject a Bill, and she may still dismiss a Minister or a Parliament, thus offering the electors a chance to express their second thoughts . . . the Queen's prerogative remains as it were a communication cord in the cause of liberty.

Neither of these views is acceptable; but it is of some significance that they could be held in such quarters. There is, indeed, a strong monarchical sentiment in Britain: it is part of British political culture. It does not seem to have much influence on political activity and virtually none on the distribution of political power. Still, it cannot wholly be ignored.

The history of the monarchy since the Tudor period is of the slow growth of Parliament's power in relation to the Crown, and then of popular power in relation to Parliament. First the Monarch had to manage Parliament; then Parliament had to manage the people (the electorate); political parties were developed to manage Parliament and people, and power was thus decisively shifted to an organised majority party in Parliament. But the last stages of this development have taken place only in the last hundred years or so. Until 1832 at least, Britain was governed by the Crown-in-Parliament, with the balance only slowly tipping in favour of Parliament (see chapter 5, p. 170). It is remarkable that as the powers of the monarchy declined, so hostility to the monarchy and republican sentiment declined. When Queen Victoria died in 1901, the monarchy was weaker politically but more popular than ever before.

The power of the monarchy

Choice of Prime Minister. The Crown plays an essential part in the formalities of establishing a new government, but normally has no influence on the choice of Prime Minister. The Prime Minister must have the support of a majority in the House of Commons, and it is there consequently that the essential choice is made. It is just possible, but hardly likely, that the House might not produce a clear majority and would throw the choice to the Queen. This possibility does not really justify the claim that power and freedom of choice lies with the Crown. For the Monarch cannot choose a Prime Minister; she must invite to form a government the person most likely to carry a majority in the House. On this point she must take advice, being in no position to judge.

There have been occasions recently when the Queen may appear to have exercised some choice of her own. In January 1957, she invited Mr Macmillan to succeed Sir Anthony Eden, though Mr R. A. Butler was the expected heir. During the time when the choice was being made, the Queen received in audience two elder statesmen of the Conservative Party, Sir Winston Churchill and Lord Salisbury. But it seems the invitation to Macmillan was the result of a hasty and informal poll of the Conservative Party. The consultation with Churchill and Salisbury was presumably by way of confirmation.

In 1963, the Conservative Party had once more to choose a new Leader/Prime Minister; and this time there was even greater confusion about the available candidates, following the unexpected announcement during the Party's Annual Conference of Mr Macmillan's retirement. Again there was a hasty, informal poll, and the Queen was advised to send for Lord Home (who was to renounce his peerage). Lord Home was not acceptable to some Conservatives, and two former Ministers refused to serve. The Party was indeed in disarray; there was no obvious candidate for the leadership, but some were less in disfavour than others.

It has been argued (by R. T. McKenzie, for example) that

the Queen in effect intervened in the choosing process by sending immediately for Lord Home: had she waited, Home's opponents in the party would have been able to make their preferences known. This may be so; but it seems much more likely that the Queen and her advisers acted with unusual speed in order to end the uncertainty and secure a new government. She was surely right to think that further delay might make choice more, not less, difficult.

These incidents show that the Crown is an essential part of the mechanics of choice; further, that if the majority party is not agreed on a candidate then the possibility of influencing the choice is opened up. These are, however, unusual circumstances. Significantly, the Conservative Party in 1965 adopted a formal election process for the selection of its Leader. It seems likely that in future the Conservative Party, like the Labour Party, would hold an election before the Queen made her choice. The Queen would thus be told ('advised') whom she must choose.

Dissolution of Parliament. Can the Queen insist on the dissolution of Parliament and the holding of an election—which is equivalent to the dismissal of a Ministry? No Monarch has done this since George III (or possibly William IV). Theory, constitutional law, and precedents give some support to such monarchical power. But, again, the conditions of modern politics go right against the possibility. First, the Monarch must find a Government with a majority in the Commons; a forced dissolution would be acceptable only if the Government had lost its majority and a dissolution was likely to provide a new majority. But, second, the Monarch cannot insist on a dissolution in circumstances in which the move might fail to provide a majority administration, thus damaging the prestige of the Crown. Third, the Monarch cannot act in a way which may appear to be partisan—these are conditions of survival, not conventions; matters not of constitutional right but of what the Monarch can 'get away with'.

Within these limitations, it is in normal circumstances impossible for the Monarch either to insist on a dissolution or to refuse one. Thus, Queen Victoria, pursuing her intense dislike of the Gladstonian Liberal Party, enquired seriously (of the Opposition) about a dissolution in 1892 and 1895. She was advised correctly that she would thereby damage the monarchy. In 1949 there was a brief campaign in part of the Conservative press to persuade King George VI that he must replace Attlee by Churchill as his Prime Minister, and then dissolve Parliament in order to secure a majority for his new Government. Of course, he did not do so: it would have been a highly partisan action and the election results of 1950 suggest that it would have failed.

Power over policy and legislation. It follows from the principles and conditions already indicated that the Monarch has no power over policy or a veto over legislation. The Ministry, not the Monarch, carries the responsibility to Parliament, hence the final power. Non-partisanship, neutrality, imply non-involvement, inaction. Victoria's great fall from constitutional good manners, in sending an uncoded telegram criticising her Prime Minister after the death of General Gordon, is unlikely to be repeated. The Queen's Speech will continue to be written by her Government. It will not be generally accepted that the Monarch has a right to intervene to prevent her Ministers from stepping outside their election mandate: neither the theory of the mandate nor indeed the theory of democracy will stand such usage.

The possibilities of influence

The Queen thus has virtually no power in normal circumstances in the important matters of politics, the choice and dismissal of Ministers, policy and legislation. However, she might still have influence on lesser matters and in conditions of unusual political uncertainty and instability. The classic formulation of monarchical influence, as distinct from power, was Bagehot's: 'To state the matter shortly, the sovereign has, under a constitutional monarch such as ours, three rights—the right to be consulted, the right to encourage, the right to warn. And a King of great sense and sagacity would want no others. He would find that having no others, would enable him to use these with singular effect.' Bagehot's view was correct for the late Victorian monarchy, and George V (who had taught Bagehot's ideas as an undergraduate) seems to have adopted a similar though weaker rule. The notion of the Monarch as a consultant and adviser in statecraft looked sound enough. The Monarch has constitutional status and strength, and could build up a continuous experience of government denied to politicians. Some matters, such as foreign and imperial affairs, and the armed forces, seemed appropriate special fields for a royal statesman. Victoria, certainly, and George V to a less extent, attempted to exert influence in these fields. For example, both fought against Irish Home Rule; Victoria held and expressed strong views on such topics as the Sudan and relations with Germany; George V intrigued with Haig, the British Commander in France. George also gave encouragement to the formation of the National Government in 1931.

However, Bagehot's formula hardly fits the mid-twentieth century monarchy. There is, in fact, little evidence that any Monarch in the last hundred years has had any significant (or even insignificant) political influence. Where there appears to have been monarchical influence, the truth is that the Monarch was simply encouraging (blessing if you like) a course of action already approved by politicians. This is the case, for example, in the 1931 crisis. The King helped to arrange meetings at Buckingham Palace to discuss the formation of a National Government, but he took only a formal part in such meetings. It was known that he favoured a coalition, but so did the party leaders. Again, Victoria had some influence in ministerial appointments. She kept Dilke out of office in 1880, describing him (in, for her, very strong words) as 'a democrat—a disguised republican'.

Another Radical, Labouchère, was also excluded at her insistence. But these were not fundamental concessions for Gladstone to make. There is some disagreement about whether George VI was responsible for Bevin's appointment to the Foreign Office in 1945. Lord Attlee maintained he had already decided on the appointment before the King made his suggestions. Others say it was not a good appointment anyway.

Indeed, the evidence for monarchical influence is thin because the theory behind it is weak. Governments need good advice; but it is unlikely, given the circumstances of royal upbringing, training and mode of life, that a Monarch will have really valuable advice to offer.

The uses of monarchy

(a) The monarchy is an essential piece of constitutional machinery. The formalities of instituting a Ministry, summoning and dissolving Parliament, and giving final approval to laws all need to be carried out by an independent institution of high status. The monarchy perfectly provides this.

(b) A State requires a formal head for ceremonial purposes—and ceremony can be an important part of the sentiment and loyalty needed in any political system. The monarchy in Britain carries out state ceremonial superbly; and relieves the effective government of much laborious and unrewarding effort.

Thus, the ceremonial monarchy helps to stabilise society and politics, binding the people to a general support for the system as a whole. At the same time, the politicians who actually govern the country are not normally the object of irrational and non-political loyalty: the citizen is invited to see his politicians as fallible human-beings, not demi-gods. This is an invaluable achievement.

(c) It is only in unusual circumstances that the monarch has any serious political power. First, there may be occasions of political uncertainty and instability, in which the existing political parties have lost cohesion, and majorities, leadership and programme are in doubt. In these circumstances the formal constitutional mechanisms of the monarchy may provide significant guidance and influence towards the integration of politics. The Monarch does not take over the government, but has to take positive initiative to secure the con-tinuance of government. It seems in practice unlikely that British politics should fall apart in this way and require rescue by the Monarch; and even the disintegration of 1931 did not lead to com-plete abdication by the politicians.

Second, the monarchy may be regarded as having some scope for action in a national emergency involving the overthrow of the con-stitution. In such a situation the rules of politics are in abeyance and the Monarch has a duty, and may have the capacity, to use his status and popularity in defence of the State. King Haakon of Norway showed the possibilities of resistance during the German occupation 1940–5. To some extent, King Constantine of Greece has more recently demonstrated this ultimate role of the Monarch in defence of the constitution. But neither Monarch was able to do much more than defy the usurpers, thus depriving them of the legitimacy they sought.

Constitutions, it seems, need stronger defences than mere mon-archy. There is another difficulty. There is sometimes a tendency to raise the cry 'the constitution in danger!' and seek the alliance of the Crown, when the threat is only to tradition and prejudice. Thus, it was argued that granting Home Rule to Ireland and limiting the powers of the House of Lords were both fundamental attacks on the constitution, which should be resisted by the Monarch. Because of this temptation to bring the Crown into politics, it is best not to regard the Crown as having a formal reserve power. If the Revolution comes, constitutional niceties will not matter much anyway!

Of course, the monarchy has its critics—why should it not? It is certainly an expensive institution, though there is a good return for the money, and the sums involved are minute by the standards of any one of the great spending Departments. It is also inevitably an institution which tends to reinforce one of the English vices—

snobbery. England has not yet fully emancipated itself from its feudal, aristocratic and imperial past. The institution of monarchy belongs to this past; but it is clearly within the capacity of British political genius (illogical and pragmatic as it is) to develop a genuinely democratic monarchy.

2 GOVERNMENT AND THE ECONOMY

It should be clear from every chapter of this book that few acts of government proceed from a simple pattern of power—as if the Prime Minister, struck by a bright idea at Chequers one weekend, returns to Downing Street, pulls a lever (or summons a secretary) and, lo!— the life of every citizen is thereby changed. Major decisions, we know, normally involve Cabinet and colleagues, party and Parliament, press and public, groups and individuals. If the levers of Downing Street are connected to an engine (to continue Mr Wilson's analogy), other people sometimes control the signals and the points.

If we analysed a major decision in any field, we should find a complex interaction of persons and groups. Examining a major decision in economics, the pattern is particularly complex. There are, first of all, the participants or actors we have just noted, those we most readily associate with politics. This part of economic decision-making is basically similar to all decision-making, but there are certain features which differentiate it.

(a) The Prime Minister is almost certainly involved.

(b) The political parties will have principles or programmes relevant to the decision.

(c) The pressure groups are particularly powerful and prominent, notably the TUC, the CBI and the major industrial groups.

(d) The influence of economic advisers (usually academics) may be apparent.

(e) Several Ministries are usually involved, thus:

the Treasury—of course, as the national financial manager, responsible for the Budget, for the public sector of industry, and for short-term planning;

Department for Employment and Productivity—including incomes policy;

Board of Trade—overseas trade;

Ministry of Technology—development of technology;

also Departments concerned with Power, Transport, Housing, Education, Scotland, Wales, local government and regional planning.

These are the normal components of the political system, functioning in a particular way in relation to the making of economic policy.

However, governments, in addition, have created special institutions to contribute towards economic policy. These stem from the acceptance in the early 1960s of the need to plan the British economy much more positively in order to make it more competitive. Such planning has to be carried out with the consent, indeed with the advice and cooperation, of industry and the unions. In consequence, governments have devised institutions which are either joint with industry, or at least a little aside from government itself. These are:

(a) The National Economic Development Council ('Neddy') (1962). This is a joint body, with a full-time staff (paid by the Government). It provides for communication between government and industry, and has sufficient standing to attract the Prime Minister as occasional chairman, as well as other senior Ministers. It is influential and, for example, secured modification in the National Plan of 1965.

(b) Development Councils for particular industries, known as 'little Neddies'.

(c) The National Board for Prices and Incomes. This was established in 1965, a successor to at least two earlier attempts by government to regulate incomes via a semi-independent body. The PIB is appointed by the Government and reports to it (specifically to DEP). Its pronouncements on prices and incomes are well-researched and delivered in reports which, by the side of mealy-mouthed government statements, are always direct and sometimes trenchant. The Board has a full-time Chairman. In 1966–7 the Government took statutory powers over prices and incomes and these were meant to give statutory force to the recommendations of the Board.

(d) Regional Economic Planning Boards and Councils. These were established in 1965 to provide machinery for regional economic planning. The Councils are advisory bodies made up of local notabilities (broadly interpreted) serving part-time, and appointed by the Government. The Boards are composed of civil servants representing the Government Departments concerned in regional planning. The Boards help to formulate regional plans, and forward and coordinate the planning aspects of their Department's work in the regions.

(e) There is also the Bank of England, formally a nationalised institution, but with substantial independence. The Government relies on the Bank for advice and for the technical management of its currency and banking needs. At this point, the actions of government acquire international complications, which in some fields provide the most serious limitations of all on its freedom of action.

Thus, major economic policy is developed within a complex array of advisory, influence-bearing and decision-taking bodies. This is, in a special and heightened form, an exemplar of the complex processes from which any major government decision derives.

3 THE NATIONALISED INDUSTRIES AND THE GOVERNMENT

The Nationalised Industries are important in the study of politics because they show the Government at work in an important field of economics; because they operate in a special administrative device, the public corporation; and because their parliamentary accountability has been provided for in a new Committee of the House of Commons, the Select Committee on Nationalised Industries.

Nationalised Industries are not new. If the Army and Navy are not counted, there is still the Post Office, as well as the public corporations of the 1930s, notably the BBC, the London Passenger Transport Board and the Central Electricity Board. The older examples have been conducted as Departments of State, accountable to Parliament through a Minister. The Boards of the 1930s have functioned independently, though this is less true of the BBC, which has been dependent on the Government for money.

The extension of nationalisation to several great industries under the Labour Government of 1945-51 has raised the problem of combining public accountability with efficiency. It is generally thought that efficiency requires independence, yet accountability implies the restriction of independence. The problem has not yet been answered. It makes an excellent set-piece problem in the arrangement of responsible government; neither Magna Carta nor the Declaration of Independence will help much.

The problem is this: Nationalised Industries should be both efficient and responsible, i.e. answerable to the public—these were the objectives of nationalisation. The first object is best achieved by appointing a Board (a public corporation) and giving it power to get on with the work; the second objective, by giving Parliament some power over the Board, a power of oversight and even of intervention. The contradiction can only be resolved by making the parliamentary power as limited as possible. It is by no means clear that the right balance has been struck.

The powers of the Minister

(a) *Statutory.* The Nationalisation Acts generally give the Minister powers:

to appoint and re-appoint to the Board;

to give general directions in matters relating to the national interest;

to call for information, returns, accounts from the Board;

in matters of development and reorganisation involving substantial capital outlay;

in matters of education, training and research.

(b) *Actual.* In practice, Ministers have sometimes gone beyond their strict statutory powers in relation to the Nationalised Boards. They have been particularly concerned to influence wages and prices, and sometimes purchasing policy. Thus, coal prices have not been varied without the agreement of the Minister; in transport, both wages and prices have been subjected to ministerial intervention; the air corporations have been instructed to buy certain British aircraft. In many cases, the Government's directions have been contrary to the industry's commercial need to pay its way, but might be defended as 'in the public interest'.

These directions are conveyed by private and informal methods; in the case of coal prices, there is a recognised 'gentleman's agreement'.

This seems a confused and unsatisfactory situation. The main arguments are as follows:

(i) There is some agreement on the overriding responsibility of the Minister for the national interest. This is a political argument about parliamentary democracy: '. . . The responsibility of deciding what is in the overriding interests of the nation rests with the Minister because it is only by resting with him that it can rest here' (Aneurin Bevan in the House of Commons, H.C. Deb., vol. 496, 25 February 1952, col. 818).

(ii) There is further a measure of agreement that the Board is the best judge of its commercial policies.

(iii) The sharpest disagreement is about the distinction between commercial and 'national interest' policy. According to a government-appointed advisory committee of 1955 (the 'Fleck' Committee), the Boards should not be expected 'to embark in the supposed national interest on any course other than a purely economic course'.

(iv) So the dispute is ultimately about the manner in which ministerial directives are conveyed to the Boards. These, it is argued, should be open and avowed so that the conflict of commercial and national objectives may be clarified, and the responsibility for unprofitable operation should be fastened on the Minister. Alas! Ministers are visible and highly vulnerable; they are not enthusiastic about taking on public responsibility for, say, the price of coal or the cost of a commuter's season ticket.

Accountability to Parliament

(a) *Forms of accountability*. In theory, as Aneurin Bevan argued, responsibility to the Minister leads to responsibility to Parliament.

The Boards, except for the BBC and the Bank of England, have been established by statute, and thus have an historical attachment to Parliament.

More important, the Boards need parliamentary approval for major borrowing and capital outlay.

There are occasional opportunities for debate arising from the Report and Accounts of the Boards.

A Minister may well regard these points of accountability as sufficient. The backbencher, however, will take a more sceptical view: 'answering to the Minister' is not the same as answering to Parliament. For the backbencher, other forms of accountability have been developed: Questions; the Public Accounts Committee; the Select Committee on Nationalised Industries; and letters directly from Members of Parliament to the Boards. Of these, Questions and the Select Committee are of particular force and interest.

(b) *Questions*. Parliamentary Questions on the Nationalised Industries are similar to Questions on other subjects, but there are special restrictions on the admissibility of Questions. Roughly, Questions are limited to matters broader than day-to-day administration, and must be within the recognised responsibility of the Minister. Thus, a Question on the closing of one pit in Glamorgan would not be admitted; but a Question on the planned closure of twenty pits would be admissible.

The Boards have expressed anxieties about the effects of the possibility of Parliamentary Questions on the vigour and initiative of their staffs. Lord Hurcomb told the Select Committee of 1951: 'The inevitable effect of constant Parliamentary Questions is to centralise . . .' He spoke of the paralysing effects of Parliamentary Questions on provincial station-masters.

Students of the British Parliament may feel that such views represent a wholly unjustified tribute to the effectiveness of Question Time.

(c) *The Select Committee on Nationalised Industries.* A permanent Select Committee on the Nationalised Industries was first proposed in 1951. The Government responded tardily and established such a Committee in 1955; but the Committee decided that its terms were too restrictive. The following year (1956), a new Select Committee was established. Its formal charge was quite simply and broadly 'to examine the Reports and Accounts' of the Industries; but the Government emphasised that the Committee was excluded from considering major government policy (for which a Minister was responsible), and day-to-day administration and wages. This still left some matters of considerable significance, for example, financial performance; organisation, including devolution and managerial efficiency; relations with consumers, and the unremunerative responsibilities of the Boards. The Select Committee has survived and is re-appointed each session.

The Select Committee has thirteen members, and is assisted by two House of Commons clerks. Its procedures, meetings, questioning of witnesses and methods of reporting are similar to the other Select Committees; it deals mainly with voluminous and complex material, and can only work slowly around the whole field of its responsibility. It cannot claim to have had a dramatic impact on the Nationalised Industries. But it has elicited information from previously obscure places, including Government Departments; it has occasionally secured modifications of government policy (e.g., on railway regionalisation); above all, it has distinguished and emphasised the relations of the Minister to the Board and the extent of the Boards' operations undertaken for social, not commercial reasons. These matters have been reported to the House, which is now better informed (and less prejudiced) about the Nationalised Industries than it was before 1955.

In many ways, the Select Committee on Nationalised Industries has demonstrated that it is both possible and desirable for a back-benchers' committee to concern itself effectively with administration, the execution of policy and even the grounds of policy, without breaching the limits of 'government policy'. The Committee has not normally divided on party lines—a sufficient indication that it has kept to the limits. It has been a model for the development of specialist committees (see chapter 7).

However, the Committee still has its critics among those concerned specifically for the health of the Industries, not Parliament. Lord Morrison told the Select Committee of 1955: 'I do not think it is the kind of body to which you could entrust this [i.e. nationalised industries] to the point of alteration of the actual management of a complex industrial concern.' Lord Reith, the great architect of the BBC, told the same Committee that Parliament had renounced the right of direct interference.

It is certainly true that the Select Committee is more properly and more effectively concerned with lay accountability than with efficiency. The *Economist* once said, rather sourly: 'Politicians are no more qualified to teach good management, blue book in hand, than they are qualified, pick in hand, to teach miners how to dig coal' (19 May 1956). Efficiency may best be secured in other ways, for example, by the internal procedures of the industries themselves, by the oversight of the Treasury's section on public enterprise, or by an efficiency unit established for all the Nationalised Industries (similar to the Comptroller and Auditor-General).

If accountability to Parliament is not the same as an efficiency audit, nor does it amount to effective representation of consumers in the day-to-day matters of complaints about service and quality. Here the intentions of the nationalisers have hardly been realised, and the nationalised industries are little more amenable to public criticism and complaint than the most entrenched private industry.

4 A PRIVATE MEMBER'S BILL

(The Public Bodies (Admission of the Press to Meetings) Bill, 1960, which became Public Bodies (Admission to Meetings) Act, 1960).

Introduction

This account illustrates the hazardous course of Private Members' legislation; also the operation of local authority pressures in both Houses, and the liking of both central and local government for secrecy.

The Private Member has few opportunities to initiate legislation: the most effective way he can do it is through the Speaker's ballot at the beginning of each parliamentary session. In the session 1959–60, 311 Members put their names in the hat and one of the twenty who drew a place was Mrs Margaret Thatcher, the newly-elected Conservative Member for Finchley. Her name came out second and she was able, therefore, not only to choose one of the six Fridays allotted for the Second Readings of Private Members' Bills, but also, most important, to take priority on that day.

Second Reading (Friday, 5 February 1960)

There are plenty of chances to obstruct a Private Member's Bill. Business in the House finished at 4 p.m. on the six Fridays: if a Member is speaking at that hour the Commons proceeds automatically to the half-hour Adjournment Debate, and the Bill goes to the bottom of the list for a subsequent Friday. Any Member can, however, move at any time that the 'question be now put'. If the Speaker thinks there has been sufficient debate he will accept the motion. Not only must a majority be obtained, but there must be at least one-hundred Members in support of the closure. There is usually a thin attendance on a Friday, and a Private Member cannot rely on the discipline of the Whips to provide a quorum, let alone a majority. But Mrs Thatcher and her supporters had done a good job. The Bill was not 'talked-out', and when the closure was moved, after a debate of almost five hours in which sixteen Members spoke, the motion was carried by 155 votes to 12.

In a maiden speech, Mrs Thatcher outlined the main principles of the Bill, which were to provide for the admission of the press to the full meetings of certain public bodies, particularly local authorities, and to the meetings of their committees, when these had substantial delegated powers. There was provision for excluding the press by resolution, when the body concerned thought that to be in the public interest. The debate revealed that Mrs Thatcher had inter-party support, but strong opposition came from a group of Members active in local government who argued that the Bill would inhibit discussion in committee by both representatives and officials; that it would upset existing good relations between the press and local authorities (and was therefore unnecessary); that it would be far better for the Minister to draw up a voluntarily-operated code of conduct with the local authorities and the press; and—a final ominous threat—that the Bill could only operate if it had the goodwill of the local authorities, which it would not have in its present form. These arguments were to be reiterated in Committee: Mrs Thatcher had been warned that she must expect a rough passage for her Bill, though perhaps she was comforted by the fact that the Minister himself spoke in the debate and gave the Government's qualified blessing. The motion for the Bill's rejection was defeated by 152 votes to 39; it was read a second time and sent to a Standing Committee.

Standing Committee (16 March to 13 April)

The Committee consisted of forty Members—twenty-three Conservative, sixteen Labour and one Liberal, together with a Chairman from the Chairmen's panel. Special interests were to the fore: at least twenty-six Members were or had been on local councils, and they included the Presidents of the Urban District and Rural District Councils Associations. The press had its representatives too. The Committee met five times on successive Wednesday mornings for a total of 12¾ hours.

A Standing Committee is concerned primarily with the details of a Bill, but principles do get discussed again. In this case, opponents of the measure, fortified by memoranda from the local authority associations, tried immediately to have the Bill put aside. They moved (a) that the Committee should not meet for a fortnight so that the Minister could negotiate a code of conduct with the local authorities and the press; and (b) the deletion of various sub-sections of the Bill and the addition of another, which would have had the effect of handing over to the Minister the working-out of details with outside bodies. The intention seemed to be to by-pass both the Committee and Parliament.

It is the sponsor's responsibility to obtain and keep a quorum, to decide attitudes to amendments, and to get the Bill through the Committee Stage in time for the Report and Third Reading on one of the later Fridays set aside for these stages of Private Members' Bills. Mrs Thatcher's difficulties were increased by the fact that, owing to faulty drafting, she had to move extra amendments and so gave greater scope for delaying tactics. Drafting is a difficult job, and the Private Member does not have the help of official draftsmen. He must rely on his own skill, or that of his legal colleagues, or pay for the work to be done. The fees must come out of his own pocket or from an organisation backing the Bill.

Mrs Thatcher got into difficulties because she wished to amend the Bill so that it applied to the 'public' and not just the 'press'. But the original long title did not permit this. 'Who drafted the long title?' asked one member rather fiercely. Poor Mrs Thatcher replied, 'I am afraid that I drafted the long title, having been here about a fortnight.'

However, the House gave instructions that, notwithstanding the long title, the Committee could if it wished include the public in the Bill's operations and could amend the title accordingly. As a result Mrs Thatcher moved at the beginning of the second sitting that the word 'public' should be inserted for the word 'press' in page 1, line 8. This was the first of a number of exactly similar amendments. Discussion on it continued into the third and fourth sittings; at the end of the second, the closure was moved so that the question could be put; but the voting was 9–9. The Bill's critics were assiduous in their attendance. Virtually no progress had been made after four sessions, yet it was so rapid at the fifth meeting that the Committee was able to complete its work that morning. This was due to Mrs Thatcher's willingness to sacrifice one of the main sections of the Bill—clause 2, section 2, whereby all committees with substantial delegated powers would have been within the scope of the Act—and substitute a section which only affected those committees on which all members of the parent body served. The main criticism of the local authority associations had been accepted.

Report Stage and Third Reading (Friday, 13 May)

The House spent two hours on the Report Stage and 1¼ hours on the Third Reading. Much of the Report Stage was taken up with technical amendments, but changes of some substance were also made. For instance, the date when the Bill would become effective was put back from 1 September 1960 to 1 June 1961. The much-amended Bill was given a Third Reading without a division and sent to the House of Lords.

The Bill in the House of Lords

On Second Reading (26 May) the House debated the Bill for one hour, and though the speeches were generally favourable, it was evident that some amendments would be moved at the Committee Stage. The Bill was read a second time without a division. At the end of June the Bill was considered by a Committee of the Whole House (the usual procedure in the Lords). The Committee considered the Bill for 1½ hours and passed four amendments. The most important was one moved by Lord Morrison of Lambeth, which excluded police authorities from the schedule, so that the press and public would not have a statutory right to attend their meetings. Lord Morrison, as an expert in local government matters and in his capacity as President of the Association of Municipal Corporations, was very active in the Lords' discussions. (In moving an amendment Lord Morrison said, 'I have been asked to move this amendment on behalf of the Association of Municipal Corporations.')

The Bill completed its progress through the House of Lords in July. At the end of October, the Commons accepted the Lords' amendments and the Bill received the Royal Assent—almost a year from the date of the Private Members' ballot.

5 THE LIBERAL PARTY

The Liberal Party last constituted a government in 1915. The 1929 election was the last occasion when it won a substantial number of seats (59, compared to 287 Labour, 261 Conservative). The Party has never recovered from the parliamentary collapse of 1931, when it split. Since 1945 it has never held more than thirteen seats; these do not reflect its voting support, which in 1964 was as high as three million. The Party's membership is about 300,000.

Clearly the electoral system works against the Party, once decline has begun. The reasons for the decline lie in the social and political conditions which gave rise to the Labour Party, and in the faults of the leadership of the Party after 1915, when Lloyd George pursued personal and coalition politics.

The policies of the Liberal Party are not wholly distinctive. The Party's old principle of free trade is no longer a satisfactory rallying cry, nor, for that matter, entirely acceptable economics. The issue of Irish Home Rule which split the Gladstonian party in 1886 is long dead. The principles associated with religious nonconformity no longer have any political impact. Liberalism in the sense of maximum freedom is generally accepted by all parties, though the Liberals have given a new and relevant content to the principle by developing policies of industrial co-ownership and regional devolution. The Party is strongly committed to Britain's joining the Common Market, but so are sections of the other parties. However, the Liberal Party's lack of electoral success has little to do with the comparative merits of the party programmes. There simply is not room for three major national parties, and history has passed the Radical torch to the Labour Party.

In structure, the Liberal Party is similar to the Conservative Party; but with the difference that it has no immediate chance of forming a government. It is, in consequence, less unified and disciplined, and open to occasional policy raids by bands of youthful and vigorous members.

The Leader is elected by Liberal Members of Parliament, and annual re-election is normally a formality. The Leader of the Parliamentary Party is also now Leader of the Party as a whole; but the Liberal Parliamentary Party is regarded otherwise as separate from the Liberal Party organisation.

The Assembly is the annual mass meeting, attended by about a thousand people. As with the other parties, its place in the constitution is unclear, ranging from a formal and theoretical predominance ('the final voice on matters of policy') to a mere mass rally (not able to 'dictate to the Parliamentary Party'). It was once described by a newspaper correspondent as a 'loose confederation of anarchist cells'.

In addition there is a Council of about 160 members—too large to be very important—and an executive Committee which does not seem to be a very powerful body. There are other smaller committees, the Standing Committee and the Party Committee; also the Liberal Central Association, which is important in candidate selection; and a regional organisation. There is a professional organisation, which, if anything, works for the Leader.

In candidate selection the constituency associations have very great freedom, but subject to the practical difficulties of persuading people to stand at all. Policy-making seems to rest with the Parliamentary Party, and especially the Leader. The mass party organisation counts for very little.

Thus, the Liberal Party is not substantially different in structure from the other major parties. The absence of responsibility for the policy of a government or an alternative government permits it greater freedom, even sometimes a degree of anarchy, and relieves it of the tensions, disputes and conflicts of a party with its hands on power.

6 DELEGATED LEGISLATION AND THE SELECT COMMITTEE ON STATUTORY INSTRUMENTS

When government acts upon the citizen, it normally does so under the authority of a Statute. But often the Statute allows discretion to the Government to make its own detailed rules and regulations in carrying out the general objectives of the Statute: Ministers may be empowered to vary, extend, adapt or even substitute for particular clauses by making an Order. Such orders under a 'parent' law are classed as 'delegated legislation'. This class of legislation includes: Orders in Council; rules, orders and regulations made by a Minister; Provisional and Special Orders (a form of private legislation); and bye-laws (made by local authorities, public corporations and similar bodies). The first two, known as statutory instruments, are of importance in national politics.

Mostly, however, even these are concerned with minor matters. For example, a list at the end of 1967 included Orders about evidence in Courts Martial, Pensions for Aden Widows and Orphans, Baking and Sausage Making (Christmas and the New Year), the Construction and Use of Motor Vehicles, Restrictions arising from Foot and Mouth Disease and the Wild Birds (Collared Doves) (Scotland) Order. These are small matters, but some of them (e.g., on motor vehicles) are important to a large number of people, and most of them will be of high importance to some people. So the manner in which such orders are made is of some political significance.

It is clear, first, that a modern government, heavily involved in economic and social affairs, cannot do without delegated legislation. Parliament has neither the time nor the expertise to deal with such detailed regulations; indeed, it has difficulty in dealing effectively with its present legislative load, and ought perhaps to delegate more. Departments, on the other hand, can manage the detail, carry out consultations where necessary, and vary their regulations to meet changing circumstances. The case for delegated legislation on grounds of efficiency is a good one.

Nevertheless, there are obvious objections to the process by which Parliament passes its legislative authority to the executive. In a famous book published in 1929, Lord Justice Hewart denounced this (and other similar developments) as iniquitous—a 'New Despotism'. Such language was injudicious, exaggerating the faults of the system, on the basis of an extreme *laissez-faire* philosophy, an unrealistic concept of the separation of powers and an undue regard for the virtues of judicial control of government. Still the system of delegated legislation does have faults. The main objections are first, that the power of the executive must be subject to the scrutiny at least of Parliament; second, that the citizen may properly require that the law which touches him is reasonably certain, clear and well-publicised. There is a remedy available through the courts—an application to have an order quashed as *ultra vires*, beyond the statutory authority of government—but this is a difficult and costly process. There also needs to be a check carried out by Parliament.

Parliament is of course responsible for the original delegation of power, and has an opportunity then to see that the scope allowed to the executive is reasonable from the point of view of the effectiveness of the law and the freedom of the citizen. To control the actual use of delegated powers, Parliament has established special procedures. Orders have to be laid before the House and are subject to the approval of the House either by an affirmative Resolution, or by a 'negative' procedure under which the Order becomes effective unless the House moves a 'Prayer' annulling it.

The House also has (since 1944, and owing a little to Lord Justice Hewart's book) a Select Committee on Statutory Instruments, which is charged with drawing the special attention of the House to Orders which:

impose a charge or require payments;

will not be open to challenge in the courts;

appear to make some unusual or unexpected use of powers conferred in the Statute;

are retrospective where this is not expressly provided for in the parent Statute;

have been unjustifiably delayed in publication;

require elucidation;

are defective in drafting.

These constitute an important inquest on Statutory Orders, but do not permit an assessment of the merit of the Order; the concern is with form, clarity, legality, not with policy or effect. The Committee has eleven members and an Opposition Chairman, and is assisted by the Counsel to Mr Speaker.

In most cases the Committee 'passes' the Orders before it; that is, sees no reason to draw special attention to them. But in a few cases, it will 'draw attention' under one of the heads given. It may request the Department concerned to comment on or explain the regulation in question, and the Department's memorandum will be put before the Commons.

The procedures have had a salutary effect on the making of statutory instruments. Departments are careful to draw their Orders within the bounds of the parent Statute, and to clarify and publicise their provisions. It is doubtful whether Lord Hewart's despotism ever existed, but there was perhaps slackness and an excessive use of regulations. These are now subject to a reasonably effective check by Parliament.

7 ADMINISTRATIVE TRIBUNALS

In the last forty years, alongside the expansion of delegated legislation, and for the same reasons, the number of administrative tribunals has risen fast. These are tribunals set up to adjudicate disputes arising over administrative action. In some cases the disputes are between an individual and the State, e.g., a tax dispute appealed to the Commissioners of Inland Revenue; a pensions dispute settled by a National Insurance Tribunal; a route-licensing dispute settled by the Transport Tribunal. In other cases, the tribunal arbitrates between an individual and a semi-independent corporation, e.g., the producer boards in agriculture; or the dispute may be between two individuals, e.g., landlord and tenant in dispute over the application of a Rent Act.

All these cases are dealt with by specially established tribunals, not by courts of law. This procedure has been severely criticised in the past, especially by lawyers. It was argued that administrative tribunals offend against the principle of separation of powers, providing for a party to a dispute (the State) to be responsible for, in some cases in control of, the settlement of the dispute. In particular, the members of a tribunal do not have the permanence of tenure, and hence the independence, of the judiciary. Again, tribunals have not always followed legal procedures in providing for the representation of both sides, hearing evidence, publishing the reasons for their decisions and providing for appeals.

At the same time, there is a good deal to be said for the administrative tribunal. It is accessible, quick, informal and cheap, in short, available and comprehensible to the layman who would be confused and deterred by the costly procedures of a court. Moreover, most of the questions decided by tribunals are of a technical or specialist nature. There is little case-law to guide the tribunal, which needs instead a combination of specialist knowledge and common sense. It may be argued that lawyers and judges have no obvious place in administrative tribunals.

Still, some concern was felt that the system as it existed in the mid-1950s did not entirely secure its proper objectives: to be open, fair and impartial. This was the view of the Franks Committee on Administrative Tribunals and Enquiries, which reported in 1957. The Committee rejected the argument that most disputes should be referred to ordinary courts: this was both unnecessary and destructive of the special, and high, position of the judiciary. Instead it was proposed that the existing system of tribunals be retained but modified.

Since then, and especially under the Tribunals and Inquiries Act of 1958, some major reforms have been accomplished. Normally, now, the chairmen of tribunals have legal qualifications; hearings are in public (except where privacy needs to be protected); the citizen is informed of his rights, is told of the departmental policies relating to his case, and subsequently of the grounds of the tribunal's decision and of his rights of appeal. The working of tribunals is kept under review by a Standing Council on Tribunals.

Thus, perhaps, the system of tribunals now has the best of both worlds, the administrative and the judicial. Some of the special safeguards of judicial procedures have been attached to a process which is otherwise accepted as administrative, being quick, fair, and, if a little arbitrary, yet ultimately within the political responsibility of the Government.

8 THE PARLIAMENTARY COMMISSIONER FOR ADMINISTRATION (THE OMBUDSMAN)

The problem

The problem in general is that governments intervene more and more in the life of the citizen, without those interventions being subject to effective control, scrutiny, complaint or appeal by the citizen or by Parliament or some other body on his behalf. The concern is not with the major political questions, e.g., the Bank Rate, Health Service charges or the reorganisation of secondary schools, but the lesser matters of administration in individual cases. (There are difficult problems of definition here.)

The available remedies

(a) Governments should intervene much less. This is the old *laissez-faire* argument and is not now widely accepted. There would seem to be a strong case for government intervention for certain economic and social ends (management of the economy, ensuring minimum standards of welfare, control of the environment). This case appears to have been accepted by the electorate, which has voted for governments with interventionist programmes.

(b) The political system already constitutes a check on intervention by the Government; all that is required is an improvement of existing procedures, that is:

(i) the parliamentary procedures of Committees, Questions Adjournment Motions, and the correspondence of Members of Parliament with the Departments;

(ii) the political procedures of parties and elections. (These matters have been discussed in Parts III and IV of this book.)

(c) A greater measure of devolution. This accepts broadly the assumptions of (b), but proposes devolution to local or regional government on the grounds that a smaller scale of operation and greater proximity of government to citizen secure more effective checks on government. This is an important argument which cannot be fully discussed here; its proponents often seem to expect too much of devolution.

(d) The extension and improvement of the existing system of administrative justice—tribunals, inspectors, rent officers, planning appeals (see note above on administrative tribunals).

(e) The extension and improvement of the legal system, so that the aggrieved citizen may seek redress through the courts. There are strong arguments for this view, notably:

(i) that the judicial system provides a check on both executive and legislature by a separate and coordinate power (the theory of separation of powers); and,

(ii) that the system provides acceptable procedures for hearing and deciding contentious cases.

The objection to this view is that the judicial system may be unsuited to the trying of matters which do not depend on law and its interpretation, and that the system is slow and expensive and its procedures complicated for the layman. It may further be objected that the system is irresponsible in the political sense, and unresponsive to changing social needs and assumptions.

(f) The establishment of an administrative device which is judicial in style and authority, but fitted into a system in which Parliament is central. A model is the office of Comptroller and Auditor-General, and the related Select Committee on Public Accounts. This is the beginning of the case for an Ombudsman (a Swedish term) and such an office was established in Britain in 1967 under the title of Parliamentary Commissioner for Administration.

The Parliamentary Commissioner for Administration

The Act establishes the office of Parliamentary Commissioner for Administration (PCA) on the terms used for judges and the Comptroller and Auditor-General, i.e. the PCA is appointed 'during good behaviour' not 'at the Queen's pleasure', and cannot be dismissed by a Government which is displeased with his activities. (The first holder of the office, Sir Edmund Compton, was a former Comptroller and a much respected one, and his appointment is likely to set a standard of judicial independence for the office.)

The Commissioner and his small staff (sixty-three altogether) consider only cases referred to him by Members of Parliament. He has access to departmental officials and their files. He reports on each case to the Member who raised it; any conclusion he comes to has a certain moral force but is not binding on the Department concerned. Parliament appoints a Select Committee to which the Commissioner makes annual and other general reports.

There are broad areas of government administration from which he is excluded: all local authority, Health Service, Nationalised Industry and Police matters; all matters concerned with government employment, appointments, dismissals, pensions. These are all areas where the citizens' grievances are likely to be numerous and profound.

But what is it that the PCA is to scrutinise?—the problem of definition is difficult. The Labour Party's Election Manifesto in 1964 used the phrase 'any misuse of Government power as it affects the citizen'. But the word 'misuse' is too wide to be a definition at all. The Act uses the word 'maladministration', and a government spokesman mentioned 'bias, neglect, inattention, delay, incompetence, ineptitude, perversity, turpitude, arbitrariness' as examples of what might constitute 'maladministration'. The Act goes on quite specifically to exempt from the Commissioner's purview 'the merits of a decision taken without maladministration by a government department . . . in the exercise of a discretion vested in that department'. This is perhaps too restrictive a definition, for it confines the Commissioner's powers to impropriety in procedure, thus excluding a decision which may be correctly arrived at but mistaken or unfair or unjust, especially having regard to its consequences.

Thus the scheme established in 1967 was especially hampered by its exclusions of areas of complaint and by its restriction of scrutiny to administrative procedure only.

The scheme in practice

The Parliamentary Commissioner has so far done useful but modest work. Complaints have been investigated at the rate of about two-hundred or so a year. About a tenth of these have yielded examples of maladministration in the view of the Commissioner, and these have all been remedied by the Departments concerned. The most notable case was the investigation of a Foreign Office decision to exclude certain claimants from a share in compensation payments for internment in a concentration camp (Report of December 1967). This seemed to be a case in which the PCA would be bound by the terms of his office to report that the procedures were satisfactory, although the decision seemed wrong and unfair. In fact, he found the procedures at fault, and so was able to recommend a review of the case. This was carried out, and the Foreign Office rescinded its previous decision. The report in *The Times* was headlined 'Triumph for Ombudsman'.

Continuing problems

The establishment of the Parliamentary Commissioner has certainly not brought about a political and administrative revolution. Some critics believe that the problems have hardly yet been touched. This depends on an assessment of the extent of the problem of maladministration, and reliable assessments are hard to find. *Laissez faire* and collectivist philosophers have their prejudices, and so do the administrators and the man who has just had his pensions appeal or planning application turned down. However, given the extent of government intervention, the fallibility of administrators (and all human beings) and the average citizen's passivity and ignorance of his rights, it seems a reasonable guess that a civilised society might do a good deal more to provide forms of scrutiny, appeal and arbitration.

This could be done by extending the Parliamentary Commissioner system. The Commissioner's area of scrutiny could be enlarged; and his terms of reference could be widened to include the quality or merit of a decision. The office itself could be enlarged to include more Commissioners specialising in particular fields, and machinery for helping the citizen to formulate his grievances. The Parliamentary Select Committee must provide the publicity which will give force to the Commissioner's recommendations.

Governments are likely to resist such developments on the grounds of 'ministerial responsibility' and 'Civil Service anonymity'. Thus, the Foreign Secretary, Mr Brown, while accepting the PCA's criticisms in the compensation case, went to great lengths to emphasise the constitutional difficulties. He said: (H.C. Deb., vol. 578, 5 February 1968, col. 112):

. . . I think that we have the best Parliamentary democratic system in the world and one of the reasons for this is that our Ministers are responsible to Parliament. If things are wrongly done, then they are wrongly done by Ministers and I think that it is tremendously important to hold to that principle.

If things have gone wrong, then Ministers have gone wrong and I accept my full share of the responsibility in this case . . . It is Ministers who must be attacked, not officials.

The Office of Parliamentary Commissioner was intended to strengthen our form of democratic Government, but let me say that if that Office were to lead to changing this constitutional position so that officials got attacked and Ministers escaped, then I think that the whole practice of Ministers being accountable to Parliament would be undermined. I think that the morale of the Civil and Diplomatic Services would be undermined.

The problem of ministerial responsibility was discussed in chapter 3 (p. 95). It was shown there that the full claim for ministerial responsibility leads to the position that civil servants are absolutely protected from criticism in Parliament, and Ministers need not treat their responsibility very seriously as long as they are not personally implicated in the administrative action under question. The extent of actual answerability is thus quite limited.

However, the constitutional difficulties of extending answerability do seem to have been exaggerated. First, civil servants may properly be answerable in private to the Parliamentary Commissioner, as they are already to the Comptroller and Auditor-General. These officials are not constantly at the administrator's elbow, and their occasional scrutiny is likely to be much less restrictive than the continuing oversight that a civil servant must expect from his departmental superiors. Second, the existing limited answerability to the Parliamentary Select Committees is already accepted and has not led to disaster. The Minister's responsibility for policy has been accepted, and civil servants have been questioned about administration. Third, the House of Commons may be expected to behave with restraint. It would, indeed, be unfair to individuals, damaging to the morale of the public service, and a great waste of Members' time to pillory by angry speeches some wretched Principal or Chief Executive Officer who had made a mistake. The anonymity of civil servants below the highest rank should be preserved, but this must not be allowed to annul the public responsibility of the public service, Thus it should be possible, if not easy, to reconcile the doctrine of ministerial responsibility with an enlargement of the work of the Parliamentary Commissioner for Administration.

9. LOCAL AND REGIONAL GOVERNMENT

There is very little about local and regional government in this book. This is not to imply that the subject is without importance. But it does imply that the British system of government can still be described, understood and assessed with little reference to anything but central government. The British system is highly centralised, and almost all the *big* decisions are taken centrally.

Of course, we are much affected in our daily lives by the *little* decisions of local government—a new primary school or swimming-pool, a pot-holed road or an ancient sewage works. We ought to be interested in these matters for academic reasons too—local politics can be as complex and as fascinating as national politics. So perhaps we should offer another justification for saying no more about local politics—that this book is quite long enough already.

Select list of books for further study

The following is a list of books suitable for a student beginning the study of politics. For more advanced and detailed study consult the bibliographies and references in these books, and in the text.

The official publications indicated in the text provide continuing and invaluable sources. Periodicals, notably *Parliamentary Affairs*, *Political Quarterly* and *Political Studies* are also of great value.

INTRODUCTION

MILLER, J.D.B., *The Nature of Politics*, Penguin, 1965

CRICK, B., *In Defence of Politics*, Penguin, 1964

DAHL, R.A., *Modern Political Analysis*, Prentice Hall, 1963

BIRCH, A.H., *Representative and Responsible Government*, Allen & Unwin, 1964

DICEY, A.V., *Introduction to the Study of the Law of the Constitution* (10th ed. by E.C.S. Wade), Macmillan, 1960

BOYD, A., *British Politics in Transition 1945–63*, Pall Mall, 1964

GUTTSMAN, W.L., *The British Political Elite*, MacGibbon and Kee, 1963

ROSE, R., *Politics in England*, Faber, 1965

BAGEHOT, W., *The English Constitution*, Fontana, 1963

BIRCH, A.H., *The British System of Government*, Allen & Unwin, 1967

STACEY, F., *The Government of Modern Britain*, Oxford University Press, 1968

PUNNETT, R.M., *British Government and Politics*, Heinemann, 1968

MORRISON, H., *Government and Parliament* (3rd ed.), Oxford University Press, 1964

STANKIEWICZ, W.J., *Crisis in British Government*, Collier-Macmillan, 1967

BENEWICK, R., and DOWSE, R.E., *Readings on British Politics and Government*, University of London Press, 1968

KING, A., (Ed.), *British Politics: People, Parties and Parliament*, D. C. Heath, Boston, 1966

LE MAY, G.H., *British Government 1914–63, Select Documents*, Methuen, 1964

FAIRLIE, H., *The Life of Politics*, Methuen, 1968

BUTLER, D., and FREEMAN, J., *British Political Facts 1900–1967*, Macmillan, 1968

THE EXECUTIVE

CARTER, B.E., *The Office of Prime Minister*, Faber, 1956

MACKINTOSH, J.P., *The British Cabinet*, Stevens, 1962

— *The Prime Minister and the Cabinet*, Allen & Unwin (forthcoming)

ROSE, R., *Policy making in Britain, a reader*, Macmillan, 1969

KING, A., *The British Prime Minister, a reader*, Macmillan, 1969

HUNT, N., *Whitehall and Beyond*, BBC, 1964

BRIDGES, LORD, *The Treasury* (2nd ed.), Allen & Unwin, 1967

MACKENZIE, W.J.M., and GROVE, J.W., *Central Administration in Britain*, Longmans, 1965

BRITTAN, S., *The Treasury under the Tories 1951–64*, Penguin, 1964

STRAUSS, E., *The Ruling Servants*, Allen & Unwin, 1961

THE LEGISLATURE

YOUNG, R., *The British Parliament*, Faber, 1962

RICHARDS, P.G., *Honourable Members* (2nd ed.), Faber, 1959

WALKLAND, S.A., *The Legislative Process in Great Britain*, Allen & Unwin, 1968

HANSON, H., and WISEMAN, H.V., *Parliament at Work*, Stevens, 1962

BOARDMAN, H., *The Glory of Parliament*, Allen & Unwin, 1960

BUTT, R., *The Power of Parliament*, Constable, 1967

WISEMAN, H.V., *Parliament and the Executive*, Routledge & Kegan Paul, 1966

WHEARE, K.C., *Government by Committee*, Clarendon, 1955

HUGHES, C., *The British Statute Book*, Hutchinson, 1957

JOHNSON, N., *Parliament and Administration*, Allen & Unwin, 1966

COOMBES, D., *The Member of Parliament and the Administration*, Allen & Unwin, 1966

CRICK, B., *The Reform of Parliament*, Weidenfeld and Nicolson, 1968

HANSARD SOCIETY, *Parliamentary Reform* (2nd ed., revised), Cassell, 1967

BROMHEAD, P.A., *The House of Lords in Contemporary Politics*, Routledge & Kegan Paul, 1958

REPRESENTATION

JENNINGS, I., *Party Politics* (3 vols.), Cambridge University Press, 1960–2

BULMER THOMAS, I., *The Party System in Great Britain*, Phoenix House, 1953

MCKENZIE, R.T., *British Political Parties* (2nd ed.), Heinemann, 1963

BLONDEL, J., *Voters, Parties and Leaders*, Penguin, 1963

FINER, S.E., *Anonymous Empire* (2nd ed.), Pall Mall, 1966

POTTER, A., *Organized Groups in British National Politics*, Faber, 1961

STEWART, J.D., *British Pressure Groups (Their role in relation to the House of Commons)*, Oxford University Press, 1958

ECKSTEIN, H., *Pressure Group Politics, the case of the B.M.A.*, Allen & Unwin, 1960

LEONARD, R. L., *Elections in Britain*, Van Nostrand, 1968

BUTLER, D.E., *The Electoral System in Britain since 1918* (2nd ed.), Oxford University Press, 1963

BUTLER, D.E., and ROSE, R., *The British General Election of 1959*, Macmillan, 1960

BUTLER, D.E., and KING, A., *The British General Election of 1964*, Macmillan, 1965

— *The British General Election of 1966*, Macmillan, 1966

PULZER, P.G.J., *Political Representation and Elections in Britain*, Allen & Unwin, 1968

BUTLER, D.E., and STOKES, D., *Political Change in Britain*, Macmillan, 1969

NORDLINGER, E.A., *The Working Class Tories*, Macgibbon & Kee, 1967

ABRAMS, M., and ROSE, R., *Must Labour Lose?*, Penguin, 1960

BIRCH, A.H., *Small Town Politics*, Oxford, 1959

ROSE, R., *Studies in British Politics*, Macmillan, 1969

References in the text

ABRAMS, M., and ROSE, R., *Must Labour Lose?*, Penguin, 1960

ATTLEE, C.R., *The Labour Party in Perspective*, Gollancz, 1937

— *As It Happened*, Heinemann, 1954

BAGEHOT, W., *The English Constitution (1867)*, Fontana, 1963

— *Works* (Ed. Mrs Russell Barrington), Longmans, 1915

BRAITHWAITE, R., *Lloyd George's Ambulance Wagon* (Ed. Sir H. Bunbury), Methuen, 1957

BRIDGES, SIR EDWARD, *Portrait of a Profession*, Cambridge University Press, 1953

BUNBURY, SIR H. (Ed.), *Lloyd George's Ambulance Wagon*, Methuen, 1957

BURKE, E., *Speech to the Electors of Bristol, 1774*, in *Speeches and Letters on American Affairs*, Dent, 1908

BUTLER, D., and FREEMAN, J., *British Political Facts*, Macmillan, 1963

BUTLER, D., and KING, A., *The British General Election of 1964*, Macmillan, 1965

— *The British General Election of 1966*, Macmillan, 1966

BUTT, R., *The Power of Parliament*, Constable, 1967

CECIL, LADY G., *Life of Robert, Marquis of Salisbury*, Hodder and Stoughton, 1921

CHAPMAN, BRIAN, *British Government Observed*, Allen & Unwin, 1963

CHRISTIANSEN, ARTHUR, *Headlines All My Life*, Heinemann, 1961

CHURCHILL, W.S., *The Gathering Storm*, Cassell, 1948

COOPER, DUFF, *Old Men Forget*, Hart-Davis, 1953

CROSLAND, C.A.R., *The Future of Socialism*, Jonathan Cape, 1964

CROSSMAN, R.H.S., *Planning for Freedom*, Hamish Hamilton, 1965

DALTON, HUGH, *Call Back Yesterday*, Muller, 1953

— *The Fateful Years*, Muller, 1957

— *High Tide and After*, Muller, 1962

EDELMAN, MAURICE, *The Mirror, A Political History*, Hamish Hamilton, 1966

EDEN, SIR ANTHONY, *Full Circle*, Cassell, 1960

FEILING, K., *The Life of Neville Chamberlain*, Macmillan, 1946

FINER, S., *Anonymous Empire*, Pall Mall, 1966

FRANKS, SIR OLIVER, *The Experience of a University Teacher in the Civil Service*, Oxford University Press, 1947

GARDINER, A.G., *Life of Sir William Harcourt*, Constable, 1923

GRIGG, SIR JAMES, *Prejudice and Judgement*, Jonathan Cape, 1948

HILL, LORD, OF LUTON, *Both Sides of the Hill*, Heinemann, 1964

HOGG, QUINTIN, *The Case for Conservatism*, Penguin, 1947

HUNT, NORMAN, *Whitehall and Beyond*, B.B.C., 1964

JENNINGS, W.I., *The British Constitution*, Cambridge University Press, 1941

JONES, THOMAS A., *Diary with Letters, 1931–1950*, Oxford University Press, 1954

KEYNES, J.M., *The General Theory of Employment Interest and Money*, Macmillan, 1951

LAKEMAN, E., and LAMBERT, J.D., *Voting in Democracies*, Faber, 1959

MCKENZIE, R.T., *British Political Parties*, Heinemann Mercury Books, 1963

MACKINTOSH, J.P., *The British Cabinet*, Stevens, 1962

MARQUIS, F., *Memoirs of the Earl of Woolton*, Cassell, 1959

MARTIN, KINGSLEY, *Harold Laski*, Gollancz, 1953

MORLEY, J., *Life of Gladstone*, Macmillan, 1903

MORRISON, LORD, *Government and Parliament* (3rd ed.), Oxford University Press, 1964

NICOLSON, NIGEL, *People and Parliament*, Weidenfeld and Nicolson, 1958

OXFORD and ASQUITH, EARL OF, *Memories and Reflections*, Cassell, 1928

PARKINSON, C.N., *Parkinson's Law*, Murray, 1958

POTTER, ALLEN, *Organised Groups in British National Politics*, Faber, 1961

RANNEY, A., *Pathways to Parliament*, Macmillan, 1965

REITH, LORD, *Into the Wind*, Hodder and Stoughton, 1949

RICHARDS, P.G., *Honourable Members: A Study of the British Backbencher*, Faber, 1959

ROSE, RICHARD, *Influencing Voters*, Faber, 1967

— *Studies in British Politics*, Macmillan, 1966 and (revised edn.) 1969

ROSS, J.F.S., *Elections and Electors*, Eyre and Spottiswoode, 1955

SELF, P., and STORING, H.J., *The State and the Farmer*, Allen & Unwin, 1962

SAMPSON, ANTHONY, *Anatomy of Britain Today*, Hodder and Stoughton, 1965

SHORE, PETER, *Entitled to Know*, MacGibbon and Kee, 1966

SIMON, LORD, *Retrospect*, Hutchinson, 1952

SISSON, C.H., *The Spirit of British Administration*, Faber, 1966

STEWART, J.D., *British Pressure Groups*, Oxford University Press, 1958

STRANG, LORD, *Home and Abroad*, André Deutsch, 1956

TAWNEY, R.H., *Equality*, Allen & Unwin, 1952

TAYLOR, SIR HENRY, *The Statesman* (in *The Works*), Kegan Paul, 1878

TRENAMAN, J., and MCQUAIL, D., *Television and the Political Image*, Methuen, 1961

VANSITTART, LORD, *The Mist Procession*, Hutchinson, 1958

WALDER, DAVID, *The Short List*, Hutchinson, 1964

WILLIAMS, F., *A Prime Minister Remembers*, Heinemann, 1961

— *A Pattern of Rulers*, Longmans, 1965

— *Dangerous Estate*, Arrow Books, 1959

WILLIAMS, R., *Communications*, Penguin, 1962

WILSON, H.H., *Pressure Group*, Secker and Warburg, 1961

WINDLESHAM, LORD, *Communication and Government Policy*, Jonathan Cape, 1966

WRENCH, J.E., *Geoffrey Dawson and Our Times*, Hutchinson, 1955

YOUNG, G.M., *Stanley Baldwin*, Hart-Davis, 1952

Index

Note: Bold figures indicate main reference.

477